KOREA
OLD AND NEW
A History

Carter J. Eckert
Ki-baik Lee
Young Ick Lew
Michael Robinson
Edward W. Wagner

Published for the
KOREA INSTITUTE, HARVARD UNIVERSITY
by
ILCHOKAK, PUBLISHERS
Seoul, Korea

Distributed by
HARVARD UNIVERSITY PRESS
Cambridge, Massachusetts
and London, England
1990

FOREWORD

Korea Old and New is an attempt to meet the need for a general history of Korea that provides detailed treatment of the post-1945 period while at the same time describing at some length the traditional historical-cultural milieu from which modern Korea has developed. It is perhaps surprising that such works have begun to appear in English only quite recently. But for understandable historical reasons the history of Korea always has been under-chronicled. In the present century, Korea's long suffering under Japanese colonial rule and, since liberation in 1945, a multiplicity of both domestic and external factors have resulted either in tendentious history or in coverage badly skewed in its emphasis on such dramatic events as the Korean War or South Korea's remarkable economic successes. The need for a more balanced survey, then, and one concerned equally with the old Korea and the new, is clear.

Several years ago, in 1984, my English rendering of Ki-baik Lee's *A New History of Korea* was published in both Korea and the United States, and its appearance has been met with a response that is truly gratifying. Unfortunately, however, its coverage of the modern era stopped at 1960 and, moreover, its discussion of historical Korea tended to be far too detailed for many among its English-language readership. But given the book's manifest strengths and the time and effort that would be required to prepare a new treatment of the long and complex history of traditional Korea, it was decided that, by and large, *Korea Old and New* should simply condense the account in Professor Lee's time-tested book. This has been done, with only an occasional emendation and with an eye to preserving more fully intact the richness of its discussions of cultural and artistic developments. And for the new book, Professor Lee has rewritten the opening chapter on the pre-history of Korea, taking into account the many recent archaeological discoveries.

More than half of the 419 pages of text of *Korea Old and New* is devoted to the tumultuous history of Korea's past century or so. The period 1864~1910, from the section in Chapter 12 on "The Reforms and Isolationist Policy of the Taewŏn'gun" (p.192) through Chapters 13 and 14, has been the responsibility of Professor Young Ick Lew, Hallym University. While retaining the structure of *A New History of Korea*, he has added both new materials and new analysis derived from his own intensive studies of the events of that period. The remainder of the book, covering the period 1910~1990, has been written expressly for *Korea Old and New* by two American authorities on the modern history of Korea. Professor Michael Robinson of the University of Southern California has authored Chapters 15~17 on the Japanese colonial period, while Chapters 18~20, on post-liberation Korea, are the work of Professor Carter J. Eckert, Harvard University.

It is, finally, my thankful task to record the debt *Korea Old and New* owes for assistance rendered it by several individuals. For vital help in manuscript input and index preparation we are grateful to Harvard graduate students Miranda Shaw, Scott Snyder, and Milan Hejtmanek. We also wish to acknowledge the editorial and substantive suggestions made by Professor Key-hiuk Kim.

Edward W. Wagner

Harvard University
Summer, 1990

CONTENTS

FOREWORD

Chapter 5. The Age of Powerful Gentry Families

Chapter 6. The Hereditary Aristocratic Order of Koryŏ

Chapter 7. Rule by the Military

Chapter 8. Emergence of the Literati

Chapter 9. The Creation of a Yangban Society

Chapter 10. The Rise of the Neo-Confucian Literati

Chapter 11. Economic Advances and Intellectual Ferment

Chapter 12. Dynastic Disarray and National Peril

Chapter 1

The Communal Societies of
Prehistoric Times

The Paleolithic Age

However long the history of man on earth may ultimately prove
to be, it was around two and one-half million years ago that he
began to use tools. During the long, long period called the
Paleolithic Age these were no more than smaller pieces of stone
struck off from larger, and it was only in comparatively recent
millenia that man began deliberately to shape these primitive tools
to his increasingly varied purposes. Archaeologically speaking,
then, the history of mankind begins from this former era, known
as the Paleolithic ("Old Stone") Age.

Korean history too, of course, has a Paleolithic period, but
its existence has been established unequivocally for scarcely a single generation. In 1933 a report appeared on a site at Tonggwanjin in the far northeastern tip of the Korean Peninsula, where
fossils of extinct mammals such as the mammoth were found in
close juxtaposition with a number of bone and stone fragments
thought to be implements shaped by human hand. The proximity of Neolithic remains at the same site induced caution in many
scholars, but the existence of undisputed Paleolithic sites in not
so very distant areas of northeastern China by now has persuaded most archaeologists to accept the Tonggwanjin evidence as
genuinely Paleolithic.

Further reports on excavations of Paleolithic sites in Korea began to appear only from the 1960s. The earliest concerned the
finds at Kulp'o-ri, Unggi, in North Hamgyŏng province in 1962
and those at Sŏkchang-ni, Kongju, South Ch'ungch'ŏng province
in 1964. Subsequently the results of investigations of Paleolithic

sites in nearly every region of Korea have appeared, and a number of further Paleolithic excavations have been undertaken. Thus it has become clear that Paleolithic man lived widely throughout the entire Korean Peninsula.

The chronology of the Paleolithic Age in Korea is not yet certain. The ages of two cultural layers at the Sŏkchang-ni site belonging to the Late Paleolithic have been confirmed to be respectively 30,000 and 20,000 years before the present. However, among the sites already excavated are two at least that date from the Early Paleolithic, and so it may be surmised that Paleolithic man began his life and cultural development in Korea at least 400,000 to 500,000 years ago. Recent excavations at several sites for the first time have revealed human bones from the Paleolithic era, including the complete skeletal remains of two small children. The predominant view, however, is that the Korean people of today are not the ethnic descendants of these Paleolithic inhabitants of their land.

Paleolithic man in Korea lived in caves, or in the shelter of overhanging rock, or else built dwellings on level ground. Habitations always were sited so as to take advantage of sunlight, and they also were located in close proximity to a fresh water source that game animals would frequent. That fire was used, probably for warmth and cooking both, is known from the remains of a hearth found at the Late Paleolithic site at Sŏkchang-ni.

The Paleolithic people lived by gathering fruit, berries, and edible roots, and also by hunting and fishing. The implements they needed for procuring and preparing food mostly were fashioned by chipping stone, although tools or implements made of bone and horn also are found. Stone tools were of many varieties, depending on the particular purpose for which they were made—handaxes, choppers, and points used in hunting and butchering, scrapers used in preparing food, gravers for working stone and wood. And in fact at one site there is clear evidence that the making of stone tools on a rather large scale was concentrated in one particular place within the settlement area.

Since a concerted group effort would have been required for hunting, it is likely that some form of communal life developed among Paleolithic man. Additionally there is some evidence suggesting that crude figurines or incised drawings of animals were made in connection with magical practices designed to secure success in hunting.

The Appearance of Neolithic Man

By about 8,000 B.C. the glacial climate of the most recent ice age had substantially moderated and the run-off from the melting glaciers gradually had raised ocean water levels. At the same time, smaller and nimbler animals like the rabbit and deer appeared in the newly ice-free regions that also were the habitat of primitive man. To catch such animals the bow came into use and spear-like implements were fashioned by attaching sharpened stone points to bone or wood hafts. These developments took place in the period known as the Mesolithic that marks the transition from the Paleolithic to the Neolithic Age. In Korea no definite Mesolithic remains have yet been found, although some argue that the lowest layer of the shell mound on Sangnodae Island, South Kyŏngsang province, dates from this time.

The lingering effects of the ice age continued to be felt for some time, and it was not until about 5,500 B.C. that temperatures and ocean levels became substantially what they are today. It was essentially at this moment that Neolithic man first appeared in Korea, with his characteristic artifacts of ground or polished stone tools and pottery. It is the appearance of these objects, as the end-products of an almost immeasurably long, slow process of human development, that tells us the Neolithic Age had dawned. And it is changes in the forms and shapes of pottery that archaeologists use in describing the processes of historical change during the Neolithic Age.

The Neolithic Age in Korea generally is divided into three periods. The Early Neolithic is marked by the making of simple, undecorated, small vessels, and of a pottery decorated haphazardly by adding short strips of clay to the body of the bowl or pot. Pieces of these types have been found at both northern and southern extremes of Korea's eastern littoral, in mid-peninsular locations as well, and also in Manchuria and Tsushima Island. The dates of these remains are variously put between 5,000 and 6,000 B.C., but they may be even older.

The Middle Neolithic period is defined in terms of the characteristic geometric-design pottery, usually called "comb-pattern pottery," it produced, starting around 4,000 B.C. It was made either by adding circular strips one upon the other or by the more advanced technique of wrapping a single long coil round and round from bottom to top. Comb-pattern pottery is gray in color with a V-shape pointed bottom or rounded base, and it was decorated by designs of parallel lines on the outer surface that resemble markings made by a comb. Comb-pattern pottery has been unearthed at many sites up and down the peninsula, especially along ocean shores and river's edge, and from Siberia through Inner Mongolia and Manchuria and on to Japan.

Then, about 2,000 B.C., a new pottery culture characterized by painted designs spread into the Korean Peninsula from China, and this marks the advent of the Late Neolithic period. The prevalent comb-pattern pottery now underwent changes in both shape and design. Flat-bottomed vessels appeared, while wave and stylized thunderbolt designs also are seen. And, again, the remains of this period have been found at widely scattered sites in the Korean Peninsula.

Neolithic culture in Korea thus experienced three major stages of development, quite likely reflecting three successive waves of migration down into the peninsula. Unlike the case of Korea's Paleolithic populations, the ethnic stock of these Neolithic people is seen as continuing unbroken to form one element of the later Korean race. It is believed, then, that in the course of a long historical process these Neolithic inhabitants merged with one another and, combining with the new ethnic groups of Korea's Bronze Age, eventually came to constitute what we now think of as the Korean people.

Neolithic dwelling sites in Korea are found mainly at water's edge, and the marine life in the adjacent rivers or seas supplied most of the food. Food was procured by hunting as well, and bones of such animals as deer and wild boar have been found, while arrowheads and spear points appear among the stone artifacts discovered. Thus at first having relied for their food on hunting, fishing, and gathering, these Neolithic people subsequently began to practice agriculture. This is known from the discovery among later remains of stone hoes used in turning over the soil and of stone sickles for harvesting, together with kernels of grain. Needless to say, this change from a hunting and gathering economy to one of agriculture was a development of the utmost significance.

Neolithic man in Korea lived mainly in pit dwellings. These usually were dug in circular or in rough square form, posts then being set up to support a straw thatch covering. In general the hearth is found in the center of the floor, while storage pits for grain or various implements are located next to the hearth or near the entrance. It is not yet clear in what way the pit dwellings of that time were grouped together to form small communities. It is evident, though, that Neolithic man in Korea at times also lived in natural or man-made caves.

Clothing at first consisted of animal skins, sewn together by the use of bone needles. Later cloth came to be woven by a primitive spindle technique from animal fur or such fibers as hemp, and the clothing made in this way was adorned with shells and decorative bits of stone.

Society and Culture in the Neolithic Period

There is almost no direct evidence suggesting what form society took in the Neolithic period. Judging from the fact that a number of dwellings are found clustered at a single site, it may be supposed that already some form of settled communal life was being practiced. Beyond this, one can only make judicious use of myths, legends, and traditional patterns of behavior described in records from later periods to conjecturally reconstruct certain features of the society of this much earlier age.

The basic unit of the society of this time was the clan. These consanguineous social groupings, each bound together by its distinct blood line, are thought to have been totemistic. The close identification with a particular totem, an object in the natural world, would not only serve to strengthen lineage solidarity but also would sharply differentiate one lineage from another. These clan entities formed distinct communities and decided important matters at clan assemblages. It is widely supposed that the later *Hwabaek* (Council of Nobles) institution of Silla represents a continuation of this ancient tradition. To be sure, the clan was headed by a chieftain, but he was chosen by his clansmen and, if he was thought to have erred, he always was subject to removal from his position. And as may be surmised from the *ture* form of communal labor arrangements found in Korean villages in later times, the primary productive activities of hunting, fishing, and agriculture likely were performed in common in the Neolithic period. The conduct of religious ceremonies too on a communal basis is suggested by later customs involving shamanistic ceremonies and ancestor worship rituals.

The clan community was an economically independent and self-sufficient entity. Economic activities, whether gathering or hunting and fishing, were not permitted within the territories claimed by other clans. Nevertheless, some economic exchange among different clan communities did take place, as can be seen in the example of a particular kind of stone being brought from a considerable distance for use in fashioning certain implements.

It will be evident that the consanguineous clan communities as postulated above possessed a markedly closed character. Nevertheless, exogamous marriage was practiced, with partners invariably sought not within the community but from other clans. It also is asserted by some, on the basis of several later social and political arrangements, that descent was determined by the mother's lineage during some part of the Neolithic period.

The general structural features of the clan community have been described as they now can be surmised, but the clan was not the only form that social organization took in the Neolithic period. Larger social configurations, or tribes, came into being with the merging either of related clan units that had split off from one another as populations increased, or of clans linked by marriage ties. These tribes tended to find their unity in territorial as well as in blood ties, but the principles governing the structure of their societies were substantially the same as those of the clan. That is, matters of concern to the tribe as a whole were decided at assemblies of the clan chieftains, and the leader of the tribe was chosen by these same clan representatives. The raising of Pak Hyŏkkŏse to kingship by an assembly of the clan leaders of ancient Silla's "six villages" is thought to be an embellished account of such a practice of selecting a tribal leader.

Neolithic man in Korea held animistic beliefs, being convinced that every object in the natural world was possessed of a soul. Man, too, of course had a soul and it was believed that this soul was immortal. Accordingly, in burying the body of one who had died, a variety of special attentions were shown, such as burying with him articles that the deceased had used during his lifetime. The souls of natural objects such as mountains, rivers, and trees were thought of in the same way as those of men, and certain of these were accorded status as divinities. The sun is the foremost example of this, and its worship as early as the Neolithic Age is thought to be reflected in later Korean myths of miraculous birth. Pak Hyŏkkŏse's birth is described as being from an egg, and it is related that the name he was given, Pak (or *palk,* "brightness") is owed to the fact that light radiated from his body. Clearly he was thought to be a child of the sun.

While good spirits like the sun were believed to bring good fortune to human beings, it also was believed that evil spirits such as those who dwelled in darkness brought misfortune upon man. Accordingly, it was necessary that there be adepts in magic, intermediaries with the ability to drive off evil spirits and invoke the gods so as to bring about a happy outcome. It is supposed that these tribal magicians performed ceremonies designed to forestall individual or collective calamity by means of chants and dancing. Primitive religious practices of this same form are found throughout the world, and in the area of Northeast Asia they are known by the general term of shamanism.

Comb-pattern pottery may be said to be the representative art form of the Neolithic period. The outer surface of this pottery was decorated by drawing series of parallel slanted lines, the direction of different groupings of lines being varied to create geometric patterns such as the common fishbone design. Another decorative device was to bring opposing sets of fine-line patterns into juxtaposition, thus creating symmetrical designs that possess a beauty of unity and harmony. These designs, however, rather than being simply decorative, seem to have had a religious significance. In most primitive art parallel slanted lines are thought to symbolize water, and so it may well be that the decorations on comb-pattern pottery also were intended to represent water, the major source of early Korean Neolithic man's food. But with the advent of agriculture straight line designs gave way to curved, and maze-like jagged broken-line designs suggesting thunderbolts also began to appear. This design is thought to symbolize lightning as the heavenly force that brought forth all creation.

Only two sculptured objects have as yet been found from the Neolithic Age. One, the head of a small clay figurine of an animal, was done in a strikingly graphic manner. The other is a simple rendering of the features of a quite unremarkable human face. A mask made from a shell, with holes put in it for the eyes and mouth, also has been found, and bits of stone that probably were used for ornamentation also have been discovered. All of these objects, it may be supposed, were made to serve religious purposes, such as ceremonies to pray for a bountiful supply of food or to drive away evil spirits.

Thus the art forms of the Neolithic period were closely bound to religious practices. And the art objects produced by Korean Neolithic man are rather characterized by abstraction than by realism, for their purpose was to give expression to some symbolic meaning.

Chapter 2

Walled-Town States and Confederated Kingdoms

Bronze Age Culture

The Bronze Age in Korea lasted from about the ninth or eighth century B.C. until about the fourth century B.C., but this time span varied to some extent in different areas of the peninsula. The Sungari and Liao river basins in southern Manchuria and the Korean Peninsula circumscribe the arena in which Korean Bronze Age culture played out its historical role. Dolmen and stone cist tombs are the predominant forms of burial that survive from the Bronze Age. The existence of these dolmen, together with numerous menhir (large upright stones), has caused this culture also to be characterized as megalithic.

Representative among the variety of Bronze Age artifacts that have been unearthed are the mandolin-shaped bronze dagger and the multi-knobbed coarse-lined bronze mirror. Polished stone daggers often were placed in tombs as burial objects, while the characteristic pottery of the age is undecorated, brownish-red ware. The occurrence of geometric-motif pottery of Neolithic design at some of the same sites indicates that there was a transition period when the two cultures were in contact. Similarly, the use of these geometric motifs in the decoration of the bronze daggers and mirrors bespeaks cultural continuity between the Neolithic and Bronze Age cultures. Yet a gradual disappearance of the geometric-design pottery signifies that the Bronze Age people had become the arbiters of the emergent social order in Korea.

Bronze Age man was a slope dweller, inhabiting the higher ground that overlooks flatlands along river courses, a terrain suitable for the agriculture on which the Bronze Age population depended. Rice cultivation began to be practiced from this time, as evidenced by the use of crescent-shaped stone knives for cutting rice stalks and grooved stones for hoeing. Since both these tools were used in rice culture in China, it is thought that rice agriculture itself may have been transmitted to Korea from China. These Bronze Age people also hunted and fished, but their cultivation of rice implies a considerable degree of sophistication in their agriculture.

Korea's Bronze Age people lived mainly in dwellings, now generally of rectangular design, sited in shallow pits. Dwellings were grouped into settlements of increasing size, but their precise arrangement is not yet clear. The habitations of this period increasingly show evidence of damage by fire, and this is likely to reflect both its heightened use and also destruction by burning in the course of warfare. The existence of bronze weapons, most notably spear points and arrowheads, suggests that the Bronze Age people were easily able to gain ascendancy over the Neolithic inhabitants, who had only stone weapons.

In terms of social organization, the Korean Bronze Age artifacts indicate a stratified society. Bronze implements were precious articles, difficult to obtain. Bronze daggers and mirrors would have been the possessions of only a privileged few, whose authority thus was symbolized by their ownership. This consideration holds true for dolmen burial as well. Dolmen tombs with capstones weighing up to seventy tons were constructed, and in some cases these huge slabs had to be brought from sites many miles distant. Clearly, a person buried in such a tomb had the power to command the labor services of a large number of people. Moreover, the authority of such a figure appears to have passed to subsequent generations. Dolmen are found in clusters of at least three or four, sometimes in groups of thirty or forty, and in rare cases of over one hundred, built in orderly array along a straight line—all of which suggests that their construction was organized and sustained over time. Therefore, the individuals buried in dolmen tombs were not simply leading members of a communal social structure but rather were those who wielded authority in a stratified society. Who, then, owned the bronze symbols of authority and enjoyed enough power to be buried in dolmen tombs? Most likely they were the successors to the tribal chieftains of the Neolithic period. However, the leaders of Bronze Age societies would have obtained a more plentiful product from agriculture and seized greater spoils in war, thus being able to command greater economic wealth.

The territories ruled by Bronze Age chieftains were not very extensive. They controlled a modest agricultural population that farmed the narrow plains beyond the earthen fortifications they built on hillside plateaus. Although these small walled-town states (sometimes called tribal states) retained a tribal character, their political structure was built around a territorial unit that subsumed populations other than the tribe alone. These walled-town states were the earliest form of state structure to exist in Korea, and thus they represent the origins of Korean political culture.

Old Chosŏn and Wiman Chosŏn

Societies with articulated political structures now began to develop around the walled-town states that had been formed with the advent of the use of bronze implements. These societies included Puyŏ, Yemaek, Old Chosŏn, Imdun, and Chinbŏn, while south of the Han River the state of Chin emerged. By about the fourth century B.C. these states had developed to the point where their existence was known even in China. Among them the most advanced was Old Chosŏn, which had established itself in the basins of the Liao and Taedong Rivers, the region where bronze artifacts are most plentifully found.

The early leaders of Old Chosŏn seem to have borne the title *tan'gun wanggŏm,* and it is likely that they combined political and religious functions in a single personage. The *tan'gun wanggŏm* is said to have descended from a sun god, a claim of divine origins that would have enhanced the dignity and authority of his political leadership. By the beginning of the fourth century B.C. at the latest, Old Chosŏn had combined with the other walled-town states to form a single large confederation, the head of which came to be designated as its king. It was about this time that Old Chosŏn and the North China state of Yen were confronting each other across their Liao River boundary, and in the light of Yen assertions that Old Chosŏn was arrogant and cruel, it can be surmised that Old Chosŏn boasted formidable strength as an independent power in northeast Asia.

The development of Old Chosŏn as a confederated kingdom coincided with the advent of the Iron Age in that relatively remote region of northeast Asia. In fact, two new metal cultures of differing provenance were transmitted to Korea in the fourth century B.C. One was the iron culture of China and the other was a bronze culture of Scytho-Siberian origin. The two cultures intermingled in Manchuria and came to the Taedong River basin, from where they soon spread in all directions, penetrating even into Japan, where they gave rise to the Yayoi culture.

The use of iron implements wrought a variety of changes. First of all, agriculture underwent striking development with the introduction of sophisticated farming tools like iron hoes, plowshares, and sickles. In this way food production increased markedly in comparison with that of the Bronze Age. The increased output doubtless was monopolized by the ruling class, and accordingly the gap between the rich and the poor must have been further widened.

The artifacts from the Iron Age in Korea include Chinese coins, Scytho-Siberian style animal-shaped belt buckles, a new type of gray stoneware pottery, and molds for casting bronze and iron. Other frequently found artifacts include a range of weapons, such as iron daggers and spear points, and bronze daggers, spear points, and spears. Such horse trappings as iron bits and bronze bells, as well as axle caps and other components of horse-drawn vehicles, also have been unearthed, and it seems clear that these objects of metal manufacture would have been possessed only by a small elite stratum. It is not difficult to imagine how this ruling elite, armed with sharp weapons made of metal and mounted on horseback or riding on horse-drawn vehicles, must have imposed its authority, while objects like their multi-knobbed fine-patterned bronze mirrors would have served as symbols of their authority.

At the end of the fourth century B.C., Old Chosŏn entered a period of gradual decline, due to pressure from the powerful Chinese state of Yen, which invaded the Liaotung Peninsula at that time. This strategic region was taken and attached as a commandery to the Yen domain, but in the ensuing century it fell successively under the dominion first of the Ch'in empire and then of the Han dynasty of China. During this turbulent period refugee populations migrated eastward, and among them a leader by the name of Wiman emerged, who succeeded in driving King Chun of Old Chosŏn from his throne (sometime between 194 and 180 B.C.) and assumed the kingship himself.

Wiman Chosŏn, as this kingdom is known, bore some of the hallmarks of the Chinese political, economic, and cultural influences that had permeated the region since 300 B.C., but Wiman continued to use "Chosŏn" in the name of his kingdom, dressed and wore his hair in Chosŏn style, and placed many men of Old Chosŏn in high positions in his government. Therefore, the kingdom of Wiman Chosŏn was not simply a Chinese colonial regime, but rather took the form of a confederated kingdom grounded on the former Old Chosŏn power structure.

Militarily and economically strong, Wiman Chosŏn expanded northward, eastward, and southward, controlling a territory stretching over some several hundred miles. But the threat posed by Wiman Chosŏn's strength and expansion, and the economic role it sought to play as intermediary in the trade between Han China and the outlying territories beyond its northeastern borders, before long provoked a Han invasion. For a year or more Wiman Chosŏn fought the Chinese armies to a standstill, but weakened by defections and internal dissension within the ruling class, the ambitious kingdom of Wiman Chosŏn finally fell, in 108 B.C.

Han China now established the three commanderies of Lolang, Chen-fan, and Lin-t'un within the former domain of Wiman Chosŏn, and in the next year completed the formation of the so-called Four Chinese Commanderies by creating Hsüan-t'u in the former territory of the Ye. The territorial extent of the Four Chinese Commanderies seems to have been limited to the area north of the Han River, and the opposition of the local populations soon forced Han China to make major adjustments in the boundaries of each of these four administrative units.

Lo-lang was the core area in which Chinese colonial policy in Korea was carried out. As its administrative center the Chinese built what was in essence a Chinese city where the governor, officials, merchants, and Chinese colonists lived. Their way of life in general can be surmised from the investigation of remains unearthed at T'osŏng-ni, the site of the Lo-lang administrative center near modern P'yŏngyang. The variety of burial objects found in their wooden and brickwork tombs attests to the lavish life style of these Chinese officials, merchants, and colonial overlords in Lo-lang's capital.

China's colonial policy does not seem to have been marked by severe political repression. It appears that the Chinese were content to exercise a certain degree of control while permitting substantial political freedom to the people they governed. Nonetheless, the Chinese administration had considerable impact on the life of the native population and ultimately the very fabric of Old Chosŏn society became eroded. The Chinese were able to command the labor services of the native population they governed, for example for the large-scale cutting of timber. It is known, too, that iron ore from deposits in the southeast corner of the peninsula was supplied to Lo-lang. And an impact of quite another sort may be seen in the record that the eight laws of Old Chosŏn, said to be all that earlier society had needed, multiplied to sixty provisions in the period of Chinese domination. Ultimately a new China-oriented elite class emerged among the native population within the area under Chinese control, and this meant that the disintegrative process in Old Chosŏn was well under way.

The impact of the Chinese commanderies also was felt in neighboring states, which coveted the fruits of the highly advanced Chinese culture. This is apparent from the fact that for the most part the leaders of the Han states in the southern half of the peninsula willingly accepted the grants of office and rank, official seals, and ceremonial attire that constituted formal tokens of their submission to Lo-lang's authority. The ability to absorb Chinese culture while maintaining their political independence allowed these native societies to weather the crises that at times confronted them and achieve impressive new development.

The Formation of Confederated Kingdoms: Puyŏ, Koguryŏ, and the State of Chin

Puyŏ (Chinese: Fu-yü) emerged in the flatlands of the Sungari River basin in Manchuria [see map p. 16]. The first clear reference to Puyŏ concerns events of about the fourth century B.C., and from the beginning of the first century A.D. the name appears frequently in the historical records. By this time Puyŏ had grown in power to the point where it was regarded, along with the Hsiung-nu and Koguryŏ, as a potential menace to Wang Mang's brief dynasty (8-23 A.D.) in China, and this indicates that by now Puyŏ had succeeded in forming a confederated kingdom. Further evidence of this is the record that not long thereafter, in 49 A.D., the Puyŏ ruler was using the Chinese appellation for "king" (*wang*). China soon came to welcome the rise of Puyŏ on the Manchurian scene. Because Puyŏ lay between the Hsien-pei on China's northern frontier and Koguryŏ to China's northeast, an alliance between Puyŏ and China would be able to check the expansion of these two powerful peoples. At the same time, Puyŏ sought friendly ties with China as a potential ally in Puyŏ's struggles with Koguryŏ to its south and the nomadic peoples to its north.

Puyŏ's frequent embassies to China, first sent in 49 A.D., were received with the utmost cordiality. Clashes between Puyŏ and the Chinese commanderies in Manchuria occurred on several occasions over the centuries, but on the whole the relationship reflected their mutuality of interests and so remained close. But when the Chinese Chin Kingdom was driven south by the nomadic tribes to its north in 316, Puyŏ found itself isolated and exposed, and within little more than a half century Puyŏ had passed under the protection of Koguryŏ. Subsequently, with the rise of the Malgal people in northeastern Manchuria, the Puyŏ royal house was driven from its ancient territory and surrendered itself to Koguryŏ, thus removing the last vestiges of the Puyŏ kingdom.

Koguryŏ was founded in 37 B.C. by Chumong and a band of his followers from Puyŏ, according to legend, in a region centered on the middle Yalu and the T'ung-chia River basin. The

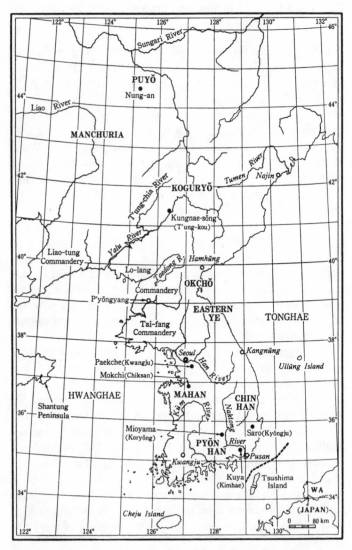

KOREA IN THE CONFEDERATED KINGDOMS PERIOD
(ca. 1ˢᵗ — 3ʳᵈ CENTURIES A.D.)

leadership elite of Koguryŏ was not native to the area it came to rule, but the state that evolved there represented a coalescence of this new force with the indigenous population, who were Yemaek people. Koguryŏ proceeded to develop in a context of conflict with the Chinese. Accordingly Koguryŏ was in need of strong military forces, and in the course of its early armed struggles the military character of Koguryŏ's ruling elite was continuously reinforced. It would appear that even in times of peace this warrior aristocracy did not engage in any kind of productive activities, but devoted itself entirely to training for combat. Only through warfare, it seems, could the warriors of Koguryŏ compensate for the inadequacy of the resources within their boundaries.

By the beginning of the first century A.D. the Koguryŏ state already had developed to the point of adopting the Chinese title of "king" for its ruler, and Koguryŏ now sought to expand its territory in all directions—toward the basins of the Liao River to the southwest and the Taedong River to the south, to the Sungari River basin in the northwest and into the plains along the northeast coast of the Korean Peninsula. Since these regions at that time were all either directly administered by China or within its sphere of influence, open warfare between Koguryŏ and China was inevitable. Such clashes intensified in the reign of Koguryŏ's King T'aejo (53-146?). By subjugating the Okchŏ to his southeast, T'aejo secured a base to his rear which could give meaningful support to Koguryŏ's warfare against China. The northeast littoral of Korea thus now was brought under the dominion of Koguryŏ. Koguryŏ, however, permitted the chieftains of the native communities to retain their authority and levied tribute through them. King T'aejo also mounted repeated attacks against the Chinese Liao-tung and Hsüan-t'u Commanderies as he pursued his plans to advance westward. T'aejo's successors continued Koguryŏ's incursions into the Liao-tung region. And when the Kung-sun house sought to extend its sway from its base in Liao-tung in the late second century, Koguryŏ opposed this Chinese thrust with fierce tenacity.

The first recorded mention of the state of Chin, south of the Han River basin in Korea, refers to an event of the second century B.C., when Wiman Chosŏn occupied the Taedong River basin. At this time Chin sent a communication to Han China seeking to open direct contact between the two. This suggests a strong desire on the part of Chin to enjoy the benefits of Chinese metal culture. Due to the obstruction of Wiman Chosŏn, which dominated international trade in the region at that time, Chin's hopes were frustrated. However, when refugees from the territory of Old Chosŏn streamed into the Chin domain they brought with them their more advanced knowledge of metalworking, the arts of governing, and rice agriculture. The absorption of these migrants into its society enabled Chin to take advantage of a more advanced iron culture and thus to develop at a rapid rate. This process eventually led to the restructuring of the Chin territory into three new political entities, known collectively as the Samhan: Mahan, Chinhan, and Pyŏnhan.

Society and Polity in the Confederated Kingdoms

Agriculture was the principal food source in this period. Rice cultivation became particularly prevalent in the Samhan states, and it is believed that reservoirs for rice irrigation already were being constructed at this time. Another important economic activity, especially in Puyŏ and the Samhan, was the raising of livestock on a large scale. Hunting of animals like wild boar and deer also was widely practiced, particularly in states like Koguryŏ situated in mountainous terrain. A rock drawing at Pan'gudae depicting whales and other marine life provides evidence that coastal peoples engaged in fishing too. This would have been regarded as a particularly vital source of food by societies like Okchŏ and Eastern Ye, which inhabited the narrow eastern coastal plains.

Still, the principal productive activity in this period unquestionably was agriculture, and the basic unit for carrying on the work of farming was the village community. Most of the farming population in these village communities possessed freeman, or commoner, social status. Above this preponderant component of free peasants were the village headmen and below them there were slaves in some number. Private ownership of land by the individual peasant likely already had developed, but it is believed that the free peasants also tilled communal fields. That the village had a communal character is a speculation based on the evidence of large buildings that may have served as community gathering places and written references to institutions that may represent assemblies of youth and communal labor practices. Although for the most part peasants performed their labor as free men within the communal structure of the farming villages, they were heavily burdened with taxes in kind and with obligations to provide labor service to the state. Moreover, the freeman peasant was not permitted to bear arms, a privilege reserved to the members of the governing class.

The peasant population was governed by a ruling elite who lived in walled towns apart from the village communities. To be sure, a kingly authority had emerged at the apex of society in the walled-town state, but at this time power in reality was exercised by this ruling elite. How this came about can be inferred from information in the historical record concerning the walled-town state of Saro. Situated in the Kyŏngju plain in the southeast, Saro appears to have been formed by the descendants of six clan groupings, two of which eventually rose to prominence. Tradition has it that Pak Hyŏkkŏse, the leader of one of these clans, was elevated to the position of first ruler of Saro, while his queen came from the other. Subsequently leadership of Saro was seized by T'arhae, a man from the coastal region east of Saro who was a skilled metalworker and also a shaman. Apparently by this time Saro already had broken out of the confines of the Kyŏngju plain and had developed a federative relationship with other walled-town states in its region. The terms used to designate Saro's rulers during this period are to be interpreted as having meant "chief," "shaman," and "successor prince" and are not to be taken as representing kings of a centralized aristocratic state such as Saro, in the form of Silla, was later to become. Again, evidence from the study of dolmen and other old tombs also strongly suggests that power in the confederated kingdoms of Korea was shared among a number of elite lineages.

The Korean confederated kingdoms, such as Wiman Chosŏn, Koguryŏ, Puyŏ, and the Samhan all represent the joining together of a number of walled-town states, but the formative process did not adhere to a uniform chronology, since some developed earlier or more rapidly than others. In the case of the Samhan, the process was relatively slow. The numerous walled-town states of the Samhan had entered into a confederated relationship in the third century A.D., but the Chinese commanderies formed diplomatic ties with each of the walled-town states on an individual basis, a divisive policy that disrupted the process of union among them and hindered their political development in varying degrees. Walled-town states like Okchŏ and Eastern Ye, which were under the direct dominion of Koguryŏ, are instances of still more retarded development of states that never reached the stage of entering into a federative relationship.

In contrast, the political restructuring of both Puyŏ and Koguryŏ went forward at an unusually rapid pace. In both these states it appears that at first kings were chosen by an elective process. If this assumption is correct, then the kingship in these two states may have alternated among two or more royal houses. A distinctive feature of succession to the throne in this period was that it often followed the principle of younger brother succeeding older brother, and this too suggests that the institution of kingship still was in an early stage of development.

Subsequently, the right to the throne came to inhere in a single royal house and succession became hereditary, passing from father to son. These developments occurred in conjunction with the energetic wars of conquest launched by these emerging kingdoms. The newly acquired territories were ruled as subject domains and tribute was levied upon them, and this further enhanced kingly power. At about the same time there is evidence indicating that systems of regional government under centralized control were put into effect in both Puyŏ and Koguryŏ, developments also suggesting that kingly authority was in the process of being strengthened.

Yet these new institutional arrangements retained features of the former federative patterns. In Koguryŏ and Puyŏ actual political authority for the time being still lay less with the king than in the hands of the senior members of the royal clan or of the various lineages from which the queens were drawn. These highborn aristocrats not only possessed political power but great economic wealth as well.

Thus they constituted the elite stratum of their societies, but they were an aristocratic political force in a centralized state that concurrently was undergoing an increase in kingly authority. For clearly the transformation of these two northern confederated kingdoms into centralized aristocratic states with the kingly authority paramount already was well underway.

Culture in the Confederated Kingdoms Period

The chief characteristics of law in the confederated kingdoms period were simplicity and severity. The societies of this age were content with the minimum degree of legal regulation necessary to maintain the norms of social order. Whatever prohibitions were needed to maintain social order were considered good, and any violation of such prohibitions was deemed to be evil and so to be punished, with little adjustment for differing degrees of transgression. Since it was believed that gods had ordained that good be upheld and evil punished, law had religious underpinnings, and criminal judgments were passed and executions carried out in conjunction with the performance of religious ceremonies.

Some specific provisions of the law codes of both Puyŏ and Old Chosŏn are known, but there are virtually no similar records for Koguryŏ, the Samhan, Okchŏ, and Eastern Ye. Nevertheless, what little evidence exists suggests that in all of the Korean confederated kingdoms the crimes of murder, bodily injury, thievery, female adultery, and jealousy on the part of a wife were commonly held to be the most serious offenses.

The known legal provisions provide important evidence of the social values of this age. Severe penalties for murder and bodily injury indicate a high regard for individual human life and productivity, and the penalties for thievery show considerable respect for private property. In addition, harsh penalties for female adultery and jealousy are thought to have served the purpose of safeguarding a patriarchal family system characterized by the widespread practice of polygamy.

Religious and political leadership gradually diverged during the period of the confederated kingdoms, as political power became more concentrated and the earlier primitive beliefs in animism or shamanism became more sophisticated. The duties of the religious leader now no longer were simply those of a practitioner of magic who believed that he could move the gods by the power of his own invocations, but rather had become those of a master of ritual who supplicated the gods for their favor. Nor was there any further need for these duties to be undertaken by the political powerholders themselves.

The autumn harvest thanksgiving festival was the most lavish religious observance, while an equally important ceremony was performed in the spring to pray for a bounteous year. For celebrations such as these song and dance were essential, and on these occasions the entire populace gathered together to celebrate by eating, drinking, singing, and dancing for days on end.

The religious ceremonies of this age, including the performance of song and dance, represent traditions handed down from the earlier clan-centered societies. And the fact that high and low alike, without class distinctions, could celebrate these religious festivals together, indicates that in the sphere of religion the traditions of the earlier egalitarian lineage-centered communities still had some force.

Belief in the immortality of the soul and the lavish burial rites that were its corollary were common features of the religious life of this period. In Puyŏ numerous burial objects were placed in the tomb and in some cases sacrificial burial was practiced, with as many as one hundred attendants being buried with their master. Burial was lavish in Koguryŏ too, marked by a multiplicity of burial objects and the covering of graves with pyramidal piles of stones. In the Samhan, the wings of large birds were buried with the deceased to supply the means for the soul to fly from the body. In general, such elaborate burial practices went hand in hand with the belief that the living soul of an ancestor exerts a continuous influence on the well-being of descendants of a later generation. Thus, as the social pattern of family headship and father to son royal succession evolved, the performance of ancestor rites came to be an important prerogative, as well as obligation, for the lineal successor. Divination too was practiced in this period. At first a duty incumbent upon the king, with the expansion of his political authority the arts of divination gradually came to fall within the specialized province of the shaman.

As bronze implements came into use and agriculture developed apace during the confederated kingdoms period, activity in the realm of fine arts also increased. In general, the traditions of the Neolithic Age remained strong and art retained its close link with religion. A conscious effort to achieve beauty of expression can be perceived in the design and decoration of many bronze artifacts, and a truly impressive variety of such creations in bronze has been discovered: dagger hilts decorated with carvings of birds or horses or flanked by a pair of bells, belt buckles in the shape of horses or tigers, shoulder armor incised with deer and other animal designs, intricately incised bronze mirrors decorated with geometric patterns, and many others. On the whole, this decorative work is characterized by realistic carvings of animals and by incised linear geometric patterns. Among the bronze artifacts are numerous ceremonial implements made for religious purposes, and even the decorations on articles intended for the secular use of political leaders probably had a magico-religious significance.

Recently discovered incised rock drawings from this period have drawn a great deal of academic attention because of the evidence they provide for the mode of life and perhaps even the religious outlook of the confederated kingdoms period. The one noted earlier at Pan'gudae portrays hunting scenes on land and by boat on the sea, with pictures of whales, tortoises, and other marine life, of wild animals like the deer, tiger, bear, boar, and rabbit, and of humans as well. Others offer a variety of geometric designs—concentric circles, triangles, and diamond shapes, as well as sketches of animals. These drawings may be seen as expressing religious beliefs or practices, such as sun worship, prayers for bounty in nature, or supplications to assure success in the life-sustaining activities of hunting and fishing.

Chapter 3

Aristocratic Societies Under Monarchical Rule

The Development of the Three Kingdoms: Koguryŏ, Paekche, and Silla

The right to the throne in Koguryŏ was permanently secured in a single royal house in the time of King T'aejo (53-146?), and from the reign of Kogukch'ŏn (179-196) the processes of strengthening the kingly authority and centralizing the governmental structure proceeded rapidly. In the first place, the five tribal enclaves of the earlier traditional society were restructured into five provinces. Secondly, succession to the throne on the whole no longer went from brother to brother but changed to a father to son pattern, and this represents a further enhancement of the power of the kingship. Thirdly, it became established practice for queens to come from one particular aristocratic house, whose interests, then, were no longer served by opposition to the growth of monarchical authority. Koguryŏ now pressed ahead with its advance toward the basins of the Liao River to the west and the Taedong River to the south. Eventually, under King Mich'ŏn in 313, Koguryŏ seized the territory of the Lo-lang Commandery and occupied the Taedong River region. At the same time, Koguryŏ came into sharp confrontation with Paekche, which had pushed northward to gain hold over the domain of the Tai-fang Commandery (established a century earlier in the area of the former Chen-fan Commandery) lying immediately to the south of Lo-lang.

Paekche originally developed out of one of the walled-town states that comprised the Mahan area, over which the ancient Chin state had ruled. It is not certain just when this original

Paekche emerged as a confederated kingdom incorporating the various walled-town states in the Han River basin, but it is known that in the year 246 the Lo-lang and Tai-fang commanderies (then under Chinese dominion) launched a large-scale attack in an effort to prevent the further consolidation of Paekche's growing power in the Han River region. The newly confederated kingdom of Paekche was led at this time by King Koi (traditional reign dates 234-286) whose reign displays the unmistakable marks of successfully consolidated centralized authority. He appointed six ministers to conduct the affairs of state along appropriate functional lines, created sixteen grades of official rank, and, in 262, decreed harsh penalties for venal officials. King Koi himself displayed his majesty by holding audience bedecked in dazzling finery. All this conjures up a vivid image of a powerful political leader.

The structuring of Paekche into a centralized, aristocratic state appears to have been completed in the reign of King Kŭn Ch'ogo (346-375). A formidable warrior king, in 369 he destroyed Mahan and took possession of the whole of its territory. In 371, Paekche struck northward into the Koguryŏ domain as far as P'yŏngyang, killing the Koguryŏ king, Kogugwŏn, in the course of the campaign. Paekche thus came to hold sway over a sizeable portion of the Korean Peninsula, including the modern provinces of Kyŏnggi, Ch'ungch'ŏng, and Chŏlla, as well as parts of Hwanghae and Kangwŏn. Furthermore, King Kŭn Ch'ogo solidified his international position by making overtures to the Eastern Chin state in the Yangtze River region and to the Wa people in Japan.

It is not surprising that from the time of this warrior king the power of the throne in Paekche came to be increasingly authoritarian. Father to son royal succession to the kingship is thought to have begun from King Kŭn Ch'ogo. It was also from his reign that Paekche kings began to choose their consorts exclusively from a single aristocratic house. Kŭn Ch'ogo's command to the scholar Kohŭng to compile the *Sŏgi,* a history of Paekche, clearly reflects the king's desire to exult in his expanded royal authority and his well ordered state. Shortly after his death, his grandson adopted Buddhism as the state religion (in 384) and the implanting of the new value system of that faith now proceeded apace.

Koguryŏ had been dealt a severe below by invasions from the continent and the ensuing attack by Paekche, and it now became necessary for Koguryŏ to reshape the pattern of its institutions. This task was undertaken by King Sosurim (371-384), who adopted Buddhism and established a National Confucian Academy in 372 and promulgated a code of administrative law in 373. Buddhism would give the nation spiritual unity, the National Confucian Academy was essential to instituting a new bureaucratic structure, and the administrative code would systematize the state structure itself. In this way Koguryŏ completed its initial creation of a centralized aristocratic state.

These internal arrangements laid the groundwork for external expansion. King Kwanggaet'o (391-413) vigorously added new domains to Koguryŏ by conquest. The huge stone stele still standing at his tomb (at modern T'ung-kou on the Manchurian side of the mid-Yalu River) records the great military campaigns of this king. Leading his cavalry forth across all of Koguryŏ's land boundaries, in the west he occupied the long-contested Liao-tung region, in the northeast he subdued Manchurian peoples, to the south he attacked and incorporated part of Paekche, and far to the southeast he crushed a Wa (Japanese) force attacking Silla. In the end, he created a vast kingdom extending over two-thirds of the Korean Peninsula and much of Manchuria as well. Kwanggaet'o thus merited his name, which means "broad expander of domain."

Kwanggaet'o was succeeded by his son, King Changsu ("the long-lived," 413-491), who during his seventy-nine year reign brought Koguryŏ to its flourishing height. He held China in check by strategically maintaining ties with both the contending Northern and Southern Dynasties. In 427 he moved the Koguryŏ capital from T'ung-kou, where it had served primarily as a military encampment in a region of narrow mountain valleys, to the broad riverine plain at P'yŏngyang. In this new metropolitan center other institutional arrangements now were perfected.

This shift of Koguryŏ's capital so far southward posed a serious threat to Paekche and Silla. Paekche allied with Silla in 433 and

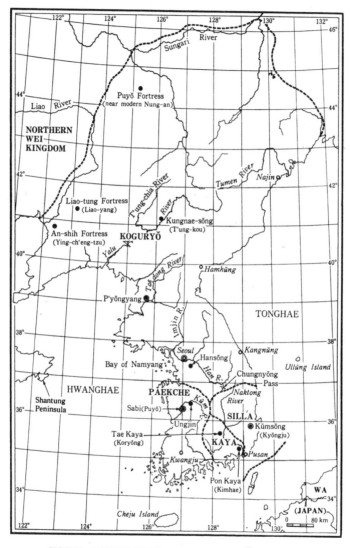

**KOREA AT THE HEIGHT OF KOGURYŎ EXPANSION
IN THE 5ᵗʰ CENTURY**

appealed to a Chinese kingdom in 472 for military support against Koguryŏ's southward aggression, but in vain. For in 475 Koguryŏ seized the Paekche capital at Hansŏng (just south of Seoul), captured the king, and beheaded him. Paekche then moved its capital south to Ungjin (modern Kongju), barely managing to preserve its national existence. The Koguryŏ empire thus had come to embrace a vast territory stretching far into Manchuria and well down into the Korean Peninsula, and so now came to contend for supremacy on the field of battle with China.

The third of the Three Kingdoms, Silla, evolved out of the walled-town state of Saro in southeastern Korea. By the time of King Naemul (356-402), a rather large confederated kingdom had taken shape, through both conquest and federation, in the region east of the Naktong River (in modern North Kyŏngsang province). Originally alternating among three royal houses, the kingship now was monopolized on a hereditary basis by Naemul's Kim clan. In the course of his reign Naemul enlisted the help of Koguryŏ in thwarting the designs of Paekche, which was making use of both Kaya (a confederated kingdom that had arisen along the lower reaches of the Naktong River) and Japanese Wa forces to harass the fledgling Silla Kingdom. This effort was successful, but Silla's difficulties with external enemies led to a slowed pace of internal development.

The first major steps toward centralization of governmental authority in Silla were carried out sometime in the latter half of the fifth century. At this time post stations were established throughout the country, and markets were opened in the capital featuring the products of different locales. Meanwhile, to counter the pressure being exerted on its frontiers by Koguryŏ, Silla had formed an alliance with Paekche in 433, and as the ties with Paekche became further strengthened, the two countries carried out joint military operations on several occasions.

Under King Chijŭng (500-514), Silla achieved important advances in its agricultural technology. Plowing by oxen was introduced and extensive irrigation was undertaken. The resulting increase in agricultural production promoted the social and cultural development of Silla society. In the political sphere, the nation's name was declared to be "Silla" and the Chinese term *wang* ("king") was adopted for its ruler. The foundation thus having been prepared, an administrative structure fully characteristic of a centralized aristocratic state was created in Silla in the reign of King Pŏphŭng (514-540). In 520 he promulgated a code of administrative law that is believed to have delineated the seventeen-grade office rank structure, prescribed proper attire for the officialdom, and instituted the "bone-rank" system. The official adoption of Buddhism as the state religion, which took place about 535, is another important event of King Pŏphŭng's reign. Buddhism provided an ideological underpinning for national unity and solidarity in the newly centralized Silla state.

At this point it became possible for Silla too to go on the offensive in its relations with its neighbors. This expansionist process had already begun, but it was King Chinhŭng (540-576) who pushed ahead most vigorously with Silla's territorial expansion. In 551 Silla attacked the Koguryŏ domain in the Han River basin region, in concert with King Sŏng, the architect of Paekche's recent resurgence. After seizing for itself the upper reaches of the Han River, Silla then drove Paekche forces out of the lower Han region. The enraged King Sŏng retaliated with a frontal assault on Silla in 554, but was himself killed in battle. Silla's occupation of the Han River basin brought with it additional human and material resources and provided a gateway through which Silla might communicate with China across the Yellow Sea. In 562, King Chinhŭng destroyed the Tae Kaya state (the modern Koryŏng area), completing Silla's acquisition of the fertile Naktong River basin. In the northeast, Chinhŭng advanced Silla's frontiers into the Hamhŭng plain, thus crowning his achievements as a conqueror king.

After moving its capital southward to Ungjin (modern Kongju) in 475 Paekche had struggled to survive, and if a foundation for renewed national development were to be laid, it was essential for Paekche to move its capital from mountain-ringed Ungjin to a more favorable location. With this objective in mind King Sŏng (523-554) moved his capital to Sabi, on the broad plain at modern Puyŏ. He then reorganized the administrative structure, fostered the spread of Buddhism to solidify the nation's spiritual foundation, and strengthened Paekche's ties with the Southern

Dynasties of China.

Having restructured his kingdom and built up its strength, King Sŏng turned his efforts toward recovery of Paekche's former territory in the Han River basin. But when Silla betrayed their alliance and seized this fruit of his long and arduous endeavors, King Sŏng saw his dreams end in failure, as has been recounted. Thereafter Paekche looked upon Silla as its mortal enemy and, making common cause with its former foe, Koguryŏ, launched one attack after another against Silla.

The Foreign Relations of the Three Kingdoms

In the relations of the Three Kingdoms with their neighbors in northeast Asia, the relationship with China was pivotal. Three general policies characterize the stance adopted by the Three Kingdoms toward China. First, as they vigorously pursued their expansionist policies of conquest, the Three Kingdoms at times launched bold military assaults against China itself, and naturally they in turn had to face Chinese attacks. This was the case particularly with Koguryŏ, whose frontiers bordered on China. Secondly, in the process of mapping out their own strategies for the unification of the peninsula, all of the Three Kingdoms took appropriate advantage of the conflict within China between the Northern and Southern Dynasties and, moreover, at times formed ties with the nomadic peoples of the northern regions or with the Wa (Japanese) to the south. Thirdly, none of the Three Kingdoms showed any hesitation in adopting whatever elements of Chinese culture and statecraft might be needful for its own development. The relations between the Korean states and China during the Three Kingdoms period, then, unfolded within the framework of these general characteristics.

The conflict of the Three Kingdoms with China was both continuous and intense, but it did not diminish the ardor of the Korean states for the introduction of Chinese culture. The most notable illustrations of this are the adoption of Chinese legal and other institutions, of the Buddhist and Confucianist ideologies, and of the Chinese written language. Nevertheless, the history of the warfare between Korea's Three Kingdoms and China constitutes the principal theme of the relationship. And it is the struggle between Koguryŏ and the Sui and T'ang dynasties that marks the climax of this violent conflict.

In the latter half of the sixth century a major change occurred in the balance of power among the Three Kingdoms and on the continent as well. The T'u-chüeh (Turks) from the steppe region of north-central Asia pressed in upon the recently unified (in 589) Sui dynasty. With its kingdom extending over the northern half of the Korean Peninsula and far into Manchuria, Koguryŏ now sought to form ties with the Turks to confront Sui, and at the same time its Paekche ally was in contact with the Japanese across the sea. Thus to oppose the north-south alignment of forces represented by the Turks, Koguryŏ, Paekche, and Japan, Sui and Silla joined hands to form an east-west axis. The confrontation between these two power blocks foreboded the great storm that soon would break over northeast Asia, and it was the showdown between Koguryŏ and Sui that represented the first decisive test of strength.

Koguryŏ opened hostilities with a bold assault across the Liao River in 598. The Sui emperor, Wen Ti, launched a retaliatory attack on Koguryŏ but met with reverses and turned back in mid-course. Yang Ti, the next Sui emperor, proceeded in 612 to mount an invasion of unprecedented magnitude, marshalling a huge force said to number over a million men. And when his armies failed to take Liao-tung Fortress (modern Liao-yang), the anchor of Koguryŏ's first line of defense, he had nearly a third of his forces, some 300,000 strong, break off the battle there and strike directly at the Koguryŏ capital of P'yŏngyang. But the Sui army was lured into a trap by the famed Koguryŏ commander Ŭlchi Mundŏk, and suffered a calamitous defeat at the Salsu (Ch'ŏng-ch'ŏn) River. It is said that only 2,700 of the 300,000 Sui soldiers survived. The Sui emperor was forced to withdraw his forces to China proper, and before long his war-weakened empire crumbled.

When the T'ang dynasty succeeded the fallen Sui, Koguryŏ anticipated further attacks from China and so fortified itself with a wall a thousand *li* in length across its northwestern frontier. At about the same time, internal schism developed within the Koguryŏ aristocracy, and military strong man Yŏn Kaesomun seized absolute political power (642) in a bloody coup, killing the king and anyone who opposed him. Taking an aggressive posture in foreign relations, Yŏn Kaesomun set Koguryŏ on a collision course with both T'ang and Silla, and before long, in 645, Koguryŏ's defiant stance provoked a large-scale T'ang invasion.

Crossing the Liao River, the Emperor T'ai Tsung reduced the Liao-tung Fortress and a number of others, but he suffered a massive defeat at An-shih Fortress, where as many as six or seven T'ang assaults a day for more than two months all were repulsed. Emperor T'ai Tsung thus turned back, and his further attempts to invade Koguryŏ also met with defeat.

Koguryŏ's victories over the Sui and T'ang invasion armies occupy a special place in the annals of the resistance of the Korean people to foreign aggression. The conquest of Koguryŏ was to be but one stage in the grand imperial design of both Sui and T'ang to achieve hegemony over all of East Asia. Accordingly, had Koguryŏ been beaten, Paekche and Silla as well likely would have fallen under Chinese dominion. But Koguryŏ held firm, serving as a breakwater against which the repeated Chinese invasions foundered, and the peoples of the Korean Peninsula thus were saved from the grave peril of foreign conquest. It is for this reason that Koguryŏ's triumphs hold such importance in the pages of Korean history.

Political and Social Structure of the Three Kingdoms

The period of the Three Kingdoms was an age in which an extremely limited number of aristocratic lineages consolidated their dominant positions over their respective societies. Power in each of the three societies was concentrated in those who lived in the kingdom's capital, and among these it was the aristocratic families, headed by the lineages of the kings and queens, that dominated the rigid and hereditary social status systems and occupied a position of primacy in the political, economic, and cultural spheres.

The "bone-rank" *(kolp'um)* institution of Silla provides the clearest example of the actual structure of aristocratic society in the period of the Three Kingdoms. This was a system that conferred or withheld a variety of special privileges, ranging from political preferment to economic advantage, in accordance with the degree of respect due a person's bone-rank, that is, hereditary bloodline. There were two levels of so-called bone-rank itself, "hallowed-bone" and "true-bone." The hallowed-bone status was held by those in the royal house of Kim who possessed the qualification to become king. Those of true-bone rank also were members of the Kim royal house but originally lacked qualification for the kingship. The distinction between hallowed-bone and true-bone rank within the same Silla royal house of Kim originally seems to have been made on the basis of maternal lineage, but eventually the two bone-ranks coalesced into a single true-bone rank. In addition there were six grades of "head-rank," "head-rank six" down through "head-rank one." Head-rank six was just below true-bone status, while head-ranks three, two, and one probably designated the common people, that is, the non-privileged general populace.

Differential access to official rank and government position was based on the various bone and head-ranks. Only those of the true-bone rank could head a governmental ministry or be named to a high-ranking military post, while those of head-rank four were restricted to the lower third of offices and ranks. Bone-rank also was linked to social and economic privilege. For example, sumptuary regulations based on bone-rank and head-rank governed the size of residences, the color of official attire, vehicles and horse trappings, and the use of various utensils. Needless to say, then, in such a hierarchic society as Silla's, predominant power was wielded by those who enjoyed the highest hereditary social status, namely those of true-bone rank.

The political structures of the Three Kingdoms evolved from early pluralistic systems to monolithic bureaucratic structures centered upon the kingship. In the case of Koguryŏ's transformation into a centralized aristocratic state, those who in former days had been tribal or clan chieftains were given rank appropriate to their earlier positions and in this way were integrated into the new socio-political structure. And it appears that the holders of certain lower office ranks emerged from among those who had been the actual administrators of the powerful royal and aristocratic houses that they served. Thus, the pluralistic political structure of Koguryŏ's past was converted into a unitary office rank system. Similar processes of structural integration occurred in Paekche and Silla, where diverse social elements also were incorporated into a monolithic, hierarchic political system.

The most significant feature of the political process in each of the Three Kingdoms is the role played by conciliar bodies in political decision making. The *Hwabaek* institution, Silla's Council of Nobles, provides the clearest illustration of this phenomenon. The *Hwabaek* was a council headed by the single aristocrat who held "extraordinary rank one" and was composed of those of "extraordinary rank two," all of whom are thought to have been of true-bone lineage. Its function was to render decisions on the most important matters of state, such as succession to the throne and the declaration of war; the original decision to formally adopt Buddhism also was made by the *Hwabaek* council. The principle of unanimity governed the *Hwabaek,* which convened at sites around Kyŏngju having special religious significance. Koguryŏ and Paekche developed analogous conciliar institutions, and their function as corporate and consensual assemblies of the high aristocracy is one of the distinctive features of the political process of the Three Kingdoms.

In the military sphere, each of the Three Kingdoms organized its military units on the national level and put them under the authority of the king as commander-in-chief of his nation's military forces. In fact, the monarchs of the Three Kingdoms frequently led their soldiers in person and fought alongside them in battle. In the case of Silla, garrisons were established in each provincial jurisdiction, commanded by generals of true-bone status. But they were composed of men who lived in the capital and so had the character of elite units drawn from elite lineages. In addition to this garrison army nucleus in Silla, there also were "oath bannermen" who, something like feudal retainers, pledged their individual services and loyalty to their commanders.

These elite units were supplemented by companies of quite young men, often in their mid teens, like the *hwarang* ("flower of youth") of Silla. These bands cultivated an ethos of loyalty, service, and strong moral values. The *hwarang* warrior youth honored the "five secular injunctions" laid down in the early 600s by the famed Buddhist monk Wŏn'gwang. These were: (1) to serve the king with loyalty, (2) to serve one's parents with filiality, (3) to practice fidelity in friendship, (4) to never retreat in battle, and (5) to refrain from wanton killing. There was also a religious dimension to the activities of the *hwarang,* as they made pilgrimages to sacred mountain and river sites in Silla and prayed for their nation's tranquility and prosperity by performing ceremonial singing and dancing. But the most important function of the *hwarang* was military. In time of peace the *hwarang* cultivated the military arts, and in time of war they joined in the fighting at the front lines. The many tales of valor and prowess in battle told of such *hwarang* heroes as Kim Yu-sin are among the most famous episodes in all of Korean history.

In each of the Three Kingdoms the authority of the central government extended over the countryside, which gradually came to be divided into administrative districts. Fortresses were built in the regions where formerly tribal communities had claimed territorial rights, and these were made the centers of local administration. The governor of such a district bore the title "castle lord." Eventually numbers of districts were combined to form larger, provincial-type administrative units, the governors of which generally also served as military commanders. In the capitals of the Three Kingdoms, where the ruling aristocracies resided, special administrative districts were created. The residents of the capital in each case enjoyed a position superior to that of people who lived in the provincial areas, as will be seen below.

With the emergence of centralized aristocratic states centered on monarchical power, the new concepts evolved that all of the nation's land belonged to the king and that all of the people were his subjects. Nevertheless, this does not mean that private ownership of land disappeared, or that the people of the nation all alike came under the direct dominion of the king. Large grants of land and numerous prisoners of war were given to commanders for their victories in battle and to the aristocratic holders of government office, and in consequence the private land and slave holdings of the aristocracy increased continuously. At times prisoners of war or criminals were forcibly resettled in separate villages, where they formed communities of low caste laborers. In fact, the social compulsion to relegate large segments of the populace to unfree status constitutes a notable characteristic of the aristocratic states of the Three Kingdoms period.

The independent peasants whose status was that of freemen comprised the preponderant class in these societies. The state levied grain and tribute taxes (in the form of local products) upon the peasants and commandeered their labor services to man local defenses or for construction projects like fortifications and irrigation works. Indeed, one might venture to say that the labor power of the free peasantry was more valuable to the state than the agricultural and handcrafted products they produced.

The peasant villages were the basic units in the provincial administrative structure, central government control over them apparently being exercised through local village chiefs or headmen. Since the peasants of the Three Kingdoms still did some farming on a cooperative basis, it is clear that the earlier communal traditions persisted. Nevertheless, on the whole they were self-reliant farmers who each worked his own land independently, and consequently considerable social differentiation developed among them. Some peasants, for example, lost their land and thus fell into a new class of landless tenant farmers. For their part, village headmen were not incorporated into the structure of office ranks held by residents of the capital. Accordingly, they were denied access to other government office, and aspects of their daily lives, too, were subject to restrictive regulations.

The Aristocratic Culture of the Three Kingdoms

The Chinese writing system was introduced to Korea in much earlier times, along with continental iron culture, but it came into much more widespread use during the Three Kingdoms period. The use of this foreign written language without modification entailed a number of difficulties, so the Koreans began to devise ways to adapt Chinese characters to suit their own needs. The system known as *idu* used certain characters in a fixed way to put a sentence partially into Korean syntax, while the more sophisticated *hyangch'al* method involved using a corpus of

Chinese characters only for their sounds to create a kind of syllabary for the Korean language.

With the development of ways of writing, a variety of state-supported compilation activities were undertaken, chief among which were national histories. None of the Three Kingdom histories has survived, but their contents probably were incorporated by Kim Pu-sik into his twelfth century *Samguk sagi* (*History of the Three Kingdoms*). The compilation of these national histories reflects the common desire of the rulers of the Three Kingdoms to display the sovereign dignity of their centralized aristocratic states to the contemporary world and to posterity.

All of the Three Kingdoms laid great stress on inculcating the Confucian ethos as a means of maintaining their aristocratic social orders and cementing the solidarity of their societies. In 372 in Koguryŏ first, and subsequently in Paekche and Silla, Confucian educational institutions were established and works from the corpus of Chinese classics, philosophies, and histories began ever more widely to be read. In Silla the Confucian precept of fidelity, so valued by the members of the *hwarang* bands, was of particular importance in welding Silla society together, and, through the inculcation of loyalty, this cohesive force was directed upward to bolster the authority of the throne.

The widely accepted date for the introduction of Buddhism to Korea is the year 372, when a monk brought images of the Buddha and Buddhist sutras to Koguryŏ from China. Twelve years later Buddhism came to Paekche in the same way. In both instances Buddhism was welcomed by the royal houses as part of their overall receptivity to Chinese culture. Buddhism also was well received when it was brought to the Silla royal house from southern China early in the sixth century, but King Pŏphŭng (514-540) could not overcome the opposition of the Silla aristocracy and secure the official acceptance of Buddhism until near the end of his reign, in about 535. In all of the Three Kingdoms the principal initiative for the acceptance of Buddhism thus was taken by the royal houses, probably because it was seen to be well-suited to undergird the new governing structure centered on the authority of the throne. The concept of a single body of believers all devoted to observing the way of the Buddha, combined with the notion of the whole of the nation's people serving the king as one, surely played a major role as a force for unity and cohesion in these early Korean states. At the same time, however, it should not be forgotten that without the acquiescence of the powerful aristocracies the official acceptance of Buddhism likely would not have come about. And the reason they acquiesced may well have been that, in societies like these marked by such strict social stratification, the Buddhist teaching of reincarnation, of a rebirth based on *karma,* was welcomed as a doctrine giving recognition to the privileged position of an aristocracy.

Although Buddhism provided a vehicle for personal devotion and belief, the aspect of Buddhism as a doctrine for the protection of the state was a powerful attraction of that faith in the Three Kingdoms period. Sutras like the *Sutra of the Benevolent Kings* were held in particular esteem; in keeping with its doctrines, ceremonies called "Assemblies for Sutra Recitation by One Hundred Monks" (Inwang Assemblies) were held to pray for the well-being of the state. Among the numerous Buddhist temples in the Three Kingdoms, moreover, those dedicated to the doctrines and rituals of state protection were on the grandest scale. An example of the interrelationship of Buddhism with the interests of the state is the widespread belief that a nine-story pagoda in Kyŏngju symbolized Silla's destiny to conquer nine other East Asian nations. Another example is the conviction that Maitreya Buddha, the Buddha of the Future, had experienced several incarnations on Silla soil in the form of famed *hwarang* warriors. Moreover, there is no question that the exhortations of monks to fight bravely in battle, to safeguard not only the state and its ruler but the way of the Buddha as well, gave courage to the soldiers called upon to wage their nation's wars.

Direct state control characterizes the Buddhism of the Three Kingdoms period. Silla established a hierarchy of abbot administrators at the district, provincial, and national levels who applied the rules of the Vinaya order to control the temples and monks of the whole country. At times monks served as political advisers, offering advice on how to rule. Buddhist monks, moreover, played a pioneering role in bringing new elements of Chinese culture to Korea, since they made up the majority of those who traveled to China for study during the Three Kingdoms period (known then as "study in the West"). The monks also provided ethical guidance to the people. Wŏn'gwang's formulation of the "five secular injunctions" and the undertaking of moral instruction to *hwarang* youth by monks who lived with them in their bands exemplify this important role.

The poetry and music of the Three Kingdoms period has a strongly religious character. The *hyangga* ("native songs") that survive from Silla, with their unpretentiousness and simple rhythms, are regarded as admirable expressions of Korean literary sensibility. The *hyangga* genre represents a transformation of shamanist incantations into Buddhistic supplications; written principally by *hwarang* or by Buddhist monks, they generally invoke divine intervention in human affairs. The monk Yungch'ŏn's "Song of the Comet," the singing of which is said to have made a comet disappear and caused Japanese invaders to retreat, aptly illustrates the religious nature of Korea's earliest poetic form. Given its close relationship to poetry, the music of this age also was replete with religious overtones—the ceremonial singing and dancing that accompanied *hwarang* prayers for their country's well-being is one confirmation of this. Some thirty or forty varieties of musical instruments, including wind, string, and percussion, are known to have been in use during this age, the most famous of which was the "black crane zither" adapted from the seven-stringed zither of China.

The artistic creations of the Three Kingdoms period, an age when a new social order was being shaped by an aristocratic elite as yet unspoiled and unsophisticated, were fundamentally both forthright and robust in their aesthetic mood. Gradually, the flourishing of Buddhism both enriched the intellectual content of Three Kingdoms art and introduced markedly advanced artistic techniques, and in consequence works began to appear in which a more refined sense of beauty and harmony can be discerned.

No specimens of Koguryŏ architecture remain, apart from stone and earthen tombs that convey a sense of the unyielding strength of the powerful figures interred therein. This, no doubt, is because Buddhist pagodas and other temple buildings in that kingdom were made of wood. Paekche's legendary palaces, pavilions, and huge temples also have not survived, but several stone pagodas do evidence the fluid, graceful architectural silhouettes of the age.

In contrast to the scant, but impressive, architectural remains, the Three Kingdoms bequeathed a magnificent array of classical sculptures of timeless appeal. Most of the sculptures of the period depict Sakyamuni (the historical Buddha) or Maitreya (the future Buddha). The most renowned Koguryŏ examples are the gilt bronze standing Tathagata Buddha (dated around 539 A.D.) and the gilt bronze half-seated Maitreya in meditation pose, to both of which their sculptors gave beatific, musing smiles. In Paekche, statues like the stone Buddha carved in the cliff face at Sŏsan and the famous gilt bronze meditating half-seated Maitreya, with its low and unadorned four-peaked diadem, exhibit elegant facial contours and imperturbable, radiant smiles. Silla also can boast of a masterfully executed gilt bronze sculpture of a meditating half-seated Maitreya that is admired for the sense of spiritual strength that it conveys.

Impressive painting specimens also survive from the Three Kingdoms period, the most important of these being the murals of the old tombs of Koguryŏ. Painted on the four walls of the burial chamber of earthen tombs and on the corbeled vaulted ceilings, and treating a variety of themes, these exuberant murals provide precious documentation of the way of life and thought of the Koguryŏ people. The Koguryŏ tombs customarily are named after the theme of the paintings that adorn their walls—for example the Tomb of the Four Spirits, the Tomb of the Dancers, and the Tomb of the Hunters. Perhaps the most famous of the murals are found in the great Tomb of the Four Spirits—the azure dragon of the East, the white tiger of the West, the vermilion phoenix of the South, and the tortoise and snake of the North. The spirited lines and bold colors of the Koguryŏ murals make these paintings so pulsate with animation that the viewer feels as if the animals are alive or that a mounted Koguryŏ warrior is riding by in full gallop before his very eyes. Mural paintings are found in old Paekche tombs as well, but the Paekche murals convey a much greater sense of refinement than those of

Koguryŏ. Artists of both countries went to Japan, where their artistry was so acclaimed that such outstanding works as the murals at the Hōryūji temple and the portrait of Shōtoku Taishi, both in Nara, traditionally were attributed to them.

The old tombs of Koguryŏ and Paekche were relatively easy to pilfer, and for this reason virtually no burial objects remain—although the discovery not many years ago of the fully intact tomb of King Muryŏng (501-523) has enabled us to gain an appreciation of the superb artistry of Paekche's craftsmen. Happily, however, the Silla style of tomb construction, utilizing a vertical shaft for interment beneath an earth-covered mound of stones, made grave robbing almost impossible. Among the multitude of burial objects so far excavated, the most spectacular are those fashioned of pure gold—gold crowns and shoes, girdles and earrings, finger rings and bracelets—and sumptuous jewelry made of gemstones and molten glass. Gold crowns have been unearthed from quite a number of tombs, and they are especially prized for the unique Silla style of their form and adornment. Nevertheless, the historical significance of these artistic creations lies less in their remarkable aesthetic qualities than in the fact that they are symbols of the power and authority of the Silla kings and queens in whose tombs they are found.

Chapter 4

The Fashioning of an Authoritarian Monarchy

The Silla Unification and the Founding of the Parhae Kingdom

In the mid-seventh century, while Koguryŏ was occupied by its bloody wars with Sui and T'ang, Paekche hastened to take the offensive against Silla in campaigns led by King Ŭija (641-660). His early successes led Silla, after overtures to Koguryŏ had been rebuffed, to seek an alliance with T'ang. T'ang acceded to Silla's request and a strategy was settled upon: Paekche would first be overcome and then Koguryŏ caught in a pincers movement from both the north and south. Accordingly, in the year 660, a T'ang invasion fleet landed troops within striking distance of the Paekche capital at modern Puyŏ, while a Silla army approached from the east. Paekche had delayed in sending a force to block the Silla advance, and before long its capital fell to the combined assault.

The following year Koguryŏ beat back a Chinese attempt to sail up the Taedong River to the very walls of P'yŏngyang, but Koguryŏ's power to resist by now had been seriously weakened both by long years of continuous warfare and by internal dissension. In 667, finally, Silla and T'ang were able to mount a coordinated offensive, and, although Koguryŏ managed to hold out for another year, the end came in 668.

The intention of the Chinese in sending armies to conquer Paekche and Koguryŏ had been to bring the entire Korean Peninsula under T'ang imperial control. To this end, T'ang now established five commanderies in the regions that had been the five provinces of the former Paekche kingdom and began to administer the area directly. Shortly thereafter, T'ang created the

Great Commandery of Kyerim as the mechanism through which the Silla domain would be ruled and brazenly appointed Silla King Munmu as its governor-general. T'ang then created nine additional commanderies to govern Koguryŏ's former domains, while at the same time establishing a Protectorate-General to Pacify the East at P'yŏngyang to rule not only over the conquered kingdoms of Koguryŏ and Paekche but over Silla itself as well.

Silla was unwilling to accept this turn of events. Accordingly, almost from the moment of Koguryŏ's collapse Silla launched a campaign to win control over the former Koguryŏ domain, assisting restorationist forces trying to drive out the Chinese. Moreover, Silla sent armies into the Paekche region and in numerous battles defeated Paekche restorationist forces and T'ang occupation troops. Before long, in 671, Silla succeeded in seizing control over the whole of the former Paekche kingdom. Some years later, in 676, in a series of battles in the region of the Han River basin, Silla was able to force the T'ang armies to retreat. In the end, T'ang removed its Protectorate-General to Pacify the East from P'yŏngyang to Liao-tung-ch'eng well outside the Korean Peninsula, in effect recognizing Silla's claim to hegemony within the peninsula.

The fact that Silla repulsed the T'ang aggression by force of arms and preserved the independence of the Korean Peninsula is of great historical significance. The T'ang ambition to destroy Paekche and Koguryŏ and conquer Silla as well, which would bring the whole of Manchuria and the Korean Peninsula under its dominion, posed no less serious a crisis for the Korean people than the establishment of the Four Han Chinese Commanderies nearly seven hundred years earlier. Clearly, Korean society and culture would not have been able to develop unhindered under T'ang political domination. Fortunately, however, Silla was fully able to resist T'ang aggression and maintain its national independence. Accordingly, the importance of the Silla unification lies above all in the creation of an environment wherein the process of the formation of the Korean people might take an independent course. To be sure, Unified Silla and Parhae confronted each other hostilely much like southern and northern halves of a partitioned nation, but in the end it was the territory and people of Unified Silla, and the society and culture fashioned there, that formed the mainstream of subsequent Korean history. In this sense the historical significance of the Silla unification scarcely can be overemphasized.

Silla's unification did not include the whole of the territory occupied by the Three Kingdoms. In fact, most of Koguryŏ's vast lands remained outside Silla dominion. In the region stretching to the north beyond the Yalu and Tumen Rivers refugee emigres from Koguryŏ now established the kingdom of Parhae, and the more northerly areas of the Korean Peninsula itself also came under Parhae control. The Liao-tung region, on the other hand, had become a part of the T'ang empire.

The founder of Parhae (Chinese: P'o-hai) was a former Koguryŏ general, Tae Cho-yŏng. Upon the fall of Koguryŏ he had been taken prisoner but, seizing upon the occasion of an insurrection by Khitan people, he led a band of followers eastward and proclaimed himself king. He ruled not only over people of Koguryŏ ethnic stock but also over a large Malgal population, members of semi-nomadic Tungusic tribes scattered over a wide expanse of Manchuria, southern Siberia, and northeast Korea. The ruling class of Parhae, however, was comprised of Koguryŏ people who clearly regarded their state as representing a revival of Koguryŏ.

The international position in which the new state of Parhae found itself was extremely precarious. Having been subjected to strong Chinese pressure from the time of its founding, for some decades Parhae remained hostile toward T'ang. At the same time, Parhae also found itself in confrontation with Silla, with the result that in 721 Silla even built a defensive wall along its northern frontier. The pressure exerted by Parhae, in fact, appears to have been the major reason why Silla was forced to be content with a northern boundary limited to the Taedong River-Bay of Wŏnsan line. But despite the hostility of both T'ang and Silla, by the end of the eighth century Parhae had succeeded in expanding its domain to encompass the whole of northeastern Manchuria and the Liaotung Peninsula as well. Meanwhile, Parhae had reached an accommodation with the Chinese and proceeded to assimilate T'ang institutions and culture.

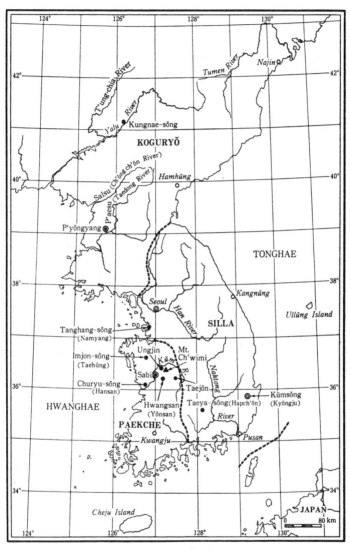

THE UNIFICATION STRUGGLE AMONG THE THREE KINGDOMS
(7ᵗʰ CENTURY)

A major change in the character of Korea's relationship with China is seen in the fact that both Silla and Parhae came to establish peaceful diplomatic relations with T'ang. This relationship can be considered under two broad headings, the first of which is economic exchange. Carried on within the framework of T'ang's tributary system, much of Korea's export trade at first comprised raw materials, but gradually a marked increase in handcrafted articles occurred. From beginning to end, however, the demand for imported goods remained the keynote of Korean trade with China, as many kinds of luxury fabrics and handcrafted goods were eagerly sought for consumpion by the members of the aristocracy.

Cultural borrowing was the other major facet of the relationship with T'ang China. Both Silla and Parhae imported large numbers of books and art works from T'ang. Moreover, Korean monks and students—at the outset mostly monks—traveled to T'ang to study Buddhism or Confucian scholarship and, after their return, contributed to cultural development in their homelands. Viewed overall, the importation of T'ang civilization was a major factor in the blooming of the native cultures of Silla and Parhae.

The Government and Society of Unified Silla

A growing authoritarianism in the power exercised by the throne was the most important change accompanying the Silla unification. During the Three Kingdoms period the throne had been occupied by rulers of "hallowed-bone" lineage, but this highest lineage rank came to an end in the mid-seventh century. The next monarch was T'aejong, King Muyŏl, a man of the "true-bone" lineage. King Muyŏl's mother was from the Kim royal house, the daughter of a king, and moreover his queen was the younger sister of Kim Yu-sin, whose Kaya royal lineage was called the "new house of Kim." Thereafter it became established practice for Silla queens to come from a narrow segment of the Kim royal house itself, and this development can be seen as evidence of the growth of the authority of the king at the expense of the aristocratic families, his rivals for power. The fact that Muyŏl was followed on the throne by his direct lineal descendants is a further indication of the heightened authority of the kingship.

It was King Sinmun (681-692) who firmly established the authority of the throne. To accomplish this he carried out a determined purge of those leading figures upon whom aristocratic power centered. The king then turned his attention to creating political and military institutions through which royal power might effectively be exercised. By the reign of his second son, Sŏngdŏk (702-737), the paramount authority of the throne in Silla finally had been secured, and with this accomplished the kingdom at last enjoyed unaccustomed domestic tranquility.

To say that the authority of the throne had become paramount is not to suggest that the bone-rank system, the linchpin of the Silla social and political order, was itself shaken. Those of the true-bone lineage continued to constitute the dominant status group, the major difference being that now their power had weakened, and as it weakened, the role of the aristocracy holding head-rank six in the stratified Silla order was correspondingly enhanced. As before, the restraints on the upward mobility of these men prevented them from serving in the topmost positions or even from being appointed as chief officers in the ministries of the central government. However, these less privileged members of the aristocracy set themselves against the true-bone nobles and so aligned their interests with those of the throne. Despite the obstacles created by the social status system, therefore, the throne and head-rank six found common cause and, accordingly, men of head-rank six now began to come to the fore in Silla society. In particular, because of their deeper learning and insight, their advice on governmental matters was sought by the king, and in this way they performed an important political role in the later years of Unified Silla.

In consonance with the greatly strengthened power of the throne, changes now occurred in the workings of the organs of the central government. The administrative structure of Unified Silla, in form at least, adhered in general to that of the Three Kingdoms period. Nevertheless, a significant change is evident in the comparative importance that came to be attached to the Chancellery Office (*Chipsabu*), created in 651 as the highest administrative organ of the Silla government. Rather than representing the interests of the aristocracy, the *Chipsabu* was a kind of executive council responsive to the dictates of the king. In consequence, the chief officer of the *Chipsabu* (called *chung-si*), who served in essence as a prime minister, stood in an adversarial relationship to the *sangdaedŭng,* the head of the *Hwabaek.* Further, the fact that the *chungsi* was regarded as politically more important than the *sangdaedŭng* indicates that the political structure of Unified Silla had become more authoritiarian.

The dominant power of the throne in Unified Silla is clearly evident in the changes in its military organization. The pre-unification "six garrisons," which were under the command of the aristocracy and organized along lines that reflected earlier tribal traditions, were replaced by nine "oath bannermen" divisions and ten garrison units. The nine oath bannermen divisions formed a national army that was stationed in the capital. They drew their recruits not only from the native Silla population but also from the former inhabitants of Koguryŏ and Paekche, and from Malgal tribesmen as well. These divisions appear to have operated under the direct authority of the king, to whom each unit took an oath of loyalty. Complementing these nine divisions in Kyŏngju were the "ten garrisons" stationed outside the capital, distributed uniformly throughout the whole of Unified Silla's nine provinces. They were entrusted with the defense of the country and internal security duties as well.

Unified Silla came into being through a process of territorial expansion, so it became necessary to create an expanded system of provincial and local government. The basic units of local administration in the Unified Silla period were the province, the prefecture, and the county. The counties were further subdivided into villages and certain special settlements for those of unfree status. There also were urbanized centers called "secondary capitals," in which Unified Silla forcibly resettled the aristocracies of the states it had conquered. It is noteworthy, though, that some of these elites from the conquered areas were accorded a bone-rank status based on the social standing they had enjoyed formerly in their own societies. The Silla aristocracy clung tenaciously to its base of power in Kyŏngju, defeating efforts to move the capital from this out-of-the-way location even so short a distance westward as Taegu. However, some members of the capital aristocracy did resettle in the secondary capitals, with the result that these came to play a special role in the social and cultural life of Unified Silla.

The great majority of the aristocratic elites of course, remained in the capital at Kyŏngju (then called by a name that means "city of gold"), where they pursued extravagant lives of pleasure. For despite their somewhat eroded political power, the aristocracy of Unified Silla continued to command vast wealth. The official history of China's T'ang dynasty contains the following record:

> Emoluments flow unceasingly into the houses of the highest officials, who possess as many as 3,000 slaves, with corresponding numbers of weapons, cattle, horses, and pigs.

It also was said that there was not a single thatched roof house within Kyŏngju's walls, while the never-ending sounds of music and song filled the streets night and day.

In continuation of pre-unification practices, the Silla aristocracy received grants of "tax villages," agricultural land to be held in perpetuity, horse farms, and grain, and it was by this means that the aristocracy accumulated its immense wealth. For their part, government officials were paid by allocation of "stipend villages," which entitled them to the grain tax from the lands within their grants and, apparently, also to the labor services of the peasants who worked these lands.

In contrast to the fortunes of the aristocracy, the years of warfare that marked the Silla unification were accompanied by increasing impoverishment of the lives of the common people. More and more of them could not repay their debts and were reduced to slavery, which was particularly prevalent in the capital. Large numbers of artisans and laborers with slave status were attached to the various palace and government agencies that supplied the requirements of the royal household at one extreme and produced weapons and ships at the other. If indeed the houses of the highest officials possessed as many as three thousand slaves, then it may be surmised that the number owned by the aristocracy in its entirety comprised a substantial portion of the total Silla population.

The ordinary farming population lived in villages normally consisting of a small cluster of peasant dwellings, and to serve the state's purposes a census register was prepared for each hamlet. A portion of one such Silla census register, believed to date from 755, has been discovered. Its contents indicate that Silla carried out a census every three years and, in addition to household and population statistics, recorded the numbers of cattle and horses, of mulberry, nut-bearing pine, and walnut trees, and the area of different types of land, such as paddy fields, dry fields, and hemp fields. Households then were classified in accordance with the number of able-bodied adults there were to provide compulsory labor service. The detailed records contained in this document leave no doubt that every effort was made to extract as much as possible from the peasant population, primarily for the benefit of the capital aristocracy.

In contrast to the free commoner population of the villages, there were separate settlements inhabited by unfree people whose status was essentially one of slavery. Either conquered people or those guilty of crimes against the state, they were transported to these special settlements to labor at such tasks as farming, stock raising, or other manual work. The existence of numerous such communities of unfree laborers located in every region of the country is one distinguishing feature of Silla society.

The Flourishing of Silla Culture

Buddhism was the dominant system of thought in Unified Silla. As the religion was revered and professed alike by all the people, from the king on high to the populace at large, Buddhism played a vital role in the intellectual and cultural life of Silla society. Many eminent monks journeyed to T'ang China or even to far away India to study the way of the Buddha. The many monks who returned to Silla after studying in China brought back with them the doctrines of the various Buddhist sects that had proliferated under the T'ang dynasty. Among these it was the Avatamsaka (Hwaŏm; Chinese: Hua-yen) that was accorded the most devout adherence by aristocratic society when Silla was in full flourish. Hwaŏm taught the doctrine of all encompassing harmony, that the one contains the multitude and that the multitude is as one, a concept that sought to embrace the myriad of sentient beings within the single Buddha mind. Such a doctrine was well suited to a state with a centralized power structure under an authoritarian monarchy, and this surely was one reason why the Hwaŏm teaching was welcomed by the ruling elite of Unified Silla's aristocracy.

The great popularity of Pure Land Buddhism, principally among the common people, is another salient feature of the Buddhism of the Unified Silla period. The Pure Land creed was a Buddhism for the masses, a faith which even the unlettered could understand and profess. No grasp of the abstruse doctrines of the Buddhist sutras was required, for it was enough only to repeat the chant of *"Nammu Amit'a Pul"* as a way to show "Homage to the Buddha of Infinite Light." If one but performed this extremely simple devotion, then one could be reborn in the "Pure Land," or Western Paradise where the Amitabha Buddha dwells. Pure Land became the Buddhism for the masses in part because of the accessibility of its practice and in part because it offered hope of an escape from the despair of lives filled with day to day suffering, a condition brought about by the gross inequities in Silla society under authoritarian rule.

Wŏnhyo (617-686), perhaps the greatest monk-scholar of the age, played a major role in the widespread propagation of Pure Land Buddhism throughout the countryside. Condemning the sense of confrontation that characterized the attitude of the various Buddhist sects toward one another, he argued the necessity of viewing Buddhist doctrine from a higher level of abstraction, so as to achieve a harmonious integration of the differing points of view. It was understandable, then, that Wŏnhyo should come to preach the Pure Land creed that all men might be reborn in paradise. Following the storied occasion when he broke his vows and fathered a son (Sŏl Ch'ong, to whom tradition attributes the creation of the *idu* writing system) by a Silla princess, he traveled in penance to hamlets in every corner of the land, preaching the Pure Land faith. And it is said that his evangelistic efforts brought about the conversion to Buddhism of eighty percent or more of the Silla population.

During the Unified Silla period Confucianism came to rival

Buddhism as an alternate system of thought. The establishment of a National Confucian College in 682 was one result of this development. As of the mid-eighth century its curriculum consisted of the *Analects* of Confucius, the *Classic of Filial Piety,* and other classical Chinese texts on rites, history, and literature. Entrance was permitted only to those members of the aristocracy who held the twelfth office rank or below, including those without office rank. This national educational institution made possible the inauguration of a state examination system for the selection of government officials in 788, and the candidates who passed this examination were given appointments on the basis of their proficiency in reading Chinese texts. The establishment of this state examination system apparently reflected a desire to emphasize Confucian learning, rather than merely bone-rank lineage, as the basis for selecting government officials.

The Confucianism in which the Silla state was displaying such lively interest essentially opposed the values of the traditional bone-rank order, with its core of true-bone aristocrats, and the Buddhist doctrine that buttressed it. It was primarily those of head-rank six background who championed Confucian thought. These men argued the paramount importance of a set of moral standards applicable to the world of human affairs, and asserted that Confucianism offered a more beneficial system of public morals and social values than Buddhism, with its emphasis on personal salvation and life in the hereafter. Accordingly, under Silla's authoritarian political structure Confucianism stood in opposition to traditional true-bone privilege and, indeed, developed in partnership with the power of the throne.

Korean scholarship and technology witnessed significant progress during the Unified Silla period. In the field of historical studies the writings of the early eighth-century scholar Kim Tae-mun are remarkable for the deep concern he shows for the native Silla tradition in an age when most were obsessed with T'ang Chinese culture. Astronomy and calendrical science already had begun to develop before the unification, resulting in the construction of the Ch'ŏmsŏngdae observatory, which still stands in Kyŏngju, by the mid-seventh century.

Mathematical knowledge also greatly advanced and was practically applied in a number of areas, most notably in Buddhist architecture. Finally, the art of woodblock printing was developed in order to reproduce a variety of texts, especially Buddhist sutras and classical Confucian writings. The copy of the Dharani sutra found not many years ago in Kyŏngju, in the base of the Pagoda That Casts No Shadow, and which therefore must pre-date the construction of the pagoda in 751, is the world's oldest extant example of woodblock printing.

The *hyangga* genre of religious poetry, which had appeared in the Silla of the Three Kingdoms period, continued to flourish in Unified Silla. A modern rendering of the concise and difficult text of the original *hyangga* "Dedication" poignantly expresses the ardent devotion with which a prayer is offered, in the form of a gift of flowers, for the compassion of the Maitreya Bodhisattva, thusly:

> Here now I sing the flower strewing song —
> Oh offering of flowers, do you
> As my pious heart commands:
> Attend and bring the Maitreya Bodhisattva
> From the distant Tusita Heaven.

Silla's *hyangga* poets composed their songs to entreat Heaven to bring tranquility to the state, to extol the virtue of the Buddha, to express longing for a deceased loved one, or simply as prayers. The *hyangga,* in sum, represents a lyrical expression of the religious feelings of the Silla people.

The hallmark of the art of the Unified Silla period is its attempt to create a beauty of idealized harmony through the application of refined artistic craftsmanship. This noble aim is nowhere more evident than in the unflawed harmonies of the Pulguk-sa temple in Kyŏngju and the nearby Sŏkkuram grotto, both built around 751. The beautiful "cloud bridge stairway" leading up to the entrance gate, the Mauve Mist Gate; the novel shape of the stone supports for the two front pillars of the Floating Shadow Pavilion; the balanced proportions of the two justly famed pagodas, the Pagoda of Many Treasures and the Pagoda That Casts No Shadow—all these alike represent the realization, in the difficult medium of stone, of an idealized beauty of symmetry and harmony. The Sŏkkuram is a man-made stone grotto designed as a setting for the worship of a principal statue of Buddha. This large Sakyamuni Buddha figure in the center of the interior chamber, the eleven-headed Goddess of Mercy and the various Bodhisattvas and Arhat (disciples of Buddha) carved in relief in a semicircle on the surrounding wall, the two *Inwang* ("benevolent kings") on the walls of the antechamber, and the Four Deva Kings standing guard along the passageway—each of these adds its own distinctive note to the symphony of beauty presented by the Sŏkkuram as an integral whole.

In discussing art forms inspired by the practice of the Buddhist faith, the castings of bronze temple bells can by no means be overlooked. The oldest extant bell from Silla is dated 725, but the best known is the so-called Emille Bell, now in the National Museum in Kyŏngju, cast in 771. The Emille Bell measures seven feet six inches (2.27 meters) in diameter and is eleven feet (3.3 meters) high, making it the largest surviving Korean bell. It also is the most exquisitely wrought, in the shape of the bell itself and in the beauty of its decoration with flying angels and lotus flower motifs. The bells of Silla have a unique shape that, together with their exquisitely executed raised designs, give them a beauty unequalled by the temple bells of China or Japan. Unified Silla has left us not only these bells but many superb examples of stone lanterns, stone stupas, stone water basins, end tiles for roofing, paving tiles, and other objects associated with Buddhist architecture. Calligraphy, as seen carved in stone at Buddhist temples, also reached a high level of development during this brilliantly creative age.

Tombs are the treasure house of Silla works of art unrelated to Buddhism. After the unification the prevalent style of tomb architecture took on a different form, characterized by a horizontal passageway leading to a stone burial chamber. The much smaller earthen mound covering the burial chamber was faced with upright supporting slabs of stone, on which were carved representations of the twelve zodiacal animal deities. These were borrowed from the ancient Chinese calendar but their use in tomb architecture is a unique Silla development. The apparent belief was that these animal figures (rat, bull, tiger, horse, etc.), all in upright human form and bearing weapons, would guard the soul of the deceased. The rendering of these fanciful subjects, which the merest inadvertence might have turned into comic figures, is done with a dexterous skill that provides yet another proof of the consummate artistry of the Silla people.

The Society and Culture of Parhae

Parhae, it has been noted, was a kingdom founded by people of Koguryŏ stock, and it was they who monopolized political power in Parhae. The majority of those over whom this elite class ruled were Malgal people and, although a few of the Malgal succeeded in moving upward into the lower echelon of the ruling elite, they mostly were a subject people. In fact, some Malgal became an unfree class serving masters of Koguryŏ origins.

The structure of the Parhae central government was modeled on the T'ang system (in contrast, Unified Silla had been content to leave the earlier, traditional administrative arrangements essentially intact). In short, Parhae appears to have sought to make manifest the authority and prestige of its governmental mechanisms by devising a carefully structured administrative system embellished by weighty Confucianist terminology.

Parhae culture incorporated both elements of T'ang and Koguryŏ derivation. A large number of students were sent to T'ang to study and, as a result of such cultural interaction, Parhae came to model not only its government structure but other institutional features as well after those of T'ang. On the other hand, elements of Koguryŏ derivation are seen in the provincial administrative structure and some features of residential and tomb architecture. Moreover, the style of Buddhist statuary found at Parhae temple sites, as well as the lotus blossom and woven cloth motifs with which Parhae roofing end tiles were decorated, also have a distinct Koguryŏ flavor.

The cultural level of the Parhae kingdom was so advanced that an official Chinese history described it as the "flourishing land in the East." But since the population was composed of a ruling elite of Koguryŏ descent and a subject class of native Malgal people, the Parhae state possessed the inherent structural weakness of a society sharply divided along ethnic lines. This instability in its social fabric was the main reason why Parhae succumbed so easily to attack by the Khitan in 926, and once Parhae fell, it proved impossible for either of its two disparate elements to transmit the Parhae culture to later historical ages.

Chapter 5

The Age of Powerful Gentry Families

Conflict within the Hereditary Status System

Although Silla civilization reached its zenith during the reign of King Kyŏngdŏk (742-765), beneath the surface signs of renewed conflict within Unified Silla society had appeared. For a movement had arisen among the true-bone aristocracy to break the authoritarian power of the throne. To thwart these efforts King Kyŏngdŏk instituted a program of political reform based on a policy of increased Sinicization, but this had no appreciable effect. Under the next king, then, a large scale rebellion broke out. Conflict of unprecedented dimensions continued for twenty years, in the course of which the line of King Muyŏl, the architect of Silla's unification, came to an end, and with it the flourishing middle period of Silla history.

That a period of decline in the history of Silla should come about little more than a century after the unification was primarily in consequence of the aristocracy's resistance to the trend toward the authoritarian rule of the throne. Members of the aristocracy originally had joined forces to break the authoritarian power of the throne, but now they found themselves torn by internecine strife. It was the increase in the individual wealth of the nobles that destroyed their solidarity. With the aim of seizing political power, ambitious nobles used their vast economic resources to create personal military forces, arming their slaves and recruiting the landless peasants who roamed the Silla countryside. At this point it was no longer direct blood lineage but political leverage and armed might that became decisive in determining succession to the throne.

Accordingly, the politics of Silla's late period is marked by the decisive role played by ephemeral coalitions of aristocratic forces. Under these circumstances, whoever might emerge victorious in the struggle for the kingship could no longer represent the aristocracy as a whole but only his own partisans, and each new king became the target of revenge of the factions he had defeated. Twenty kings occupied the throne during the approximately one hundred fifty years of Silla's decline, and a goodly number of them fell victim to the almost unceasing political turmoil.

There were serious problems elsewhere in the Silla socio-political order as well. Because of the limitations imposed by their social status, men of head-rank six could not be appointed to positions of real political power. These men all were aware of the fact that the examination system in T'ang China provided opportunity for advancement in public office in accordance with an individual's demonstrated abilities. Accordingly, criticism began to be heard from such men concerning the inequities of Silla's bone-rank system. Ch'oe Ch'i-wŏn (857-?), a man of head-rank six who had passed the T'ang examinations and served importantly there, submitted detailed proposals to the throne for dealing with the major issues of his day. But when his advice went unheeded he abandoned his official career and spent the rest of his days in unsettled retirement away from the capital. Ch'oe Ch'i-wŏn was not alone, for other scholars of head-rank six background took the same critical stance toward the bone-rank status system, in extreme cases even working actively against the interests of their Silla homeland by defecting to the new political forces that ultimately arose in the turmoil of the kingdom's last years.

The Rise of Powerful Local Gentry

Around the middle of the ninth century the intense political strife among the true-bone aristocracy that had arisen out of the struggle for the throne began to show signs of abating. A spirit of reconciliation had come to prevail among the previously warring factions, owing to the need to unite against the threat posed by emerging regional power centers. The leaders of these new forces, who found the avenues of political participation at the central government level blocked by the bone-rank system, turned their attention to maritime trade, an undertaking that reflected and also increased their economic and military power. Trade flourished with T'ang China and with Japan as well, and in fact the overseas traders and seafaring adventurers of Silla soon came to dominate the maritime shipping lanes of East Asia.

Military garrisons in Silla originally were situated at strategic locations to defend the country's land frontiers, but the threat of piracy to Silla's thriving maritime commerce led to the creation of a succession of garrisons at important coastal points. Perhaps the most important of these was the Ch'ŏnghae Garrison on Wando Island, established in 828 by Chang Po-go. After pursuing a successful military career in the service of T'ang, Chang Po-go had returned to Silla and to Wando, that strategic island athwart the vital sea lanes in Korea's southern waters, where he created a strong military base. Now at the head of a force of 10,000 men, very much in the nature of his own private army, Chang Po-go patrolled Silla's coastal waters and put an end to the depredations of Chinese pirates. At the same time, he controlled a flourishing trade with China and Japan and became, in effect, the master of the Yellow Sea.

At the height of his career Chang Po-go attempted to intrude himself into the thick of the political strife in the capital, and his support was vital in helping one aspirant seize the throne (in 839). A few years later, however, the protests of the capital aristocracy prevented the next king from making Chang Po-go's daughter his second queen and before long, in 846, Chang was assassinated.

Chang Po-go had failed in his efforts to participate directly in the politics of the capital, nor was he able to create an independent political force that might contend for supremacy with the government in Kyŏngju. The capital aristocracy was torn by schism and its power had begun to crumble, but it still was strong enough to preserve the bone-rank system on which its dominance rested. However, other military garrisons had developed in much the same way as that at Ch'ŏnghae, and before long these would serve as sources of military support for the ambitions of powerful gentry families in the Silla countryside.

At this time there were many powerful familes that for several generations had exercised de facto control over particular regions away from the capital. Typically these leading gentry houses built fortifications around the population centers from which they held sway, and so they were known as "castle lords." These castle lords commanded their own private soldiery recruited from the local populace and based at their strongholds, and they exercised economic jurisdiction in the villages over which their power extended. This shift in the locus of economic control over the countryside signified a growing erosion of the economic foundation of the central government, and this constituted a grave problem upon which the very survival of Silla hinged.

The Later Three Kingdoms

The growing strength of the castle lords weakened the hold of the central government of Silla over the countryside, and this made it impossible to collect taxes from the peasants. In an attempt to overcome its fiscal crisis, the government in 889 resorted to forced collections of taxes from the provincial and county areas. This imposed a dual burden upon the peasant population, for they now had to suffer the exactions of both the castle lords and the central government.

Silla already had a large population of landless wanderers, driven to abandon their farms by the harsh exactions to which they were subjected. Some of these formed brigand bands and lived by plundering, while others sought the protection of local gentry families. All these developments had a serious destabilizing effect on the social order. Now the government's last gasp effort to fill its treasury by force drove the peasantry into seething rebellion.

The first flames of peasant revolt flared in the Sangju area in 889, on so large a scale that the government forces sent to suppress it were loath to do battle with the powerful peasant insurgents arrayed against them. An unending succession of rebellions now erupted in every corner of the country. Moreover, a large force of brigands that called itself the Red Trousered Banditti seized control of the region southwest of the capital. And countless other peasant insurgent bands, called "grass brigands" in the records, rose spontaneously across the land.

The early rebel leaders had been no more than commanders of rebel forces in a particular limited locale. Before long, however, two leaders emerged at the head of forces strong enough to create new state entities in the areas they controlled and challenge Silla for the mantle of legitimacy. These were Kyŏnhwŏn and Kungye who, claiming that the states they founded were restorations of Paekche and Koguryŏ respectively, set in motion a three-cornered contest for mastery of the Korean Peninsula. The nearly half century span consumed by this struggle is known as the Later Three Kingdoms period.

Kyŏnhwŏn proclaimed the founding of the state of Later Paekche at Chŏnju in 892. Despite his poor-peasant background and early career as a foot soldier, once he sat on his throne he proved to be a willful and despotic ruler. Kyŏnhwŏn harbored bitter enmity toward Silla. When he pillaged Kyŏngju in 927, he killed the king, abducted the highest officials, seized large quantities of treasure and arms, and made prisoners of the capital's skilled craftsmen. Had Kungye and Wang Kŏn not stood in his way, he surely would have had little difficulty in toppling Silla.

Kungye was a Silla prince who most likely fell victim to a political power struggle, first becoming a monk and then a soldier. As a subordinate commander in the central regions of the peninsula, he succeeded in capturing wide and strategic areas and in assembling a large army under his personal control. At this point he overthrew his master and in 901, proclaiming the founding of the state of Later Koguryŏ, he set about creating an impressive state apparatus. But like Kyŏnhwŏn in Later Paekche, Kungye ruled over his domain with untempered despotism. Forced to maintain himself in power by acts of terror, Kungye in the end was driven from his throne by his own generals and was killed as he fled by the people he had ruled.

It was Wang Kŏn who was put forward to succeed Kungye as king of the northern region, in 918. Wang Kŏn emerged from a gentry family in the Kaesŏng area and his connections with the maritime activities centered around the garrison on nearby Kanghwa Island seem to have been particularly close. He had taken part in a number of campaigns as one of Kungye's commanders, but he had won greatest recognition for his seaborne operations against the southwest coastal region. And because of these achievements he had been appointed Kungye's chief minister.

Wang Kŏn too considered himself to be the successor to the mantle of Koguryŏ, and he gave his state a shortened form of that name, Koryŏ. He made his own home area of Kaesŏng his capital, not merely to secure his military and political base but to demonstrate as well his standing as a local gentry figure. As such, he could form firm ties with other local gentry, thus assuring strong and unwavering support for his effort to reunify the Korean Peninsula.

Wang Kŏn shrewdly employed a policy of friendship with Silla, both as a strategy for overcoming his rival Kyŏnhwŏn and to secure his claim to be the successor to Silla's traditions and authority. At the same time he did not neglect to develop a military strategy toward Silla, establishing a garrison as a permanent encampment for Koryŏ troops not far north of the Silla capital, Kyŏngju.

Unification by Koryŏ

Koryŏ and Later Paekche now found themselves evenly matched and in an almost unceasing state of hostilities. Their battlefield was the area just west of the Naktong River, the outer perimeter of Silla's capital region, for Silla already had completely lost control over its hinterland and now was helpless. Meanwhile the local gentry leaders in their fortified towns looked to their own interests as they made overtures to either Wang Kŏn's Koryŏ or Kyŏnhwŏn's Later Paekche.

With the victory of the Koryŏ army at modern Andong (N. Kyŏngsang province) in 930 the stalemate was broken, and the tide of battle turned to favor Koryŏ. And when Koryŏ crushed Later Paekche's forces in a battle in Kyŏnhwŏn's domain in 934, the fighting developed entirely to Koryŏ's advantage. A power struggle within Kyŏnhwŏn's own family had led to this defeat. Kyŏnhwŏn's eldest son, cheated of his inheritance by his father's fondness for another son, confined his father in a temple and seized the throne for himself. Kyŏnhwŏn managed to escape to Koryŏ and, entrusting himself to his old enemy Wang Kŏn, plotted revenge on his son. At this juncture, late in 935, the last ruler of Silla tendered formal surrender to Koryŏ. In the following year Koryŏ troops, with Kyŏnhwŏn in the lead, brought about the collapse of Later Paekche as well.

When Parhae perished at the hands of the Khitan around this same time, much of its ruling class, who were of Koguryŏ descent, fled to Koryŏ. Wang Kŏn warmly welcomed them and generously gave them land. Thus Koryŏ achieved a true national unification that embraced not only the Later Three Kingdoms but even survivors of Koguryŏ lineage from the Parhae kingdom.

King T'aejo (Wang Kŏn's posthumous title) had brought order out of the chaos of the Later Three Kingdoms and established a new unified dynasty. Regarding himself as the successor to Koguryŏ, he pursued a policy of expansion to the north, extending his borders to the Ch'ŏngch'ŏn River, and he also broke the chains of the bone-rank order which had shackled Silla's society. At the same time, he was deeply aware of the significance of his reunification of the national territory of the Unified Silla state. Accordingly, he took to wife a woman from the Silla royal house, and he treated the Silla nobility with extreme generosity. Because of this, many individuals of Silla lineage entered into the Koryŏ bureaucracy, thus initiating the tradition of elite continuity that would characterize Korean political culture down into the twentieth century.

Unification by King T'aejo, however, signified only the extinction of the competing regimes. The castle lords continued to maintain the quasi-independent status of their regional strongholds, so that officials to govern the local areas for some time could not be dispatched from the central government. There were also the men to whom T'aejo owed his throne, the military commanders of local gentry background who had shared his victories and defeats on the battlefield. With the prisoners and other spoils of war they had seized and in command of their own armed retinues, they constituted a prideful and powerful force. To ensure their consent and cooperation, T'aejo established marriage ties with more than twenty local gentry families throughout the country, and in some cases he firmed the alliance by bestowing the royal surname, thus establishing fictive family ties.

T'aejo died without being able to consolidate centralized royal power, and improved prospects for stable royal authority in Koryŏ had to await the reforms of King Kwangjong (949-975). His initial move in this direction was to enact a Slave Review Act, designed to restore to free status the many commoners enslaved during the chaos of the Later Three Kingdoms. At the same time, of course, this would weaken the economic and military power of the owners now deprived of their slave properties. Kwangjong also established a civil service examination system in 958 as another means to strengthen royal authority. The purpose was to employ in the bureaucracy a new kind of civil official, the man of learning, in place of the old military officials from the ranks of those who had participated in the founding of Koryŏ.

The greatest discontent with these reforms was felt by those high military and civil officials who had been rewarded for their services in founding Koryŏ, and by their heirs. As a result a merciless purge occurred. Even being a military commander who had fought side by side with his father, Wang Kŏn, brought no immunity, as Kwangjong liquidated all who would not submit to the authority of the throne. Thus he was able to assert royal authority over at least the aristocrats in the capital, the heart of the kingdom.

Culture of the Gentry Period

During the height of royal authoritarian rule in Silla, Confucianism gradually won wider acceptance as a doctrine providing a unique moral basis for effective government. But during the later years of Silla, when the bone-rank system was in decline, Confucianism emerged as an ideology of political reform. The number of Confucian students going to study Confucianism firsthand in T'ang China increased dramatically, and these men urged that the government appoint men distinguished by learning rather than merely by their bone-rank lineage. They hoped in this way to create a different kind of centralized aristocratic state, with men of talent who possessed a Confucian training as its core element. In the end, it was Confucian scholars of this persuasion who provided the political ideology of the new Koryŏ dynasty.

The new trend in Buddhism in the late Silla period was the

popularity of Sŏn (Zen). The Sŏn, or Contemplative School, stood in contrast to the Kyo, or Textual School. Sŏn taught that faith need not be grounded in the written word and emphasized instead that each individual may uncover the spiritual essence of the human mind by *sŏn,* or meditation. This method would bring about "sudden enlightenment," the direct, intuitive comprehension of the Buddha nature inherent in the mind of every being.

Sŏn is thought to have entered Korea in the seventh century during Queen Sŏndŏk's reign (632-647), but it was only vaguely understood at that time. At the beginning of the ninth century, the Sŏn school gradually started to spread more widely, leading to the establishment of the Nine Mountain Sects of Sŏn. The great popularity of Sŏn is attributable to the warm reception it received from the gentry families in the countryside. In fact, the Nine Mountain Sects all took root in outlying areas near the strongholds of the powerful local gentry, including Wang Kŏn, who supported them. Sŏn thus basically developed as the religion of the local gentry and understandably so, for the individualistic element in Sŏn provided an ideological basis for the assertion of their independence from the power structure centered in the capital.

Another way of thought that became widespread with the rise of the local gentry was geomancy. It was the monk Tosŏn who greatly enhanced the appeal of geomancy, for he combined it with the Buddhist idea of achieving merit through good works and with the Taoistic yin-yang and Five Elements theories. According to Tosŏn, the natural features of a land area and their configuration deeply affect a country's or an individual's fate. In the lie of the land there is decay or prosperity, and by selecting a flourishing or propitious site for a building or for constructing a tomb, the country or an individual would be able to enjoy good fortune. On the other hand, one can forestall calamity by constructing temples on a decadent or inauspicious site just as one might apply a poultice to the human body. Tosŏn is said to have wandered all over Korea divining the auspiciousness and inauspiciousness of the topographical features.

On the basis of geomantic theory, the gentry of each locality regarded their own home ground as auspicious and sought to legitimize their standing as gentry on this basis. A prime example of this is Wang Kŏn's deeply held belief that his unification of the Later Three Kingdoms was the result of Kaesŏng's virtuous topography. He left behind a testament known as the *Ten Injunctions,* precepts in the realm of government and values to be honored by later kings. In this document he asserted:

> I carried out the great undertaking of reunifying the country by availing myself of the latent virtue of the mountains and streams of the Samhan.

The later period of Silla is generally acknowledged to be a time of decline in the arts. It must not be overlooked, however, that several new trends appeared in association with the political and religious developments of this age. First to be noted is the widespread building of prayer pagodas by the nobility. With the frequent changes in power-holding accompanying the succession struggles, true-bone aristocrats competed with each other in constructing prayer pagodas to assure their good fortune. Such pagodas also were built by gentry in the local areas.

In Buddhist sculpture, the great popularity of images of the Vairocana Buddha, the Universal Buddha of Great Effulgence, characterize this age. Many of these images were cast in iron, unlike those of earlier periods. Huge stone carvings like the mid-10th century Ŭnjin Maitreya, at modern Nonsan, and others carved on the face of rock cliffs, also attest to the artistic vitality of this age.

Memorial stupas and monument stones also came into vogue in this period. Stupas were made as tombs in which to preserve the remains of noted monks. Since the Sŏn school as a matter of principle did not rely on texts but transmitted the enlightenment experience from the mind of the teacher to that of a learner, it looked upon the master-disciple relationship as being of fundamental importance. Accordingly, the cremated remains of a master were extraordinarily venerated by members of his sect or school. Memorial stupas to honor Sŏn masters were built in considerable numbers, the oldest known dating to 790. Such a stupa typically had an eight-sided pedestal and a monumental stone recording the Sŏn master's achievements, in calligraphy that often was an artistic achievement in its own right while at the same time constituting a major source for the history of Sŏn Buddhism in Korea. These stupas and monument stones, with their out-thrusting capstone elements and the vigorously carved swirl-design motifs that remind one of whirlpools, well reflect the tumultuous society of the age.

Chapter 6

The Hereditary Aristocratic
Order of Koryŏ

Beginnings of Koryŏ's Aristocratic Order

The reforms of King Kwangjong (949-975) dealt a serious blow to high officials of local gentry origin, as Kwangjong principally gave appointments to scholars without distinguished lineage background who had passed the state examination. However, the influence of these officials evaporated with the king's death, and Confucian scholars of Silla's head-rank six lineages assumed leading political roles. Ch'oe Sŭng-no was one such figure.

Ch'oe Sŭng-no aspired to create an aristocratic society with a centralized power structure. A scholar who had no base in the countryside, he had been a Koryŏ government official at the time of Silla's surrender. Therefore his concern was with advancing in the capital, an orientation that naturally caused him to favor centralization of power. But he opposed the growth of royal absolutism and abhorred the absolute monarch who would ignore the opinions of the aristocracy. He wanted to construct an aristocratic society in which the political process would operate with the aristocracy at its center.

Sŏngjong (981-997), in dealing with the political situation after the failure of Kwangjong's reforms, relied on the views of Confucian scholars such as Ch'oe Sŭng-no. Now, for the first time, officials were dispatched from the capital to head the provincial administrative units, and he instituted a reform of the local government structure that marked the inauguration of Koryŏ's county functionary system, thus effecting a downgrading of the position of the local gentry. Still, wishing to absorb into the capital aristocracy as many of the local gentry as possible, he spared no effort to educate their youth. Always attentive to the opinions of aristocratic officials well-versed in the Chinese classics, he sought to reflect these ideas in his political decisions. In this way the foundation for Koryŏ's aristocratic order was laid.

The aristocrats of Silla's head-rank six lineages contributed much to the reordering of Koryŏ's social and political structure, in the process solidifying their own position. At the same time, increasing numbers of men from gentry families in the area around Kaesŏng also appeared on the central political stage as civil officials. Unlike Silla, where the true-bone members of the royal lineage had been at the center of the political process, the Koryŏ government drew on aristocrats from many different clans. This did not mean that Koryŏ society attached any less importance to lineage background, but only that access to political power had become markedly more open and equal within the still narrow confines of a hereditary aristocracy.

Aristocratic lineages used marriage as a strategy to expand the power of their families. The more influential the family with which one formed marriage ties, the more quickly one might enhance the standing of one's own house and bring it into greater political prominence. Accordingly, the highest aspiration was to marry with Koryŏ's most aristocratic family, the royal clan. This brought with it the greatest prestige and a direct shortcut to political power. Two exalted lineages that monopolized power as marriage kinsmen of the royal family were the Ansan Kim and the Inju (Inch'ŏn) Yi families. The Ansan Kim clan monopolized power in this way under four kings, for over fifty years, while the dominance of the Inju Yi clan lasted for the next eighty years or more, until early in the reign of Injong (1122-1146). Thus in Koryŏ there emerged a society centered on new hereditary aristocratic houses, and it was these that controlled the workings of the political process.

The heartland of this aristocracy was the capital at Kaesŏng, where those who shaped the destiny of the nation all congregated. The palace was built at a site that geomantic lore regarded as highly propitious, and around it were broad streets filled with great government buildings, monasteries and temples, and the houses of the upper class. Amid this opulent splendor, the thatched houses of the ordinary populace clustered together like anthills.

The emergence of a new ruling class necessitated a remodeling of the social status system. The Koryŏ social structure was characterized by its close connection with the political system. A number of "orders" were created whose names indicated their particular political functions, and membership in them was determined on a hereditary basis. There were civil official, military officer, court functionary, and soldiering orders, as well as various clerical and artisan occupational categories that were hereditarily fixed. The peasant population was not eligible to hold government office, and below the peasants were lowborn who were slaves. A number of measures were adopted to ensure the inheritance of social status. A "protected appointment" system provided favored access to the bureaucracy to sons of higher civil or military officials. Soldiers and local functionaries passed on their occupations to their descendants. The bulk of the population, of course, the peasants and the unfree, were consigned to their lot in perpetuity by hedgerows of barriers both institutional and unspoken.

Nevertheless, contrary to the hereditary principle, in fact changes in social status in Koryŏ took place with some frequency. Especially noteworthy are instances of local clerks moving into the civil official order by passing the civil service examination, and soldiers entering the military officer order through meritorious service. Furthermore, since the ranks of the soldiery were replenished by recruits not only from the free peasantry but also from the slave population, by this route even slaves occasionally could rise into the military officer order. It is a particular characteristic of the Koryŏ period that social change of this sort was permitted within a framework of fixed, hereditary social classes.

The Aristocratic Ruling Structure

The new Koryŏ political structure began to take shape in 983 under King Sŏngjong and was completed in 1076 under Munjong. The government was organized around Three Chancelleries, the first two of which merged into a single organ called the

Directorate of Chancellors, where high policy decisions were made. The third chancellery, or Secretariat for State Affairs, was responsible for carrying out policy through Six Boards that handled actual government administration. These were Personnel, Military Affairs, Taxation, Punishments, Rites, and Public Works; it was the Board of Rites that had jurisdiction over foreign relations, education, and the state examinations. Another high-level organ was the Royal Secretariat, whose duties were to transmit royal commands and also the handling of urgent military matters.

The highest officers of the Directorate of Chancellors and Royal Secretariat met in joint sessions called "Convenings of the Privy Council," or *Todang,* to consider overall state policy. Outside the Two Directorates was the Censorate, with the important duties of evaluating administrative performance and censuring the wrongdoing of officials. By virtue of its mandate to scrutinize appointments of officials and propose changes in statutes, this key organ exerted a significant restraint on autocratic exercise of royal power.

The establishment of twelve provinces in 983 marked the beginning of the dispatch of officials from the capital to administer local government. After a number of further changes, the restructuring of local government reached a definitive stage in 1018. At this point the whole country was divided into a capital region, large circuits, and border regions, and within these were established three capitals, five regional military commands, and eight provinces, with further subdivisions into districts, counties, and garrisons. Two border districts along Koryŏ's northern boundary and the northeast littoral constituted special military zones.

Central government officials were dispatched to head all of the provincial and local administrative units. These officials could not be appointed to head their own home districts and their terms of office were fixed, precautions taken out of fear of the growth of regional power centers. Under these officials dispatched from the capital, local headmen and other petty functionaries performed the administrative tasks involving direct contact with the population at large. Originally of local gentry background, these petty functionaries constituted the elite stratum of local society, and the influence they exerted was tremendous. To check their power, central government officials were sent out to inspect their own home districts, and in addition a kind of hostage system was developed that required young male members of local influential families to do a term of duty in the capital.

Koryŏ had emerged in a setting of military conflict, had had to use military might to destroy its powerful Later Paekche foe, and had already experienced numerous military clashes with the Khitan in the north. Understandably, then, Koryŏ devoted considerable attention to military organization. Wang Kŏn himself had gone into battle at the head of a powerful army which drew on the military strength of the Kaesŏng region, and this army became the nucleus of the Two Guards and Six Divisions into which the forces of the central government now were organized, around 995. The first three of these latter were charged with defending the capital and guarding the frontiers, while the others performed the more specialized functions of participating in state ceremonies and guarding the palace and city gates and government buildings. The Two Guards units were the king's personal bodyguards.

The generals and lieutenant generals had their own joint deliberative organ called the Council of Generals, but its power was in no way commensurate with that of the counterpart Privy Council of the civil officials. The rank and file of the Two Guards and Six Divisions were professional military men from families belonging to the hereditary soldiering order. The state granted them "soldier's land" and assigned two "supporting households" to cultivate it, thus providing for their livelihood and equipment expenses. The private armed forces of the gentry in the countryside had at first been brought together under the control of the central government, but subsequently they were reorganized into provincial garrison forces. Regular army units, on the other hand, manned the frontier garrisons. They were a force at the ready, on permanent station, one that could do battle the moment called to arms.

In Koryŏ, the members of the many hereditary aristocratic houses all were entitled to participate in political life. A way also was opened for those of local functionary background to advance into the central bureaucracy. In other words, to a degree that stands out in sharp contrast with the Silla period, it had become possible for large numbers of men to become government officials in Koryŏ. This made necessary a new method of selecting personnel, namely the state civil service examinations. These were of three basic types: the Composition Examination course, the Classics Examination course, and the Miscellaneous Examination course. The composition examination tested candidates on the basis of their ability to compose in set Chinese literary forms, while the classics course examined knowledge of Confucian canonical works. Both of these were conducted for the purpose of selecting civil officials, but the Composition Examination was regarded as by far the more important, and thus fewer than one out of ten candidates elected to sit for the Classics Examination. Miscellaneous Examinations were held to select specialists in areas demanding technical knowledge, such as law, accounting, medicine, divination, and geomancy. However, as has been noted earlier, the civil service examination was not the only mechanism used for selecting officials. A "protected appointment" system, allowing direct appointment to office of sons of higher officials, worked to preserve the privileged position of the hereditary aristocracy.

The establishment of the National University in 992 under Sŏngjong laid the foundation for Koryŏ's educational system. Eventually, like a modern university, Koryŏ's National University came to contain a number of colleges within it, namely the so-called Six Colleges of the Capital. University College, High College, and Four Portals College were places to study the sources of the Chinese tradition, and they were distinguished not by curriculum but by the official rank of the families from which they drew their students. The Law College, College of Calligraphy, and College of Accounting taught these technical specialties to the sons of low-ranking officials and commoners. In his zeal for spreading education out into the countryside, King Sŏngjong at first brought youth from the local areas to study in the capital, but later he sent scholars of the Classics, medicine, and other subjects to the countryside to teach. Under Injong (1122-46), schools were set up in rural areas to educate local youth. This was only natural inasmuch as one objective of the civil service examination system was to absorb men of local gentry background into the central bureaucracy.

Aristocratic Society and the Economic Structure

The Stipend Land Law occupied a central position in the Koryŏ land system. Fully instituted first in 998, the new system allocated land to officials, in lieu of salary, in accordance with their office rank. Consequently, the collection of land rents was managed by the state and when an official died the allocated land was to be returned to the state. Besides such stipend land, so-called privileged merit land also was an important form of remuneration generally given to higher ranking officials as grants in perpetuity. Thus in effect privately owned, this land was cultivated by tenant farmers, and the grantee collected the rent on his own authority. Land allocated to local government functionaries and to soldiers also was tantamount to privately owned land, since it came to be inheritable. However, if a soldier had no male descendants he was made to return his soldier's land and was given instead a modest pension land allocation. Such pension land also was given to families of officials and deceased soldiers, including war widows, who had no other means of livelihood. In addition there was "royal estate land" that belonged to the palace, "public agency land" allotted to cover the expenses of government offices, and lands owned by the monasteries or temples.

The underlying premise of the Koryŏ land system was that all land in the country was the king's land. However, this did not mean that all land was owned by the state. To be sure, there was "public land" that the state directly managed. The rents from this land were transported to Kaesŏng by ship and were used for public expenditures, the foremost of which was official stipends. This "public" land mainly provided economic benefits to that key segment of the "public" consisting of the aristocracy as a whole. In contrast, "private land" served the private interests of the recipient. Some such land, since granted in perpetuity, generally met all of the criteria of private ownership. In other cases, despite the existence of minor hindrances, grants in the category of "private land" or "land held in perpetuity" also were, in effect, privately owned. Moreover, as the power of the aristocracy grew, "stipend land" too came to be inherited, thus turning into private land from which rents were collected directly by the aristocrats. By such stratagems as reclaiming wasteland, or by receiving special grants from the king, or by seizing the land of others by force, the aristocracy increased its holdings of private land even further. And the rents from private land, in contrast to the 25% rate on public land, amounted to half the harvest.

Based on such a foundation of private landholding, the wealth of the aristocracy steadily grew. They built granaries to store their share of the harvest, then profited by lending grain at high interest. Such granaries were operated not only by individual aristocrats, but by the state and the monasteries as well. And there were "endowments" that, while serving worthy purposes, also profited from the interest on grain loans. A principal medium of exchange, cloth too was used in these profit-making activities.

Koryŏ was built on an agricultural economy, and those who directly tilled the land, the peasantry, formed the foundation of the society. The freeborn farmers who made up the majority of the peasantry lacked any fixed role in the service of the state and accordingly were not eligible to receive a land allocation. On the public land they cultivated they paid one-fourth of the harvest to the state, but when they tilled the private lands of the aristocracy, the rent obligation was fully one-half of the yield. A tribute tax paid in cloth usually was imposed upon them as well. Furthermore, adult males from the ages of 16 to 60 were liable for corvee labor duty, and they were mobilized for all sorts of construction projects.

Treated even worse than the freeborn peasantry was the lowborn population living in special administrative districts and variously assigned to farm labor, mining, or the production of silk, paper, or pottery. It should be noted that the existence of these special aggregations of the lowborn was a legacy inherited from Silla, and that they gradually disappeared as a distinctive group as they were merged with the freeborn population.

At the very bottom of the society was the slave class. There were government slaves belonging to the state and private slaves belonging to individuals. Government slaves performed various duties in the palace and government offices or served as personal attendants to civilian and military officials. Private slaves belonged to members of the royal household, the aristocracy, and temples. Many of these were out-resident slaves paying rents to their masters for the land they cultivated in the countryside, and some of them were able to accumulate property and so rise to the status of commoners. In all cases, of course, slave status was hereditary and slaves were bought and sold. There was also an outcast population, those such as butchers, wicker workers, and entertainers, whose occupations were despised, with the consequence that they were treated socially as slaves.

The freeborn peasantry and those of lower status generally led lives of poverty, and their hardships forced many of them to run away. In response, the government developed minimal relief programs that included small monetary grants, infirmaries for the indigent sick, a public dispensary, "righteous granaries" that stored grain in normal times for public relief in years of poor harvests, and Ever Normal Storehouses that served to smooth out fluctuations in commodity prices. Buddhist establishments also functioned as relief agencies, providing food and other services to itinerant beggars.

Foreign Relations

Already in the time of its founder Koryŏ's boundary line had expanded northward to the Ch'ŏngch'ŏn River, as T'aejo sought in a variety of ways to implement a policy of recovering the ancient territories of the Koguryŏ kingdom. His sons and grandsons continued this northern expansion policy, establishing numerous garrison forts across the Ch'ŏngch'ŏn River in their push toward the Yalu. It was inevitable that these actions would bring Koryŏ into conflict with the Khitan people, who had conquered Parhae in 926 and so shared a common border with Koryŏ. Increasingly uneasy about Koryŏ's intentions, in 993 they sent an invasion force across the Yalu. This time, through the dazzling diplomatic maneuvers of Sŏ Hŭi, the Khitan were persuaded to withdraw and even gave their consent to the incorporation of the area up to the Yalu into Koryŏ's territory. To be sure, the main Khitan forces at this time were engaged in a struggle with Sung China, so that the concessions won by Koryŏ can be viewed as only prudent temporizing on the part of the Khitan.

In any case, it was not many years before the Khitan demanded that Koryŏ cede to them the Six Garrison Settlements southeast of the Yalu that Koryŏ had rushed to build after the Khitan invasion army withdrew. Koryŏ naturally rejected this demand, but at this point the Khitan took advantage of political turbulence in Koryŏ to launch a second invasion under the personal command of the Khitan emperor, who defeated the Koryŏ forces sent against him and occupied Kaesŏng, while the Koryŏ king hastily fled south. Fearing that their supply lines might be cut, however, the Khitan suddenly withdrew without gaining any advantage, stipulating only that the Koryŏ king pay homage in person at the Khitan court. This was not a commitment Koryŏ willingly would honor, and such a royal journey never was undertaken.

Subsequently the Khitan launched several small-scale attacks before mounting their third great invasion in 1018. This time the Khitan army was harassed at every turn and all but annihilated by a massive Koryŏ attack at Kusŏng executed by Kang Kamch'an. The Koryŏ victory was so overwhelming that scarcely a few thousand of the 100,000 man invasion force survived. The Khitan invasions of Koryŏ thus ended in failure, as Koryŏ had resolutely resisted foreign aggression and driven the invaders back. The result was that the two nations compromised their differences and peaceful relations were maintained between them thereafter.

About the time peace was worked out with the Khitan, Koryŏ began to be troubled by the Jurchen (a proto-Manchu people of eastern Manchuria). The long wall stretching from the mouth of the Yalu a thousand *li* eastward to the sea, laboriously built over a twelve year period from 1033 to 1044, was intended for defense not only against the Khitan but also against the Jurchen. The Jurchen had not yet achieved a level of societal development that would enable them to create their own state entity, and so, because of its advanced culture, they looked upon Koryŏ as the source of the trappings of civilization they so desired to acquire. Koryŏ supplied their needs for grain, cloth, iron agricultural implements, and iron weapons, for which they exchanged horses and furs. Many Jurchen migrated into the Koryŏ domain, and to these Koryŏ gave land, dwellings, and a means of livelihood.

The situation changed, however, when a new urge toward unification of all the Jurchen crystallized under the leadership of the chieftain of the Wan-yen tribe in northern Manchuria. As the power of the Wan-yen tribe extended even to the Jurchen who had submitted to Koryŏ, military clashes began to break out. The Koryŏ standing army, however, had deteriorated and consisted mostly of infantry, so the usual outcome was defeat by the mounted Jurchen. For this reason a new military organization called the Extraordinary Military Corps was created, consisting of cavalry and infantry units formed around members of aristocratic families and the freeborn peasantry, respectively, and a special unit of Buddhist monks. The massive assault this force was unremittingly trained for was mounted in 1107 under the command of Yun Kwan. Occupying the Hamhŭng plain, a region hitherto inhabited by Jurchen tribesmen, he constructed the so-called Nine Forts and garrisoned them for defense. Ultimately, however, the region of the Nine Forts was turned back to Jurchen control.

A few years later, in 1115, the Jurchen succeeded in founding a state, called Chin, which overran the Khitan Liao dynasty in 1125 and two years later captured the Sung capital at Kaifeng. In the course of these events Chin put increased pressure on Koryŏ and ultimately demanded that Koryŏ acknowledge Chin suzerainty. Yi Cha-gyŏm, the all-powerful father-in-law of the king, judged that peaceful relations with the continent would contribute to maintaining his own political dominance, and so he assented to Chin's demands. As a result there was no military invasion of Koryŏ by the Chin dynasty.

From the beginning Koryŏ admired the advanced civilization of Sung China and sought to satisfy its material and cultural wants by maintaining a harmonious relationship with Sung. Thus, through the visits of official embassies and the travels of private merchants, Koryŏ exported such raw materials as gold, silver, copper, ginseng, and pine nuts, and handcrafted items favored by the Sung people such as paper, brushes, ink, and fans, in return importing silk, books, porcelain, medicines, spices, and musical instruments. These imports had a significant impact on Koryŏ's culture. For example, Sung woodblock editions contributed to the development of Koryŏ woodblock printing and Sung porcelain to the development of Koryŏ celadon ware. Thus the relationship between the two countries rested on a peaceful foundation of cultural and economic exchange, and this relationship continued even after Koryŏ refused to put its own national interest at risk by aiding Sung in its life and death struggle against Khitan and Chin invaders.

Aristocratic Culture

In a state committed to the principle of rule by civil officials in accordance with Confucian political ideals, it was natural that Confucianism prospered. But in Koryŏ society the importance attached to aristocratic pedigree acted to modify certain features of Confucian doctrine. This can be seen in the rise of private academies as the principal agencies for the education of aristocratic youth. The first of a dozen such schools, known as the Twelve Assemblies, was established in the mid-eleventh century by the great Confucian scholar Ch'oe Ch'ung, a man from a leading aristocratic lineage who had held the top government post of chancellor. What attracted the sons of high-born lineages to the private academies was less the superior education they offered than the superior and enduring connections they could make by attending. In either case the result was to give the sons of the privileged still other advantages, and of course the flourishing of private academies brought on the decline of government schools. Concerned over this, a succession of kings took a variety of actions to breathe new life into the state school system. These efforts culminated under Injong in the establishment of the Six Colleges of the Capital, as described above, from which a goodly number of eminent scholars emerged.

The growing acceptance of Confucianism brought with it a mode of thought that favored a rational approach to the problems of human society. Confucianism was looked upon as the orthodox doctrine by which to order family relationships and to govern the state, and both the monarch and the aristocracy came to regard it as vital to the moral cultivation of political leaders. Native Korean values, however, dictated that the conversion of the Koryŏ aristocracy to Confucian rationalism would be less than whole-hearted. Koryŏ Confucians by no means rejected Buddhism. Regarding it as the doctrine for achieving spiritual tranquility and otherworldly salvation, they felt that it complemented and could coexist with Confucianism. Accordingly, many men were versed in both, and in this respect they differed from the Confucian scholars of late Koryŏ and the Chosŏn dynasty.

Koryŏ Buddhism achieved a systematization with the wood-block printing of the Tripitaka, the Buddhist scriptural canon as rendered in Chinese translations. Originally undertaken as a kind of ritual observance to bring a halt to the Khitan invasions, the first carving of the Tripitaka was completed in 1087 after more than a lifetime of labor. The woodblocks for this printing were destroyed in the thirteenth century Mongol invasions, and the so-called *Koryŏ Tripitaka,* which remains today at Haein-sa temple, represents a new edition completed in 1251. The *Koryŏ Tripitaka,* despite being done under wartime conditions, is regard-ed as the finest among some twenty versions of the Tripitaka originating in East Asia, in terms of its accuracy, the beauty of the calligraphic style, and the exquisite carving of the woodblocks. Meanwhile the monk Ŭich'ŏn published treatises and commen-taries found in Sung, Liao, Japan, and Koryŏ as a *Supplement to the Tripitaka,* some of which still survives.

The Buddhist world of Koryŏ found itself divided into two streams of sectarian belief, the Textual (Kyo) and Contemplative (Sŏn, i.e., Zen) Schools, and disunity and conflict arose from their respective prejudices. The Ch'ŏnt'ae (T'ien-t'ai) sect took root in Koryŏ, then, as an attempt to reform the Buddhist estab-lishment by resolving these conflicts. It was Ŭich'ŏn who estab-lished Ch'ŏnt'ae as an independent sect, and it quickly came to be a major force in the world of Koryŏ Buddhism. Ŭich'ŏn, the fourth son of King Munjong, returned from Sung China where he had studied Ch'ŏntae in 1086. Urging the unity of the Textu-al and Contemplative Schools, Ŭich'ŏn propagated Ch'ŏn-t'ae as a faith adherents of both schools might embrace since, although heavily doctrinal, it taught that a redefined process of meditation plays an essential role as the means to achieve clear perception of ultimate truth. This teaching drew many adherents from the Nine Mountain Sects of Sŏn and also inspired a revitalization within the Sŏn school, which led to the emergence within it of the Chogye sect.

Buddhism was integral to everyday life in Koryŏ society and was the major creative force shaping its cultural achievements. In particular, the belief that personal or even national well-being will be assured through the accumulated effect of pious acts was the motivating force behind Koryŏ's construction of so many temples and monasteries and its dutiful observance of the various Buddhist ceremonies. T'aejo himself expressed this belief in the first of his *Ten Injunctions:*

> The success of the great enterprise of founding our dynasty is entirely owing to the protective powers of the many Buddhas. We therefore must build temples for both Sŏn and Kyo schools and appoint abbots to them, that they may perform the proper ceremonies and themselves cultivate the way.

The proliferation of temples in Koryŏ—there were as many as seventy in Kaesŏng alone—itself conveys a clear picture of Koryŏ as a thoroughly Buddhist state.

The two largest state Buddhist festivals, held on the fifteenth of the first month and the fifteenth of the eleventh month, combined Buddhist rites with indigenous practices. With performances of music, dance, and various entertainments, the king and his subjects entreated the various Buddhas and spirits of heaven and earth to bring tranquility to the nation and the royal house. Other important annual ceremonies celebrated, for example, the birthdays of Buddha and of the reigning king. There were also "Inwang meetings" to pray for peace in the nation, in conjunction with which huge vegetarian feasts were held for up to 100,000 monks. Such pious acts as copying sutras with infinite care in gold and silver on dark blue paper were undertaken to supplicate Buddha for some tangible benefit. "Scripture processions" of monks reading sutras, or simply displaying them while walking about the streets praying for the fortune of the nation and the blessing of the people, were familiar scenes at that time.

The deep respect for Buddhism led to the establishment of examinations for its clergy, on the model of the state civil service examinations. There were separate examinations for monks of the Textual and the Contemplative schools, and those who passed were given cleric ranks. A monk might aspire to become a Patriarch of the Textual School or a Great Sŏn Mentor, beyond which were only the rare and exalted titles of Royal Preceptor and National Preceptor. Monks received land allotments from the state and were exempt from corvee labor duties, considerations that increased the number of monks. Many royal princes also entered the clergy, as well as members of the aristocracy, a phenomenon that contributed significantly to the great wealth possessed by the monasteries.

Monasteries expanded their landholdings through donations from the royal house and aristocracy, through commendation by the peasants, and by outright seizure. Because this land enjoyed tax exemption, the Buddhist establishment grew ever more powerful economically. Using income from their land, monasteries produced still more wealth by setting up Buddhist endowments, relief granaries, and similar agencles for loaning grain at high interest. And they also increased their income through commerce, wine-making, and raising livestock. In order to protect their growing wealth the monasteries trained monks as soldiers. The number of armed monks appears to have gradually increased, and they even were used as a military force for national purposes, as has been noted in connection with the Jurchen invasions.

Turning to literary and art forms, early in the Koryŏ period the Silla *hyangga* tradition came to an end, and literature written in Chinese flourished instead. The Koryŏ aristocracy, unlike their Silla counterparts, delighted in Confucian thought and Chinese literature and took pride in their ability to memorize phrases from the Chinese classics or to recite Chinese poetry. The latter skill in particular developed apace, gradually becoming an essential attainment for aristocratic youth. Originally Chinese poems simply were recited, but later they came to be sung, or chanted, just as *hyangga* had been.

Celadon ware is the crowning glory of Koryŏ artistic achievement. Koryŏ celadon ware developed under the influence of Sung celadon, but is deemed to be superior to the Sung prototype, and the Chinese themselves traditionally have praised it as the world's finest ceramic art. The excellence of Koryŏ celadon first of all is seen in its delicate color, particularly in the case of the jade-green pieces. The Koryŏ artisans produced celadon in widely varied shapes—flasks, jars, cups, wine pitchers, plates, water droppers (for use in mixing ink), brush holders, incense burners, teapots, flower vases, flower pots. Particularly delightful are the incense burners, water pitchers, and water droppers fashioned in the shapes of such plants or animals as chrysanthemums, lotus flowers, pomegranates, bamboo shoots, melons, parrots, mandarin ducks, the phoenix, rabbits, monkeys, turtles, dragons, lions, and fish. In addition to its elegant shapes, Koryŏ celadon ware is remarkable for its decorations, especially those done with the distinctive Korean slip-inlay technique. Clouds and cranes, waterfowl and willows, peonies, chrysanthemums, pomegranates, gourds, grapes, lotus flowers, arabesque scrolls, and stylized floral clusters are among the favorite motifs. Koryŏ celadon ware thus embodies a refined beauty in which shape, color, and design are harmoniously combined. These celadon pieces were made more for display than for actual use, so theirs is less a robust beauty than a subtle, exquistite loveliness. Indeed it may be said that this celadon ware expresses the yearning of the Koryŏ aristocracy for Taoistic simplicity and Buddhistic tranquility.

Not only celadon but other artistic creations too express the refined tastes of the Koryŏ aristocracy. Many objects fashioned in bronze were found in aristocratic homes—incense burners with silver inlay, *kundika* (ritual ewers), candelabra, and mirrors represent a truly beautiful art form. Stone memorial stupas much admired for their elaborate and delicate workmanship also are prime examples. In contrast, the larger the size of Koryŏ structures and sculptures, the more clumsy seems their workmanship. In time, though, a distinctive softened look came to mark the Koryŏ pagoda. There were masterpieces of Buddhist statuary, too, although not many. The art of painting flourished, it is known, but almost nothing survives from the earlier half of the dynasty. Finally, three of the "Four Worthies of Divine Calligraphy" are early to mid-Koryŏ figures.

Disturbances in the Aristocratic Order

The hereditary aristocracy of Koryŏ had created a number of institutional arrangements, the examination system and the Stipend Land Law among them, designed to restrain the arbitrary exercise of royal authority and to maintain the privileged position enjoyed by the ruling elite as a whole. But when powerful families took advantage of the protected appointment system to monopolize government posts and expand their private landholdings, the balance of power among the great hereditary houses was broken. Under these circumstances it was only natural that conflict and even armed insurrection should break out among the aristocratic ruling elite themselves. Several such disturbances occurred in rapid succession in the reigns of Injong (1122-1146) and Ŭijong (1146-1170), the very period that may be said to have marked the zenith of aristocratic culture.

The first to thus shatter Koryŏ's domestic tranquility was Yi Cha-gyŏm, the man who brought the Inju (Inch'ŏn) Yi house to the pinnacle of its power. Yi Cha-gyŏm had given a daughter as queen to Yejong and he contrived to put Injong, the son of that union, on the throne in 1122. Then to Injong as well he gave two daughters, assuring by this reduplicated in-law connection his own monoply of power. Now grown arrogant, Yi Cha-gyŏm came to cherish the ambition of deposing Injong and himself assuming the throne. Yi's forces managed to imprison the king and kill many of those around him, but then their opportunistic leader suddenly turned against Yi Cha-gyŏm (in 1127) and drove him into exile, from which he was heard of no more.

The Yi Cha-gyŏm incident had demonstrated the weakened state of royal authority and the power potential of the aristocracy. Accordingly, no sooner had this grave menace been overcome than Injong contemplated a series of political reform measures that would restore the authority of the throne. But this was the time when the Jurchen were exerting constant pressure on Koryŏ, and at this point several men of P'yŏngyang decided to take advantage of the troubled situation at home and abroad to seize power and create a new P'yŏngyang-centered dynasty. The principal figure among them was a monk, Myoch'ŏng, who now set in motion an intricate scheme the first requirement of which was that Injong be persuaded to move the Koryŏ capital to P'yŏng-yang. At first Myoch'ŏng's geomancy-inspired arguments succeeded in swaying the king, deeply disturbed as he was by Yi Cha-gyŏm's attempted treason. But when mounting opposition in Kae-sŏng made it evident that he would not be able to persuade the king after all, Myoch'ŏng determined to resolve the issue by military force and raised an army in P'yŏngyang. Early the next year (1136), however, P'yŏngyang fell to government forces and Myoch'ŏng's revolt was suppressed.

Chapter 7

Rule by the Military

The Military Seize Power

Aristocratic rule in Koryŏ was grounded in the principle of civil supremacy, and this led to an inferior position in the society for military officials. They were discriminated against politically—appointments to high command, for example, in many cases were given to civil officials—and in economic terms as well. Officers who had served with distinction against the Khitan or Jurchen often felt inadequately rewarded by a government dominated by civil officials, and in consequence some even sought to redress their grievances by force. At the same time Koryŏ's professional soldiery found its livelihood becoming increasingly precarious. Not only had many not received the government grants of land to which they were entitled, but allocations that had been made were reclaimed by the state. Moreover, often mobilized in time of peace for corvee labor, the professional soldier was looked upon as little more than a menial.

The situation worsened under King Ŭijong (1146-1170), a monarch so absorbed in pursuing the life of the aesthete that he scarcely found time to set foot in the palace. The country at last was at peace, and the king and his retinue of civil officials had no thought for the deteriorating condition of the military. Symbolically, Ŭijong even took no action when military officers were made to suffer personal indignities at the hands of civil officials—such as the storied incident of the scion of an exalted civil official lineage setting fire to the beard of General Chŏng Chung-bu.

The military revolt that broke out in 1170, then, could come as no surprise. Led by Chŏng Chung-bu and other commanders, the uprising began with the cry: "Death to all who but wear the civil official headdress!" With officers and soldiers united in common cause, the revolt met with quick success. In the course of the revolt, countless civil officials were massacred, and a second major purge occurred three years later. Subsequent attempts to oust the military junta in Kaesŏng by armed force all were thwarted, and so it was that political power passed from the civil officials into the hands of the military.

After their seizure of power the military officials managed state affairs through the central mechanism of the *Chungbang,* the supreme military council, and they sought to effect a military monopoly of all government positions, high and low alike. Then, like their civil official predecessors, they utilized their positions to expand their private landholdings and take control of the country's economic resources as well. This newly acquired political stature and economic wealth soon led to the arming of family retainers and household slaves, with the aim of developing personal military forces. It now had become an age when what mattered was no longer lineage background, but only how much force-in-being one could muster. In consequence, power shifted again and again from one military strong man to another. Within a few years Chŏng Chung-bu was gone, assassinated, and all in all all for a quarter century a kaleidoscopic succession of military men burst upon the scene, held power fitfully, and disappeared again, leaving political upheaval and social chaos in their wake.

It was Ch'oe Ch'ung-hŏn (1149-1219) who brought an end to these years of disorder. He had risen in the military, won recognition in crushing the early foes of military rule, and now he reached the pinnacle of power, in 1196. Ridding himself of all who questioned his authority, including his own brother and nephew, in the end he succeeded in establishing a personal dictatorship. Although he preserved the royal house of Wang and the monarchy, he not only directed the affairs of government himself but manipulated the throne at will—within the short span of sixteen years he deposed two kings and set four on the throne. Ch'oe Ch'ung-hŏn also used his strength to break the power of the Buddhist monasteries and temples, which constituted the sole remaining reservoir of military might with ties to the king and the civil officials. There were occasions, indeed, when several thousand armed monks stormed Kaesŏng in an attempt to overthrow military rule, but Ch'oe forced the Buddhist clergy to leave the capital, and he defeated the armed monks by military force. He also put down uprisings by peasants and by slaves that threatened his regime's stability. In addition to military means he also employed conciliatory tactics, proffering office and rank to some insurgent leaders and freeing the lowborn inhabitants of the forced labor areas.

Peasant and Slave Uprisings

The trend toward peasants abandoning the land for a life of wandering already had appeared at the beginning of the twelfth century, and from time to time these rootless people had taken to organized brigandage. Already in a state of unrest, the peasants were further agitated by the social upheaval brought about by the military revolt, and large-scale popular insurrections now came to break out in many parts of the country. Not only peasants but the soldiery and government slaves as well rose up against the oppression of local officials and their minions, as in Chŏnju in 1182. These early rebels, however, primarily sought to mitigate the harsh conditions under which they lived. They had not yet reached the stage of demanding liberation from the lowly status hereditarily assigned them in Koryŏ society.

With the insurrections of two rebel bands in North Kyŏngsang province in 1193, popular uprisings entered a new phase. Joining forces in a common front, for well over a year the rebels fought to a standstill the government forces sent against them. The scale of the insurrection may easily be imagined from the fact that more than 7,000 rebels died in their final battle. Others then rose to take their places and the struggle continued for some ten years. Such uprisings occurred not only in the countryside but in Kaesŏng as well. Although nipped in the bud, the best known of these was plotted in 1198, just two years after Ch'oe Ch'ung-hŏn seized power. The entire slave population in the capital was to rise as one in a revolt frankly aimed both at emancipation and at the seizure of power. The stirring words uttered by its leader, Manjŏk, to the government and private slaves he had assembled at Kaesŏng's North Mountain survive in the records:

> Since the events of 1170 and 1173 many high officials have arisen from among the slave class. Are generals and ministers born to these glories? No! For when the time is right anyone at all can hold these offices. Why then should we only work ourselves to the bone and suffer under the whip?...If each one kills his master and burns the record of his slave status, thus bringing slavery to an end in our country, then each of us will be able to become a minister or general.

In the end all of these popular uprisings were suppressed, but they remain of great significance. They demonstrate that the very foundation of the Koryŏ social order had been shaken, as the oppressed members of society forcefully demanded a thorough revamping of the hereditary status system. The military officers revolt not only had brought a new elite to power at the top, but had given rise as well to great ferment in the bottom layers of Koryŏ society.

The Military Rule of the Ch'oe

The authority of the Ch'oe house as military rulers rested on the strength of its own private soldiery. In the years following the military officers revolt, powerful military figures had created personal guard units by arming their household retainers and slaves. Ch'oe Ch'ung-hŏn's private armed retinue was a greatly enlarged version of this model. Not surprisingly, the regular army now deteriorated, as its most able men opted for service in the private army of the Ch'oe house. Eventually the Ch'oe regime further created separate units to take over the police and combat functions performed by the Six Divisions of the regular army. These were the "Three Elite Patrols," the *Sambyŏlch'o*. Although they were maintained at public expense and were entrusted with public functions, in reality the *Sambyŏlch'o* were tantamount to another private Ch'oe armed force. The fact that the *Sambyŏlch'o* were disbanded upon the collapse of military rule would seem to prove this point. The economic underpinning that made possible the growth of these private armed retinues was the personal landholdings of the military officer group. Private landholding already had begun to expand during the heyday of aristocratic rule, and the process became still more pronounced with the seizure of the lands of civil officials by military men following the military officers revolt. In the case of the Ch'oe, the whole of the southeast coastal region of Chinju in effect was appropriated as their own private preserve, from which they took all of the revenues.

The political mechanism through which the military had exercised control immediately following the military officers revolt was the Council of Generals (*Chungbang*). But this instrument of joint rule by the military was pushed into the background under the authoritarian rule of the Ch'oe house. In its place, new control mechanisms better suited to the Ch'oe dictatorship were established. To give formal legitimacy to his military rule, Ch'oe Ch'ung-hŏn had the king bestow on him the enfeoffment title of marquis, and he created a separate in-house governing authority. But it was still another body, the Directorate of Decree Enactment, that served as the highest organ of the Ch'oe "shogunate." Until the final collapse of military rule the position of chief of this office continued to be occupied by whatever military man actually held the reins of power.

Unlike the military strong men who preceded them, however, the Ch'oe were not content to act as overlords of a purely military regime. As the supreme arbiters of power in Koryŏ, they established a Personnel Authority in their own residence to handle official appointments. Men of civil attainments were attached to this office and this paved the way for the gradual reappearance of civil officials in positions of power. Ch'oe U, Ch'oe Ch'ung-hŏn's son and successor, further established a Household Secretariat, formed from men of letters among his household retainers. Thus surrounding themselves not only with a military retinue but with a civilian staff as well, the Ch'oe made themselves the dominant figures in both the civil official and the military official orders—they were, in short, *yangban* (officials of the "two orders") who controlled all of the affairs of government in thirteenth century Koryŏ.

The Struggle with the Mongols

The Mongols arose as a nomadic herding people in the steppe region of north central Asia. The wealth produced by the agricultural peoples to their south naturally aroused their acquisitive instincts, and so it was that the empires of Chin and Sung, and Koryŏ too, became prime targets of Mongol invasion. The first contact between Koryŏ and the Mongols came about when they joined forces to destroy a motley army of Khitan who had fled from Manchuria across the Yalu to escape the Mongols. Regarding themselves as Koryŏ's benefactors, the Mongols demanded an annual tribute. Koryŏ's refusal to always accede to these heavy demands was the immediate cause for the beginning of a rift between the two. Subsequently, a Mongol envoy was killed enroute back from Koryŏ in 1225, and the Mongols used the incident as a pretext for launching their first invasion of Koryŏ, in 1231.

The Mongol army ran into stubborn resistance at a northern border fortress, but, abandoning his siege there, the Mongol commander drove toward the capital at Kaesŏng. When Koryŏ sued for peace, the Mongols left military governors behind in the northwest region of Korea and withdrew their troops. But Ch'oe U resolved to fight the Mongols and so moved the capital to Kanghwa Island the next year (1232), an action calculated to exploit the one Mongol weakness, their fear of the sea. The Mongols could only glare across the narrow strip of sea separating Kanghwa from the mainland and exchange taunts with the Koryŏ defenders. So long as Koryŏ's military rulers were determined to resist, it would be well-nigh impossible for the Mongols to capture Kanghwa. And in the meantime, secure in their island haven, the ruling class would be able to sustain their extravagant lives of luxury. For the grain tax revenues, now shipped to Kanghwa along safe coastal routes, continued to be exacted from the hard-pressed mainland peasants much as before.

The resistance of the military regime to the Mongols at first was carried on with the support of the peasantry and lowborn classes. When the capital was moved to Kanghwa the government instructed the peasantry to abandon their village homes and take refuge in nearby mountain fastnesses or on islands off the coast. Unable to overcome the stout resistance of these redoubts, the Mongols adopted the tactic of laying waste by fire to the ripened grain fields. Moreover, when a mountain fortress fell to the Mongols, its defenders were cruelly slaughtered by their conquerors. The most severe suffering and destruction resulted from the invasion of 1254, when the Mongols took back with them more than 200,000 captives, left countless dead, and reduced the entire region through which they passed to ashes. It was also during this time that many irreplaceable cultural treasures were lost, outstanding among them the woodblocks for the Tripitaka produced two hundred years earlier.

As the Mongols devastated their land, the life of the peasants became one of extreme hardship, made still worse by the government's constant harsh exactions. This exploitation both alienated the peasants from their rulers and dampened their desire to fight against the Mongols. With popular support thus weakened, the military regime faced a grave crisis. Its trust in the power of the Buddha led the government to undertake another woodblock carving of the Tripitaka, and the result was the *Koryŏ Tripitaka,* famed for its exquisite artistry, that survives to this day at Haein-sa temple near Taegu. Anxious prayers also were offered up to the deities of heaven and earth. It was in such an atmosphere, then, that sentiment for peace with the Mongols arose among the king and the civil officials in particular.

The civil officeholders saw that in order to retain and expand their role in the governing process the power of the military men would have to be curbed, and one way to do this would be to make peace with the Mongols. Thus, in collusion with a segment of the military officials, they proceeded to bring about the overthrow of the Ch'oe regime. In 1258 the last of the Ch'oe dictators, Ch'oe Ŭi, was assassinated and authority for the moment reverted to the king. In the next year, the crown prince (later King Wŏnjong) went to the Mongols and conveyed Koryŏ's desire for peace, and to clearly signal this intent to cease resisting, Kanghwa's walled fortifications were torn down. A decade more was to pass before the opposition to peace of a hard core of military officials could finally be overcome, but by 1270 it was possible for the king to order the assassination of the then paramount military figure and return the capital to Kaesŏng.

The Koryŏ government now had completely abandoned the struggle against the Mongols, but one final drama of resistance remained to be played out. The Three Elite Patrols, the *Sambyŏlch'o,* not only had constituted the military underpinning of military rule but also had been in the forefront of the fight against the Mongol invaders. They were bitterly resentful, therefore, when the military regime was toppled and peace terms worked out with the Mongols. And when the return to Kaesŏng was announced, therefore, the *Sambyŏlch'o* immediately rose in revolt. Kanghwa Island, however, was no longer a safe bastion, and so the rebels went far south, to the island of Chindo off the southwest tip of the peninsula. Bringing the nearby islands and adjacent coastal regions under their control, they briefly created a distinct maritime kingdom. But in mid-1271 Chindo fell to a combined Koryŏ-Mongol assault, and the survivors who had escaped to Cheju Island were subjugated in 1273. This bitter-end struggle of the Three Elite Patrols provides perhaps the clearest indication of how strong was the spirit of resistance to the Mongols among the military men of Koryŏ.

The Culture of the Age of the Military

When the military seized power, men of letters had no recourse but to abandon thought of government careers, and some of them secluded themselves in mountain villages where they passed their days in the enjoyment of poetry and wine. Still others sought to again enter government service in the way that was opening to them, as retainers in the house of Ch'oe. But such careers offered limited prospects for advancement, and in this sense these men too may be counted among the disenfranchised. It was natural, then, for these two groups to come together in a unitary literary community, and the genre that developed as their common mode of expression was the prose tale. Some of these, like the "Fortunes of Master Coin," were humorous tales that personified everyday objects. Another variety was potpourris of anecdotal material, poems and stories, and casual commentary designed to entertain. Koryŏ's enhanced consciousness of national identity, aroused by the trauma of reaching accommodation with a succession of bellicose neighbors, also found its reflection in the literature of this time, in long narrative poems celebrating semi-legendary founders and heroes.

After the seizure of power by the military a new development occurred as well in Koryŏ Buddhism. This was the establishment of the Chogye sect within the Sŏn School. When the monk Ŭich'ŏn founded the Ch'ŏnt'ae (Chinese: T'ien-t'ai) sect in Koryŏ, he drew many of the promising young monks away from the Nine Mountain Sects of Sŏn, but at the same time he inspired a revival within the Sŏn sects. The Nine Mountain Sects of Sŏn now took the new name of the Chogye sect, and began to flourish under the leadership of the monk Chinul (1158-1210). Chinul made "sudden-enlightenment [followed by] gradual cultivation" his basic precept, a formula that gave priority to meditation but also attached importance to invoking the name of Buddha and reading sutras. Thus Chinul combined the appealing directness of Sŏn and the concrete gradualism of the Textual School, while the emphasis on continuous discipline lent itself to incorporation into a military ethos. The Chogye sect won substantial support from the military rulers and proceeded to develop in mountain monasteries throughout Korea as a distinct and indigenous stream of Buddhist faith and practice. Furthermore, with its emphasis on cultivation of the mind-nature, Chogye Buddhism played a key role in preparing the ground for the acceptance of Neo-Confucianism in the years soon to come.

Chapter 8

Emergence of the Literati

The Pro-Yüan Policy and the Powerful Families

The first ordeal Koryŏ suffered following the conclusion of peace with Yüan (the Mongols had proclaimed the Yüan Dynasty in 1271) was its forced participation in the Mongol expeditions against Japan. The Mongol rulers wanted to make use of Koryŏ and Japan, both of which had close maritime connections with Sung China, in pressing the Yüan attack against the stubborn Southern Sung dynasty. Yüan demands forced Koryŏ to support Mongol invasion armies on two attempts to subjugate Japan, in 1274 and 1281, but both campaigns met with stout resistance from the Kamakura Shogunate and ended in failure. Koryŏ was responsible for the construction of warships and the provision of supplies for both invasions, and this severely burdened a Koryŏ peasantry already exhausted from the thirty-year struggle against the Mongols.

As agonizing as these experiences were for Koryŏ, of still greater moment were the deleterious changes that now took place within the Koryŏ polity itself in consequence of the relationship with Yüan. A succession of Koryŏ kings was required to take princesses of the Yüan imperial house as primary consorts, while sons born to these queens normally would succeed to the Koryŏ throne. Koryŏ thus became a "son-in-law nation" to Yüan, and the Koryŏ king was no longer the independent ruler of his kingdom. This diminution of royal authority was accompanied by terminological degradation that reflected the subordination of the Koryŏ throne and government to the interests of the Yüan overlords. The most striking of these was the affixing of the

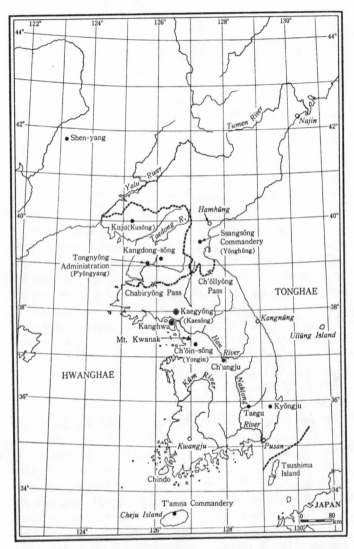

KORYŎ AND THE MONGOLS (13ᵗʰ CENTURY)

Chinese character "loyal" to the posthumous names bestowed on Koryŏ kings, thus vividly to give expression to the spirit of loyalty with which they were to serve the Mongol Yüan empire.

Nevertheless, the Koryŏ royal house maintained to the end its position as sovereign ruler of an independent nation, and the opposition of the Koryŏ officialdom defeated the more blatant Mongol attempts to interfere in internal Koryŏ politics. These successes were a legacy of the valiant struggle against the Mongols waged by the military regime. Yüan regarded it as fortunate indeed to have secured the peaceful submission of a nation that had persisted in a stubborn resistance against them for some thirty years. Thus while Yüan placed Korea under onerous restraints, it also felt compelled to soothe Koryŏ feelings.

On the other hand, sizeable portions of Koryŏ territory were, in fact, initially placed under direct Yüan dominion. While the bulk of these areas reverted before long to Koryŏ control, the Yüan Ssangsŏng Commandery that ruled over all of the northeastern quadrant of the peninsula continued in existence until recovered by force of arms in 1356. Moreover, Yüan's economic levies on Koryŏ sorely afflicted a nation laid waste by prolonged warfare. Yüan demanded Koryŏ gold, silver, cloth, grain, ginseng, and falcons, and at times even young women and eunuchs. These impositions, in the final analysis, came to rest on the backs of the peasants, who thus had to bear the double burden of exactions by Yüan and by their own government. This caused many peasants to abandon their land and wander about the countryside, whereupon the Koryŏ ruling class, with its huge agricultural estates, rounded up the wanderers and put them to work as farm laborers. Gradually, then, the Mongols came to regard this wealthy, propertied ruling class as a more reliable instrument for promoting Yüan interests than the powerless royal house.

As Yüan influence in Koryŏ grew, the Koryŏ ruling class soon came to be dominated by new forces that emerged in Koryŏ society under Yüan aegis. There were those who became powerful as Mongolian language interpreters, and there were others who rose to importance through military service to Yüan or as agents through whom Yüan tribute levies were collected and delivered.

These newly powerful families brazenly monopolized the benefits that the ruling class as a whole should have derived from the governing process, as they acquired vast estates and hundreds of slaves. This increase in private estates ate away at the government's own land resources, thus severely depleting state revenues. In consequence, if a newly appointed official lacked a private estate inherited from an ancestor, he had to lead a life of virtual poverty no matter how high his bureaucratic position might be. Furthermore, the increase in the privately owned slave population caused a reduction in the numbers of those on whom the state might impose corvee duty. This forced the government to mobilize instead the slaves of its own officials. In short, the situation had reached the point where political stability in Koryŏ became threatened by the disaffection of a significant segment of the socio-political elite, whose well-being had been seriously eroded by the economic aggrandizement of the all-powerful pro-Yüan houses.

Emergence of the Literati

A new bureaucratic class appeared following the disintegration of aristocratic government during the period of military rule. These were the literati (sadaebu), educated and knowledgeable men who also were adept in the administration of the affairs of government. After the collapse of military rule these scholar-bureaucrats strove for political advancement via the examination system, on the basis of demonstrated achievement. Literati also emerged from among the clerical force in the central government and from the ranks of the petty functionaries (hyangni) in the local administrations. The literati of this latter origin were small and middle-level landowners who possessed small-scale agricultural estates in their home localities. They lived on their land and personally directed the working of it. These literati despised the powerful absentee landlords of the capital who had acquired their huge estates by illegal means backed by political muscle. The emergence of such literati from among independent rural landowners brought a profound change to the political scene in Koryŏ.

However, so long as the powerful families were backed by the might of the Yüan dynasty, no effort to correct the abuses for which they were responsible could succeed. It was not until the reign of King Kongmin (1351-1374), at a time when Yüan was being driven northward by the rising Ming dynasty of China, that an opportunity for reform presented itself. Kongmin's reforms, then, had two facets: externally a policy directed against Yüan and internally an attempt to suppress the powerful families. Kongmin abolished the Yüan liaison organ, the Eastern Expedition Field Headquarters, purged the pro-Yüan faction, restored the old government structure, and recovered Koryŏ's lost territory by attacking the Yüan commandery headquarters at Ssangsŏng. These aggressive acts of defiance of course provoked a reaction from both Yüan and its Korean adherents. But Kongmin was able to frustrate these designs against him, and upon the founding of the Ming dynasty, in 1368, he immediately adopted a pro-Ming stance and initiated an exchange of envoys.

Internally Kongmin endeavored to undermine the dominant position of the powerful families through a variety of reforms. His first move was to abolish the Personnel Authority, that instrument of the autocratic rule of the Ch'oe house in the period of military rule. Later in his reign Kongmin grew fond of an obscure monk, Sin Ton, appointed him a National Preceptor, created for him the extraordinary post of Prime Minister Plenipotentiary, and had him carry out a sweeping reorganization of the government. Sin Ton first of all ousted officials of exalted lineage background and appointed others without such connections. Then, with the consent of the king, he established a special agency, the Directorate for Reclassification of Farmland and Farming Population, and set about returning lands and slaves seized by the powerful families to their original owners, and in many cases setting slaves free.

These actions naturally were well received by the populace as a whole, and Sin Ton was even hailed as a saint. But he so incurred the hostility of the powerful families that in the end they encompassed his downfall and death. Presently King Kongmin too was killed. A man more of artistic temperament than he was a political adept, he was unequal to the task of freeing Koryŏ from the grip of the powerful families, with their still formidable sources of strength.

The Founding of the Chosŏn (Yi) Dynasty

During the last quarter century or so of Koryŏ dynastic rule the country again was victimized by depredations from abroad. In the turmoil attendant upon the decline of Yüan, a powerful brigand force, the Red Turbans, arose and twice invaded Koryŏ. On the second occasion, in 1361, the Red Turbans swept swiftly down across the Yalu and even briefly seized the capital, Kaesŏng, before being put to rout. But these were short-lived and localized incursions, unlike the raids of Japanese marauders (*waegu*) that extended over a long century or more and ultimately affected the whole country.

Raids of the Japanese *waegu* had begun during the reign of King Kojong (1213-1259), and after 1350 they became rampant. Although armed but lightly, the Japanese came at will by sea, landed at random along the whole of the Koryŏ coast, and devastated the farming villages. Many peasants fled inland, letting the rich farmlands of the coastal regions lie fallow. Since the *waegu* might appear anywhere at any time, maritime traffic became paralyzed, cutting off the flow of grain and taxes in kind from the local areas to the capital. Thus Kaesŏng, where the aristocratic ruling class was concentrated, faced imminent economic collapse.

Repeated diplomatic representations to Japan failed to bring an end to the *waegu* attacks, and ultimately Koryŏ once again was compelled to muster the resources for a major and sustained military campaign. Two commanders in particular, Ch'oe Yŏng and Yi Sŏng-gye, rose to prominence as a result of their repeated successes against the Japanese raiders. They both soon came to enjoy great influence at the capital, but they sharply disagreed over Koryŏ policy toward the continent. This issue still had not been finally resolved when, in 1388, the newly established Ming dynasty proclaimed its intention to lay claim to the whole of Koryŏ's northeastern territory that had constituted the Yüan Ssangsŏng Commandery. Outraged, Ch'oe Yŏng determined to strike at Ming by invading the Liao-tung region of Manchuria, and with the agreement of the king troops were quickly mobilized throughout the country. Within scarcely two months an expedition was launched, with Ch'oe Yŏng as commander-in-chief and Yi Sŏng-gye as a deputy commander. But events were given an unexpected turn by Yi Sŏng-gye, who had favored a pro-Ming policy and opposed the expedition from the start. Marching his army back from Wihwa Island in the mouth of the Yalu, in a nearly bloodless coup Yi Sŏng-gye ousted the king and Ch'oe Yŏng from power, seizing political control himself. He thus had grasped the historic moment for the overthrow of Koryŏ and the establishment of a new dynasty.

Yi Sŏng-gye and his supporters used their newly won power to carry out a sweeping land reform, advocated all along by the newly risen literati class but hitherto impossible to put into effect. The literati reform advocates, by and large adherents of Neo-Confucianism, not only opposed the powerful families but also the Buddhist establishment, both on ideological grounds and because it too had amassed great estates and so was undermining the nation's economic foundation. The reform of private landholding, then, signified the destruction of the old economic order and the establishment of a new one by the rising literati class.

The land reform began with the undertaking of a cadastral survey of landholding throughout the country. Then, in 1390, all the existing registers of public and private land were set afire and destroyed. In accordance with the new, basic Rank Land Law statute, land in the Kyŏnggi region around the capital was allocated to members of the official class in accordance with their rank. Needless to say, the Yi Sŏng-gye faction in this way received substantial allocations. The land in the rest of the country all was subsumed under the category of state land, with the result that the agricultural estates were in effect confiscated. Accordingly, the economic foundation of the powerful families was destroyed, and this signaled the downfall of the Koryŏ dynasty itself. At the same time, the increase in state land brought about a corresponding increase in government revenues, and this secured the economic foundation of the new dynasty of Chosŏn.

Yi Sŏng-gye had taken political, military, and finally economic power into his own hands. The only requirement still to be met to effect the establishment of a new dynasty was the formality itself. Powerful opponents still stood in the way, but the most formidable of these, the revered Neo-Confucian scholar-official Chŏng Mong-ju, was assassinated by Yi Sŏng-gye's fifth son (the later King T'aejong). The last king of the Koryŏ house of Wang then was forced to abdicate the throne, whereupon the founder of the royal house of Yi was seated upon it.

Yi Sŏng-gye represented new forces that emerged toward the end of the Koryŏ dynasty. He was not the scion of a famous family with a long history. His immediate ancestors had been military commanders in the Hamhŭng area of northeast Korea, and Yi Sŏng-gye himself won advancement through his exploits in the numerous battles of his day. He then seized power as the champion of the new class of literati-bureaucrats and was raised by them to the kingship.

Yi Sŏng-gye named his dynasty Chosŏn, after the most ancient Korean kingdom, and moved the capital to Hanyang (Seoul), both actions important manifestations of the founding of a new dynasty. In terms of its geomantic setting and in its scale, Yi Sŏng-gye strove to ensure that Seoul would mirror the prestige of his new kingdom. From this time on Seoul has been the political, economic, and cultural center of Korea.

The Culture of the New Literati Class

The special characteristic of late Koryŏ Confucianism lies in its acceptance of Neo-Confucian doctrine. Neo-Confucianism is a philosophical Confucianism that explains the origins of man and the universe in metaphysical terms. Its political ethic stresses the mutual relationship of ruler and subject, and it is an intolerant doctrine, quick to reject all other teachings. The new literati class of that time, unable to find fulfillment either in Buddhism or in traditional Confucianism, now made Neo-Confucianism their spiritual mainstay. The spread of Neo-Confucianism gave rise to an intensifying repudiation of Buddhism. At first, rather than denouncing belief in Buddhism itself, the literati-bureaucrats attacked the abuses of the Buddhist establishment—its grasping concern with wealth and power, and the misconduct of its monks. But soon some stepped forward, like Chŏng To-jŏn, to completely reject Buddhism as destructive of family mores and ruinous to the state.

An active interest in historiography is a prominent feature of the world of scholarship in middle and late Koryŏ. Beginning with the compilation in Hyŏnjong's reign (1009-1031) of official *Annals* (*Sillok*) for the first seven kings of the dynasty, annals for all the Koryŏ rulers were prepared. Today, however, none of these survive, and we are left with the *History of the Three Kingdoms* (*Samguk sagi*), compiled in 1145 by Kim Pu-sik in response to a royal command, as Korea's oldest extant history. In annals form with separate chronological tables, treatises, and biographies, it reflects an aristocratic point of view and adopts a Confucianist historiographical perspective—that is, it is a frankly didactic work that evaluates the actors and events of Korea's early history from the viewpoint of Confucian moralism. There is also the *Lives of Eminent Korean Monks* (*Haedong kosŭng chŏn*) written in 1215, again by royal command, only a portion of which remains. A kind of orthodox history of Buddhism in Korea, this work was written from the standpoint of the Textual School that had flourished in congenial partnership with aristocratic power in Koryŏ.

Of quite a different character are *Memorabilia of the Three Kingdoms* (*Samguk yusa*) by the monk Iryŏn (1206-1289) and *Songs of Emperors and Kings* (*Chewang un'gi*) by Yi Sŭnghyu. The unique feature of both these is that they begin Korean history with Tan'gun. The suffering of the people of Koryŏ during the Mongol period, it would seem, strengthened their sense of identity as a distinct race and gave force to the concept of their descent from a common ancestor. A second characteristic is that these works clearly evidence the deep respect the authors felt for the traditions and legacy of their past history. The Sŏn monk Iryŏn's *Memorabilia of the Three Kingdoms* is a particularly rich source of information on ancient folkways and institutions.

The literary form in which the literati of this age expressed themselves was the *kyŏnggi*-style poem. This newly developed poetic form used the Chinese language, but to exalt Korea's own land and its lore. It began with the "Song of the Confucian Academicians" composed by the young Confucian officials of the Academy of Letters during the period of military rule, a poem that vividly depicts the exultant view of life held by the literati now emerging onto the political stage. At the same time poems about fishermen that depict the solitary pastimes of the literati living on their countryside estates also appeared. In contrast, the "long poem" (*changga*), the authors of which are largely unknown, was the literary form of the common poeple. These poems developed out of the folk song tradition and give full, frank, and sometimes ribald expression to the feelings and daily lives of the people. In its themes, the *changga* range from the unblushingly licentious scenes of "The Turkish Bakery" to the mournful cadences of the "Green Mountain Song" that express the sorrow of landless peasants as they are forced to abandon their farms for a life of wandering. These *changga* came to be sung frequently on such occasions as palace banquets, and so they also underwent development as songs for the enjoyment of the upper classes.

The distinctive feature of painting in the late Koryŏ period is that it increasingly came to be practiced by the non-professional, by the literati, to give expression to their sensibilities in what may be called a romantic style. This is seen in the frequency of the portrayals of the literatus as recluse, the pleasures of alfresco fellowship, the "four gentlemen" (orchid, chrysanthemum, bamboo, and plum) and, above all, of representations in black writing-brush ink of bamboo, the plant whose pliancy and tenacity symbolized the ability of an honorable official to weather political storms without losing integrity. The concept of poem and painting as a unitary mode of expression, achieved by adding calligraphed poetry to the scene depicted, is another hallmark of the literati painting of this day. But there is little opportunity to directly assess late Koryŏ literati painting today, as perhaps no more than three or four works from this period are known. Fortunately this is not the case with Buddhist painting, many specimens of which, done with both refinement and splendor, can be seen still today, in museums around the world and on temple walls in Korea.

The earliest surviving Koryŏ wooden structure is the Hall of

Paradise at the Pongjŏng-sa temple in Andong, thought to date from the thirteenth century. But the best example of Koryŏ architecture in wood is the Hall of Eternal Life at Pusŏk-sa in Yŏngju, which appears to have been built at about the same time. Its tapered columns, shapely three-tiered roof supports, the buoyant lines of the dual roof-edge, and the ceiling-less open work of the hall within give an overall solemn dignity of appearance that is characteristic of Korean wooden buildings.

An unusual late Koryŏ stone pagoda, now in the Kyŏngbok Palace grounds in Seoul, was built about 1345. A ten-story pagoda done in marble, the three-tiered pedestal and first three stories each protrude alternate square-shaped and triangular edges, eight in all, providing twenty surfaces on which to carve Buddhistic images; the top seven stories, then, are typically square. The stone memorial stupas of this late period took the unadorned form of stone bells, a marked change from the ornamental ones of earlier Koryŏ times. Finally worthy of note is the existence down to today of superb wood-crafted articles such as the masks for the Hahoe masked drama.

The great concern from the early years of Koryŏ for the establishment of libraries led not only to the acquisition and preservation of books but to their duplication as well. Tens of thousands of rare books were kept as treasured possessions in Koryŏ, so that on occasion even the Sung government sent to Koryŏ to secure works unavailable in China. Printing thus flourished and a wide variety of books were published. At first most printing was done by the woodblock technique, of which the publication of the Tripitaka is an outstanding example. Woodblock printing was an extremely convenient way to satisfy a widespread demand for one particular work. Once the blocks were carved, the printing itself was a simple matter and subsequent editions could be made as well. But when many kinds of works were needed in a limited number of copies, printing by movable type was more efficient. Thus Koryŏ directed its attention toward printing by movable type and proceeded to develop this art. In Koryŏ there is a record of the use of cast metal type in the year 1234 for the printing of the work

Prescribed Ritual Texts of the Past and Present. It is clear that the type used to print this book was metal movable type, and therefore Koryŏ's use of this printing method is the earliest in the history of the world.

Korean technology moved forward too on other fronts. Formerly, hemp had been the principal material for people's clothing, with ramie and silk also used in the more elegant wear of the aristocracy. At this point the cultivation of the cotton plant, introduced from Yüan China in 1363, began in Korea and cotton cloth emerged as a major material for clothing. Advances in the medicinal arts in Koryŏ were stimulated both by influences from Sung China and by study of Korea's own traditional folk remedies. Compilation of the work *Emergency Remedies of Folk Medicine* was an outgowth of this latter emphasis; published in 1236, it is Korea's oldest extant medical treatise.

Finally, gunpowder was manufactured for the first time in Korea during this period. Ch'oe Mu-sŏn, a minor official, worked tirelessly to formulate gunpowder in order to make more powerful weapons with which to counter the devastating raids of the Japanese marauders. Eventually learning its closely guarded secret from a Yüan Chinese, Ch'oe persuaded the Koryŏ court to establish a Superintendency for Gunpowder Weapons (1377) where cannon and weaponry of various kinds could be made. He also equipped the navy with newly built ships, which, with their cannon, achieved major successes in repulsing the Japanese.

Chapter 9

The Creation of a Yangban Society

The Development of Yangban Society in Chosŏn

Military strength was the principal factor that enabled Yi Sŏng-gye to establish a new dynasty and become its first ruler (as King T'aejo, 1392-1398). At the same time, had the literati not given him their support, he surely could not have occupied the throne. In Chosŏn's early years the "Dynastic Foundation Merit Subjects," the men of literati background who had elevated T'aejo to the kingship, wielded paramount political power from their base in the Privy Council, while he himself appears to have been content with a largely passive role. The literati powerholders then set about codifying a corpus of administrative law infused with the Confucian ideals, principles and practices by which the political process of the dynasty of Chosŏn would operate.

Because this exercise of power by the Dynastic Foundation Merit Subjects simply repeated the pattern of Koryŏ aristocratic rule, the king's more ambitious sons and the numerous literati beneath the highest levels became disaffected. The result was the liquidation of Chŏng To-jŏn, the prime architect of the new dynasty's original structure of governance, by T'aejo's fifth son, the later King T'aejong (1400-1418). T'aejong in the end took the throne for himself, having first ordered the assassination of T'aejo's designated heir, the youngest son, and then disposing of the rival claim of his own next older brother. T'aejong abolished private armed retinues, instituted centralized military control, and changed the Privy Council into a State Council with greatly diminished authority, entrusting overall conduct of government business to six ministries each authorized to approach the throne directly.

Sejong (1418-1450), T'aejong's successor, established the Hall of Worthies, assigned outstanding scholars to it, and had them study the ancient statutes and institutions of China as the basis upon which he would reorganize the political structure of Chosŏn. In consequence of this process the political voice of the scholars in the Hall of Worthies came to be heard ever more loudly, and the usurpation of the throne by Sejo (1455-1468) may well have been a reaction against this development. In the process of seizing power Sejo killed a great many of those who opposed him, beginning with two honored elder statesmen and his own younger brother. Subsequently, when a treason plot against him was uncovered, he carried out a bloodbath in which the famed "six martyred ministers" and other scholars of the Hall of Worthies met their deaths. He too then set to work compiling a statutory code that would define the structure and functioning of Chosŏn's government, producing finally the *National Code*. This set in place the administrative structure of the kingdom of Chosŏn, a dynasty characterized by a governing process directed by civil and military bureaucrats enforcing prescribed statutory procedures, rather than one dominated by a joint deliberative organ situated at the highest level.

The literati constituted the dominant social class of the Chosŏn dynasty, for they were the *"yangban,"* the members of the "two orders" of officialdom who served as civil or military officials. And because it was this *yangban* class that directed the government, economy, and culture of Chosŏn, it may fittingly be designated a *yangban* society. Chosŏn's dominant *yangban* class was much more broadly based than the ruling classes of Koryŏ or earlier ages. The increased size of the *yangban* class in turn greatly increased the importance of the state examination system for the recruitment of officials, as opportunities to enter government service via so-called protected appointments were severely curtailed by dynastic policy.

The sole duty of the *yangban* was to devote themselves exclusively to the study and self-cultivation that Confucian doctrine holds must underlie the governing of others, and their sole profession was the holding of public office. Yet they did not serve in the technical posts as medical officers, translator-interpreters, astronomer-astrologers, accountants, statute law clerks, scribes, or government artists, all of which positions became the virtually hereditary preserve of the *chungin* ("middle people") class. Nor did the *yangban* perform the routine duties of petty clerks and local civil functionaries or of military cadre members. They also were not interested in working at agriculture, manufacture, or commerce, for these were but the occupations of farmers, artisans, and merchants. Their role instead was to fashion an ideal Confucian polity through the moral cultivation of Chosŏn's people.

The *yangban* who thus enjoyed the special privilege of governing, together with its many attendant benefits, could not be other than elitist. They pursued various strategies to protect their status and limit their numbers. *Yangban* married only among themselves, thus preserving the hereditary nature of *yangban* status. They even lived in separate quarters of Seoul and in the villages in the countryside, not in the towns. Within the *yangban* class itself there also were distinctions. The civil order was more prestigious than the military, and there were members of the *yangban* class whose access to the examinations and civil office was seriously restricted, such as the numerous descendants of *yangban* by their secondary wives. There was regional discrimination as well, and residents of the northern provinces, in particular, found it all but impossible to gain appointment to the higher offices. All of these limitations may be viewed as part of a self-selection process at work within *yangban* society, designed to counteract the dilution of *yangban* privileges that would result from excessive increase in their numbers.

Administrative Structure of the Yangban Bureaucratic State

The highest organ of government in Chosŏn was the State Council, a deliberative organ whose joint decisions were made by three High State Councillors. The principal administrative agencies were the Six Ministries—those of Personnel, Taxation, Rites, Military Affairs, Punishments, and Public Works. And since the ministries came to have the authority to lay matters under their purview directly before the king, the State Council gradually declined in authority. Accordingly, Chosŏn's political structure might aptly be termed a "ministries system." The Royal Secretariat, the organ through which documents were transmitted to and from the king, at times also performed a vital advisory role.

An instrumentality designed to prevent abuses in the exercise of political and administrative authority was the *Samsa*, a combined term for the Office of Special Advisers, Office of the Inspector-General, and Office of the Censor-General. The Office of Special Advisers searched out administrative and legal precedents, authored major state documents, and so served as an advisory organ to the king. The Office of the Inspector-General was a surveillance organ, criticizing public policy, scrutinizing official conduct, and rectifying public mores. The Office of the Censor-General examined and censured when necessary the conduct of the king himself, a function that imposed restraint on the arbitrary exercise of the power of the throne. Together, these latter two organs were entrusted with a unique authority, to look into the family background and career records of those nominated for middle and lower ranking positions, preliminary to giving or withholding approval of their appointments. Taken as a whole, Chosŏn's central government constituted a system of checks and balances designed to prevent power becoming over concentrated in any one segment of the structure. This system, however, worked perhaps too well, often resulting in intra-bureaucratic strife and rendering the decision-making process dilatory and ineffective.

As for provincial and local government, the country was divided into eight provinces [see map p. 112] and within the provinces were counties of several types. A governor was appointed to each province, with jurisdiction over the various county magistrates. The county magistrate, also appointed by the central government, was the so-called shepherd of the people, the official who governed them directly. His principal duty, however, was to collect taxes and mobilize corvee labor, and so it may be said that local government in Chosŏn was designed more to serve national than local interests. A county magistrate was appointed for a term of five years and, due to potential conflict of interest, was not permitted to serve in his county of residence. On the other hand, a county's *yangban* residents exerted great influence on local administration through the so-called Local Agency. This office undertook responsibility for assisting the magistrate, rectifying public mores, and scrutinizing the conduct of the county's petty functionaries (*hyangni*), thus serving as a power base for the local *yangban*.

In each provincial and local administrative unit duties were allocated among six "chambers," on the model of the Six Ministries in the capital. The duties of these offices were discharged by a hereditary class of petty functionaries (*hyangni,* also known as local *ajŏn*) native to the area in which they served. For liaison purposes an *ajŏn* from each county was stationed in Seoul and at the headquarters of the provincial governor. Thus it was the *ajŏn*, or *hyangni,* who actually carried on the operations of the local government offices. They were an indigenous element and they also were unsalaried, a combination of characteristics that proved all too conducive to venality and exploitation of the peasant populace.

The military system had been in chaotic condition ever since the late Koryŏ period, and so Yi T'aejo established the Three Armies Headquarters to assume control over the military apparatus. However, many powerful figures still retained personal armed retinues, and this frustrated T'aejo's efforts to centralize military authority in the hands of the government. It was T'aejong who resolutely abolished these private armed forces and so accomplished this end, in 1400. The Three Armies Headquarters was reorganized by King Sejo (1455-1468) into the Five Military Commands Headquarters, to which was given authority over the fivefold division (Center, East, West, South, and North) of the forces that garrisoned the capital. The troops that formed the core of the Five Commands, such as armored soldiers, were professional military men selected through tests of their military skills.

From an overall perspective, provincial armies were a more important component of Chosŏn's defense structure than were the Five Commands in the capital. Each province had its own Army Command and Navy Command [see map p. 112], and

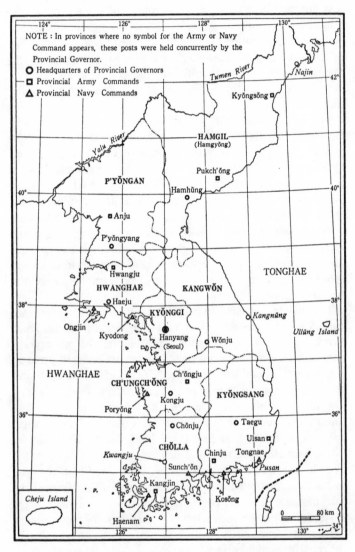

NOTE : In provinces where no symbol for the Army or Navy
Command appears, these posts were held concurrently by the
Provincial Governor.

○ Headquarters of Provincial Governors
□ Provincial Army Commands
△ Provincial Navy Commands

Tumen River

Najin

Kyŏngsŏng □

HAMGIL
(Hamgyŏng)

Yalu River

Pukch'ŏng □

P'YŎNGAN

Hamhŭng ○

□ Anju

P'yŏngyang ○

Hwangju □

HWANGHAE   KANGWŎN

Haeju ○

Ongjin   KYŎNGGI

Kyodong   Hanyang   Wŏnju ○
(Seoul)

TONGHAE

Kangnŭng

Ullŭng Island

HWANGHAE   Ch'ŏngju □

CH'UNGCH'ŎNG   KYŎNGSANG

Kongju ○

Poryŏng   Taegu ○

Chŏnju ○   Ulsan □

CHŎLLA   Chinju   Tongnae
Kwangju   □   Pusan
Sunch'ŏn

Kangjin   Kosŏng

Cheju Island

Haenam   0   80 km

**CHOSŎN'S EIGHT PROVINCES AND REGIONAL
MILITARY COMMANDS (15ᵗʰ CENTURY)**

under these were an appropriate number of garrisons. The military men attached to the garrisons in the provinces were of three kinds: the combat soldiers who defended the garrison fortifications, their support or labor battalions, and the sailors who manned the ships. The land garrison forces were by far the most important of these, with their core element of units made up of commoner peasants. Assigned to military service in accordance with a system of rotation, when they were stood down these peasant-soldiers returned to their farms.

The central government and provincial forces, which thus at first had existed under separate command structures, later came to be merged. That is, a garrison–command structure was created, centering on the fortified garrison points to which were assigned drafts of commoner peasants. Accordingly, the conscript was simply a peasant-soldier who normally went about his farming but then would be called up in turn to active duty in Seoul or at the garrison forts. Meanwhile, other peasant–soldiers would remain on the land, serving as "sustainers" who provided economic support for those on active duty. This arrangement was brought to final form by the Paired Provisioner System, under which one of a team of two or three able-bodied men was to be supported while on active service by the others, the "provisioners" supplying the conscripted soldier with a fixed amount of cotton cloth and being so supported when they in turn were called up.

Finally, in order to quickly inform the capital of military crises that might occur in the provinces, there was a system of beacon fires, and in order to speedily convey more detailed information on such situations a network of post stations was maintained. The post station system also was used for the transmission of government documents in general, for government transport purposes, and for official travel.

The examination system was of central importance in the recruitment of officials in Chosŏn Korea. Since Chosŏn restricted protected appointments to the sons of officials of the second rank and above, unless one passed through the examination system the path to higher office was for the most part closed. For the *yangban*, then, the examinations truly were the gateway to success. While it is true that anyone of commoner, or free, status possessed the legal qualification to sit for the examinations, it is clear that the *yangban* virtually monopolized the examinations leading to appointment to the civil offices so prized by Chosŏn's *yangban* society.

Qualifying examinations for appointment to civil offices were conducted at two levels, the licentiate or lower level and the erudite or higher level. The licentiate examinations were of two kinds: the Classics Licentiate Examination that examined candidates on the Four Books and Five Classics of China, and the Literary Licentiate Examination that tested skill in composing a variety of Chinese literary forms. From an early age *yangban* youth attended private elementary schools (*sŏdang*) where they learned the basic Chinese characters and practiced writing them. Then, from age seven, they advanced to one of the Four Schools in Seoul or to their local County School. After several years of study the Confucian students of these schools were thereby qualified to sit for the licentiate examinations, and if they passed a first stage examination held at the provincial level they proceeded to Seoul for a second stage examination, which determined those who would receive Classics or Literary Licentiate degrees. These Licentiates might then enter the National Confucian Academy (*Sŏnggyun'gwan*) in Seoul, the country's highest educational organ, and the students who attended the National Confucian Academy could in due course sit for the Erudite Examination. Here too the successful candidates, typically thirty-three in number, had to survive preliminary and second stage examinations. Finally a Palace Examination was held in the presence of the king to determine the final ranking of those who had passed.

What has just been described, however, represents the processes of recruitment for civil offices as they were designed institutionally, and it was by no means the case that only this one track had to be followed. As the means of preparing for the examinations, for example, *yangban* society increasingly preferred its own privately established institutions to the government's Four Schools in Seoul or County Schools in the countryside. Moreover, although it originally was prescribed that so-called regular examinations be carried out every third year, in reality examinations also were held at other times on a variety of special occasions. As these irregular examinations increased in frequency, the triennial examinations diminished in importance, to some extent being deliberately avoided by sons of capital-centered *yangban* lineages.

Military examinations had been held for the first time at the very end of the Koryŏ period, and these were continued in the Yi dynasty. The military examination tested skills in basic military arts, as well as knowledge of the Classics and military texts. Although the military examination was far less important than the civil, its establishment meant that military officials would be recruited from the same privileged lineages as were civil officials, and this in turn signified the formal completion of the *yangban* ("two orders") bureaucratic structure. But the military examination too later changed complexion and became an avenue through which even the lowborn might in some measure advance.

There also were four Miscellaneous Examinations (*chapkwa*) for the selection of technical specialists, in foreign languages, medicine, astronomy (including meteorology and geomancy), and law. Those who took degrees in these specialties were employed in the appropriate government agencies. The *yangban* literati of Chosŏn looked down on these specialized studies, calling them a "hodgepodge of learning," and from around 1600 a number of new *chungin* ("middle people") lineage segments evolved that soon came to provide an overwhelming preponderance of those who won success in the Miscellaneous Examinations, and also of those who served as government calligraphers, artists, and accountants.

Social and Economic Structure of the Yangban Bureaucratic State

The land system of Yi Korea rested on the foundation of the reform carried out by Yi Sŏng-gye (T'aejo) at the end of Koryŏ. In accordance with the Rank Land Law put into effect at that time, both incumbent and former officials were to receive stipendiary allocations of land. Such allocations were to be made only from land in the Kyŏnggi area, the province around the capital. Although in principle grants of rank land were limited to the lifetime of the recipient, an official's widow was permitted to retain a portion of her husband's land, and similarly, if both parents were deceased, "fostering land" could be kept for the upbringing of the children. Thus, from the beginning, there was a marked tendency for rank land to be held hereditarily.

These circumstances soon combined to create a shortage of land available for distribution to those newly eligible to receive rank land allocations. The problem was exacerbated by the fact that grants of "merit land," made in perpetuity, continued to increase, primarily in consequence of the several succession disputes that occurred early in the new dynasty. Before long, in 1466, Sejo revoked the Rank Land Law and in its place enacted an Office Land Law, which authorized allocations only to incumbent officeholders. But this new system too proved unworkable and was abolished by about 1556. Thenceforth officials were no longer given land but were paid salaries.

There was a variety of other types of state allocated land. "Military land" supported the *hallyang* military junior officer class that still was a force in the countryside; like rank land, it too tended to be held hereditarily, on the ground that it was needed for the care of widows and orphaned children. There were tracts of land set aside to meet the needs of the palace, while "public agency land" went to the many central government offices (soon, however, to be abandoned in favor of meeting the expenses of government out of grain tax and local tribute receipts). Land continued to be assigned for the support of local government agencies, but the "local service land" formerly given to the *hyangni*, the petty functionaries of local government, was abolished. Finally, allocations were made of "school land" to support the government's education organs, "temple land" for Buddhist temples, and "garrison land" to provide stores for provincial and local military units.

In underlying concept, the land system of Chosŏn postulated that ownership of all the nation's land formally resided in the king. The term "public land," however, did not mean land owned by the state, but rather designated land from which the state directly collected a "rent" originally set at ten percent of the harvest. Similarly, "private land" was distributed to individual rank or office holders, but what the government granted was the right to collect the rent and not ownership rights. Nevertheless, *yangban* recipients of such grants often were able to convey the right to collect the land rent to their heirs, and ultimately to convert this limited right to one of outright ownership. Despite the formal principle of state ownership, therefore, the extent of private ownership of land steadily grew.

In point of fact, private ownership of land had been widespread from the outset. Most land distributed under the Rank Land Law actually belonged to the category of "people's land," which meant that private ownership rights to it were recognized by the state. These rights generally appear to have come into existence at the end of Koryŏ, in many cases as a direct consequence of the confiscation of the large estates that preceded the Rank Land Law reform. Typical owners of "people's land" possessed only enough to cultivate themselves, but many—especially the *yangban*—had far more, and the numerous owner-tenant class had less. A half and half crop sharing arrangement normally prevailed between a land owner and its cultivator, with the owner paying the ten percent rent to the state from his share. This crop sharing system gradually spread as well to rank land, merit subject land, and other forms of land allocation. In consequence of these circumstances, from the beginning of the dynasty both landowning by the *yangban* and their income from the land continuously increased, and once again the term "agricultural estates" (*nongjang*) came to be used to describe the large holdings of the more wealthy members of the ruling class.

It was the peasants, of course, who tilled the land. The peasants of this period had mastered a far better agricultural technology than their predecessors. They knew how to use a variety of fertilizers and thus were able to cultivate the land year after year without letting it lie fallow. Moreover, although direct sowing of seed remained predominant, the method of transplanting rice seedlings had become known. Reservoirs to combat the effects of drought also were constructed, numbering over six hundred in Kyŏngsang province alone. Efforts were exerted, too, to develop strains of seed better adapted to the Korean climate. These improvements in agricultural technology inevitably resulted in increased yields.

The position of the peasant in Chosŏn Korean society also improved. It would appear that there was a significant number of independent peasants in this period, owner-operators who employed hired hands to help them cultivate their small holdings. The typical peasant, of course, still was one who toiled as a tenant farmer on the various kinds of *yangban* owned land, but his social status was that of freeborn commoner. There also were "out-resident" slaves who tilled their owner's land and who were classed as "lowborn" (*ch'ŏnmin*), but since these formed independent households and were themselves responsible for their livelihood, they did not differ particularly in the lives they led from the peasant tenant farmers.

At the same time, the peasants were fixed on the land and were unable to move as they wished. In order to prevent them from abandoning the land they worked, an "identification tag" (*hop'ae*) law was enacted. The *hop'ae*, on which was recorded the name, date of birth, class, status, and county of residence of the registrant, was like a modern citizen's identification card, and it was required to be in one's personal possession at all times. Subsequent to two mid-15th century rebellions in Hamgyŏng province, which drew support from peasants who had migrated there, the *hop'ae* law was further strengthened. Moreover, a newly enacted law organized households into units of five, each of which was responsible for ensuring that other members of the unit did not abscond from their locality of residence. In consequence, the typical peasant household in Chosŏn tended to be a self-sufficient unit living generation after generation in one place, providing its own needs for food, clothing, and shelter.

In return for having land to cultivate, the peasant farmer was required to pay a land tax. The Rank Land Law had set this at one-tenth the harvest, but when Sejong promulgated the Tribute Tax Law in 1444, the tax rate was lowered to one-twentieth. The Tribute Tax Law also sought to correct abuses that had arisen in the procedures for estimating the harvest potential of different plots of land, by stipulating that land be classified into six grades of fertility and that the effect of weather conditions be judged on the basis of a nine-fold classification. Accordingly, it would appear that the peasant paid a land tax not merely modest to begin with, but one reasonably well adjusted in his favor under adverse circumstances. But it would be a mistake to conclude, therefore, that the peasant's burden was light, for between the peasant and the state stood a landlord with whom the peasant had to share the fruits of his labor on an equal basis.

An additional burden on the peasant was the "local tribute" tax, levied on products indigenous to a particular locale. It met government needs for a variety of handcrafted items, such as utensils, fabrics, paper, and woven mats, as well as refined metals, marine products, furs, fruits, and lumber. Originally to be paid by the local magistracy, the cost of these tribute articles ultimately came to be borne by the peasants.

Finally, for the able-bodied commoner male, there was the obligation of military and corvee labor service. Military service was performed on a rotation basis, while corvee labor was required each year for a fixed period of time. Although the work obligation was to extend over no more than six days in a single year, in reality corvee drafts could be mustered whenever the government saw fit. Thus it was not merely to ensure stability in agricultural production but also an adequate supply of corvee laborers that led the government to fix the able-bodied peasant farmer in his locale of residence.

In Chosŏn, with the rapid expansion of the cultivation of cotton, the production of cotton cloth was the principal household industry, although the traditional crafts of fabricating silk, hemp, and ramie cloth of course continued to be practiced. Cotton not only was used by the peasants for their own clothing, but it also was important to the government as material for military dress and as an item in Korea's foreign trade. The making of farm implements was another major occupation of the peasant villages.

Just as in the Koryŏ period, in early Chosŏn the work of craftsmen and artisans was performed preponderantly under government aegis. For the most part, these skilled workmen were enrolled as "government artisans"—for example, some 640 were assigned to the Government Arsenal to make weapons and 91 to the Paper Manufactory to meet the government's needs for paper. Altogether some 2,800 such skilled workers were employed in Seoul and more than 3,500 in the provinces. These artisans, however, were pressed into government service only for certain periods during the year, so that in fact they normally worked for themselves on orders from private clients. Although some artisans were government slaves, they lived and worked no differently than the freeman artisans, the proportion of whom continuously increased. At the same time, in the urban areas, there was a growing pattern of work undertaken on private initiatives. While private artisans did produce luxury goods on order for *yangban* clients, in the main they made household necessities—brassware utensils, horsehair hats, and leather shoes among others—for the general populace and sold them in the markets.

From an early time there were shops in Seoul centering along the main thoroughfare of Chongno, established by the government and leased to merchants for their premises. The so-called Six Licensed Stores somewhat later came to typify this pattern of commercial activity. Granted the monopolistic privilege of purveying silk, cotton cloth, thread, paper goods, ramie cloth, and fish products, in exchange these stores were required to supply the government's needs for the item in which they severally dealt. But there were small shops as well, free of any obligation to the government, and markets were opened too in a number of places.

In local areas permanent markets had begun to develop early in the dynasty. But these soon were suppressed, since they were operated by peasants who had fled their land either because of famine or to avoid the burdens of military service or taxation. It was thus only the periodic markets that could flourish. Generally opened every five days, these markets trafficked in such items as agricultural produce, handcrafted articles, marine products, and medicinal substances. The vendors were itinerant pack and back peddlers who belonged to a guild formally sanctioned by the government. The back and pack peddlers who worked the countryside had their counterpart in itinerant peddlers who traveled the coastal sea lanes, but theirs was not so flourishing a trade.

With commercial activities in early Chosŏn conducted in this fashion, a money economy could not so easily develop. Several 15th century mintages, for example, were intended primarily for government use in collecting taxes. They did not, therefore, gain wide circulation, and as before the medium of exchange in important transactions was cloth, with the unit of exchange now shifting from hempen cloth to cotton.

In Chosŏn society, too, beneath the freeman commoner class there was a large lowborn population, predominantly comprised of slaves. There were two basic categories of slaves: public slaves owned by the government and private slaves belonging to individuals. Among both government and privately owned slaves a substantial majority, it appears, formed independent households and paid fixed fees in lieu of providing labor services to their owners on demand. Their economic position, therefore, was little different from that of the tenant farmers, but their status by law was hereditary and they could be bought and sold at the whim of their masters. It is difficult to estimate the size of Chosŏn's slave population, but one oft-cited statistic, taken from contemporary government records, is that there were "well over 200,000" government slaves on the rosters of Seoul agencies alone in 1462. And since a child became a slave if either parent had slave status, it is clear that the slave population continued to grow during the first three centuries or so of the dynasty. It may be suggested, then, that for much of the Chosŏn period Korea in fact was a slave society, with perhaps close to one-third of its people legally classed as unfree.

In addition to the slaves, as in Koryŏ lowborn status also was possessed by outcasts, *paekchŏng,* who hereditarily worked at such occupations as butchering, tanning, and wickerwork, and who lived in separate hamlets. In an effort to assimilate them to the general farming population King Sejong gave them land, and this is how they came to be called *paekchŏng*, a term originally used to designate peasant farmers in general. Although thus treated as commoners in point of law, they continued to pursue their hereditary occupations, regarded by society as before, as lowborn. Finally, there were the *kisaeng,* female entertainers assigned to duties in both capital and local jurisdictions, and who frequently were taken by *yangban* as concubines or secondary wives. Traveling troupes of entertainers too were classed as lowborn, as were the female shamans or exorcists known as *mudang.*

Foreign Policy of Early Chosŏn

Chosŏn used the term *sadae* ("serving the great") to describe its foreign policy toward Ming China, and every effort was made to maintain a friendly relationship. Chosŏn's founder, Yi Sŏng-gye, had adopted a pro-Ming stance from the outset, a policy calculated to confer legitimacy both on his new regime and also on himself as its ruler. The old aristocracy looked askance at this parvenu from so unremarkable a family background, and so Yi Sŏng-gye was in need of authoritative sanction for his regime.

Chosŏn dispatched four regular embassies to Ming each year, to offer New Year's felicitations, to congratulate the Ming emperor on his birthday, to honor the birthday of the imperial crown prince, and to mark the passing of the winter solstice. Embassies were sent additionally whenever a ruler died, a succession to the throne occurred, or a queen formally was invested in either Chosŏn or Ming. The purpose of all these missions chiefly was political, but they served also as the medium for cultural borrowing and economic exchange. Articles exported in this way by Chosŏn included horses, ginseng, furs, ramie cloth, and straw mats with floral designs, while in return Korea obtained silk fabrics, medicines, books, and porcelain ware. Thus the relationship with Ming China on the whole proceeded satisfactorily.

Having risen to power from a base in the northeast, Yi T'aejo took early steps to extend his sway over the whole of this region, and he succeeded in gaining control over all territory up to the Tumen River frontier. The native inhabitants of the area, however, a Jurchen people called Yain or "barbarians" by the Koreans, remained unruly. King Sejong (1418-1450), then, established six garrison forts in the northeast, thus making permanent the Tumen River boundary. At the same time, expeditions were sent against the Yain in the Yalu region, resulting in the creation of four outposts along the upper Yalu River. The purpose of this opening up of the north lay not only in bringing new land under cultivation but in extending the frontier to the natural defense line formed by the two rivers, and to consolidate its control the government on several occasions sent colonists from the southern provinces to settle the newly incorporated territories. Thus was fashioned the domain that Korea occupies today.

Originally the Yain maintained a half-agricultural, half-hunting economy, and they had to obtain from Chosŏn food, clothing, and other basic necessities, as well as tools of production such as agricultural implements. Accordingly, the key element in Chosŏn's pacification policy was the opening of markets where Yain horses and furs might be bartered for cloth, farm implements, and grain. Their ritual submission and immigration also were encouraged, and titular rank, food and clothing, and houses in which to live were given to those who thus pledged their allegiance. Nevertheless their pillaging activities did not completely cease, and a major rebellion broke out in 1583. Kyŏngwŏn and other garrison forts fell one after the other, but after a hard struggle the uprising was subdued by government forces under Sin Ip.

Chosŏn's sea frontier also continued to bear watching. The threat posed by Japanese marauders gradually had subsided, although in early Chosŏn incidents of pillaging still occurred from time to time. Unable to produce enough food on their mountainous, rocky islands, the Japanese on Tsushima had to provide for themselves either through trade or by launching forays against their neighbors. When Sejong sent a strong military force to attack Tsushima in 1419, his purpose was to wipe out the bases from which these Japanese marauders mounted their attacks. The Sō house, the rulers of Tsushima, then sent repeated missions to Korea to express their contrition, and in response Chosŏn granted the Japanese limited trading privileges. Three ports were opened to them along the southeast coast of Korea, and business and living quarters were provided in each to facilitate trading activities.

In consequence Japanese vessels now fairly streamed into the three ports, carrying away with them large quantities of rice and cotton cloth. This led the Korean side to seek to limit the volume of goods given or allowed to be traded to the Japanese, and such an agreement was reached in 1443. According to its terms Tsushima might send no more than fifty trading ships each year and, moreover, the amount of rice and beans granted as an

annual allowance to the lord of Tsushima was set at only enough
to feed perhaps 100 people. Sometime later, in 1510, the Japanese
residing at the three ports rose in arms against the Korean garrison commander, with whom they had been at odds. After this
was put down trade relations were severed, but Japanese entreaties
led to a new agreement, in 1512, by which trade again was permitted but with the numbers of ships and allowances stipulated
in the 1443 treaty cut in half.

Items exported to Japan in this period were necessities such
as rice and other grains, cotton, hemp and ramie cloth, and handcrafted articles like mother-of-pearl inlay, porcelain ware, and
floral design mats. Cultural items also were important and included the Buddhist Tripitaka, Confucian writings, histories, temple bells and Buddhist images. Naturally these all had considerable
impact on Japanese culture. In exchange the Japanese offered
minerals not found in Korea, such as copper, tin, and sulphur,
as well as luxury items for *yangban* consumption such as medicines and spices.

Yangban Bureaucratic Culture

The creation of *han'gŭl,* an indigenous alphabet for the Korean
people, is a monumental accomplishment of the early Chosŏn
dynasty. It was an awareness that his people must have a writing
system designed to record the language of their everyday speech,
and a concern that all his subjects easily be able to learn it, that
impelled King Sejong to devise *han'gŭl.* Called at that time the
"proper sounds to instruct the people," the preface to its explication stated clearly King Sejong's thinking:

> The sounds of our language differ from those of China and
> are not easily conveyed in Chinese writing. In consequence,
> though one among our ignorant subjects may wish to express
> his mind, in many cases he after all is unable to do so. Thinking
> of these, my people, with compassion, We have newly devised
> a script of twenty-eight letters, only that it become possible for
> anyone to readily learn it and use it to advantage in his everyday
> life.

Enlisting the services of scholars in the Hall of Worthies and brushing aside the opposition of a conservative segment of the literati-officials, Sejong thus created the *han'gŭl* alphabet, the proudest cultural achievement of the Korean people. The new alphabet was promulgated in his twenty-eighth year on the throne, in 1446.

Soon after proclaiming the new alphabet, Sejong established the Office for Publication in Han'gŭl and had it author a number of major works. Chief among these are *Songs of Flying Dragons (Yongbi ŏch'ŏn ka)*, a eulogy of the virtues of the royal ancestors; two hymns, together titled *Wŏrin Sŏkpo*, singing the praises of the Buddha; and texts for the study of Chinese characters. King Sejo, a son of Sejong, went on to establish a Superintendency for Sutra Publication which put out numerous *han'gŭl* translations of Buddhist texts. Agricultural manuals for peasant farmers and sensitive military texts also were written in *han'gŭl*. Women of the palace and the wives and daughters of *yangban* families came to use *han'gŭl* extensively, too, for example in exchanging letters. Nevertheless, the many works of major importance compiled under government auspices continued on the whole to be written in Chinese.

In Chosŏn's first century scholarship developed apace in many fields, and the state itself zealously bent its energies to the compilation and publication of a variety of scholarly works. These books, naturally enough, were mostly of a practical kind, their contents closely related to the governance of the new dynasty, which had cast itself as a Confucian state.

Foremost among works of this sort were historical compilations, for the history of the past was viewed as a mirror, or exemplar, for government in the present. The tradition of preparing a history of each reign began in 1413 with the compilation of the *Annals of King T'aejo* and continued thereafter to the end of the dynasty. This massive record is known collectively as the *Annals of the Dynasty of Chosŏn (Chosŏn wangjo sillok)*, and in order to ensure their safe transmission to posterity copies were placed in special repositories in four widely separated parts of the country. The *Precious Mirror for Succeeding Reigns,* a work that drew examples from the *Annals* of words of wisdom and acts of good government by earlier monarchs for the edification of later ages, also was continued throughout the dynasty. Chosŏn was determined, too, to prepare an official history of the preceding dynasty, for one reason to make clear the legitimacy of its own founding, and after a prolonged effort the much revised final version of the *History of Koryŏ* was completed in 1451. At almost the same time another work, *Essentials of Koryŏ History,* was compiled in strict chronological format. In 1485 Korea's first overall history appeared, the *Comprehensive Mirror of the Eastern Kingdom,* which treated the whole of Korean history from the mythical Tan'gun through the end of Koryŏ. The enhanced ethnic consciousness among Koreans at this time had been underscored by Sejong's establishment of a national shrine to Tan'gun at P'yŏngyang, and so it was natural that a comprehensive history should begin with an account of the Tan'gun era.

Gazetteers, or geographies, must next be mentioned. The *Geographical Description of the Eight Provinces* was the first to be compiled, in 1432, and it included a dozen or more categories of data deemed needful in the governing of the country. A fuller work, the *Augmented Survey of the Geography of Korea (Tongguk yŏji sŭngnam)* was compiled in 1481 under new guidelines that much expanded coverage of cultural geography, under such headings as pavilions, temples, shrines, historical remains, famed officials who had governed the particular district, other historical figures associated with the area, poetical creations inspired by the surrounding scenery, and compositions taking the local schools and shrines, for example, as their themes. This, then, was a geographical treatise designed to reflect the interests and values of the literati class.

The *Exemplar for Efficient Government* was the first manual for administrators. Compiled in 1441, it was an attempt to provide guidance for officials in the form of selections from administrative achievements and shortcomings in the past. A work that prescribed the mode of conduct of major state ceremonies was the *Five Rites of State*; completed in 1474, it dealt with rites for royal succession, funerals, and marriages, as well as with ceremonies of welcome for foreign envoys and military reviews. There was also the *Conduct of the Three Bonds,* which employed drawings and accompanying texts to portray models of the loyalty, filiality, and fidelity that ideally characterized proper relationships between ruler and official, father and son, and husband and wife. It hardly need be added that the purpose behind this work was to widely encourage those ethical values that form the basis of Confucian morality.

Science and technology also developed in many areas in early Chosŏn and a number of inventions and publications appeared. Of major importance was the agricultural manual called *Straight Talk on Farming,* compiled under Sejong in 1430. Designed to meet the specific conditions of Korean agriculture, it surveyed and reported the techniques used by the older, experienced farmers in each area of the country in storing seed, improving fertility, transplanting rice seedlings, and the like. A half century later, the high ranking scholar-official Kang Hŭi-maeng wrote a treatise on agricultural practices with which he was personally familiar in his home district just south of Seoul. The contents of the book were of such value that it was appended to a new edition of *Straight Talk on Farming* published in 1492.

At the same time astronomy and meteorology, sciences closely related to agriculture, also greatly advanced. A particularly fine example of the applied science of that day is the gauge to measure rainfall created in 1442, some two hundred years before such a device appeared in the West. Simple instruments called "wind streamers" also were in use, to gauge the direction of the wind and to assist in estimating its velocity. Further, in 1434 an observatory was built on the grounds of Kyŏngbok Palace and an armillary sphere with which to make celestial observations was mounted therein. Again under Sejong, various types of astronomical clocks, sundials, and water clocks were created, and calendrical science, too, was refined. Finally, in Sejo's reign, a triangulation device and surveyor's rod were created to measure land elevations and distances, and these were put to use in making cadastral surveys.

In the medical field, in 1433 the *Compilation of Native Korean Prescriptions* appeared. This work continued a tradition that began in the Koryŏ period, and its systematic and comprehensive coverage brought to fruition the process of establishing an independent Korean medical science based on the Korean experience. In 1445 a massive medical encyclopedia entitled *Classified Collection of Medical Prescriptions* was completed in 265 volumes, based on a wide variety of Chinese medical treatises. In turn, the landmark *Exemplar of Korean Medicine*, completed in 1610, grew out of these early Yi efforts.

These state compilation activites inevitably led to the further development of printing technology. Metal movable type, in particular, was cast in great quantities and was widely used in book publication. A type casting foundry was established first in 1403 and works printed with this copper type survive today. In 1434 Sejong ordered a new casting, the so-called *kabin* (1434) type famed for the exquisite style of its Chinese characters. And as printing continued to undergo development still other font styles appeared.

In the realm of military technology, improvement in cannon manufacture was given impetus by their effectiveness in the campaigns against the Jurchen (Yain) tribesmen that ensued from the settling of the northern regions, and the emphasis hitherto on defensive use of cannon shifted to their employment as offensive weapons. Techniques for casting and using cannon were described in detail, with diagrams accompanied by *han'gŭl* text, in a publication in 1448. A projectile launching vehicle was invented soon thereafter, in 1451, an artillery piece that used gunpowder, ignited by fuse wicks, to fire one hundred arrow-like missiles. For use in naval warfare a close-quarters attack galley was constructed by adding a protective covering to the standard Koryŏ warship used to ram and sink enemy vessels.

The *yangban* of Chosŏn held the view that art was what artisans produced, not something that *yangban* should turn their hands to, and if *yangban* did take up such pursuits it would be merely as a pastime. The result, in the realm of painting, was the popularity of ink and brush drawings known as "literati paintings." A master of this genre in the early Yi dynasty was Kang Hŭi-an (1419-1464), a well-born *yangban* official who served King Sejong. His genius has left marvelous creations for us to enjoy today, but his paintings are too small in compass for the masterful brush strokes he employed. In contrast, the most highly praised early Yi painter, An Kyŏn of Sejong's time, as well as the renowned Ch'oe Kyŏng and Yi Sang-jwa, later fifteenth and mid-sixteenth century figures respectively, all were government artists. An Kyŏn synthesized the techniques of a number of great masters to produce famous landscapes like the "Dream of Strolling in a Peach Garden," recognized then as now as a supreme achievement. Ch'oe Kyŏng was skilled in both landscape and portrait art, as was Yi Sang-jwa, born a slave but selected as a government artist when his outstanding talent was recognized. The government artists, for the most part, painted landscapes on request from *yangban* in a style suited to their patrons' tastes. These landscape paintings portrayed idealized settings not found in the natural world, most often in a Northern Sung mode. But by such devices as focusing the composition of their canvases off-center, the Korean artists created styles of their own.

In calligraphy the style of Chao Meng-fu (1254-1322) continued to be popular, as it had been in late Koryŏ, and its acknowledged master was th Prince of Anp'yŏng, the third son of King Sejong. Yang Sa-ŏn (1517-1584) for his cursive style and Han Ho (1543-1605) for his square or block style also were famed calligraphers of their day. Unlike painting, training in calligraphy was an essential adjunct of every *yangban's* education, yet at this time there were not many calligraphic creations that ventured onto untried ground.

Ceramics occupies a special place in Yi dynasty art. In the early period pieces called *punch'ŏng* ("powder blue-green") were produced, like Koryŏ celadon only with a glaze that had devolved toward an ashy blue-green tone. This was a transition stage leading to the making of white porcelain (*paekcha*), a genre that departed from the smoothly curved shapes of Koryŏ celadon in favor of simple, warm lines. These creations also stood on broader bases, resulting in more practical vessels that give the viewer a sense of sturdy repose. This Yi dynasty ceramic ware, with its varying shadings of white ranging from pure white to milky to grayish hues, is said to constitute a fitting expression of the character of the *yangban* literati.

In a Confucian state, music was a vital component of statecraft. Thus the arrangement of musical texts became a major task of early Chosŏn rulers, and the man who contributed most to this endeavor was Pak Yŏn, in Sejong's reign. Subsequently, in 1493, the *Canon of Music* (*Akhak kwebŏm*) appeared, an illustrated treatise that dealt thoroughly, from the musical notation to the staging of the actual performance, with the three categories of ceremonial music, Chinese music, and native songs.

At the urging of Pak Yŏn, a book of lyrics to be sung to various musical scores was compiled from the songs of Koryŏ and from the folk tradition. But this did not find great favor with the *yangban*, who composed many new texts, earnest and solemn celebrations of the founding of the new dynasty and the leading role of the literati, to replace the traditional ones. The "*kyŏnggi*-style poem*," popular among the literati from the late Koryŏ period, also belongs in this category.

In 1478 Sŏ Kŏ-jŏng (1420-1488), an eminent official and literary titan, put together his *Anthology of Korean Literature (Tongmun sŏn)*, a selection from past ages of poetry and prose written by Koreans in Chinese. At the same time, the literature of tales and anecdotes came to be in great vogue as a manifestation of the way the literati bureaucrats occupied their leisure hours. Probably the best known of these is the mid-16th century work by Ŏ Suk-kwŏn, *Miscellany from a Storyteller (P'aegwan chapki)*. This literature is considered also to be important as a rich source for the oral tradition of Korean history and culture. The *New Stories of the Golden Turtle* (*Kŭmo sinhwa*) by Kim Si-sŭp (1435-1493), a man of nonconformist spirit who turned away from the ordered world of Confucianist authority, also belongs to this period and is valued as the precursor of the novel in Korea.

In a society where Confucianism was paramount Buddhism could not but wither. T'aejo himself instituted a registration system to prevent the monk population from increasing, and he banned any new founding of temples. But his son T'aejong soon inaugurated a severe suppression of Buddhism, leaving only 242 temples and monasteries throughout the whole country and disestablishing the rest, at the same time confiscating their lands and slaves (1406). This dealt Buddhism a blow of such magnitude that it never could recover. A brief revival was brought about through the deep personal faith of kings Sejong and Sejo, but under Sŏngjong (1469-1494) and Chungjong (1506-1545) further harsh measures were taken against what remained of the Buddhist institutional church. In the reign of Myŏngjong (1545-1567), under the regency of the Queen Dowager Munjŏng, the famous monk Pou was given important responsibilities in the encouragement of Buddhism, and for a time the Buddhist world again displayed some vitality. With the death of the queen dowager, however, Buddhism again suffered suppression, becoming a faith practiced principally by women.

Chapter 10

The Rise of the Neo-Confucian Literati

Changes in Society under Rule by the Meritorious Elite

The class that dominated political, economic, and cultural life in the early Chosŏn period of course was the *yangban* literati, and in particular it was those usually designated as the meritorious elite who designed and implemented high state policy. The meritorious elite originally were men who had played prominent roles in assisting Yi Sŏng-gye to found the dynasty and who had been amply rewarded for the support they had given him. Soon they were joined by those who had sided with the eventual winners in the succession disputes that erupted in the dynasty's early years; many of these, too, had been enrolled on "Merit Subject" rosters and given sizeable awards. Then, in the middle decades of the fifteenth century, primarily in consequence of Sejo's usurpation of the throne, several additional merit rosters were promulgated, enrolling for their loyal services unprecedentedly large numbers of the *yangban* elite and, in many cases, bestowing upon them unprecedentedly lavish rewards. In a number of cases, indeed, a single individual was named on as many as four separate merit rosters and thus was given unimaginably rich rewards. Chŏng In-ji (1396-1478) and Sin Suk-chu (1417-1475) were two such figures who, with others much like them, constituted the political force that held the reins of power, occupying high office and possessing an abundance of lands and slaves. These men, together with a preponderance of their colleagues in the core elite, were representatives of powerful, growing *yangban* lineages that were bound to one another by an expanding network of interrelationships through marriage, including numerous and close marriage ties with the royal house. Moreover, they also were scholar-bureaucrats proficient in branches of learning having practical applications, and they had taken part in many of the government's compilation enterprises. And very largely, they were a Seoul-centered force.

The majority of the *yangban* literati, however, inevitably had had to content themselves with less highly visible symbols of their status as elite members of Chosŏn society. Many lesser talents, or less fortunate talents, met with failure in the always harshly competitive pit of central government politics. Others simply opted out of the competition, preferring the more certain pleasures of good fellowship or perhaps rusticity. But a substantial number of the elite of early Chosŏn took a stern moral stance against what they saw as a political ethos of unbridled ambition and unprincipled pursuit of personal gain. Sejo's usurpation, in particular, was widely judged to have been an immoral, unrighteous act, and many men of this persuasion felt that, in good conscience, they should not serve a king who had seized the throne by force. Accordingly, they viewed those who supported or served Sejo not as political realists but as amoral men all too ready to violate the ancient Confucian code of conduct. And before long, after Sejo's death, a new breed of officials—men with a new and more rigorous Confucian commitment, men steeped in the doctrines of Neo-Confucianism—appeared in increasing numbers on the national stage and launched what developed into a political vendetta against those in high places.

At this time, when the rule of the meritorious elite came to be seriously challenged, they not only enjoyed a solid political position but they also had gained possession of large agricultural estates, in this way securing their economic foundation. The *yangban* bureaucrats who comprised the meritorious elite first of all had received "rank land" from the government, but then they had been given large amounts of "merit land" as well. The former, as has been noted, did not, in fact, often revert to the state, while land granted to merit subjects from the beginning was intended to be held in perpetuity. There were other ways, too, by which the *yangban* bureaucrats expanded their holdings—by purchase, outright seizure, and reclamation. Their eyes fastened in particular on the abundant state-owned lands in the three provinces of the fertile southern third of the country, and they steadily encroached upon these.

The expansion of agricultural estates brought about a reduction in government tax receipts, on the one hand, and this in turn led to the imposition of greater tax burdens on the peasant-farmers. The hardship thus endured by the peasants was aggravated further by the tribute tax on special items of local provenance and craftsmanship. Not only was the amount of this tax a heavy burden, but a number of evils developed in the process by which it was levied and collected, resulting in a doubling or even tripling of the amounts that had to be paid. Unable to meet their tax obligations, more and more peasants abandoned their land, only to have collection enforced upon their kinsmen or upon their neighbors. Proposals eventually were aired to reform these abuses, but the government of the *yangban* bureaucrats was painfully slow to take action on this problem.

Changes in the military service system added further to the woes of the peasantry. With the great enlargement of military rosters attendant upon adoption of the "paired provisioner" system (the arrangement requiring alternate duty and direct provision of support for paired peasant conscripts called in turn to active duty), it became impossible to fill the quotas for corvee labor duty. Inevitably, then, the soldiers themselves were mobilized for corvee duty, and the only way they could escape this double burden was to hire someone to do corvee service in their place. But since the payment required for corvee labor substitution was excessively harsh, the number of conscript soldiers and provisioners who took to flight to escape this burden steadily increased, to the point where the ranks of the military were emptied and villages abandoned.

Finally, the grain loan system evolved into a form of usury at the expense of the peasants, causing them further distress. Designed to provide grain to the needy peasant-farmer during the spring hunger season, before the winter barley crop came in, grain loans were to be repaid from the harvest in the fall. But when grain was repaid an interest charge called "wastage grain" was added, and a number of ruses were used to increase the ten percent fixed rate of interest. This constituted still another heavy burden on the peasantry.

The result of all this was to make the lives of the peasantry unsettled in the extreme. Many turned to a life of wandering, and all over the country brigandage became rampant. The most famed brigand leader was Im Kkŏk-chŏng, who was active for three years, between 1559-1562, in the region of Hwanghae province.

Emergence of the Neo-Confucian Literati

Hitherto dominated by the meritorious elite, Chosŏn dynasty society underwent a succession of upheavals with the appearance in the ranks of central government bureaucrats of a new ideological force—men ever more deeply committed to the abstract doctrines of Neo-Confucianism. By and large, these were younger men, nurtured in the changed intellectual atmosphere of the new dynasty, and freshly successful in the highly competitive state civil service examinations. Numbers of them were from families with roots outside the capital, lacking close ties with the entrenched lineages of the capital elite and also lacking the substantial socio-economic resources on which the latter's power rested. But for these very reasons, the rural Neo-Confucian literati proved to be less important and less enduring in their impact on the politics of the capital.

To be sure, modern Korean historiography overwhelmingly holds to an opposing view, asserting that rural Neo-Confucian literati, known as *sarim,* emerged into political prominence through the civil examination process, repeatedly attacked the power-holding meritorious elite and, despite being crushed bloodily and repeatedly in four convulsions called the Literati Purges, by the last quarter of the sixteenth century succeeded in taking dominant political power into their own hands. This view, however, can be shown to be fundamentally flawed. A better understanding of the political culture that developed during Chosŏn's first two centuries posits instead a single, unitary sociopolitical force, one that lived scattered throughout the whole of the country but whose core lineages lived in the capital and its relatively near environs. It was a force that held to a shared ideology and set of values, although the timing of the process of ideological commitment may well have varied. In short, the term *sarim* ultimately defines an attitude, or a political posture, rather than one of two opposing, discrete socio-political forces.

The first literati purge was the Purge of 1498 (*muo sahwa*), sometimes also called the "History Purge of 1498." The ostensible reason for the purge was the thinly veiled condemnation of Sejo's usurpation written by a venerable Kyŏngsang province Neo-Confucian scholar-official, Kim Chong-jik, and incorporated by one of his disciples into a history draft for the official *Annals of King Sŏngjong* (1469-1494; a grandson of Sejo). A more plausible explanation of the purge, however, is to be found in an examination of the nature of the political process at the central government level during the preceding twenty years or so. What had been taking place, essentially, was both an ideological and institutional challenge to the authority of the higher administrative organs of government and even to the authority of the throne. The challenge was mounted by younger officials deeply committed to an abstract Neo-Confucian ethos that demanded adherence to unrealistically high moral standards in the formulation and execution of public policy. The principal vehicle of this challenge was those organs of government charged with the remonstrance function—that is, the agencies whose duties were to scrutinize, and criticize, government policy and performance, focusing on issues related to official and royal conduct. When it worked properly, of course, exercise of the remonstrance function was conducive to good government. But when remonstrance was carried to an extreme, as it tended increasingly to be in this period of institutional and doctrinal consolidation in early Chosŏn, it could lead to administrative paralysis and bitter factional conflict.

At this point in 1498, then, the throne was occupied by a king, Yŏnsan'gun, more inclined than most toward autocratic exercise of his powers, and the upper echelons of the central government were filled by men whose backgrounds made them highly vulnerable to charges of failure to adhere to required norms of political and personal morality. These high officials, a great many of whom were meritorious elite, found it difficult to counter charges leveled against them, in essence, on moral grounds, since it was not possible to call into question moral dogma that was an integral part of the Confucian system of belief proclaimed to be the state ideology of Chosŏn. Accordingly, they instead took advantage of the issue of Kim Chong-jik's "treasonous" impugning of Sejo's conduct as ruler (that monarch whom they all had gladly, and profitably, served) to rid the government of both the symbol and substance of the excessive and perilous abuse of the remonstrance function by younger officials in the Censorate and related organs. For his part, Yŏnsan'gun was more than pleased to order the offending historian and several more disciples of Kim Chong-jik executed, and to banish or dismiss from office numbers of other Neo-Confucian literati linked to them.

In the years that followed, Yŏnsan'gun's addiction to a life of luxury and pleasure seeking led to massive squandering of the state's fiscal resources. Ultimately, in an effort to overcome his financial difficulties, Yŏnsan'gun would even attempt to confiscate the lands and slaves possessed by the meritorious elite, who naturally sought to frustrate the royal will. Yŏnsan'gun in turn looked for an opportunity to eliminate all sources of resistance to the exercise of his kingly authority. He already had launched a purge when a group of courtiers closely connected to the throne by marriage dredged up the incident in the previous reign of the ouster and subsequent execution of Sŏngjong's consort, the Lady Yun, who was Yŏnsan'gun's mother. Yŏnsan'gun thus was spurred on to decree death or banishment for many members of the meritorious elite as well as hundreds of literati officials who had survived the 1498 purge. This massive second purge is known simply as the Purge of 1504 (*kapcha sahwa*).

After two years of often whimsical, and gruesome terror, the king's cruelty and dissolute life having exceeded all bounds, Yŏnsan'gun was removed from the throne by opportunists who had survived or even abetted his purges, and replaced by Chungjong (1506-1544). The new monarch, unlike his half-brother Yŏnsan'gun, was inclined to refrain from arbitrary exercise of royal authority and to respect the views of his literati officials. It was Chungjong who brought forward the young Neo-Confucian scholar Cho Kwang-jo (1482-1519) and rapidly appointed him to a succession of ever more influential positions. Cho Kwang-jo took as his political objective the establishment of a pattern of government by moral suasion, in accordance with the Confucian ideal. He rooted out superstitious beliefs that ran counter to Confucianist manners and mores, and he put into effect the so-called "village contract" (*hyangyak*), a mode of local self-government infused with a spirit of basic justice for all and mutual assistance in time of need. He also encouraged the preparation of a number of vernacular translations of basic Confucianist writings, in an effort to inculcate Confucianist ideals among the populace at large. It was he, too, who proposed and secured the enactment of the "examination for the learned and virtuous," whereby the responsible administrators in the capital and provinces were to recommend men of model integrity for recruitment into the bureaucracy by means of a much simplified examination held in the presence of the king. In consequence, numbers of like-minded Neo-Confucian literati were enabled to secure appointment to prestigious government positions.

As the influence of Cho Kwang-jo and his faction grew, however, they used their power to attack higher administrative officials, members of the meritorious elite, and anyone else who stood in their way or simply disagreed with their policies. And presently, those whom the Cho faction had attacked or antagonized found an opportunity to turn the king against the young zealots. Cho Kwang-jo had launched a campaign to rescind the awards bestowed on a large number of those rewarded for their merit in bringing Chungjong to the throne. Labeling their awards excessive, Cho succeeded in forcing the king to delete seventy-six names, nearly three-quarters of the total, from the merit roster that had been promulgated some thirteen years earlier. In the space of the next four days, however, the enraged Merit Subjects had so worked on Chungjong's fears that his own position might be in jeopardy, that he ousted the reform faction and even sanctioned death sentences for Cho Kwang-jo and his leading supporters. This event was the Purge of 1519 (*kimyo sahwa*), the repercussions of which continued to haunt the political process in Chosŏn for a half-century or more to come.

Still another purge, that of 1545 (the *ŭlsa sahwa*), occurred in consequence of events surrounding the successive enthronement, within the span of only eight months, of two sons of Chungjong by different queens. Even before Chungjong's death, factions of *yangban* officials had formed around brothers of the two queens, although both in fact were from the same leading aristocratic clan. The accession of Injong, Chungjong's eldest son, in significant measure meant a return to power of men identified with Cho Kwang-jo and the "men of 1519." A purge ensued, however, when Injong's untimely death brought the eleven year-old Myŏngjong to the throne and his strong-willed mother to power behind it. Once again, many officials widely regarded as more public-spirited and of superior virtue were executed, banished, or removed from government, while those who set the purge in motion liberally rewarded themselves for their meritorious service to the state.

All four of the Literati Purges can be understood in part, though in differing degrees, as the consequences of factional struggle for political power (and indirectly for the economic perquisites that accrue to the powerholder). In the first three purges in particular, however, a fundamental ideological catalyst also was at work. That is, a conscious effort was made by deeply indoctrinated and high-minded younger officials, who also were politically ambitious, to take advantage of the sacrosanct character of Neo-Confucian dogma to cleanse the government of all moral impurity and also, surely not just incidentally, rid it of their political rivals and opponents. Ironically, and fetefully, although the political battle was on each occasion lost, the ideological war gradually but ultimately was won. By the time the young King Sŏnjo assumed the throne in 1567, no real disagreement remained on the theoretical proposition that good government must rest on strict adherence to Neo-Confucian political norms and moral strictures.

At the same time, the repeated and traumatic failure of the efforts to apply these norms too rigidly had set in motion a process of institutional evolution that resulted in a more cautious and responsible exercise of the political power potential of the organs of remonstrance. The ills of political factionalism had not been cured, far from it; what had changed was the dynamics of factional disputation. Dominant political power thus was not, as traditional historiography has it, now grasped by Neo-Confucian literati whose background was small and middle land-holding in the countryside. Quite the contrary. Dominant political power now was in the hands of a Seoul-centered core group of Neo-Confucian literati who, in large part, were members of the very same lineages the so-called meritorious elite had represented. Future factional conflict, then, arose within this rather restricted core *yangban* group, and the root cause of such factional disputation, endemic to the very end of the dynasty, was the quest for dominant political power in the central government. Looked at another way, as a contemporary aphoristic analysis puts it: "In the Literati Purges the evil elements persecuted the good; in the [post-1575] Factional Strife, the good fought with the good." That is, by the latter years of the sixteenth century, the entirety of the ruling elite had become, ideologically, homogenized as "good" Neo-Confucians, so that there was no longer a "bad" element with which they might quarrel.

A Chosŏn dynasty phenomenon closely related to the deepening commitment to Neo-Confucian thought and, it is widely believed, also to intensifying factional schism, was the appearance of private academies, *sŏwŏn*. Private academies had existed from the end of Koryŏ, but schools that, like the *sŏwŏn*, also were shrines dedicated to worthies of an earlier period now appeared for the first time. Among the early *sŏwŏn* the most famous was that established by Chu Se-bung in 1543 in honor of An Yu, the famed Koryŏ advocate of Neo-Confucianism. Subsequently, when Yi Hwang (1501-1570; the foremost Korean Confucianist philosopher of his age) became Magistrate of P'unggi, the site of this *sŏwŏn* in Kyŏngsang province, his memorial to the court persuaded the king to bestow on it a hanging board inscribed in the king's own hand with the four characters "academy of received learning" (*Sosu Sŏwŏn*). Thenceforth known by this name, this was the first of the so-called royally chartered private academies.

Sŏwŏn now sprang up everywhere, and by the end of Sŏnjo's reign in 1608 they already numbered more than 'one hundred. The number of royally chartered *sŏwŏn* also increased at the same time, and it soon became a matter of course for the state to bestow on them grants of books, tax-free land, and slaves. Thus the *sŏwŏn* came to occupy a position in Chosŏn society very much like that enjoyed by the Buddhist temples in the Koryŏ period, as institutions supported by the state but without obligation, or productive contribution, to the state.

The village contract or code (*hyangyak*) was another new institution that owed its creation to Chosŏn's commitment to Neo-Confucian statecraft. The spirit of the village contract was embodied in the four objectives that it emphasized: mutual encouragement of morality, mutual supervision of wrong conduct, mutual decorum in social relationships, and mutual succor in time of disaster or hardship. Cho Kwang-jo had sought to put the village contract into wide effect in 1519, but his personal downfall brought failure to this effort as well, and it was only in Sŏnjo's time that it was instituted broadly. The general farming population automatically was included in the workings of the village contract, but its activities normally were directed by the local Neo-Confucian literati. These local elites, in most if not all counties, were bound to the government in Seoul through reduplicated ties. In many cases leading local lineages had been founded by sons of officials resident in the Seoul area on land acquired by wealth accumulated during service in the government. Another sort of bond was forged through official service in Seoul by sons of local elites who had passed the competitive government examinations. These men all but invariably retired to the area of their birth, thus re-cementing their locality's ties with the central government. Finally, especially in areas less remote from Seoul, marriage ties with capital lineages could also serve to provide such linkages. It thus was through the mechanism of the village contract, and through the instrument of the local literati-gentry, that the conservative, state-sustaining values of public-mindedness and social order were maintained in the countryside.

The political upheavals known as the literati purges and their relationship to ongoing factional strife already has been noted. Only a single generation after the last of these traumatic events factional strife again erupted, this time in a strain so virulent that it became quasi-institutionalized and, in one permutation or another, afflicted the dynasty to its very end. The factors that contributed to this development are many and diverse—and are but poorly understood. Among them, certainly, are such considerations as the rigidity of Neo-Confucian doctrine as interpreted and applied in Chosŏn; the relative weakness of the monarchic institution; structural flaws in the central government's design seriously diluting the authority of the administrative ministries and also impeding the policy formulation and decision-making processes; and the rapid natural increase of the *yangban* elite portion of the population and a consequent swelling of the numbers qualifying for office in the government service examinations. Still other, case-specific reasons for the intensification and continuation of factional strife will be apparent in discussions that follow of the more important manifestations of this unfortunate phenomenon.

Factional strife in the formal sense as defined by traditional Korean historiography (which labeled the phenomenon *tangjaeng*) began in 1575 with a confrontation between two segments of the officialdom. The immediate cause of the conflict was a quarrel over appointments to powerful and coveted middle-rank positions in the Ministry of Personnel, and before long the *yangban* bureaucrats of that day had begun to take sides and to regard their opponents with hostility and contempt. The fact that the two factions known as Easterners (Tongin) and Westerners (Sŏin) came into being in this way, in consequence of an incident centering on the government office having authority over personnel, offers useful insight into the nature of factional strife in Chosŏn Korea.

The dominant characteristic of factional strife in Chosŏn is that it was a struggle among political cliques in which membership ultimately became foreordained and permanent. The descendants of those identified with a particular faction came to inherit their factional affiliation generation after generation, so that factional politics became inextricably bound to blood lineage. Factional strife of this nature was not likely to be brought to an end by a single incident, by one victory or defeat. Even if a faction was ousted from power, descendants of the victims would await the time when they might again obtain office in the capital and vindictively exonerate their ancestors.

Master-disciple relationships, formed in the course of study for the rigorous government service examinations, contributed much to the rigid and intractable nature of factional strife in Chosŏn. The hierarchical Confucian value system meant that the ties formed between student and teacher constituted a stifling restraint on individual initiative and freedom of action. The views of a teacher, however much in error they might be, could not easily be opposed by his young disciples. Furthermore, those who had studied under the same master, or in the same private academy, formed fellowships that not only preserved the bond created by their shared experience, but also gave cohesion to their attitudes and actions on factional matters and on issues they might face later as government officials, a solidarity that transcended all question of right or wrong.

The Struggle Against the Japanese and Manchus

When Korea began to suffer sporadic attacks on its coasts by the Japanese in the mid-sixteenth century, the government created a Border Defense Council and entrusted to it all matters in respect to the country's defenses. But the *yangban* bureaucrats, accustomed to the ways of peace and not easily bestirred, were content to take only temporizing measures. At this very time, a new situation was unfolding in Japan, as Toyotomi Hideyoshi brought an end to internal disorder and succeeded in unifying the country. He then directed the energies of his armies outward into the wider world beyond Japan's shores, having conceived the reckless ambition to launch an invasion through Korea against the Ming empire itself.

The Japanese forces landed at Pusan in overwhelming numbers in the spring of 1592. Chŏng Pal, commander of the Pusan garrison, and Song Sang-hyŏn as the magistrate of Tongnae, defended the two beachhead areas to the death, but in vain, and the Japanese quickly launched a three-pronged attack northward toward Seoul. The stunned government now pinned its hopes on Sin Ip, who had won repute in his successful campaign against Yain tribesmen in the north. But when Sin Ip met defeat in a battle at Ch'ungju, the king and court took flight toward Ŭiju on the Yalu River.

The populace at large was infuriated at the government's incompetence and irresponsibility. As Sŏnjo and his high officials abandoned Seoul in flight, the people blocked their way, hurling insults at them. Once the king and his retinue had left Seoul, the city's slave population set fire to the registry where the slave rosters were kept and to the offices of the Ministry of Punishments. Two princes sent to raise fresh troops found none who would respond to their call to arms, and in the end they were captured by the Japanese. The blame for this wretched state of affairs lay with the government officials, who had failed to concern themselves with the welfare of the people. Nearly the whole of the country, now defenseless, was trampled over by the Japanese armies. They were a military force experienced in land warfare, blooded in the many campaigns of Japan's Warring States period, and moreover they possessed firearms. There was no reason to expect that Korea's meager, poorly trained battalions might hold out against them.

It was at this point that Yi Sun-sin (1545-1598), Naval Commander of Left Chŏlla province, began to make his presence felt in the struggle. Appointed to his post the year before, Admiral Yi had energetically set about strengthening the country's naval forces, building warships and training their crews. In particular, on the model of vessels already in use in the mid-fifteenth century, he built his famed "turtle ships" (*kŏbuksŏn*) with a protective covering (thought to have been iron plated) to ward off enemy arrows and shells, and in addition with numerous spikes implanted to prevent the enemy from boarding. He also emplaced cannon around the entire circumference of the ships, so that attack could be made at will from any side. His preparations made, Yi Sun-sin set forth with his warships to destroy the Japanese fleet whenever and in whatever waters it might appear. Victorious in his first encounter at Okp'o, he continued to carry the day in successive battles off the southern coast [see map p. 145]. The battle in the seas near Hansan Island is especially famous as one of the three great victories of the war against the Japanese. Admiral Yi's successes gave complete control of the

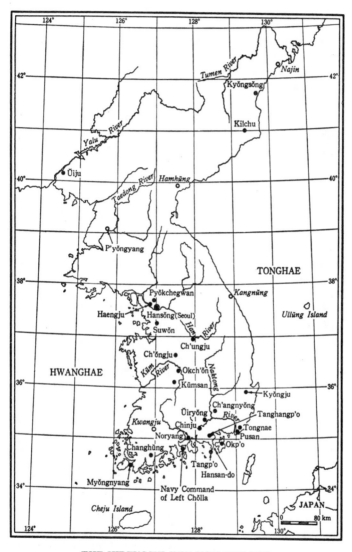

THE HIDEYOSHI INVASION (1592-1598)

sea lanes to the Korean forces, with three important results: the Japanese were unable to move north by sea and effect a link with their land armies; Japanese supply routes were cut; and the grain-rich region of Chŏlla province remained safely in Korea's hands.

Meanwhile, within the borders of the country, guerrilla forces (known as *ŭibyŏng*, "righteous armies") sprang up on all sides. The same populace that had reacted indifferently to the government's efforts to muster fresh troops now spontaneously took up arms in defense of their homes. Typically, a force of *yangban*, peasant-farmers, and slaves in a single district coalesced around a guerrilla leader and then gradually expanded the area of its operations. The guerrilla leaders generally were Neo-Confucian literati of high repute in their locales, among them such outstanding figures as Cho Hŏn, Kwak Chae-u, Ko Kyŏng-myŏng, Kim Ch'ŏn-il, and Chŏng Mun-bu. Cho Hŏn rose in Ch'ungch'ŏng province and routed the Japanese from Ch'ŏngju, only to be killed in an assault on Kŭmsan. Kwak Chae-u assembled a guerrilla force in the southeast and went on to join with Kim Si-min in repulsing the enemy's first attempt to take Chinju. Ko Kyŏng-myŏng led a guerrilla force northward from his home in Changhŭng, in the extreme southwest, but he too died in the attack on Kŭmsan. Kim Ch'ŏn-il repeatedly harassed the Japanese forces around Suwŏn and later took part in the second battle of Chinju, where he was killed. Chŏng Mun-bu, on the other hand, was active and highly successful in Hamgyŏng province in the north and in the east-central province of Kang-wŏn. There were even bands of Buddhist monks led by such honored figures as the monks Sŏsan Taesa and Samyŏng Taesa. The hit-and-run thrusts of these and the hundreds of other Korean guerrilla units dealt severe blows to Japanese military operations.

Moreover, a Ming Chinese relief army had arrived, 50,000 strong. The Ming army recaptured P'yŏngyang but suffered a reverse just north of Seoul and pulled back. Korean forces under Kwŏn Yul meanwhile had taken up positions in the mountain redoubt at Haengju on the north bank of the Han River, but they now had to face alone repeated large-scale assaults against their bastion. They succeeded in repulsing the Japanese in each of these bloody battles, and the victory they won there at Haengju early in 1593 is remembered too as one of the three great Korean triumphs in the struggle against the Japanese invaders. A few months later the Japanese, who had been beaten back in an earlier assault on Chinju, attacked the town once again, and despite a heroic defense in the end Chinju fell. Nevertheless, the first successful defense of Chinju occupies a special place among the three great Korean victories of the war.

In the first flush of their invasion the Japanese land forces had swept over nearly the whole country, but their navy had been defeated and control of the seas wrested from them. Moreover, harassed by Korean guerrilla attacks and threatened by the cautious advance southward of the Ming army, the Japanese were beating a steady retreat. Peace negotiations between a Ming envoy and the Japanese commander now were underway, and the Japanese forces proceeded to withdraw all the way to the southeastern littoral of Kyŏngsang province, where they sheltered themselves behind intricate, castle-like fortifications. The negotiations, however, eventually were broken off. On the one hand, the Chinese sought to resolve the situation in their favor by accommodating Japan within the Chinese tributary system— enfeoffing Hideyoshi as the "king" of Japan and granting him the privilege of formal tribute trade relations with Ming. Hideyoshi, for his part, regarded himself as the victor, and so he responded with the absurdly unrealistic proposal that a daughter of the Chinese emperor be given to wed the emperor of Japan, that a portion of Korea be ceded to him, and that a prince of Korea and several of its high officials be sent to Japan as hostages.

After the rupture of the long drawn out peace talks, the Japanese launched a second campaign to conquer Korea in 1597. This time, however, the Korean army was equipped and ready, and the Ming relief army too moved quickly into action. In consequence, the Japanese land forces could achieve no more than local successes. At sea, on the other hand, the Japanese navy now was operating with unaccustomed audacity. Admiral Yi Sun-sin had been dismissed as the result of intrigue against him in Seoul, whereupon the new commander had been overwhelmingly defeated in an encounter with the Japanese fleet. The dismayed government hastily reinstated Admiral Yi who, with the mere dozen warships remaining in his command, engaged a Japanese flotilla as it was sailing toward the Yellow Sea off Mokp'o, and won a resounding victory. The Japanese now found themselves hemmed in both by land and sea. Presently, in mid-1598, Hideyoshi died, and before the year was out the Japanese had withdrawn completely from the peninsula. But as he was harassing the retreating Japanese forces, Admiral Yi Sun-sin's heroic career was ended by a chance enemy shot.

In the course of the seven-year struggle, nearly the whole of Korea's eight provinces became an arena of Japanese pillage and slaughter, but Kyŏngsang province suffered most severely. The population markedly decreased, and famine and disease were epidemic. As a consequence of the terrible suffering the war had visited on the populace at large, uprisings also broke out on all sides. Moreover, with the destruction of land and census registers, the government was hard put to collect taxes and enforce corvee levies. The loss of cultural treasures in fires set by the Japanese troops also was substantial, including the wooden structures at Pulguk-sa in Kyŏngju and Kyŏngbok Palace, while the volumes stored in three of the four History Archives were reduced to ashes. On the other hand, the war with Japan brought advances in military tactics, and new weapons such as the "heaven-shaking explosive shell" and a kind of mobile rocket launcher were developed.

The impact of the war with Japan was felt not alone by Korea, for it was a conflict of a magnitude that shook the whole of East Asia. The Jurchen people who grew powerful at this time in Manchuria, while Ming was busied in Korea, were soon to conquer Ming and make themselves masters of China. In Japan, too, the Tokugawa house established a new military regime. At Japan's request Korea entered into friendly relations with the Tokugawa shogunate from 1609, but the animosity of the Korean people toward Japan remained alive long thereafter. Not only did the war bring about political changes in the countries of East Asia, but it had a marked cultural impact as well. Japan benefited in particular from the abduction of skilled Korean potters as prisoners of war, who then became the instruments of great advance in the ceramic art of that country. The numerous books seized by the Japanese in Korea also contributed to the development of learning in Japan, especially the study of Neo-Confucianism.

The beleaguered throne that Sŏnjo had occupied passed next to Kwanghaegun (1608-1623), a monarch who displayed uncommon capacities in directing both domestic and foreign affairs. He rebuilt the History Archives, printed many books, and reinstituted the *hop'ae* "identification tag" system, among other noteworthy domestic accomplishments. Beyond Korea's borders, Kwanghaegun's adroit foreign policy kept Korea from being drawn into the developing conflict on the continent, where the rise of the powerful Jurchen Manchus had created a perilous new situation for Chosŏn. When Ming sent an army to strike at the Manchus, Kwanghaegun was unable to refuse the Ming request for help. But as the Korean force of some 10,000 troops was about to set forth, the king gave its commander certain secret instructions, and when the tide of battle turned against Ming, the Korean contingents found an opportunity to surrender, thus for the moment averting the danger of Manchu punitive action against Korea. Meanwhile, Kwanghaegun spared no effort to enhance his country's state of military preparedness, repairing defensive strongpoints, renovating weaponry, and instituting training programs. But in the midst of this endeavor Kwanghaegun was forced from the throne by the Westerners faction, to be succeeded by King Injo (1623-1649).

Under the influence of those who had put him on the throne, Injo abandoned Kwanghaegun's posture of watchful waiting in favor of a blatant pro-Ming, anti-Manchu policy. This change was taken by the Manchus as a serious affront, and they were further alarmed when a Ming general encamped on a small Korean island near the mouth of the Yalu River. It was at this point, at the beginning of 1624, that the insurrection of Yi Kwal erupted. Yi Kwal was one of those cited for merit in bringing Injo to the throne but, believing his services to have been inadequately rewarded, he rebelled and for a time even occupied Seoul. When presently he was defeated by government forces some of his followers fled to Manchuria, where they appear to have urged the Manchus to invade Korea to redress the injustice of

Kwanghaegun's removal from the throne. At any rate, it was under the pretext of righting this wrong that the Manchus launched their first invasion in 1627. The main Manchu force penetrated quickly well below P'yŏngyang, whereupon Korea sued for peace. In exchange for a Korean pledge to do honor to the Manchu throne as would a younger to an older brother, the Manchus now withdrew.

Before long, the Manchu emperor changed the name of his new state to Ch'ing and sent an embassy to Korea with the demand that Chosŏn acknowledge his suzerainty. The Korean response was to refuse either to receive the Ch'ing envoys or the documents they carried. This unpardonable act of hubris brought on the second Manchu invasion, an assault led by the Ch'ing emperor himself in 1636 (the *pyŏngja horan*) at the head of a large force. The royal family and much of the court sought refuge on Kanghwa which, however, quickly fell to the Manchus. The king himself had gone to the Namhan-san fortress just south of Seoul, but there was no hope of mounting an effective resistance. Injo thus capitulated to the Manchu emperor, in a ceremony on the southern bank of the Han staged in full view of the enemy encampment. Chosŏn was required to sever its ties with Ming, to deliver Injo's two eldest sons as hostages, to do homage to Ch'ing as the suzerain power, and to dispatch troops to assist the Manchus in their campaign against Ming. The Manchus further seized and executed three scholar-officials, those who had argued most forcefully against making peace, and subjected Kim Sang-hŏn, a venerable scholar and high official already sixty-seven years of age, to harsh confinement in a Manchu prison.

In comparison with the war against the Japanese, the Ch'ing invasion was of short duration, only a small part of Korea became a battlefield, and the damage suffered was relatively slight. But the northwest region of Korea through which the Manchus had passed was ravaged by plunder and killing, and the smoldering enmity this aroused was fanned by Korea's feelings of cultural superiority to give rise to an intense hostility toward Ch'ing. The quixotic scheme of one military official to attack Ch'ing in concert with the waning Ming dynasty, and the plan of Injo's successor, King Hyojong (who had been held as a Manchu hostage for eight years), to launch a northern expedition both were born of this festering hostility. At the same time, Hyojong was moved to strengthen Korea's defenses by repairing the mountain fortresses atop Pukhan-san and Namhan-san.

The Culture of the Neo-Confucian Literati

The successive literati purges and the subsequent intensification of factional strife led many Neo-Confucian literati to abandon thought of careers in government and instead to devote themselves to scholarly inquiry and the education of the younger generation. Having thus turned their backs on official life, it was natural for these men of learning to interest themselves in speculative and theoretical studies rather than in practical scholarship. To be sure, Neo-Confucian doctrine seeks to establish an ethical basis for an enlightened, Confucian political order through substantiation of the premise that the nature of man is fundamentally good, but it also endeavors to find the roots of this premise in the natural order of the cosmos. The exigencies of the time, then, produced a number of great thinkers whose writings represent the efflorescence of Neo-Confucian doctrine in Korea.

Neo-Confucians divide all existence into two inseparable components, *i* and *ki* (*li* and *ch'i* in Chinese). The one, *i*, is a patterning or formative element that accounts for what things are and how they behave, or normatively should behave, while the other, *ki*, is the concretizing and energizing element. The two are interdependent and inseparable, since *i* could not exist concretely without *ki* and *ki* would be but formless and directionless energy without *i*. Based on this dualism, two distinct schools of Neo-Confucian thought developed in Korea, one giving primary emphasis to *i*, the other arguing the primacy of the role of *ki*.

The thinker who first put forward a full explication of the view that stressed the primacy of *i* was Yi Hwang (T'oegye). Yi T'oegye is a giant figure in the history of philosophy in Korea, and he is known as Korea's Chu Hsi. In his elaboration of Chu Hsi's thought he further defined the role of *i* in the function of the human psyche, and he established a position that gave emphasis to personal experience and moral self-cultivation as the essence of learning. This was because of his belief that one's spiritual essence and personal integrity are found in individual apperception of moral principle and its realization in practice. Yi Hwang did follow the dualistic position of Chu Hsi, which views *i* and *ki*, the forces that constitute the foundation of the universe, as inseparably related one with the other. But he stressed particularly the role of the formative or normative element, *i*, as the basis of the activity of *ki*. This school of thought exerted great influence on Confucian scholarship in Japan as well, eventually constituting one of the main streams in Japanese Confucian thought.

This emphasis on the role of *i* was countered by the school of thought that gave primary emphasis to *ki*, as the concretizing, energizing, more material element. The man who completed the formulation of this view was Yi I (Yulgok, 1536-1584), famed not only as a philosopher but for the many reform proposals he put forward in regard to government, the economy, and national defense. Fundamentally, the theory of the primacy of *ki* looked upon the material, energizing force of *ki* rather than the mysterious formative power of *i* as the fundamental factor in the existence of the universe. Ultimately this view leads to seeing *i* as nothing but the laws of motion or activity inherent in *ki*. Its advocates also attached importance to the search for moral principles, but their approach emphasized looking outward rather than inward, intellectual rather than spiritual perception, and so they valued external experience and breadth of learning. Thus within Korean Neo-Confucianism two markedly different schools of thought developed, and to a degree the argument between the two was not only philosophical but mirrored contemporary factional political differences as well.

In Korea's *yangban* society of this age, now thoroughly Neo-Confucian in outlook and also strife-torn, the consanguineous clan unit comprised of descendants from a single patrilineal ancestor, and even identification with one of the branch or sub-lineages of which it was composed, had become major determinants of position in the society. The delineation of an individual's relationship with others in his lineage was to be found in the clan genealogy (*chokpo*). Thus, the widespread compilation and publication of clan genealogies from around the beginning of the seventeenth century was due not only to the desire to demonstrate one's privileged standing as a *yangban*, but also to the fact that it made explicit one's connections with respected or powerful figures in the same lineage. The gradual development of a field of study called by Koreans *pohak* ("lineage-ology"), reflected this need of the *yangban* for detailed knowledge not only of the structure of his own lineage but also of those lineages with which he might wish to form ties.

Just as knowledge of lineage relationships was an important field of learning, so was knowledge of the funerary and memorial rituals that had to be observed in consequence of these relations. From the time Neo-Confucianism had been introduced into Korea, family rituals had been performed in accordance with the prescriptions of the *Family Rites of Chu Hsi*, but Korea's *yangban* had observed these rites rather perfunctorily. At this point, with the appearance of such works as *Exposition of Family Rites* by Kim Chang-saeng (1548-1631), a theoretical foundation was given to the study of ritual as a scholarly discipline, and new emphasis was placed on the individual's conscious practice and deliberate involvement in ritual. Kim Chang-saeng became known as the "luminary" of this school in Korea, and in the ensuing centuries many treatises were written in this new field of study.

In mid-Chosŏn the lyrical form known as *kasa* was widely composed. Although written in Chinese as a kind of prose-poetry, in its form the *kasa* exhibited characteristics of typical Korean lyric verse. Through the *kasa*, then, the Neo-Confucian literati were able to vividly express their attachment to the beauties of nature that were a part of their life. Chŏng Ch'ŏl (1536-1593) is the poet who perfected the *kasa* form, but there were many other renowned literary figures who composed poems of this genre.

A major genre of native literature, written in the Korean language, is the *sijo* poetic form, born in the late Koryŏ period but brought to its flowering in the early-middle years of Chosŏn. Although at times it was labeled the poetry of dilettantes, it became a necessary component of the education of every *yangban*, and statesmen, scholars, and military men alike have left to us their *sijo* compositions. *Sijo* literature reached the peak of its perfection in the hands of Yun Sŏn-do (1587-1671). There were numberless other composers of *sijo* too, of course, and the themes of which they sang were many and varied. There are *sijo* that express loyalty to the sovereign and those that inculcate moral precepts, those that sing of the valiant spirit of the warrior and, in contrast, other *sijo* that depict the feelings of bitter rancor of those who suffered through the Japanese and Manchu invasions. Still others extol the beauties of nature, or give voice to a yearning to find solace in the natural world. Such a work is Yun Sŏn-do's "New Songs from My Mountain Fastness." In one of its verses, the "Song to Five Companions," he writes:

> How many friends have I, you ask?
>   The streams and rocks, the pines and bamboo;
> Moon rising over eastern mountain
>   You I welcome too.
> Enough. Beyond these five companions
>   What need is there for more?

In this way he expresses his desire to experience the tranquil pleasures of life in the company of five friends—the streams, the rocks, pine trees, bamboo, and the moon. He had left behind the world of political striving and sought to console himself in a life of upright but unrewarded endeavor. The fact that the greatest works of *sijo* literature were written on such themes as this surely is a reflection of the troubled age in which their authors lived.

Chapter 11

Economic Advances and Intellectual Ferment

Government by Powerful Lineages

When the factional split between Easterners and Westerners first developed, the Easterners quickly achieved dominance and proceeded to suppress the Westerners. Within the Easterners, however, two sub-factions developed over the issue of a leading Westerner's proposal for designating an heir to the throne then occupied by King Sŏnjo, who had no legitimate son. These new groupings became known as Northerners (Pugin) and Southerners (Namin), the former urging harsh condemnation and punishment of the Westerners while the latter took a more moderate stance. Consolidating their power in the years following the war with Japan, the Northerners threw their weight behind the succession of Kwanghaegun, and accordingly they dominated the political scene during his reign (1608-1623). Meanwhile the political outs, the Westerners, were biding their time, and when Kwanghaegun was charged with misrule and deposed in 1623 they rallied behind the accession of King Injo. For a long time thereafter the Westerners had things essentially their own way, and during the reign of Hyojong (1649-1659) in particular, with the king's former tutor, Song Si-yŏl (1607-1689), occupying a high position, they made their political base even more secure.

This is not to say that the Westerners met with no challenges to their exercise of power. In a dispute over the length of the period of mourning to be observed by Hyojong's mother, the Westerners were driven from power and the Southerners took their place, in 1674. Again when King Sukchong (1674-1720), long without an heir, proposed to invest the newborn son of his favorite concubine, Lady Chang, as crown prince, the unyielding opposition of the Westerners once more brought about their downfall, while Song Si-yŏl paid with his life. Meanwhile, the Westerners themselves had split, into an Old Doctrine (Noron) faction and a Young Doctrine (Soron) faction.

In the course of this prolonged political conflict along factional lines certain paramount lineages emerged, especially in the dominant Old Doctrine faction, that retained their grip on political power generation after generation. They were able to perpetuate their preeminent position by manipulating the appointment process, and by taking advantage of flaws in the workings of the examination system, so as to assure their own preferment.

At this point, many Neo-Confucian literati became virtually excluded from meaningful participation in the political process, and some of these sought fulfillment by establishing *sŏwŏn* (private academies) in the countryside localities where they lived, both to educate their youth and also to carry on the teachings of earlier generations of Neo-Confucian literati. The result was that nearly three hundred *sŏwŏn* were founded during Sukchong's reign. Content now to forgo official careers, the scholars associated with the *sŏwŏn* came to represent the mainstream of Confucian scholarship and to win great respect as "rustic literati" (*sallim*). At the same time, as a matter of government policy aimed at preventing their further alienation, they sometimes were appointed to special sinecures such as votive officiant in the National Confucian Academy, the officer who presided over rites honoring Confucius. But a greater number of these "idle" literati found satisfaction in playing roles as advisers and enablers in the formal and informal administration of local affairs.

Reaction against the political dominance of the Westerners, the Old Doctrine faction in particular, and the consequent exercise of governmental power by a few great families, took other forms as well. Many lost faith in the justness of Chosŏn's social order and harbored resentment against it. These men criticized the elevation of Neo-Confucianism to a position of unassailable dogma, and they discovered in themselves resources of spirit that made possible free and unorthodox thinking. It was in this milieu that ideas rejecting the established order of that day took root—the geomantic and portentous formulations of the *Chŏnggam nok* (a book of prognostications), the subversive creed of Western Learning (Catholicism), and the individualist doctrines of the Wang Yang-ming school of Neo-Confucianism, anathema to the orthodox Chu Hsi philosophy. At the same time, monarchic authority had become threatened by the ongoing dominance of a single political coloration. The policy adopted to overcome the grave danger to the state implicit in this development was the *t'angp'yŏngch'aek* ("policy of impartiality").

First adopted by King Yŏngjo (1724-1776) and continued under Chŏngjo (1776-1800), the policy of impartiality aimed at according equal favor in official appointments to men of all the so-called four colors (*sasaek*)—to those of the Old Doctrine and of the Young Doctrine, to the Southerners and to the Northerners. As a result, factional strife became relatively quiescent and a new equilibrium was achieved among the *yangban* officials. Royal authority thus was greatly enhanced, with a consequent political stability during these two long reigns.

But the "policy of impartiality" could not eradicate the root cause of factional strife, and in 1762 a new conflict arose between the Party of Expediency (Sip'a) and the Party of Principle (Pyŏkp'a). These factions took shape over the issue of Yŏngjo ordering his son, Crown Prince Changhŏn, cruelly put to death, the Party of Expediency deploring his fate and the Party of Principle justifying the king's act. The conflict between the two groupings cut across factional lines, so that the phenomenon of political strife now took on the added complexity of factions within factions.

Changes in the System of Tax Collection

During the period that political power was becoming concentrated in the hands of a few great lineages, the most serious problem facing the nation was the dismal fiscal situation. Farmland had been laid waste in the wars and the area under cultivation had decreased. To make matters worse many land registers had been destroyed and the number of "hidden fields," those kept off the government registers, had increased. Accordingly, the amount the government collected in land taxes had shrunk substantially, and measures to make good this deficiency were desperately needed.

In this context a radically different concept was proposed, a "rice payment law" that would take the place of the tribute tax, thus automatically relieving the peasant-farmers of the single most onerous burden they hitherto had had to bear. At the same time, it was anticipated that a fair and uniform system of land tax assessment would ultimately lead to a satisfactory increase in government revenues. By the terms of the new enactment, known as the Uniform Land-Tax Law (*taedongpŏp*), only about one percent of the harvest was to be collected from each *kyŏl* unit of land, and the tax could be paid in cotton cloth or in coin as well. The government continued to collect tribute products from the peasants as necessity required, but in essence the tribute tax system had been abolished. The Uniform Land Tax Law was first put into effect in Kyŏnggi province in 1608, and in 1623 it was extended to Kangwŏn province, in Hyojong's reign (1649-1659) to Ch'ungch'ŏng and Chŏlla, and finally in 1708 it was enforced throughout the whole country.

This shift to a land tax had a not inconsiderable impact on Chosŏn society. In the first place, the economic burden on the peasant was lightened. Not only this, it fostered the accumulation of commercial capital by the government-designated merchants, known as "tribute men" (*kongin*), who served as purchasing agents for government requirements, and it concomitantly led to the emergence of independent artisans who produced goods on order for these "tribute men." These related phenomena combined to bring about a major transformation in Chosŏn's economy and society.

At the time of the Japanese invasion Chosŏn no longer possessed any military force worth mentioning. During the course of the war, however, a Military Training Command was established to train fighting men. There soldiers who formed a new garrison unit of musketeers, archers, and lancers and swordsmen were taught their skills. From this beginning, over the next century or so a total of five new army garrisons had been created in the capital area, and from this time on these Five Army Garrisons constituted the core elements of Chosŏn's army.

Although it had not been the original intention, the ranks of the new Five Army Garrisons were filled predominantly by a system of paid recruits. This did not mean, of course, that the able-bodied male population was simply exempted from the military service obligation. Instead of being called up for military duty themselves, the peasant-farmers now were asked to pay two bolts of cotton cloth per year to defray the expense of keeping the soldiery under arms. This tax was by no means an insubstantial burden at best. But some were able to wangle exemptions and a number of unlawful practices further added to the afflictions of those poor households who had no way to avoid paying the cloth tax. As peasants fled their land to escape these onerous obligations, their unpaid taxes were forcibly collected from their neighbors or from their kinsmen.

However, the Chosŏn state rested on its agricultural economy, and it was clear that the dynasty could not remain standing on a foundation of ruined farm villages. The government was aware that changes had to be made in the military cloth tax system, but it was the principal source of government revenue and often a source of illicit private profit as well. Finally in 1750, after much agonizing and delay, Yŏngjo decreed that the cloth tax be reduced from two bolts to one, the loss in revenue to be made up by a variety of minor levies, including a minuscule grain surtax. This enactment represented an attempt to equalize the tax burden, and accordingly the new measure was called the Equalized Tax Law (*kyunyŏkpŏp*). Its administration was marked by all of the inevitable abuses, but it appears to have had some effect in counteracting the flight of impoverished peasants from their land.

Economic Growth

Agricultural technology underwent considerable advancement from early in the seventeenth century. First of all, the technique of transplanting rice seedlings was developed. That is, rice was first planted in a small seedbed and then transplanted to the paddy field, enabling the same plot of land to be used meanwhile for the ripening winter barley crop. Such a double-cropping system required a reliable supply of water, and to this end many new reservoirs for irrigation were constructed. By the end of the eighteenth century about 6,000 reservoirs were in existence, and a marked increase in agricultural production had been achieved. Moreover, a comparable advance took place in dryfield cultivation techniques as well.

These advances in agricultural techniques dramatically reduced the amount of labor required, so that the area of land one farmer could cultivate increased severalfold. In consequence the phenomenon called "enlarged scale farming" soon became common, and those who practiced it became small agricultural entrepreneurs, producing for the market as well as for their own consumption. These developments also led to a gradual improvement in the economic situation of tenant farmers as well, because the labor they sold to their landowners had become so much more productive. This in turn gave rise to simple-fee farming as the means by which the tenant farmer paid for his use of land owned by others. That is, the tenant paid a fixed amount for his use of the land, agreeing to bear the costs of production and the risk by himself. The advantage to the tenant was that he thus was free of the landowner's supervision and, for the first time, could farm as he thought best. At the same time, the gradual change from share-cost farming to a simple-fee system laid the foundation for the further change to a system of payment in cash instead of in kind.

Commercial production of specialized crops also now developed, in particular ginseng, tobacco, and cotton. The ginseng grown in the Kaesŏng area was especially sought after and nearly all of it was grown for the market, some of the crop being exported even to China and Japan. Tobacco, first introduced in the early seventeenth century, also came to be widely cultivated and exported to China in some quantity. The profit from tobacco was greater than that from grain, and so some of the most fertile land was devoted to growing it. The production of cotton, too, was no longer only for home consumption but also for the market.

In this way a new class of commoner-landlords emerged,

composed of peasant-farmers. They were able to accumulate wealth through the increased production that resulted from advances in agricultural technology and improvements in methods of farm management, and through the growth of farm production for the commercial market. But these developments also produced a more complex stratification of rural society, with the newly rich peasant class at the top, the successful tenant farmers forming an intermediate group, and the rural unemployed, whose labor was no longer in demand, at the bottom. Some of these latter became wage laborers but others were forced to take up lives of vagrant begging or joined robber bands. A further dimension was added to the new structure of rural society by the fact that increasing numbers of descendants of *yangban* lineages were sinking to the status of peasant-farmers, and even to the level of tenant farmers. Quite plainly, slow but significant changes were underway in the status system of Chosŏn society.

In the realm of commerce during this period, the development that first commands attention is the active role of the *kongin*, or "tribute men." With the elimination of local tribute payments following enactment of the Uniform Land Tax Law, goods required by the government came to be procured through purchasing agents known as *kongin*. In the process the *kongin* gradually accumulated capital and so, although they continued to act as agents of the government, their economic function was far broader. They did business with the Six Licensed Stores in Seoul and with the inland market and coastal trade brokers, and they also dealt directly with the craftsmen who produced the goods. In time, then, they developed into a specialized class of wholesale merchants, each handling large quantities of one particular type of good.

At the same time, the activities of private merchants were becoming more evident in Seoul and throughout the country. For example, the river merchants of Seoul marketed their grain, salt, and fish all along the reaches of the Han River in Kyŏnggi and Ch'ungch'ŏng provinces. Since they transported their wares by boat they began to invest their capital in boat-building, thus coming to dominate that industry. Again, the merchants of Kaesŏng extended their activities over land routes into regions to their north and into southern provinces as well, and in all these areas they established branches known as "Kaesŏng Shops." The Kaesŏng merchants themselves contracted for the cultivation of ginseng, a major item in their trade, and they also undertook the processing of it into "red ginseng," the steamed and dried form in which it often is consumed. Similarly, the government-licensed merchants in Seoul also controlled the production of handcrafted articles and, by taking advantage of the privileges given them by the government, gained monopolies in dealing in particular goods.

The merchants of this time were active not only within Korea but in foreign trade as well. In particular, the merchants of Ŭiju near the mouth of the Yalu carried on private trade with the Chinese at island sites in mid-river and at designated markets well inside Manchuria. At Tongnae, too, near Pusan, merchants dealt privately with Japan. Somewhat later a triangular trade developed, with the merchants of Kaesŏng, Ŭiju, and Tongnae serving as middlemen in transactions involving in the main Korean ginseng, Chinese silver, and Japanese copper. Through such international dealings many private merchants grew extremely wealthy.

As the activities of private merchants grew in scale, the appearance of Seoul's commercial streets also changed. After the special privileges granted to the licensed merchants were largely withdrawn in 1791, three great markets operated by private merchants developed in Seoul—one inside East Gate, another in the modern Chongno area, and the third outside South Gate. These three markets also dealt in goods from China and Japan, and it was from these markets that the citizenry of Seoul bought their daily needs.

Markets in the countryside also underwent much development. Markets existed at over a thousand locations in Korea in the eighteenth century, and the larger ones already had been established on a permanent basis. It was in these latter that wholesale merchants emerged to provide services to the itinerant pack and back peddlers. These were not simply wholesalers but engaged in warehousing, consignment selling, transportation, and innkeeping activities on the one hand, while also performing banking functions such as making loans, issuing checks or money drafts, and accepting deposits.

Expanded commercial activity necessitated wider use of metal currency. Following the minting of copper coins in 1678, large quantities of coins continued to be issued, and by around the end of the seventeenth century coins were in use throughout the whole country. Merchants began to amass wealth in cash rather than putting their money into land, and they increased their wealth by loaning out their hoards at high interest. "Coin famines" developed because of widespread hoarding, but nevertheless their use penetrated into the far corners of the country and accelerated the commercialization of production. In this way marketing transactions, payment of wages, and payment of taxes in coin all gradually became more common, and eventually regulations came into effect requiring that land rents too be paid in money.

As artisans and craftsmen broke away from government control during this period, production under state auspices gradually declined. In large measure, therefore, the government's rosters of artisans became no more than lists of those on whom the "artisan tax" was to be assessed. Near the end of the eighteenth century, moreover, the keeping of these rosters was itself abolished, a good indication that craftsmen of all kinds had become private producers independent of government control. Nevertheless, craftsmen at this time had not yet reached the stage of financing their operations with their own capital. Instead, the merchant, as the financier, controlled production, and the craftsman found himself in the position of a wage laborer.

Although this was the most prevalent form of handcrafted production in the seventeenth and eighteenth centuries, at the same time some craftsmen were beginning to produce and sell goods on their own, using their own capital. Fashioners of fur clothing and knife makers, for example, produced and sold fur neckpieces and decorative knives for women on their own, in competition with the licensed merchants. This was the case in particular with ironware and brassware manufacture. Pig iron artisans themselves enjoyed a monopoly on the manufacture and sale of cooking cauldrons. Similarly the makers of brassware used their own capital to employ labor and sold their output to merchants on periodic market days. They employed their labor under contract and they paid wages in cash.

As for mining, in order to produce silver for the illicit trade with China, the government permitted private mining activity and taxed it. However, the tax was so heavy that the number of officially sanctioned mines soon decreased. Subsequently, gold mining, especially the extraction of placer gold by panning, surpassed silver in importance. The government authorized copper mining, too, to supply the need for copper coins, but poor methods of refining the ore and excessive taxation made much development impossible. As a result, copper mining came to be carried on without the government's knowledge, and these covert operations employed a wage labor force.

Sirhak and Other Intellectual Concerns

As political power came to be monopolized in the seventeenth and eighteenth centuries by a small number of *yangban* houses, many *yangban* who did not belong to these select few lineages became frustrated by their inability to share in the country's governance. In the countryside, meanwhile, along with the emergence of peasants grown rich through the practice of enlarged-scale farming, poor peasants were being forced to give up their land, and the number of rural vagrants for whose labor there was no demand was increasing. In urban areas too a variety of changes were underway, as wholesale merchants amassed wealth through their control of trade and handcrafted production, while small merchants faced ruin and prices soared. As the numerous social ills attendant upon these phenomena became more grave, the problems Chosŏn society now faced demanded serious reflection on the part of the members of its educated class. Their response is embodied in the scholarship and thought known today as "Practical Learning," or *Sirhak*.

The birth of *Sirhak*, therefore, connoted censure of those who held political power and a consequent intent to bring about changes in the political and social order. There were, of course, government officials too who labored to effect reforms, but the chief critics were those who could not easily participate in the political process. Thus many *Sirhak* thinkers appeared from among the Southerners (Namin) faction that had been largely excluded from important government positions.

The major concern of the *Sirhak* scholars was to illuminate the history and contemporary workings of political, economic, and social institutions. First preparing the ground by painstaking scholarly inquiries, they proceeded to elaborate their visions of how an ideal society might be achieved. By no means limiting their scholarship to fields of social science, such as politics and economics, they extended their inquiries to embrace many other areas—Chinese classical studies, historiography, geography, natural science, agriculture, and many more.

Although the objects of their study were many and diverse, there was a common ground on which all *Sirhak* scholars stood. Namely, the point of departure for their studies was the actual manifestation of things, their reality. Pragmatic scholarship naturally requires a pragmatic methodology, and so the *Sirhak* scholars sought always for explicit verification. Since the realities with which they were concerned were precisely those confronting their society in their time, their thought inevitably had a Korea-centric thrust to it. Thus the *Sirhak* thinkers impelled scholarship in Chosŏn rapidly ahead in new directions.

It was to reform of the condition of agriculture that *Sirhak* scholars first addressed themselves, and their institutional approach to reform laid stress on the vital areas of the land system, administrative structure, and military organization, with the aim of promoting the sound development of an agricultural economy based on the independent, self-employed farmer. The scholar who systematized this institutional approach was Yu Hyŏng-wŏn (Pan'gye; 1622-1673). He passed his years in isolation in a farming village, engrossed in observing and comprehending the realities of the local society. The fruit of this lifetime of study was his treatise titled *Pan'gye surok,* completed in 1670. In it he examined and criticized in detail such institutional features of the dynasty as the land system, education, appointments, government structure, official salaries, and the military service system.

Yi Ik (Sŏngho; 1681-1763) followed in Yu Hyŏng-wŏn's

footsteps, extending his inquiries in both breadth and depth. His basic work, *Sŏngho sasŏl*, displays the diversity of his scholarship. Almost encyclopedic in coverage, its section on the human condition which treats such subjects as government, the economy, and the family, makes detailed proposals for reordering each aspect of Chosŏn society. But it was his *Record of Concern for the Underprivileged* that laid down the main principles of his reform ideas. Yi Ik attracted many disciples, and thus *Sirhak* gradually emerged as the dynasty's dominant school of thought.

Chŏng Yag-yong (Tasan; 1762-1836) was the scholar who applied the institutional approach in the most comprehensive fashion. While living in banishment for eighteen years and forced retirement for seventeen more as a result of the Catholic Persecution of 1801, he wrote many works in which he analyzed and criticized conditions in contemporary Korean society. In his *Design for Good Government* he put forth his views on government structure, in his *Admonitions on Governing the People* he proposed reforms in local administration, and in his *Toward a New Jurisprudence* he offered his ideas on penal administration. In other works as well, such as the *Treatise on Land,* he further revealed his thinking on reforming the ills of his age. His is rightly judged to be the greatest name among *Sirhak* scholars.

Sirhak thinkers like Yu Hyŏng-wŏn, Yi Ik, and Chŏng Yag-yong, in their approach to the solution of the problem of the farming villages, focused their attention on those who actually cultivated the soil. Accordingly, Yu Hyŏng-wŏn advocated a "public land system" under which the state would hold title to the land and allocate a fixed amount to each farmer; Yi Ik proposed an "equal field system" that would guarantee in perpetuity to each peasant household the amount of land minimally necessary to maintain its livelihood; and Chŏng Yag-yong urged adoption of a "village land system" whereby land would be owned and tilled in common by each village unit, the harvest then apportioned on the basis of the labor actually performed by each individual. Their common objective was to create a single class of independent, self-employed farmers who themselves held and tilled their lands. In this way, they thought, the disintegration of rural life resulting from the development of commerce and the change to a money economy could be prevented.

A second school of thought developed within *Sirhak*, one that arose in the urban surroundings of Seoul and so took issue with the proponents of institutional reform aimed at fostering a healthy agriculture-based society. This alternative view owed much to the gradual expansion of commercial and manufacturing activities, and it sought to bring about prosperity in Chosŏn society precisely through such activities. This doctrine is frequently called Northern Learning—i.e., a school of thought influenced by contemporary trends in scholarship in Ch'ing China.

The first important scholar of this persuasion was perhaps Yu Su-wŏn (1695-1755). His major work, modestly entitled *Idle Jottings,* presents a systematic plan for political, economic, social, and cultural reform. The author of *Jehol Diary,* Pak Chi-wŏn (1737-1805), next deserves mention. Pak Chi-wŏn kept a diary of his 1780 journey to Peking in the entourage of a Korean embassy, and in it he set forth his views on how poorly conditions in Korea compared with those in Ch'ing China. Hong Tae-yong (1731-1783) also wrote a *Peking Memoir,* but his work *Dialogue on Mount Iwulü* especially commands attention as a critique of conventional beliefs regarding the natural world, human society and institutions, and the thrust of history. Pak Che-ga (1750-1805) and Yi Tŏng-mu (1741-1793), too, wrote about their experiences in Peking, in works entitled *Discourse on Northern Learning* and *Peking Diary* respectively. Pak Che-ga's work is not merely a journal of his travels but addresses itself to reform of a variety of ills the Korea of his time confronted.

The significance of the views expressed by the proponents of Northern Learning did not lie in their admiration for the achievements of Chinese civilization but in their ardent wish to bring about change in Korea. Accordingly, their writings constituted a severe indictment of the *yangban* society of that age. They assailed the parasitic life of the *yangban* Confucianists who performed no productive labor themselves, and in contrast they attached great value to commercial and manufacturing activity and to agricultural work as well. They urged that production be expanded, through the introduction of new technology, and that means of transport and distribution by wagon and by ship be developed. The making and trading of goods, they argued, were activities that ought to be pursued by people of whatever social status, of course including *yangban*. And they put forward the radical proposal that a bureaucratic structure be created around a core of professional public servants recruited through educational opportunities open to all.

Since the actual conditions that the *Sirhak* thinkers wanted to reform were those of the society in which they lived, they could not but be deeply interested in their own history, geography, and culture. Yi Su-gwang (Chibong; 1563-1628) must be accounted to be the first *Sirhak* scholar to display an interest in Korean history. In a wide-ranging work (*Chibong yusŏl*) discussing such subjects as astronomy, geography, Confucianism, and botany, he offers, too, his own candid views on society and government in earlier Korean dynasties.

The major work of purely historical scholarship is the superb *Annotated Account of Korean History* by An Chŏng-bok (1712-1791), in which he presents a full chronological treatment of Korean history from Tan'gun through the end of Koryŏ, based on painstaking research. An equally imposing figure as a historian is Han Ch'i-yun (1765-1814); his *History of Korea* is a remarkable account, in the annals-treatises-biographies format, that incorporates an exhaustive selection of records on Korea found in Chinese and other non-Korean histories. The *Yŏllyŏsil Kisul*, by Yi Kŭng-ik (Yŏllyŏsil; 1736-1806), is a description of major events in the history of Chosŏn through the reign of Sukchong (1674-1720), drawn from hundreds of individual accounts, often contemporary.

It must be noted, too, that there was great interest in the history of Manchuria at this time, a phenomenon arising out of the shared view of *Sirhak* thinkers that the stage of the Korean historical experience extended northward beyond the Korean Peninsula. The most important work of this kind surely is the *Study of the Parhae Kingdom* written by Yu Tŭk-kong (1748-1807). In it the author propounded the view that the so-called Silla Unification period instead should be known as that of the "Northern and Southern Kingdoms," since the independent Korean kingdom of Parhae existed simultaneously in the north.

The study of historical geography was also a flourishing *Sirhak* pursuit. The pioneer work of this sort is *Treatise on Korean Geography* by Han Paek-kyŏm (1552-1615), but several other outstanding works appeared around two centuries later. An exceptionally fine cultural geography is the *Ecological Guide to Korea,* written by Yi Chung-hwan (1690-?). In this work the author treats political and economic matters, as well as customs and community values, from the perspective of the advantages and disadvantages of establishing residence in a particular local area. And several specialized geographical treatises appeared in Yŏngjo's long reign (1724-1776). The *Sirhak* thinkers also approached geography from the standpoint of firsthand investigation of actual conditions, and as the network of commercial activities spread over the whole country, their interest in such areas as topography and cartography, and transport and communications, also steadily expanded. At the same time there was marked interest in the study of the Korean language, and pioneering works on the *han'gŭl* writing system appeared.

The *Sirhak* scholars were not alone in wanting to achieve a new understanding of their own country and its history, for such studies also were accorded a high priority in government circles as well. Kings Yŏngjo and Chŏngjo (1776-1800) were particularly supportive of this endeavor. Chŏngjo, in fact, established a research library and institute within the palace, called the *Kyujanggak*, and assigned scholars to it to prepare a large number of works of practical application in the administration of the country. Major works compiled under government auspices during Yŏngjo's reign include the *Supplement to the National Code,* the *Supplement to the Five Rites of State,* the *Revised Illustrated Manual of Military Training and Tactics* that updated a fifteenth-century prototype, and the *Reference Compilation of Documents on Korea.* This last, prepared initially in 1770, is a true encyclopedia of Korean studies that provides a chronological overview of the nation's geography, government, economy, and culture. Under Chŏngjo many other important compilations were produced: the *Exemplar of Documents and Letters of State,* a selection of proclamations, royal admonitions, edicts, foreign relations documents and other state papers authored over the course of the dynasty; *Documents on Foreign Relations;* the *Records of the Ministry of Punishments;* the *Records of the Ministry of Taxation;* and others. A number of new castings of movable type were made in connection with this massive government compilation effort.

Catholicism, known then as "Western Learning" (*Sŏhak*), came to Korea in the early stages of the transmission of Western culture, which first was introduced to Korea through European Jesuit missionaries residing in Ming China. It was the *Sirhak* thinkers who initially took an interest in the new religion, but theirs was mainly an intellectual curiosity—they showed little disposition toward belief in Catholic doctrine as they understood it and, in fact, they leveled criticism at it.

During Chŏngjo's reign, however, the first stirrings of belief soon developed into a strong current, especially among Namin (the Southerners faction) scholars. A particularly significant event occurred in 1784 when Yi Sŭng-hun, who had accompanied his father in a diplomatic entourage, returned from Peking after being baptized by a Western Catholic priest. During the next few years the number of converts grew rapidly, especially among the Sip'a faction of the Namin and among the *chungin* class of technical specialists. These early believers had, as it were, converted themselves, through reading treatises brought back from China. What they seem to have sought in Catholicism was a means to grapple with the host of evils that then beset Chosŏn's social and political order. One can well imagine that those reform-minded *Sirhak* thinkers took fresh hope for creating a heavenly kingdom on earth through belief in the new religion. Accordingly, the acceptance of Catholicism may be seen as constituting a challenge to the grasping and predatory nature of the Chosŏn state and the intellectual rigidity of Neo-Confucianist orthodoxy.

The issue that brought to the surface Catholicism's challenge to the existing order was the so-called Rites Controversy, which arose in consequence of a papal ruling in 1742 that ancestor worship and belief in Christianity were incompatible. Chŏngjo had designated Catholicism a heresy and proscribed it in 1785, and in the next year the importation of books of any kind from Peking was banned. Then a few years later, in 1791, a *yangban* convert was sentenced to death for failing to prepare an ancestral tablet for his mother and not performing the standard Confucian memorial ritual. Catholicism thus came to be suppressed on ritual grounds, but the activities of a Chinese priest who entered Korea secretly in 1795 revived the fortunes of the new religion, and before long the number of converts had reached about four thousand.

While Chŏngjo remained on the throne a course of tacit tolerance of Catholicism was followed. But when Chŏngjo died, a cruel suppression known as the Catholic Persecution of 1801 almost immediately ensued. There was a political motive for the persecution as well, in that the Pyŏkp'a segment of the Old Doctrine faction saw an opportunity to use the issue of Catholicism to bring down its rival Sip'a Southerners. The 1801 persecution also was the occasion when Hwang Sa-yŏng secretly attempted to present his famous "silk letter" to the Catholic bishop in Peking, a European, but was found out and executed. His letter, written on silk, asked Western nations to dispatch naval and land forces to compel the Korean government to grant religious freedom.

Science and Technology

In consequence of the paramount interest in the development of agricultural technology in the seventeenth and eighteenth centuries, a great variety of works on agriculture appeared during this period. Deserving mention among these are the *Manual on Farming* by Pak Se-dang (1629-1703), in which primary attention is given to the cultivation of fruit trees, raising of livestock, horticulture, irrigation, and weather; *Farm Management* by Hong Man-sŏn (1643-1715), dealing with the problems any farmer might face in the course of his daily activities, including food processing and storage; and *Farming in Korea,* an attempt to systematize the whole range of Korea's agricultural science, which Sŏ Ho-su (1736-1799) compiled by royal command. At the same time much attention was given to the sweet potato as a famine distress food, and a number of works on its cultivation appeared from the eighteenth century.

Two quite different studies, both remarkable, need next to be mentioned. One is the *Register of Hŭksan Fish* by Chŏng Yak-chŏn, written in 1815 in banishment on Hŭksan Island off the southwest Chŏlla coast. In it he records the name, distribution, morphology, habits, and uses of 155 varieties of marine life, knowledge he gained through personal observation and analysis of specimens gathered from the seas around him. The other is a medical text, the *Comprehensive Treatise on Smallpox,* written by Chŏng Yag-yong in 1798. This timely work refers to numerous Chinese writings on the subject in presenting a full discussion of the symptoms and treatment of smallpox, a widespread disease that would continue to scourge Korea throughout the nineteenth century.

Like Catholicism, Western science and technology initially entered Korea through Ming China, whence it had been brought by European Jesuit missionaries. The frequent Korean embassies to China provided the principal channel of transmission, but there were others as well. Crown Prince Sohyŏn, Injo's eldest son, became acquainted with the Jesuit missionary Adam Schall von Bell while he was a Manchu hostage, and in 1644 he brought back to Korea a number of works on Western science. In 1628 a Dutchman was shipwrecked on Korean shores; experienced in casting cannon, he contributed to Korean knowledge in that area. He was followed in 1653 by Hendrik Hamel and his company of Dutch sailors who were cast ashore on Cheju Island. Some of them eventually escaped to Nagasaki, thus giving them the opportunity to make the reverse contribution of providing the West with its first direct knowledge of Korea.

Among the specific scientific advances that were owed in some measure to knowledge gained from the West were new methods of calendrical computation, which culminated in the promulgation of a revised calendar in 1653, and the pulley mechanisms devised by Chŏng Yag-yong and put to use in constructing the fortifications at Suwŏn near the end of the eighteenth century. Similarly, the insights they gained from Western science led several Korean thinkers, most notably Hong Tae-yong, to put forward their own views on terrestrial movement within a solar system.

During these two centuries of intellectual ferment, dissenting views also emerged within the Neo-Confucian school itself. Two scholars who made known their dissatisfaction with the orthodox interpretations were Yun Hyu (1617-1680) and Pak Se-dang. In his *Exegesis of the Doctrine of the Mean* Yun Hyu attacked Chu Hsi's interpretations, earning for himself the appellation of "traitor to true Confucianism." And when he lost out to Song Si-yŏl in the great mourning rites controversy of that day, he was executed. Pak Se-dang not only deviated from Chu Hsi's interpretations of the Chinese Classics, but through his own analysis of the *Lao-tzu* and *Chuang-tzu* he offered a fresh view from the perspective of Taoist thought. For this temerity he too was branded a heretic. Chŏng Yag-yong was another creative interpreter of the Classics who likewise sought to discover the original intent and meaning of Confucius' formulations.

Meanwhile the "heretical" ideas of Wang Yang-ming began to gain acceptance from some Korean scholars. Interest in Wang Yang-ming doctrine appears to have been especially strong among scholars from segments of *yangban* society who were disadvantaged politically, including members of the royal house and men of illegitimate descent (that is, descendants of *yangban* by their secondary wives). Rather than seeing the ideas of Wang Yang-ming as antithetical to those of Chu Hsi, these scholars generally regarded the two schools of thought as mutually reinforcing. On the other hand, Chosŏn's leading exponent of the Wang Yang-ming school, Chŏng Che-du (1649-1736), disassociated himself completely from orthodox Chu Hsi-ism. He could do this, it would seem, because he was able to move to Kanghwa Island and spend his life away from the political hazards of the capital. Although these thinkers, for the most part, presented their critiques with understandable caution, their scholarship marked a new departure in its determination not to accept uncritically the orthodoxy of the Chu Hsi school.

New Modes of Expression in the Arts

The spirit of *Sirhak* manifested itself not only in scholarly writings but also appeared in new literary forms. The fictional works attributed to Pak Chi-wŏn perhaps best exemplify this.

He wrote down several short pieces, all bitingly satirical indictments of *yangban* values and conduct. The best known are probably "The Tale of Hŏ Saeng" and "Tale of a *Yangban*." He told these stories in a natural, free-flowing style that avoided the overly mannered phrasings of earlier writing in Chinese.

It is also important to note that men of *chungin* or petty clerk (*sŏri*) background, and others of commoner status, produced anthologies of poetry. Already in the time of Sukchong (1674-1720), Hong Se-t'ae (a *chungin*) had compiled *Pearls from the Real Korean Poetry,* and in 1737 Ko Si-ŏn (also a *chungin*) supplemented this with his *Poems of a Peaceful People.* The term "poems of the people" was intended to indicate poetry of the non-*yangban* social classes, and such anthologies were published thereafter at sixty-year intervals. At this time there also appeared collections of short stories that represented transcription in Chinese, in a quite unaffected style, of tales that had passed down orally among the people.

The greatest change in the literature field in the seventeenth and eighteenth centuries, however, was the outpouring of works written in *han'gŭl.* Most of the new *han'gŭl* fiction, drawn as it often was from the storyteller's repertoire, was new in style as well, being written in such genre as the novel and a "long form" narrative *sijo.* Authorship changed too, away from the *yangban* class to those of lower social status such as petty clerks. These developments took place, in short, because this literary output was for a new, non-*yangban* clientele of readers. Novels in *han'gŭl* treated a variety of themes. Hŏ Kyun's *Hong Kiltong,* written in the reign of Kwanghaegun (1608-1623) and considered to be the first vernacular novel, is a work of social criticism that scathingly attacked the inequities of Chosŏn society, in particular its discriminatory treatment of illegitimate offspring. Such works as *Rose Flower and Pink Lotus, That Goodness Be Manifest and Righteousness Prized, Tale of Sim Ch'ŏng,* and *Tale of Hŭngbu* may be seen as morality tales, wherein evil is punished and virtue rewarded. There also were novels like *The War With Japan* and *General Im Kyŏng-ŏp* that related military exploits. The most widely read novels, however, *Dream of the Jade Chamber, The Story of Sukhyang,* and *The Story of Ch'un-*

hyang, all deal with themes of love. Many of these novels, the authors of which almost all are unknown, express the discontent of the non-*yangban* classes with the society in which they lived. Considered the greatest of the novels of this period, *The Story of Ch'unhyang* takes the stance that commoners and those of mean birth are no different in their human qualities than the *yangban.* Thus, the heroine of its title is led to exclaim: "How can loyalty and filiality, or womanly virtue, differ between high born and low?"

The same tendency is apparent in *sijo* poetry as well. The early *sijo* were *yangban* literature, short poems that sang of Confucian virtue, or the joys of rusticity, or the heroic spirit of the warrior. Now, however, the *sijo* was taken over by those of status other than *yangban,* and their desire was to let the *sijo* express their feelings in unrestrained fashion. Accordingly, the *sijo* became a long poem and its themes too changed, to portray love between the sexes, the hardships of family life, and even unabashed lewdness. The authors of the new *sijo* who are known (many creations were left unsigned) most frequently were government clerks, "fallen" *yangban,* or those of low social status such as female entertainers.

> Pass where the winds pause before crossing over,
>   Pass where the clouds too pause before crossing,
> High peaks of Changsŏng Pass where
>   Wild hawks and trained hawks and
>   Highest soaring falcons all,
>   All must pause before crossing over.
> Were but my love waiting me across yonder pass,
>   I should pause not once in my crossing over.
>   Anonymous

The two major compilations of new *sijo* were by the government clerks Kim Ch'ŏn-t'aek and Kim Su-jang, whose *Enduring Poetry of Korea* and *Songs of Korea* appeared in 1728 and 1763 respectively. All in all, the appearance of the new *sijo* verse, like that of the new novel, gives ample evidence of the emergence of a fresh, new literature.

In painting too the new trends are plain to see. First of all, this period marks the appearance of realism in landscape painting, as Korean artists now came to depict Korea's natural surroundings as seen with their own eyes. Chŏng Sŏn (1676-1759) was the painter who developed this realistic landscape style. He had to work out his own approach to composition, and he learned how to portray the craggy features of the Korean landscape with forceful splashes of black, to give a sense of looming mass. Paintings that perhaps best exhibit these characteristics are "Storm Lifting Over Inwang Mountain" and "The Diamond Mountains." Although also a painter of the realism school, Kim Hong-do (1745-ca. 1818) depicted mountains, trees, and streams with swift brush strokes, conveying with the beauty of his lines a style that contrasts with that of Chŏng Sŏn. Typical of his landscape paintings is "The Steepled Rocks off Kŭmgang's Shore."

Genre painting also flourished during this period. Kim Hong-do and Sin Yun-bok (1758-?) are the most famed masters of genre painting, the art that depicts scenes from the ordinary events of everyday life, and it is noteworthy that both were *chungin* professional painters in government employ. Kim Hong-do was adept at delineating mountains and streams, Taoist immortals, flowers and grasses, and he is especially known for his way of depicting the branching of trees. His principal genre themes are the workaday lives of everyday people, as they till the fields, gather the harvest, or labor in a smithy, but his "Dancer with Musicians" and "Wrestling" are especially well-known works. Kim Tŭk-sin (1754-1822) is another genre painter of the same bent in style and subject matter as Kim Hong-do, while the paintings of Sin Yun-bok depict mainly the mores of the townspeople of his time, with a focus on the activities of women. The best examples of his work are "A Beauty" and *An Album of Genre Scenes,* in which are to be found girls on swings, housewives washing clothes in streams, women selling wine, and suggestive scenes of disporting libertines. The popularity of genre painting, in sum, constituted an artistic protest against *yangban* Confucian society, an assertion of the worth of all humanity.

A noteworthy development in ceramics was the production of blue on white porcelains. In the past, the pigment known as "Mohammedan blue" had been imported from China and was very expensive, and its use among the common people was forbidden. During the reign of Chŏngjo, however, when a pigment produced in Korea began to come into use, "blue on white porcelain" gained wide acceptance among the whole population and underwent considerable development. Quick brush strokes using only the blue pigment limned in mountains and streams, flowers and birds, grasses and trees. When fired, this blue on white porcelain ware was possessed of a beauty far different than that of the contemporary Chinese or Japanese ceramics of varied hues that employed blue, red, green, purple and other colors. From these Korean porcelains there emanated a simple poetry, an intrinsic Korean flavor of unaffected naturalness.

Chapter 12

Dynastic Disarray and National Peril

Government by Royal In-Law Families

So long as Yŏngjo and Chŏngjo maintained their policy of appointment of officials without regard to factional affiliation, the political scene generally remained stable. But upon the death of Chŏngjo in 1800 and the accession of Sunjo, a boy of just ten years, the power of the royal in-law family became predominant, and the era of so-called in-law government (*sedo chŏngch'i*) began. As Sunjo's father-in-law, Kim Cho-sun of the Andong Kim clan was able to concentrate political power in his own hands, and in consequence a number of his close clansmen rose rapidly to occupy vital positions in the government. Subsequently, the Andong Kim for a time had to yield power to another formidable in-law lineage, the P'ungyang Cho clan. This was because the mother of Hŏnjong (1834-1849), Sunjo's grandson and successor, was a daughter of Cho Man-yŏng, a leading P'ungyang Cho figure. Following the new established pattern, Cho In-yŏng (Cho Man-yŏng's younger brother) became chief state councillor and many of his clansmen secured appointments to important posts. But power once again reverted to the Andong Kim after the accession of Ch'ŏlchong (1849-1863), since his queen was the daughter of Andong Kim Mun-gŭn whose close kinsmen Kim Hŭng-gŭn and Kim Chwa-gŭn now came in turn to head the officialdom as chief state councillor. And as the dynasty approached its end, the close kin of Queen Min, King Kojong's consort, took their turn at exploiting their proximity to the throne.

Concentration of power in the hands of a succession of royal in-law families brought with it grave disorder in the governing process, and the suffering that ensued therefrom fell mainly on the shoulders of the peasantry. This is because the large sums offered in bribes to obtain appointments to office had to be recovered through exactions levied on the common people. The instruments employed for this nefarious purpose were the so-called three administrations, the agencies that administered the three prime sources of government revenue—land tax, military service tax, and the state granary system. These agencies, one feels, now served less as fiscal managers for the state than as embezzlement facilities for the rapacious officialdom.

The land tax actually was made up of a variety of charges levied on the basis of the number of *kyŏl* under cultivation. Despite the multiplicity of these taxes the total amount came to less than twenty *tu* (about ten bushels), under one-tenth of a typical harvest and so by no means a large amount. Nevertheless the land tax indeed was a heavy burden, and the reason for this was a variety of surcharges and handling fees. Although practices differed from region to region, the addition of these further charges and fees raised tax collections in some cases to as much as one hundred *tu* per *kyŏl*, an amount equal to about half the harvest. On top of all this, officials might levy taxes on abandoned fields, and they frequently extorted payments above the fixed amounts so that they might replace the public funds they had spent for private purposes.

The military tax, for its part, levied payment of one bolt (*p'il*) of cloth on each able-bodied male. To be sure, the rate had been cut in half by the Equalized Tax Law, but one *p'il* was equivalent in value to six *tu* of rice, and so the military tax added about a third to the average tax obligation. Moreover, as noted earlier, there were always an assortment of illegal exactions, such as levying the cloth tax on family members who had died. In fact, then, since the military tax involved the production of cloth by the peasants themselves, it imposed a greater hardship, perhaps, than the land tax.

Finally, under the grain loan (*hwan'gok*) system, loans were made from government stores in the lean spring months and were to be repaid at harvest time with a "wastage" charge of ten percent. But what was supposed to be a means of giving relief to hard-pressed peasants was converted into an instrument for making usurious loans, and the abuses of the grain loan system became the most flagrant of all among the three tax administrations.

Local officials thus grew fat on what they illegally extorted from the farm population in their charge. It was not the county magistrate alone, for the local functionaries (*hyangni*) at the bottom of the administrative ladder also profited. In order to obtain an appointment, the *hyangni* were required to pay a fee in advance to the local magistrate, and to recoup this amount they had to find suitable ways to collect taxes by force. They were only *hyangni* but they wore the cloak of governmental authority, and the peasants had no way to refuse their demands.

The corruption of local administration not only brought grief to the peasantry but threatened the fiscal soundness of the central government as well. The government's response was to dispatch secret inspectors (*amhaeng ŏsa*) to bring charges against officials guilty of corrupt practices. Fear of a visit from a secret inspector may sometimes have served as a restraint, but it was not an effective way to get at the roots of the rampant corruption.

Tremors in the Yangban Status System

In broad conception, the society of the Chosŏn dynasty had been structured as a highly stratified society dominated by the *yangban* class. But in reality the system was never so rigid as it often appeared. There were many reasons for this, but in general it may suffice to remember that a society is a living organism, constantly in flux, always interactive collectively and individually with the totality of its members. However inert the society of Chosŏn may at times have seemed, as the dynasty aged it became apparent that change was taking place in a number of directions, some of them of fateful significance. The status system was one such area where important processes of change were underway.

One major phenomenon that had been visible from the very beginning of the dynasty was that a great many individuals born into *yangban* lineages were unable to maintain their claims to that status. The most numerous such group, no doubt, were those who have been called "fallen" *yangban*. These may be defined as those with impeccable *yangban* lineage antecedents but whose claim to the privileges of the *yangban* status had eroded. Typically these were men living in the rural areas who for many generations had been unable to pass the government service examinations, or secure official appointment, and who in the meantime had lost some or all of the economic underpinning that even the most abbreviated *yangban*-like life-style requires. Such *yangban*, at best, had fallen to the status of a kind of local gentry, while others among them had been forced by circumstance to become small-scale farmers. These latter sometimes are called "ruined" *yangban* (*chanban*), and their numbers were steadily increasing.

At the same time, the distinction between legitimate and illegitimate (*sŏja*) lines of descent was slowly breaking down. Opportunities to sit for even the civil service examinations had been given to *sŏja* already early in the seventeenth century. Now, in the latter of the eighteenth century, Chŏngjo had appointed such men to positions as editor-compilers in the prestigious *Kyujanggak* (the palace library). The *chungin* too, especially the hereditary class of technical specialists in the capital, were improving their position. Not only were interpreters widening their horizons through coming into contact with a new culture on their travels to Ch'ing China, but they were amassing wealth through private trading activities and thus were expanding their influence in the society. And other elements of the *chungin* class, such as those who held clerical posts in government agencies, were joining these professional men in pressing fresh claims to the position in Chosŏn society to which their skills entitled them.

Another changing aspect of social class relationships was the growing strength of provincial gentry, who always had been less favored than capital elites. For example, the number of successful higher civil service examination candidates from P'yŏngan province in northwest Korea increased sharply, to the point where the not very large county of Chŏngju came to produce more such degree-holders than any other county north or south. To be sure, these men found it difficult to go on to have careers of importance in the central government, but the fact that such new elements were appearing at all must be accounted a significant change.

Currents affecting the *yangban* ruling structure also were rising at the base of Chosŏn society. There were in fact instances of peasants becoming rich farmers and achieving the outward trappings of *yangban* status, but with the expansion of the landholdings of the royal house and in-law families many more peasants were reduced to precarious tenancy. At the same time, others lost their land entirely and became agricultural wage laborers, as has been seen. Many, too, left their villages to take up new lives as non-agricultural laborers, often as handcraft workers or miners. In the case of mine workers this sometimes resulted in the formation of new communities with periodic markets to service them.

Even if they lost their land, however, free peasants no longer fell into slavery, for slavery was gradually disappearing. The number of slaves on the government's rosters had fallen from 350,000 in the fifteenth century to less than 200,000 by the seventeenth century, and from some time in the early to middle eighteenth century, the number of privately owned slaves had begun to drop precipitously. This was a dramatic development, since there are strong indications in recent scholarship on the subject that slavery increased markedly throughout virtually the whole of the seventeenth century. The principal process at work in reducing slave numbers was manumission in exchange for military service. Slaves had come to be permitted to perform military service because it was becoming increasingly difficult to fill the ranks of the military with freeborn commoners. Those who thus were enlisted in due course were set free on the basis of passing a test of their military skills, or on the ground of two successive generations of military service. And some were able simply to buy their freedom. As for the government slaves still carried on the rosters, they no longer in fact performed labor for the government, nor did they pay a labor remission fee, so that they too were in effect free.

Under these circumstances the government itself decided to free its remaining slaves, and in 1801 the rosters of government slaves were ordered burned. True, slaves attached to local government agencies remained unfreed, and the institution of private slavery would not finally be abolished until 1894. Nevertheless a social change of major dimensions was taking place in Chosŏn's traditional social status system.

Ideologies of Change and Acts of Resistance

The forces of change thus clearly at work in Chosŏn society inevitably engendered changes in beliefs and values as well. A major evidence of this is seen in the manner in which the further spread of the Catholic faith took place. At the outset, as noted earlier, Catholicism had attracted many *yangban* converts, especially from among Namin (Southerner) scholars, but after the Persecution of 1801 most converts came from among people of commoner status. A decided majority were peasants, craftsmen, or those in commercial occupations, but there were even substantial numbers of converts from among wage laborers, while women adherents also increased remarkably. Still, Catholicism remained a faith for urban dwellers rather than a religion of the villages.

It is clear that what attracted Koreans to Catholicism was above all its creed of equality, its tenet that the whole of humankind are alike the children of God. It must have been a moving experience for *chungin* and commoners to be able to number themselves among God's children and worship Him on a basis of equality with the *yangban*. For women as well, Catholicism surely had a corresponding appeal. Moreover, those who found themselves in circumstances of despair doubtless responded with joyous belief to sermons about the kingdom of God. Indeed this vision of an afterlife likely constituted a powerful inducement to embrace Catholicism. In short, belief in Catholicism was in itself a grave and growing indictment of *yangban* society and of the values it cherished.

It was fundamentally for this reason, because of the challenge that Catholicism represented to the ideological underpinning of the Chosŏn social and political order, that the severe Persecution of 1801 had been carried out. However, once the Andong Kim lineage led by the young king's father-in-law, Kim Cho-sun, had secured power early in the reign of Sunjo (1800-1834), Catholicism no longer was severely suppressed. During the ensuing years the Vatican appointed a vicar apostolic for Korea, three French priests entered the country, and the Catholic faith began to win wider acceptance. But a policy of suppression again was employed by the Pyŏkp'a P'ungyang Cho, who had come to dominate the court as the current in-law family, and in the ensuing Catholic Persecution of 1839 the three foreign priests and many Korean converts were executed. A few years later the first Korean priest, Kim Tae-gŏn, who had been trained at a seminary in Macao, secretly returned to Korea and began to proselytize. He tried to maintain contact with missionaries in China by sea rather than via the long and dangerous land route, but he soon was apprehended and suffered martyrdom, in 1846. With Ch'ŏlchong (1849-1863) on the throne the Andong Kim again held power, and again the anti-Catholic policy was relaxed. As a result a number of French priests entered Korea, the number of converts reached perhaps 20,000, and a variety of Catholic books and tracts were published.

Meanwhile, increasingly aware of the need to gain control over their own destinies in a society ground down by *yangban* misrule, the peasantry came to adopt a number of strategies for survival. First mention should be given to the development of the *kye*, a voluntary association formed to provide a structure for mutual assistance activities or for a specific kind of social interaction. In its earlier stage of development, lineage *kye, kye* organized by those born in the same year, wedding and funeral *kye,* and neighborhood *kye,* were among the most common such compacts. It is known, too, that many *yangban* and wealthy households participated in *kye* of these sorts. But later the dominant form of *kye* became those organized to overcome economic hardship through the pooling of resources. Such *kye* were formed to repair a reservoir indispensable to all, for the common purpose of paying the military cloth tax, or to purchase an ox or farm tools for shared use.

The great interest aroused in the potato and sweet potato as famine foods also is a phenomenon closely related to village life around this time. Sweet potato seeds were brought to Korea from Tsushima in 1763 by an official returning from a diplomatic mission to Japan. Its cultivation spread, then, through the efforts and encouragement of a number of dedicated people, until it became a meaningful adjunct to the Korean diet. But the sweet potato is not easy to cultivate in Korea, and so the white potato spread more widely from the moment of its introduction from China around 1840.

Despite all their efforts at self-help, the life of peasants reduced to tenancy on small plots of land was one of grinding poverty. In poor harvest years there were multitudes of famine-stricken people everywhere, and thousands died of hunger. Forced to abandon their villages, large numbers of peasants took up lives of vagrant wandering. Some peasants sought to survive as "firefield people" (*hwajōnmin*) in the upland areas. They moved from place to place, with no fixed abode, burning off the vegetation cover and farming the hilly land as best they could, but the harvests of course were small and their lives were poor. In all these circumstances it is hardly surprising that the numbers of peasants who migrated across Korea's borders into the Chientao (Korean: Kando) region of Manchuria or the Russian Maritime Province were rising.

The discontent and grievances of the peasantry now began to be made manifest in covert ways. One expression of this was the repeated appearance all over the country of inflammatory streamers (usually hung from trees) and wall placards. Among many examples of this form of protest that might be cited, perhaps the most revealing episode is the hanging of a streamer in Ch'ōngju in 1826. Its written text cursing the government for its corruption and abuses was considered so seditious that Ch'ōngju was downgraded in the hierarchy of local administrative jurisdictions and its name changed. These and many other similar incidents offer clear insight into the state of mind of the common people at this time.

Given such grounds for discontent, it is understandable that peasant protest did not long remain so passive. First of all, many peasants turned to brigandage, shattering the public peace on all sides. Such bands roamed the countryside and ranged up and down the coastlines. Gradually this lawlessness became better organized, and more destructive, as smaller bands that had arisen separately merged into more powerful forces.

A rash of popular uprisings now broke out, centered naturally on the peasantry. Leadership generally was provided, however, by discontented *yangban* elements, the "fallen" *yangban*, and in a number of instances originally localized disturbances grew into large-scale rebellions. This was the case with the Hong Kyŏng-nae Rebellion in 1811. A fallen *yangban* from P'yŏngan province, Hong Kyŏng-nae conspired with others representing a variety of disaffected elements of intermediate social position in his locale. Declaring that discrimination against the populace of P'yŏngan province must end, they decided to attempt to achieve their purpose by force of arms. Just at this time the people of P'yŏngan were in a volatile mood, due to severe famine conditions and an unusually large number of landless wanderers. Under the pretext, then, of assembling laborers for mining operations, Hong Kyŏng-nae and his fellow conspirators gathered and drilled their motley force and rose in open rebellion. Nearly the whole region north of the Ch'ŏngch'ŏn River immediately came under their control, but presently they were defeated by government forces and were forced to fall back to the fortified town of Chŏngju, where they continued to hold out for some months. But Hong himself was killed in the final battle for the town and his rebellion was suppressed.

The Hong Kyŏng-nae Rebellion was put down, but its result was only to fuel the deepening popular discontent. Rumors that Hong Kyŏng-nae was still alive were widespread, and over the years small-scale outbreaks continued almost uninterruptedly throughout the whole country. The Chinju Uprising of 1862 was the most serious of these. Unable to endure the rapacious exploitation of the provincial army commander, the populace armed themselves with bamboo spears and rose under the leadership of a peasant of fallen *yangban* background. The rebels killed local government functionaries, set fire to government buildings, and wrought considerable destruction. The Chinju Uprising too was suppressed, but it ignited a succession of similar outbreaks. The tide of uprisings spread up and down the land, with even the fishermen on Cheju Island rebelling against the local authorities. These popular uprisings mostly were spontaneous, and both their causes and their objectives were local in character. But it would not be long before a truly national rising, with national aims, would threaten the very survival of the fading dynasty.

If it was Catholicism that propagated its faith in the region of the capital, then it was Tonghak that was nurtured among the people of the farming villages. For the grievances of the peasants against the society in which they lived found expression in a religious movement called Tonghak, or "Eastern Learning." Tonghak began to be propounded by its founder, Ch'oe Che-u (1824-1864), from 1860. Although he asserted he had taken the best precepts of Confucianism, Buddhism, and Taoism so as to oppose "Western Learning" (Catholicism) with "Eastern Learning," his doctrine included elements from Catholicism and also embraced features of popular shamanistic beliefs.

Ch'oe Che-u believed in the unity of man with God, that mankind and the Supreme Being are one and the same. He preached that the mind or spirit of man was a replica of that of God and that, accordingly, serving man constituted service to God. His ideas thus proclaimed an equality for all human beings that transcended social status or class, and this is the primary reason why his doctrine was welcomed by the oppressed peasantry. Another factor in the acceptance of Tonghak by the peasant population was that it incorporated such practices as the chanting of magical formulas and worship of mountain deities, aspects of traditional shamanistic beliefs that were readily understood by village people.

Tonghak was not simply a religious movement but a social movement as well, one concerned primarily with the peasantry and the betterment of the conditions in which the villagers lived. Tonghak urged that the nation be strengthened and the livelihood of the people be ensured, and it called for reform of the corruption-ridden government. Moreover, Tonghak went on to assert that the turning wheel of time had brought near the day when these goals might be achieved. It was this millenarian aspect that led the government to view with alarm the spreading popularity of the Tonghak faith. Accordingly, in 1863 Ch'oe Che-u was arrested on charges of misleading the people and sowing discord in the society, and he was executed the following year. His trial and execution sent many of his followers into hiding in the mountains, and for a time the popularity of Tonghak waned. But the discontent of the peasantry, the hotbed that had nurtured Tonghak, had not been alleviated, and the Tonghak faith soon was revived, infused with new vigor.

Development of a Popular Culture

Out of the *Sirhak* (Practical Learning) tradition of the seventeenth and eighteenth centuries came new scholarly achievements in the nineteenth century. The basic thrust of scholarly endeavor remained the same, an attempt to find ways to treat the ills of that day by searching for their roots in the Korean historical process. But the nineteenth-century Korean scholars felt a stronger sense of urgency to bring the results of their work to bear on the pressing problems of fundamental dynastic change. Their scholarship thus served to link *Sirhak* thinking with the "enlightenment thought" of the close of the century.

The most noteworthy aspect of the scholarship of this period was the effort to give it an overall structure. It was in the early nineteenth century that the thought of Chŏng Yag-yong, the great synthesizer of the full range of *Sirhak* scholarship, ripened into maturity, and now in Sunjo's reign (1800-1834) appeared two remarkable compilations encyclopedic in nature: *Sixteen Treatises Written in Retirement* by Sŏ Yu-gu (1764-1845), and *Random Expatiations* by Yi Kyu-gyŏng (1788-1856). The former treated agriculture most comprehensively but also dealt with the full spectrum of life in Chosŏn society, from daily activities to economic output to *yangban* intellectual and recreational pursuits. Yi Kyu-gyŏng's broader-gauge work is a vast assemblage and meticulous examination of data in virtually the whole range of scholarly endeavor. Then at the very end of the dynasty, in 1908, a group of scholars completed an expanded version of the late eighteenth-century *Reference Compilation of Documents on Korea,* a work that truly may be called an encyclopedic collectanea of materials for the study of traditional Korea. Again, in 1865, a team of scholars prepared the *Comprehensive National*

Code, a systematic updating of the dynasty's corpus of administrative law.

Another characteristic of nineteenth-century scholarship lies in its research methodology. Yi Kyu-gyŏng's striking concern for substantiating the data he used, his efforts at empirical verification, already have been remarked, but Kim Chŏng-hŭi (1786-1856) was the leading practitioner of this methodology. He adopted the approach of the Ch'ing empirical school and is known in particular for his deeply learned studies of historical inscriptions. A work typical of his meticulous scholarship is the *Observations on Examining Two Stone Inscriptions,* a study of two of the monument stones erected by Silla King Chinhŭng in the mid-sixth century as he toured the expanding frontiers of his kingdom. In the field of cartography Kim Chŏng-ho completed his "Detail Map of Korea" in 1861 on the basis of a lifetime spent in direct observation of the geographical features of the whole of the Korean Peninsula.

It is important to note next that numbers of scholars now emerged from among the fallen *yangban* and from the *chungin,* and that their work contained points of view that reflected the interests of the social class of their origin. Foremost among this group was Ch'oe Han-gi (1803-1875), a scholar of fallen *yangban* background. In a typical work completed in 1860, *Personnel Administration,* he argued that the way to restore good government was through proper recruitment of officials, and he proposed that men of talent be educated and employed from *yangban,* peasant, craftsman, or merchant backgrounds, without discrimination. He had a progressive view of history, one that made him confident the future held a better life for mankind in an enlightened world. Accordingly he urged that Korea abandon its policy of isolation, open its doors, and live in concert with the other nations of the world. Ch'oe Sŏng-hwan was a *chungin* who advocated reform and rationalization of government administration in a work called *Brief Words of Counsel.* Among the positions he took were that the traditional practice of forced mobilization of commoners to labor on state construction projects should be replaced by a wage labor system, and that taxes should be paid in cash, not kind.

A history of the social issue created by the large numbers of disadvantaged men who belonged to *yangban* secondary lines of descent (*sŏja*) also appeared. Called *Sunflowers,* it was compiled in 1859 by men who suffered this stigma and it urged an end to all discriminatory treatment directed against them. A little earlier, about 1848, a *History of the Clerkly Class* was published. Put together in the course of the previous century principally by a man of *hyangni* (local functionary) origin, this work argued that since the bloodlines of *hyangni* and *yangban* originally were the same, the two classes ought to be accorded the same treatment. Moreover, in such works as *Chronicles of Forgotten Men* by Cho Hŭi-ryong (1789-1866), a noted painter, calligrapher, and writer, *Excursions Into Byways* by a government clerk, and *Those This Age Has Overlooked* by a *yangban* from an impoverished family, are found biographies of men of outstanding accomplishments or virtuous enterprises whose lower social origins prevented their recognition by inclusion in the conventional compilations. Representing a new phenomenon in Korean historiography, all these works reflect the changes that were taking place in the society of that time.

As an example of native Korean literature, the *Anthology of Korean Poetry,* an imposing collection primarily of *sijo* poetry, appeared in 1876. But the "one-man opera" or *p'ansori* form is the most noteworthy achievement in Korean literature of this period. *P'ansori* were tales sung by professional artists to an outdoor audience in a performance extending over several hours. The origins of the *p'ansori* form can be traced rather far back in time, but it only flourished in the nineteenth century when masterly singers emerged to bring *p'ansori* to the peak of its popularity. The lyrics sung by the *p'ansori* performers were adapted from earlier Korean vernacular novels, and eventually a repertoire of twelve tales was created. The man who contributed most to the development of this corpus of *p'ansori* texts was Sin Chae-hyo (1812-1884), who put his own creative stamp on his story material by transforming mere words into emotion-charged phrasings. *P'ansori* texts contained satirical passages that lampooned the *yangban* class, thus providing a vehicle for the artists who performed them, as well as the populace who heard them, to give vent to their grievances against the inequities of late Chosŏn society.

Literature written in Chinese by members of the commoner class already had begun to appear and now it truly flourished. In 1857 the compilation of the *Third Selection of Poems of the People* was completed. It included works by monks and by women, and it contained poems by an impressive total of some three hundred five different authors. These literary artists formed "fellowships of poets," and one well-known such company was the group of seven that included Chang Chi-wan, a *chungin*. The creations of satirical poets like Kim Sakkat also provide insight into the nature of literature in Chinese produced during this period.

Masked dance, a drama form aimed at an audience of the common people, also flourished at this time. Interspersing dance and song and narrative, masked drama contained shamanistic elements, and this made it still more appealing to the mass audience. Furthermore, satirical passages contained in the narrative usually mocked the *yangban* class, as in this passage from the drama *Festival at Naval Headquarters* spoken by a snake-like creature:

I'll eat them raw at low tide, cram my maw at high tide,
Devour my *yangban* masters nine and ninety.
Then I'll eat one more and lo!
A dragon now become, mount the throne of Heaven.

Painting by men of letters in an abstract style derived from the art of calligraphy was the dominant genre of this period. Kim Chŏng-hŭi (mentioned above for his empirical scholarship) is the most renowned such artist, and in his outstanding work "Winter Scene" one sees not the real landscape of Korea but a portrayal of an other-dimensional idealized world. The orchids of the Taewŏn'gun and Min Yŏng-ik also exemplify such expressionism. This predilection for subjective representation was not limited to the *yangban* literati but spread as well to the professional painters in government employ, to the point where it became the predominant trend of this age. It appears, moreover, that the earlier trend toward naturalism in landscape painting, and in portrayal of scenes from everyday life, was arrested by the development of this new expressionist school. At the end of the nineteenth century the most renowned figure is Chang Sŭng-ŏp (1843-1897), a painter frequently accounted one of the three great masters of the dynasty, along with An Kyŏn and Kim Hong-do. Chang Sŭng-ŏp was an orphan who learned to paint by looking over the shoulders of his foster brothers, but his talent soon was recognized and he was given employment as a government artist. A genius who would not take up his brush for anyone he did not like, no matter in how high a station, Chang Sŭng-ŏp is best known for such paintings as "Plum Blossoms Red on White," a depiction that quickens into life the ethereal beauty of its subject.

In calligraphic art, the hidebound style of the past, one that had degenerated into mere formalism, was swept away and new modes of brushwork appeared. Kim Chŏng-hŭi, the great painter and scholar of epigraphy, was a foremost master of the new calligraphy. He studied the work of famed calligraphers of the past and fused their different characteristics into a style bursting with boldness of spirit, a form generally called the Ch'usa style after his penname. And there were other extraordinary talents who also contributed greatly to the innovations in calligraphic style.

The art of woodworking also underwent considerable development. Wardrobes, chests, mirror stands, cabinets for storing writing materials, stands for displaying ceramic art, bookcases, dining tray-tables, and other items of furniture are famed for their simple, unadorned elegance that preserves the natural beauty of the wood grain. At the same time, many superbly crafted articles were fashioned from bamboo, and bone, and lacquered wood with mother-of-pearl inlay.

The Reforms and Isolationist Policy of the Taewŏn'gun

King Kojong (1864-1907) succeeded King Ch'ŏlchong in 1864 at the tender age of twelve, whereupon power devolved into the hands of his ambitious father, Yi Ha-ŭng (1821-1898), better known in history as the Taewŏn'gun. The Taewŏn'gun faced the task of strengthening a dynasty well on the road of decline and confronted by the twin perils of internal rebellion and foreign invasion. As de facto regent during the decade of 1864-1873, he thus bent his energies toward effecting a dynastic "restoration" parallel to the contemporary Tung-chih Restoration of Ch'ing China.

No sooner had he assumed direction of the government than he set in motion a vigorous program of reform aimed at enhancing royal authority at the expense of the powerful lineages and consort families that had controlled the ruling mechanisms of the country since 1800. To this end, he appointed high officials on the basis of personal merit, regardless of their factional and regional background, and sought to strengthen official discipline by sentencing to death or banishment those officials who had enriched themselves at public expense. Aware of its symbolic value for elevating dynastic prestige, he set about to reconstruct the Kyŏngbok Palace, which had been destroyed during the Hideyoshi Invasion in the late sixteenth century and never rebuilt. He completed this project by mobilizing a large force of unpaid laborers for the construction, levying irregular taxes, and exacting excessive "voluntary" contributions from the people. He tried to replenish the government treasury by converting the military cloth tax, hitherto levied on commoners only, into a household tax assessed alike against *yangban* and commoners, and by minting a highly debased coin, in addition to imposing miscellaneous commercial taxes. To alleviate the economic burdens of the peasantry, he reorganized the grain loan system by establishing a network of locally administered village granaries. Primarily as a means of striking at the very roots of *yangban* power in the countryside, but also in part for fiscal considerations, he ordered the closure of all but forty-seven of some six hundred private Confucian academies *sŏwŏn*), which owned large tax-exempt agricultural estates and slaves to work them.

The Taewŏn'gun was quite successful in restoring both the authority of the throne and the financial health of the government. He also succeeded in repelling foreign intruders by upgrading the defenese capabilities of the country, as discussed below. In addition, some of his egalitarian reforms favoring the non-*yangban* segments of Chosŏn society gained him considerable popularity among the people, despite the economic hardship they suffered because of his ambitious projects. The Taewŏn'gun, however, was a pragmatist whose remedies offered only symptomatic relief, and he failed to effect fundamental changes in the country's economic, military and educational systems along the lines proposed by the *Sirhak* scholars since the eighteenth century. In the end, the impact of his reforms on vested *yangban* interests aroused bitter opposition from the Confucian literati of that day. This became the crucial factor in the set of circumstances that forced him to relinquish power in 1873.

From early in the nineteenth century, Western nations had come knocking at the doors of the "hermit kingdom," displaying an ever-growing interest in establishing contact with Korea for trade and other purposes. English merchant ships and men-of-war began appearing off the coast of Ch'ungch'ŏng province from 1832. In 1846, three French warships dropped anchor off the Ch'ungch'ŏng coast, left a letter to be forwarded to the court, and departed. In 1854 two armed Russian vessels sailed along the Hamgyŏng coast, causing some deaths and injuries among the Koreans they encountered. In August 1866, an American trading ship, the *General Sherman*, sailed all too brashly up the Taedong River to P'yŏngyang, only to be set afire by a mob of local residents and soldiers, resulting in the death of all twenty-four crewmen on board. In 1868, a Prussian adventurer, Ernst J. Oppert, who had been fruitlessly seeking to trade with Korea for two years, nearly succeeded in a bizarre scheme to pressure the Taewŏn'gun by violating the tomb of his father in coastal Ch'ungch'ŏng province.

Koreans were aware of the fate that had befallen China as a consequence of continuing clashes with Western nations, such as the Opium War of 1839-1842 and the Arrow War of 1856-1858. The Chosŏn government under the Taewŏn'gun, therefore, rejected Western demands for trade in the belief that this would prevent such disasters from overtaking Korea. The government also feared the spread of the Catholic faith. It has been seen that Catholicism, which had initially attracted mainly disaffected Namin *yangban* scholars, subsequently gained more and more converts from among *chungin,* commoners, women, and other disadvantaged or oppressed segments of the population. By the early years of the Taewŏn'gun's rule, there were over

20,000 Catholic converts and twelve French priests engaged in clandestinely proselytizing this officially proscribed alien faith. At the outset, the Taewŏn'gun was relatively tolerant of Catholicism. Concerned about Russia's southward advance, he even adopted a Korean Catholic's proposal to attempt to block Russian expansion by enlisting the aid of France. Eventually persuaded by his conservative counselors to follow an exclusionist policy, he launched a full-scale anti-Catholic campaign early in 1866. Before it was over, nine of the French missionaries and a reported 8,000 Korean converts had been martyred.

Korea's doors were now tightly closed. The Taewŏn'gun's policy of seclusion, and his persecution of Catholics in particular, resulted in two major "foreign disturbances," i.e., military clashes with Western nations. The first was the "French Disturbance of 1866," which was ignited by his suppression of Catholicism. One of the French missionaries who had survived the persecution and escaped to China, sought out the commander of the French Asiatic Squadron and persuaded him to take punitive action against Korea. After a brief reconnoitering mission to the Han River, the French admiral entered Korean waters in October 1866 with a flotilla of seven warships and seized the administrative center of Kanghwa Island, pillaging it and carrying away the weapons and documents stored there. A French force attempting to make its way toward Seoul, however, was beaten back by Korean troops at a fortress on the mainland just opposite the town of Kanghwa. Moreover, the French troops sent to attack the fortifications at the southern end of Kanghwa also were repulsed [see map p. 196]. In the end, the French squadron was forced to withdraw without having accomplished its mission.

Five years later, the "American Disturbance of 1871" occurred, in consequence of the destruction of the *General Sherman* on the Taedong River in 1866. Now the U.S. government decided to force Korea to open its ports to trade by recourse to the same gunboat diplomacy that had been successfully used against Tokugawa Japan in 1854. Accordingly, the U.S. Asiatic Squadron was ordered to send a detachment of five warships into Korean waters. By this time, however, in the aftermath of the French expedition, the T'aewŏngun had repaired the coastal

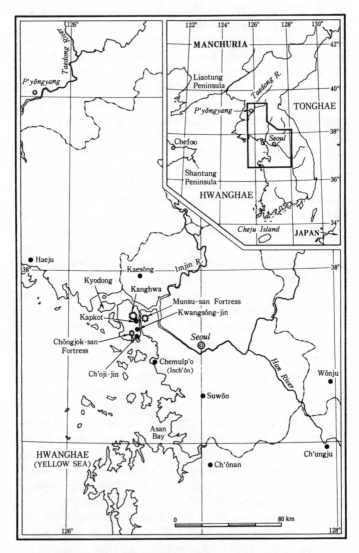

THE "FOREIGN DISTURBANCES" OF 1866 AND 1871

fortifications, built new gun emplacements, cast more cannon, and additionally strengthened Korea's defenses. When the American warships attempted to steam boldly up through the Kanghwa Strait, Korean shore batteries opened fire. Although U.S. marines succeeded in capturing the forts on southern Kanghwa in the face of stubborn Korean resistance, it had become apparent that the Korean government would not yield to a show of force. Accordingly, the U.S. fleet withdrew and returned to its station in China.

The two "foreign disturbances" contributed to a hardening of Chosŏn's isolationist policy. Exultant at his "victories" over the attacking French and American warships, in 1871 the Taewŏn'gun had stone markers set up on the main thoroughfare in Seoul and at other important sites throughout the country, incised with this admonition: "Western barbarians invade our land. If we do not fight, we must then appease them. To urge appeasement is to betray the nation."

The Taewŏn'gun's seclusion policy was anachronistic and myopic in view of the fact that China and Japan had already opened their doors to the West in the 1840s and 1850s. But his actions were supported by a preponderance of the nation's Confucian literati, who had long been clamoring for "rejecting heterodoxy [i.e., Christianity]." One widely esteemed ideologue, Yi Hang-no, set forth in his memorial of 1866 the extreme Confucianist argument for uncompromising armed resistance against foreign inroads. He asserted that to advocate peaceful relations with Western "barbarians" would be to abandon the values on which all civilization rests, thereby causing man to sink to the level of animal behavior. He further argued that men of standing in local areas should form guerrilla bands, or "righteous armies" (*ŭibyŏng*), to fight in concert with government forces against the foreign enemy.

The failure of the two Western attacks on Kanghwa was due in part to the stubborn Korean resistance. But neither the French nor the Americans had had determinedly aggressive purposes. At that time, France was preoccupied with the problems of consolidating control over its Annam (Vietnam) colony, while American energies, in the aftermath of the Civil War, were consumed in the settling of the West. Similarly, England was engaged in putting down revolt in India, and Russia was occupied in the colonization of the Maritime Province of Siberia. They too, therefore, had no strong desire or need to force Korea to open its doors.

In contrast, however, Japan was ready to pursue a forward policy toward Korea. Having overthrown the Tokugawa shogunate in 1867 through the Meiji Restoration, the leaders of the new Meiji government adopted an increasingly aggressive stance towards Korea for a number of reasons: the political necessity of finding an outlet for the energies of the disestablished *samurai,* the economic motive of acquiring a captive market for Japanese consumer goods, the strategic consideration of preempting Russian encroachment into the Korean Peninsula, and the chauvinistic impulse of the Restoration leaders to spread Japan's "imperial glory" abroad. As early as 1873, then, some hotheaded Meiji leaders went so far as to advocate mounting an "expedition against Korea." Thus the Japanese desire to invade Korea was apparent, the only remaining question being that of a suitable opportunity.

Chapter 13

Growth of the Forces of Enlightenment

Enlightenment Policy and Reaction Against It

Beginning in the late eighteenth century, some progressive thinkers of *Sirhak* persuasion had argued for an open-door policy towards the outside world with a view to increasing national wealth and strengthening Korea's defenses. For example, the late eighteenth-century scholar of Northern Learning, Pak Che-ga, maintained that only by developing trade relations with Japan and the Western nations could Chosŏn become a rich and powerful nation. Another *Sirhak* scholar, Ch'oe Han-gi, wrote *Descriptions of the Nations of the World* in 1857, a book based on contemporary Chinese works, in which he informed his readers about Western lands and suggested that it was necessary for Korea to open itself to foreign intercourse.

The argument for foreign trade was expounded even more forcefully by such officials as Pak Kyu-su and O Kyŏng-sŏk, who had opportunities to learn about the outside world during frequent visits to China on tributary missions. Pak Kyu-su, grandson of the *Sirhak* titan Pak Chi-wŏn, argued that Korea should open its doors to Western ideas and ways. O Kyŏng-sŏk, a Chinese language interpreter of the *chungin* class, brought back from China a number of books on the Western nations and urged his countrymen to read them. An increasing number of young *yangban* intellectuals in Seoul heeded their words, and the voices urging entering into relations with the West thus grew louder and more insistent. At the same time, changing conditions within Korea were creating an environment more favorable for the adoption of an open-door policy.

One such change occurred in December 1873, when the staunchly isolationist Taewŏn'gun at last relinquished his decade-long hold on power. Actually, he was compelled to do so by the combined force of the Confucian officials whom he had so antagonized and the newly rising consort family of the Yŏhŭng Min lineage. The Taewŏn'gun, mindful of the abuses that had developed under the ascendancy of the Andong Kim, had arranged for the young king to take a queen from a branch of the Yŏhŭng Min clan that lacked powerful political connections. Kojong, however, was weak-willed and easily manipulated by Queen Min. When a Confucian scholar-official, Ch'oe Ik-hyŏn, submitted a memorial denouncing the Taewŏn'gun, the king and queen adroitly seized the opportunity to effect his retirement from government. The departure of the staunchest advocate of isolationism naturally facilitated the abandonment of Korea's seclusion policy.

Aware of the changing conditions in Korea, the Japanese government seized the opportunity to force a commercial treaty on Chosŏn that would further Japan's aggressive designs. To this end, Japan deliberately provoked a confrontation with its neighbor by creating the so-called Unyō Incident in 1875. The Japanese navy vessel Unyō was sent into the waters off Kanghwa where it promptly was fired upon by Korean defenders on the southeast tip of the island [see map p. 196]. Although the Japanese government charged that Korea was guilty of an unprovoked attack upon a ship engaged in a peaceful mission, in fact the Japanese commander had been instructed to provoke some sort of incident that might serve as a pretext.

The following year, then, Japan dispatched General Kuroda Kiyotaka as minister plenipotentiary, with a force of three warships and four transports carrying about eight hundred soldiers. Landing on the east coast of Kanghwa Island, General Kuroda demanded that Korea enter into treaty negotiations. Although a majority of Chosŏn's high officials maintained there should be no dealings with Japan, Pak Kyu-su persuaded the king to adopt a conciliatory policy. The result was the Treaty of Kanghwa, concluded on February 22, 1876.

The Treaty of Kanghwa was Korea's first modern treaty.

Signed under foreign pressure, it featured provisions typical of an unequal treaty. The most important of its twelve articles proclaimed that, as an autonomous nation, Korea possessed equal sovereign rights with Japan. The objective behind this declaration of Korean independence was to open the way for Japanese aggression without inviting interference from China, which had historically claimed suzerainty over Korea. Another article stipulated that Korea open Pusan and two other ports within twenty months following the signing of the treaty. In addition, the treaty permitted Japan to survey Korean coastal waters at will and authorized establishment of Japanese settlements in the open ports, with the extraterritorial provision that the Japanese residents would be subject to Japanese law as applied by Japanese courts. A Supplementary Treaty and Trade Regulations signed on August 24, 1876, granted additional economic privileges to Japanese merchants in Korea.

Although the Treaty of Kanghwa paved the way for Japan to advance its political, economic, and military aims on the Asian continent, it nevertheless was of great historical significance for Korea. It brought Korea for the first time onto the international stage and opened the country to the outside world. The introduction of Western civilization to Korea was an inevitable consequence. The Korean people, however, faced the twofold task of advancing modernization while struggling to preserve their national independence.

King Kojong and his reform-minded coterie quickly began taking measures designed to promote the "enlightenment" and "self-strengthening" of the nation. In the same year the Treaty of Kanghwa was concluded, the government dispatched a high official as a special envoy to Japan to observe and report on the course Japan was following in adopting new Western ways. In the meantime, protracted negotiations got under way that led to the opening of a Japanese legation in Seoul in 1880, the first such establishment in Korean history. An important impetus to change came from a leading Chinese statesman, Li Hung-chang, who began handling Korean affairs for the Chinese court from late 1879 as Governor-General of Chihli Province and Imperial Commissioner for the Northern Ports. Alarmed by the Japanese annexation of the Liu-ch'iu (Ryūkyū) kingdom, one of China's tributary states, and by the Russian threat on China's northern border, Li wrote to Korean government figures, urging them to adopt concrete measures to bolster Korean defenses by emulating the Chinese self-strengthening policies.

Another important stimulus to the Korean enlightenment or self-strengthening movement came from the mission to Tokyo in 1880 undertaken by Kim Hong-jip. Having observed the startling evidence of Japan's progress and learned of developments elsewhere in the world, Kim desired to promote similar changes in Korea. He brought back two treatises that would have a considerable impact on the shaping of opinion in Korea. One of them, written by a Chinese legation official in Tokyo, Huang Tsun-hsien, argued that Korea must adopt Western institutions and technology and tolerate Protestantism, while following a foreign policy of close friendship with China, treaty ties with Japan, and a diplomatic "alliance" with the United States. The other work was by a Chinese comprador thinker, Cheng Kuan-ying, who asserted that to strengthen a nation such as China it was not merely enough to import Western technology; the political and other institutions that underlay Western technological development would have to be adopted as well. Influenced by such arguments as these, in October 1880 the Korean government made the momentous decision to establish diplomatic ties with the United States and take other measures necessary to promote reform and strengthen the nation.

As a first step, early in 1881, King Kojong established a new office at the highest level, the Office for the Management of State Affairs (*T'ongni Kimu Amun*), to oversee and coordinate the government's program of reform. Modeled on a contemporary Chinese administrative innovation, the Tsungli Yamen, this office took charge of such vital and diverse matters as diplomatic relations, military affairs, foreign trade, production of arms and weapons, and foreign language education. Soon thereafter, the government undertook a thoroughgoing reform of the military system. Most notably, a Special Skills Force composed of eighty cadet soldiers was created and a Japanese army lieutenant was invited to instruct this elite unit in the tactics of modern warfare.

Also in 1881, the king selected twelve younger officials to undertake a study mission in Japan. Known as the Courtier's (or Gentlemen's) Observation Mission, for over seventy days the delegation traveled about Japan, inspecting a wide range of Meiji Japan's modernized institutions and facilities. Some youthful members of the mission's retinue, such as Yu Kil-chun and Yun Ch'i-ho, remained in Tokyo as students, thus becoming the first Koreans to study in modern Japan. Almost concurrently, another reform-minded official, Kim Yun-sik, led a group of thirty-eight students and artisans on a training mission to China, in late 1881. They studied the methods of modern weapons manufacturing and military applications of the basic sciences at the schools and factories of the Tientsin Arsenal.

One of the most significant enlightenment measures undertaken by the Chosŏn government at this time was the conclusion of the Korean-American Treaty in 1882. The United States had taken the initiative after learning of Korea's treaty with Japan, but there were serious obstacles to be overcome. On the one hand, the U.S. failed to secure Japan's good offices, while the Korean side was compelled to proceed with caution in the face of the strident movement "to reject heterodoxy (Christianity and other Western values) in defense of orthodoxy (Confucianism)," mounted nationwide by chauvinist Confucian literati to block any Korean rapprochement with the West. Consequently, the Korean king asked Li Hung-chang to mediate the treaty, a role the Chinese statesman was happy to undertake—for such an agreement would not only provide a U.S. counterweight to Russian pressures but also would undercut Japan's monopolistic position in the Korea trade. The terms of the treaty, then, were worked out in Tientsin between Li Hung-chang and the American negotiator, Commodore Robert W. Shufeldt. The resulting "Corean-American Treaty of Amity and Commerce" was signed at Inch'ŏn on May 22, 1882.

The treaty was the first Korea had signed with a Western power. Although it was an unequal treaty typical of the age of imperialism, it featured three provisions that sought to meet Korea's interests and needs. First, the United States promised to provide its "good offices" to Korea in the event of a threat from another power. By this clause Korea understood an American commitment to come to Korea's aid under whatever circumstances. Another provision fixed import tariffs on articles for daily use at 10 percent *ad valorem* and 30 percent on luxury goods. These relatively high tariff rates were obviously in Korea's interest, since they would serve to protect Korea's infant industries while at the same time yielding badly needed revenue. Thirdly, the U.S. gave an explicit pledge to abandon its extraterritorrial rights when "the Korean statutes and judicial procedures could be reformed in conformity with those in the United States." In addition, the conspicuous omission of any provision regarding the propagation of Christianity made the agreement less objectionable to the traditionalist Confucian diehards.

Korea and the United States exchanged instruments of ratification in Seoul in May 1883, and it was reported that the Korean king "danced for joy" when the first U.S. minister to Korea arrived. In 1883, an eight-man diplomatic mission was dispatched to the United States under Chief Envoy Min Yŏng-ik and Deputy Envoy Hong Yŏng-sik. In addition to the general aim of cementing Korean-American ties, the mission's more specific objective was to obtain American advisers, teachers, and loans. The mission met with President Arthur in New York and made an extensive tour of modern facilities in major cities of New England. One mission member, Yu Kil-chun, remained in the U.S. as a student at the Governor Dummer Academy in Massachusetts— the first Korean to study in the United States. Back in Seoul, several members of the mission, including Hong Yŏng-sik and Sŏ Kwang-bŏm, became champions of radical reform and leaders of the Enlightenment Party.

The U.S. treaty was followed by generally similar agreements with Britain (1883), Germany (1883), Italy (1884), Russia (1884), France (1886), and Austria-Hungary (1889). Among these, the Korean-British Treaty became the standard for assessing customs duties for all imported goods, because of its relatively low rates, while the Korean-French Treaty contained an ambiguously phrased clause permitting the propagation of Christianity in Korea.

The strong undercurrent of anti-foreignism continued to grow while the government pursued its policy of enlightenment. The movement "to reject heterodoxy in defense of orthodoxy" was its most virulent expression. The conceptual basis for "rejecting heterodoxy" was that Chu Hsi's Neo-Confucianism was the sole valid system of belief; thus civilizations based on any other ideology must be kept from Korean shores. This belief was held most strongly by those Neo-Confucian literati, particularly outside the capital, who did not actually participate in governmental affairs. It was inevitable that these worthies would react with unmitigated hostility toward most reform measures introduced by the proponents of "enlightenment."

By 1881, these guardians of Chosŏn's traditional values were so outraged that they came to look upon the Taewŏn'gun, whose policies they earlier had abominated to the point of securing his ouster from political power, as someone around whom they might rally. Taking advantage of the situation, the Taewŏn'gun made plans for a comeback. His first scheme, in 1881, was to replace Kojong with another of his sons, and then proceed to remove from office the advocates of enlightenment. The plot became known, however, and only the Taewŏn'gun's status as the father of the reigning monarch saved him from official investigation and, no doubt, severe punishment.

The eruption that then ensued was the Soldiers' Riot of 1882 (*Imo Kullan*). The elite Special Skills Force, established the previous year, had been regarded with special favor by Kojong, and it was assumed that the traditional military units would soon be scrapped entirely. Treatment of the old-line units had worsened, and for some thirteen months the troops had not received their pay and rations. At this point, several transports arrived carrying tribute grain from the Chŏlla region, and it was decided to use these supplies first to pay out the arrears to the soldiers. But depot clerks of the Tribute Bureau, with an eye to personal profit, adulterated the rice rations with chaff. When the infuriated soldiers assaulted the ration clerks, the director of the Tribute Bureau, Min Kyŏm-ho, had the ringleaders arrested and sentenced to death.

Thus further outraged, the soldiers stormed Min Kyŏm-ho's house on July 23, forcing him to flee to the palace and Queen

Min's protection—for his older brother was the queen's adoptive brother. The soldiers then appealed to the Taewŏn'gun in the hope of gaining his support. Although outwardly he offered only soothing words, the Taewŏn'gun proceeded to plot secretly with the leaders of the riot, and instructed his own trusted aides to direct their actions. The soldiers now seized weapons from the government armory, attacked the prison where their comrades were held, and freed them. Then they murdered the Japanese training officer and descended in force on the Japanese legation. The Japanese minister, Hanabusa Yoshimoto, barely escaped with his staff, but the legation building was burned to the ground. The next day, the rioting soldiers invaded the palace premises and killed Min Kyŏm-ho. They tried to find Queen Min for the same vengeful purpose but she managed to hide and escape unharmed in the melee.

Faced with this perilous situation, Kojong had no choice but to bring his father back into the palace, and an edict was issued ordering that henceforth all governmental matters be submitted to the Taewŏn'gun for decision. Thus, once again the Taewŏn'gun could rule as he pleased. At the same time, the riot subsided. Granting the demands of the soldiers, the Taewŏn'gun dismantled the Special Skills Force and abolished the recently created Office for the Management of State Affairs. The initial efforts to institute a policy of enlightenment had come to naught.

The Taewŏn'gun's return to power was a victory for proponents of a reactionary isolationist policy. His triumph was short-lived, however, for both Japan and China intervened in Korea's affairs. Hanabusa returned with powerful army and navy escorts, prepared to press forward with harsh demands for reparations for damages suffered during the riot. But the military show of force he likely had intended soon became out of the question, because Chinese military contingents had arrived on the scene in greatly superior numbers.

Ch'ing China was alarmed by Japan's dispatch of armed forces to Korea, and with the approval of Korean emissaries in Tientsin, a force of 4,500 men immediately was dispatched under the command of General Wu Ch'ang-ch'ing. This constituted the first instance of Chinese military intervention in Korea since the

Manchu attack in 1636. What the Chinese sought to do, of course, was to use this opportunity to restore China's position of supremacy in Korea that had been undermined in recent years by Japan. Entering Seoul, General Wu stationed Chinese soldiers at strategic points in the capital, then seized the man responsible for the rioting and its consequences, the Taewŏn'gun, and sent him under secure escort to Tientsin. China's abduction of the Taewŏn'gun on August 26 brought a swift change in Japan's high-handed attitude. Japan was not prepared to confront the Chinese military, but it was now possible to reopen negotiations with Korea and to quickly secure a favorable settlement. Most significantly, the resulting Treaty of Chemulp'o (Inch'ŏn), signed on August 30, 1882, gave Japan the right to station a company of troops to guard the Japanese legation in Seoul.

With a strong military force firmly entrenched in Seoul, the Ch'ing government began to interfere boldly in Korea's internal affairs, claiming the authority to do so on the basis of the traditional suzerain relationship. The Min family, the dominant force in the Korean court, expediently adopted a pro-Chinese stance and looked to China for support in dealing with Korea's many vexing foreign relations problems. In response, the Chinese recommended the appointment of two special advisors on foreign affairs, a Prussian diplomat, Paul G. von Möllendorff, who had served in the Chinese maritime customs, and the Chinese diplomat Ma Chien-ch'ang. As the two advisers took up their posts another administrative reorganization was effected, this time creating two offices to plan and coordinate Korea's self-strengthening measures at the highest level: one for handling foreign affairs and so known simply as the Foreign Office, and another usually referred to as the Home Office to deal with internal matters. With regard to the military establishment, a Capital Guards Command was created with Four Barracks Commands under it. The new force was trained along Chinese lines by Yüan Shih-k'ai, who served under General Wu as the "chief of the military secretariat and concurrent associate director of Korean military affairs."

The Ch'ing government also sought to expand Chinese economic interests in Korea with a view to offsetting the growing influence of Japanese merchants. On the heels of its armed intervention China imposed on Korea a set of Regulations for Private Maritime and Overland Trade, whereby Chinese merchants obtained the right to reside, conduct business and to travel freely within Korea. Under the terms of the Regulations, China also dispatched a High Commissioner of Trade whose task it was to promote Chinese commercial penetration into Korean markets.

The Enlightenment Party's Abortive Reform

As knowledge of the outside world spread, in spite of intense reaction and resistance against it, what Koreans call "enlightenment thought" (*kaehwa sasang*) began to exert a powerful influence on the *yangban* officialdom. Prominent political figures, such as Kim Hong-jip, Kim Yun-sik, and Ŏ Yun-jung, as well as members of the royal consort family like Min Yŏng-ik, who led the Korean mission to the United States in 1883-1884, supported enlightenment policies. These men, however, favored a gradualist approach and, moreover, they wished to carry out their plans with the aid of Ch'ing China. They believed that Korea must preserve its traditional values while at the same time mastering Western technology—a concept sometimes encapsulated as "Eastern ways, Western machines." In contrast, ambitious men such as Kim Ok-kyun, Pak Yŏng-hyo, Sŏ Kwang-bŏm, and Hong Yŏng-sik—*yangban* officials whose advance was blocked by the Min faction's control over appointments to high positions—pushed for rapid change. The reform ideas espoused by men such as these had been influenced by Pak Kyu-su and Yu Hong-gi, a learned figure from a leading *chungin* lineage. The appeal of such ideas transcended social class divisions, as progressive thinkers now banded together under the banner of enlightenment and searched for ways to bring about reform.

Firm believers in the principle of equality, the Progressives (as they sometimes are called) sought to abolish class distinctions, reform the political process by following the model of Japan's Meiji Restoration, and achieve genuine national independence for Korea by ending China's interference in Korean affairs. They believed that their goals could be achieved only by extraordinary measures, and they hoped to obtain foreign support for their plans. Although few in number, the Progressives were a conspicuous element in the politics of the time and were referred to as the Enlightenment Party, or the Independence Party.

The Progressives first became active after the Soldiers' Riot of 1882, when Pak Yŏng-hyo was sent as a special envoy to Japan, accompanied by Kim Ok-kyun and Sŏ Kwang-bŏm. Because of their knowledge of the outside world, these men won the confidence of King Kojong and, as their influence grew, succeeded in winning royal approval for a number of reform measures. For example, it was in response to their proposals that an Office of Culture and Information was created in 1883, where a thrice-monthly gazette, the *Hansŏng Sunbo,* was published. Also, about forty students were selected and sent to Japan to study military and technical subjects; a Postal Administration was established to provide modern postal service; and a modern army unit was formed at Kwangju near Seoul (although opposition from the Min clique quickly led to its dissolution). Aware of the importance of diplomacy for the preservation of Korea's independence, the Progressives took every opportunity to cultivate contacts with foreign representatives, particularly members of the American legation.

The Progressives had earned the enmity of the Min clan faction, however, and could not secure appointments to pivotal positions. Japan's attitude toward them, too, became decidedly cool, and when the Progressives asked for a loan to meet the cost of the new army unit and other planned reforms, Japan refused. Thus, despite their desire to bring about rapid reform, in the end they were able to effect only a few real changes. Before long, then, the Progressives became ready to consider taking whatever extreme steps might be necessary to put their policies into effect. They seem to have begun to lay their plans in 1883, around the time Kim Ok-kyun went to Japan in an attempt to secure a loan of three million yen. His efforts to obtain the loan, which was essential to his plans, were unsuccessful, but when he returned home he brought gunpowder back with him.

In 1884, hostilities broke out between France and China over Vietnam, and the Progressives viewed this as an opportunity to drive the Chinese presence out of Korea. They rushed ahead with a detailed plan for a coup and succeeded in recruiting Sŏ Chae-p'il, who had just returned from study at a Japanese military academy, into the core group of conspirators. They also tried, but in vain, to secure support for their plan from the American legation in Seoul. In the meantime, however, Japan's attitude toward the Progressives had changed, and the Japanese minister, Takezoe Shin'ichirō, promised that in the event of a coup the Japanese legation guards in Seoul would render assistance. The Progressives' plans were now complete. It was a serious miscalculation, however, to allow the fate of the enterprise to hinge on the support of less than 200 Japanese troops when, even after the withdrawal of some contingents, there were at least 1,500 Chinese soldiers stationed in Seoul.

The ill-starred Coup d'Etat of 1884 (*Kapsin Chŏngbyŏn*) took place on December 4, 1884. The conspirators chose a banquet in celebration of the opening of the new Postal Administration, hosted by its director, Hong Yŏng-sik, as the occasion for their coup. The guests of honor were various foreign diplomats, and the commanding officers of the Four Barracks Commands also had been invited. The plan was to set fire to the nearby detached palace in An'guk-tong in order to create confusion, dispose of the four commanders, and then to seize the person of the king. Although things did not go as planned at the banquet hall, Kim Ok-kyun and his cohorts rushed to the palace, falsely told the king that the Chinese troops had created a disturbance, and asked him to summon the Japanese legation guards for protection. After escorting the king to the Kyŏngu Palace, a site better suited to defense against attack, they summoned the Barracks commanders (who held the authority to call out the troops) and other senior officials of the conservative faction, killing them one by one as they arrived at the palace gate. Returning finally to the Ch'ang-dŏk Palace, they promulgated a fourteen-point reform program.

In this document the reformers called for the immediate repatriation of the Taewŏn'gun from China, termination of Korea's tributary ties to China, curtailment of *yangban* privileges, appointment of officials on the basis of merit, central control of fiscal and military administration, and the concentration of decision-making power in a state council. In short, they aimed to establish an independent and efficient modern state with an egalitarian social order, to replace the oligarchic, *yangban*-centered sociopolitical structure of the Chosŏn dynasty.

Even before their reform measures were made public, however, on December 6 Chinese troops went into action and the fate of the Progressives was sealed. In the meantime, the Japanese minister reneged on his promise of military support. Kim Ok-kyun and eight fellow conspirators accompanied the retreating Japanese legation guards and escaped to Japan, while the others chose to remain behind and die at the hands of the Chinese soldiers. Minister Takezoe set fire to his legation building and joined in the flight. In addition to the intended victims, over one hundred eighty people, including thirty-eight Japanese and ten Chinese, had lost their lives.

The coup itself had lasted a mere three days, but its ramifications affected Korea's increasingly parlous foreign relations for a decade or more to come. The Korean government accused Takezoe of wrongful interference in Korea's internal affairs and demanded that he be held fully accountable. For its part, the Japanese government knew that Takezoe's conduct was improper but nevertheless tried to sidestep this issue. Thus the chief Japanese delegate to the ensuing talks, Foreign Minister Inoue Kaoru, sought a solution that would ensure appropriate redress for Japanese losses while evading the question of responsibility for the violent incident. The resulting agreement contained provisions for indemnities to the Japanese victims as well as compensation for the cost of rebuilding the Japanese legation.

The failed coup represented a major setback for Japan's forward policy in Korea, and so the Japanese aim now became to salvage what it could of the situation. To this end, Japanese leaders proposed a simultaneous withdrawal of Chinese and Japanese troops from the peninsula. Japan's leading statesman, Itō Hirobumi, went to China to discuss the matter with his Chinese counterpart, Li Hung-chang, and the resulting Convention of Tientsin, signed April 18, 1885, resolved the issue. The agreement stipulated that both nations withdraw their troops from Korea within four months of its signing; that neither signatory send military instructors to Korea; and that, should either party decide to send troops to Korea in the future, it notify the other of this intention in advance.

Although the Convention of Tientsin removed foreign troops from Korean soil, it did not fully remove constraints on the Korean government's sovereign freedom of action. On the contrary, China intensified its intervention in Korean affairs by appointing an all-powerful resident agent in Seoul. In October 1885, Li Hung-chang selected Yüan Shih-k'ai to be "Director-General Resident in Korea of Diplomatic and Commercial Relations," and assigned him the mission of preventing any future political disturbance or diplomatic development harmful to Chinese interests. It was China's further intention to promote Sino-Korean trade by having Yüan use his dominant influence to destroy the monopolistic position Japanese traders had come to hold in the peninsula.

During his decade-long tenure in Seoul, Resident Yüan Shih-k'ai succeeded in significantly raising the level of Chinese commercial activity in Korea, at the expense of Korean as well as Japanese merchants. By interfering in Korean domestic politics, moreover, he dealt a serious blow to Korea's enlightenment and self-strengthening movement. First of all, he crippled the movement's leadership by forcing the removal of reform-minded officials such as Kim Hong-jip, Kim Yun-sik, and Ŏ Yun-jung and by supporting the more conservative pro-Chinese members of the Min faction, who possessed neither zeal for reform nor concern over China's infringement on Korea's independence. Secondly, Yüan sought to block any development that might foster enhanced nationalist sentiments among the Korean people or that might otherwise pose a potential threat to China's suzerain position in Korea. To this end, he tried to limit Korean diplomatic and cultural contacts with the non-Chinese world, discouraged the development of capitalistic economic enterprise, and even sabotaged Korean attempts to reform the military system. Consequently, almost all of the enlightenment projects launched by King Kojong and his reformist officials in the early 1880s had to be abandoned and the few scattered reform projects that the king was able to initiate with American assistance, including the Royal Academy in 1886 and the Military Training School in

1888, were short-lived. In sum, the decade of Yüan's residency was a dark age for the Korean enlightenment movement.

While China was striving to consolidate its dominant position in the peninsula, a new power appeared on the Korean scene. After the conclusion of a treaty between Korea and Russia in 1884, Karl I. Waeber was stationed in Seoul as the Russian representative. An able diplomat, he paid frequent visits to the court in an effort to create a pro-Russian force in the government. In reaction to China's excesses, pro-Russian sentiment in fact gradually began to appear among Korean leaders—a development given further impetus by von Möllendorff, the foreign affairs adviser China had recommended to the Korean government. Von Möllendorff believed that Chinese and Japanese influence in Korea needed to be balanced by that of a third power, and to that end he worked to build a Russian presence. The king and queen, too, began to lean toward an anti-Ch'ing, pro-Russian policy, and rumors spread in early 1885 and again in mid-1887 that they had reached a secret agreement with Russia.

Not only China but England too was aroused by the inroads of Russian power in Korea. In confrontation with Russia along the length of its southern perimeter, England could not look lightly upon Russia's southward advance into the Korean Peninsula. Accordingly, England dispatched a naval force and attempted to counter the Russian advance by occupying Kŏmun-do (Port Hamilton), a strategic island off the southern coast of Chŏlla province, in April 1885. England's intention to frustrate Russian designs thus was evident, and alarmed Russian authorities made it ominously clear to the Korean government that the English action would not be tolerated. When at the same time Russia warned China that it too would occupy Korean territory, Li Hung-chang interceded. After nearly two years of negotiations, England withdrew its forces from Kŏmun-do early in 1887, first obtaining a Russian pledge to respect the inviolability of Korean national territory. The Kŏmun-do Incident had revealed that Korea was not the arbiter of its own destiny, but that its fate would be decided by outside powers pursuing their particular selfish interests.

China's initial response to Korea's tilt toward Russia in 1885 was to repatriate the xenophobic Taewŏn'gun as a means of promoting anti-Russian sentiment among Korean leaders. Presently, too, von Möllendorff was replaced as foreign affairs adviser by an American, Owen N. Denny. China also put the Korean Maritime Customs Service, which owed its inception in 1883 to von Möllendorff, under the supervision of the Imperial Chinese Maritime Customs Service. Unexpectedly, however, Denny too undermined the Chinese cause in Korea during his five-year tenure from 1886 to 1890. He helped Korea enter into treaty relations with France in 1886, he played a key role in bringing about a Russo-Korean Overland Trade Agreement in 1888, and he openly criticized the unwarranted interference of Yüan Shih-k'ai in Korean internal affairs. Acting on Denny's advice, moreover, King Kojong attempted to shore up Korea's fragile independence by establishing a permanent legation in Tokyo, in 1887, and another in Washington D.C. in 1888. The king's desire to establish a legation in Europe, however, was thwarted by Chinese meddling, and the Korean legations in Tokyo and Washington were unable to function properly because of incessant Chinese interference.

The Uprisings of the Tonghak Peasant Army

As Yüan Shih-k'ai tightened China's control over Korea, political power increasingly came into the hands of pro-Chinese members of Queen Min's lineage. The resulting Min oligarchy was notoriously incompetent and corrupt. Under their self-serving rule no progress could be expected in carrying out the wide-ranging reforms that the country so badly needed, while the nation's chronic financial difficulties rapidly worsened. The sale of offices was widely practiced, with those who purchased official positions customarily compensating themselves by gross peculation and extortion. The civil service examinations, held more frequently than ever, also had been corrupted so as to benefit members of the Min clan and those who associated themselves with it. Tax levies were increased by local and national governments until they reached three to four times the legal rates. In the meantime, extravagance, license, and debauchery were the order of the day at court. Popular discontent with the prevailing moral decadence and the inequities of the time was reflected in a well-known couplet: "As the drips of the candle on the banquet table fall, so do the tears of the people; and as music swells in merry-making, the outcry of the discontented masses becomes the more clamorous."

Life for the peasantry worsened under the Min oligarchy for a number of fundamental economic reasons. Special exemptions, abandoned fields, and tax evasion diminished the government's receipts, while developments subsequent to the opening of Korean ports, such as the exchange of diplomatic missions, the payment of indemnities to Japan, the acquisition of modern military weapons, and the construction of modern facilities, required new and heavy expenditures. These were paid for in part by customs receipts and foreign loans, but government activities still had to be financed primarily by tax collections from the farming villages. The burdens on the peasantry doubled or even tripled, as every pretext was used to impose fresh levies upon them, while the petty functionaries who collected the taxes resorted to increasingly harsh methods of extortion.

Meanwhile, Japanese economic penetration was further eroding Korea's rural economy. Japan had been the first foreign power to exploit Korea, and while Japan's economic position in the peninsula had suffered as a consequence of the failed 1884 coup, by the early to mid-1890s Japanese economic activity had reached astonishing levels. Japanese commercial establishments could be found in overwhelming numbers in each of the open ports, Inch'ŏn, Pusan, and Wŏnsan; in 1896, 210 of 258 such businesses were Japanese-run. Japan also dominated the carrying trade in Korean waters: of 1,322 merchant ships with a gross tonnage of 387,507 entering Korea's ports in 1893, 956 ships weighing a total of 304,224 tons were Japanese. Thus 72% of the vessels and over 78% of the gross tonnage came in under the Japanese flag. Japan's proportion of Korea's foreign trade volume loomed correspondingly large—over 90% of exports went to Japan while more than 50% of imports came from Japan.

Moreover, most ordinary Japanese traders in Korea were from the lower and depressed elements of Japanese society, with few scruples about getting rich quick at the expense of the Korean peasant. Taking advantage of the fact that the village people could buy Japanese cotton goods, kettles, pots and pans, farming tools, kerosene, dyestuffs, salt and other items only by selling their rice, they would advance money to the peasants for their purchases and then at harvest time claim part or all of the debtors' crops. The Korean government attempted to curtail Japan's economic penetration by banning the export of rice from certain provinces, but Japanese protests vitiated this effort.

As rural Korea continued to sink into destitution, the peasantry harbored a mounting hostility towards its exploiters, Korean and foreign alike. In the early 1890s, popular uprisings against the Min oligarchy began to break out in many areas, while armed bandits raided periodic markets and other rural commercial centers of goods distribution with alarming frequency. The seemingly endless patience of the stoical Korean peasant soon must find its limits.

After the execution in 1864 of its founder, Ch'oe Che-u, the Tonghak ("Eastern Learning") movement for a time could not operate in the open. But under its second leader, Ch'oe Si-hyŏng, in spite of great difficulties, the *Bible of Tonghak Doctrine* and the *Anthology of Ch'oe Che-u's Hymns* were compiled, thus systematizing the tenets of the new religion. At the same time, a network of Tonghak churches was successfully established, organizing members into "parishes" and creating a hierarchy of church leadership. The movement to bring new converts under Tonghak discipline owed its success to the peasantry's deep hostility toward the *yangban* class in general and the Min clan oligarchs in particular, as well as to its spirit of resistance to foreign intrusion.

As the Tonghak grew to be a force in Korean society, a vigorous campaign was launched to clear the name of the founder, who had been put to death under false charges. This effort took overt form first in 1892, when several thousand Tonghak members gathered at Sammnye in Chŏlla province [see map p.219] and made demands on the governors of Chŏlla and Ch'ungch'ŏng that Ch'oe Che-u be posthumously exonerated and that suppression of the Tonghak be ended. The governors lacked authority to accede to the former demand, but a pledge was made that local functionaries would be ordered to stop their persecution of Tonghak believers. Not satisfied, the assembled Tonghak followers resolved to petition the throne directly. This too failed, with the petitioners in fact being dispersed by force from in front of the palace gates.

Thereupon, the order was given for Tonghak members to assemble again, and more than 20,000 heeded the call to Poŭn in Ch'ungch'ŏng province in April 1893. There they proceeded to erect defensive barricades, hoist banners, and call for a "crusade to punish venal officials in the government and expel the Japanese and Westerners." The disconcerted authorities barely succeeded in dispersing the Tonghak throngs in Poŭn by threatening the use of force, while at the same time soothing them with further promises. But this proved to be only a momentary peace. The Tonghak movement had become distinctly political, aiming at the overthrow of the Min oligarchy and at driving out all foreign intruders. And in the spring of 1894, an expanded and better organized Tonghak movement erupted into a large-scale armed peasant uprising.

The spark that inflamed the peasantry to the point of open rebellion was a local but typical case of venal exploitation and cruel treatment of the peasant population by a *yangban* magistrate, in this instance in Kobu county of Chŏlla province. The enraged people of Kobu had petitioned repeatedly for redress of their grievances, but to no effect. At this point, under the leadership of Chŏn Pong-jun (1853-1895), a Confucian village teacher who recently had become the head of Kobu county's Tonghak parish, the peasants occupied the county office, seized weapons, distributed illegally collected tax rice to the poor, and then destroyed a new reservoir built with their own forced labor. When news of the incident reached the government, a special investigator was dispatched to Kobu, but he arbitrarily charged the Tonghak with responsibility for the uprising, imprisoning some Tonghak members and summarily executing others. Furious at this added injustice, the peasants rallied around Chŏn Pong-jun and other local Tonghak leaders, and launched an armed insurrection.

Peasants from all surrounding areas joined with the Tonghak

forces, swelling its ranks to some several thousands. They tied multicolored cloths around their heads and waists, and armed themselves with the few rifles, swords and lances they had seized, but mostly with bamboo spears and cudgels. After occupying Kobu, they paused to group themselves into battle formations. On April 26, 1894, Chŏn Pong-jun assumed overall command and on his banner in large letters inscribed the exhortation to "sustain the nation and provide for the people." Chŏn then issued the following four-point manifesto:

(1) Do not kill the [innocent] people; do not destroy [the people's] properties.
(2) Fulfill the duties of loyalty [to the sovereign] and filial piety [to parents]; sustain the nation and provide for the people.
(3) Drive out and eliminate the Japanese barbarians and thereby restore the Way of the [Confucian] Sages.
(4) Storm into the capital in force and thoroughly cleanse [the government of] the powerful families—so as to strengthen [Confucian] moral relationships, to rectify names and roles, and to realize the teachings of the Sages.

In short, the Tonghak intent was to destroy the corrupt Min oligarchy then in power and drive the Japanese from Korean soil. Their political program, however, smacked of conservatism: they wished to restore the Confucian moral and political order which had been eroded by the influx of modern Western and Japanese culture following the opening of the country. Like the Neo-Confucian literati of the early 1880s who waged the campaign "to reject heterodoxy in defense of orthodoxy," Chŏn Pong-jun hoped that the Taewŏn'gun, a xenophobe and mortal enemy of the Min faction, would regain power and carry out needed reforms, but within the strictures of Chosŏn's long Confucian tradition.

Now massed in battle array, the Tonghak army first crushed government troops sent from Chŏnju in a battle in Kobu county, and went on to seize control of a number of counties of southern Chŏlla [see map p. 219]. The government meanwhile dispatched an elite battalion of about 800 men from the capital garrison, but by the time it reached Chŏnju its numbers had been reduced to half by desertions. Despite superiority in weapons and the time-

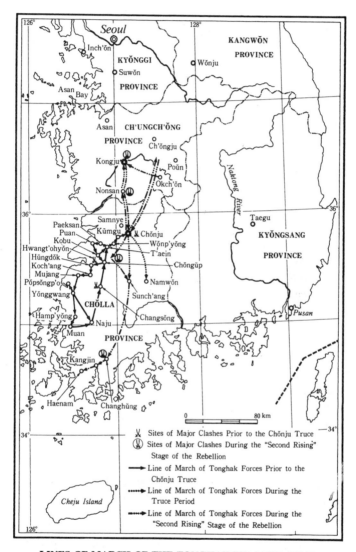

LINES OF MARCH OF THE TONGHAK PEASANT ARMY

ly arrival of reinforcements, the government force was routed by the confident and spirited Tonghak soldiery. The Tonghak army then pushed north against virtually no resistance and captured Chŏnju, the capital of Chŏlla province, on May 31.

In panic, the government hastily appealed to China for military support. China's response was immediate, and within a month a sizeable force had landed at Asan Bay. Japan, however, also sent troops to Korea, with the result that the two powers faced each other in an increasingly tense confrontation. Convinced that the Tonghak must be appeased by whatever means and its army of peasants dispersed, the Korean government proposed a truce. Regarding the government's willingness to negotiate as an opportunity to achieve Tonghak objectives without inviting foreign intervention, Chŏn Pong-jun agreed to disband his forces and to withdraw from Chŏnju on June 11. His condition was that the government implement a number of political and economic reforms, so as to end its chronic misrule.

As agreed, the Tonghak peasant troops withdrew from Chŏnju and returned to their homes. The Tonghak then proceeded to establish administrative offices in the fifty-three counties of Chŏlla province, with a headquarters in Chŏnju headed by Chŏn Pong-jun, and set about restoring order in the countryside and redressing local government abuses. On the whole, positions in the Local Administrative Centers went to those with knowledge of administrative matters, that is, the "fallen" *yangban* and county-level petty functionaries. They carried out social and economic reforms in cooperation with the government in Seoul, newly organized under the nominal leadership of the Taewŏn'gun on July 23. Their principal aims were to end the oppressive treatment of the Tonghak by the government, alleviate the economic burdens of the peasantry by rescinding the excessive taxes imposed during the Min clan's rule, abolish the *yangban*-centered class system, and protect Korea from further Japanese aggression by punishing those guilty of collusion with the Japanese. These reform measures were welcomed with great enthusiasm by the peasantry at large. As a result, the powerful impact of the Tonghak movement was felt not only in Chŏlla but in the other provinces as well, even as far north as P'yŏngan and Hamgyŏng.

The cease-fire, however, worked to the disadvantage of the Tonghak army, for the explosive situation created by the presence of both Chinese and Japanese troops in Korea soon led to the outbreak of the Sino-Japanese War in late July, 1894, whereupon Japan took virtual control over all internal security matters in Korea. Chŏn Pong-jun and his followers were outraged when they heard that the Japanese army had seized the Korean royal palace and that a pro-Japanese "puppet" regime was carrying out fundamental institutional reforms with little regard for Korean popular wishes. In October, after learning that the Japanese and pro-Japanese Korean officials had forced the Taewŏn'gun from power, the Tonghak decided to take up arms once again. They rose this time as an anti-Japanese "righteous army" (*ŭibyŏng*), with the specific purposes of driving out the Japanese invaders from Korean soil—in the time-honored tradition of the righteous armies during the Hideyoshi Invasion—and purging pro-Japanese officials from the government.

The Tonghak righteous army, however, was defeated in a series of battles near Kongju against government troops and a Japanese army contingent specially dispatched to crush them. The Tonghak fighters suffered thousands of casualties, while many of their leaders, including Chŏn Pong-jun, were captured. Chŏn and three comrades were tried by a special tribunal in Seoul presided over by a pro-Japanese minister of justice, Sŏ Kwangbŏm, and put to death on April 23, 1895—five days after the cessation of hostilities in the Sino-Japanese War.

The Tonghak uprisings of 1894 constitute the largest scale peasant insurrection in Korean history. The leaders of the movement, particularly Chŏn Pong-jun, were inspired by the traditional Confucian ideal of realizing the "Way of the Sages," not by any vision of a modern popular democratic society. But the Tonghak peasant army was infused with a strong patriotic ardor, a burning desire to protect the nation from foreign aggression, and with the egalitarian dream of abolishing the *yangban* class system. The Tonghak peasant movement, an incipient form of modern nationalism, had the potential to develop into a fullfledged social revolution, if only foreign intervention had not brought it so abruptly to an end. Ironically, the Tonghak reform program soon was to be realized, though only in part, by the pro-Japanese officials who carried out the Kabo Reform Movement during 1894-1896.

The Reform Movement of 1894-1896

Unable to suppress the Tonghak Uprising by itself, the Korean government had requested assistance from Ch'ing China. Chinese leaders, regarding this as an opportunity to strengthen China's position in Korea, dispatched a force of 3,000 men, landing them at Asan Bay. In accordance with the terms of the Convention of Tientsin, China notified the Japanese government of its action.

Japan too saw an opportunity to expand its influence in Korea, an outcome it found attractive for a complex of reasons. The Japanese army desired to create a solid base on the continent before Russia could complete the construction of the Trans-Siberian Railway; Japanese businessmen were demanding protection from their Chinese competitors in Korea; and the Tokyo government badly needed a foreign war to divert public attention from the domestic political crisis created by an opposition-dominated Diet. Thus, under the pretext of protecting Japanese residents in Korea from the Tonghak insurgents, Japan landed 8,000 troops at In-ch'ŏn in early June. By the time the Japanese forces reached Korea, however, the Tonghak peasant army had dispersed of its own accord, leaving no legitimate reason for Chinese and Japanese troops to remain in Korea. Recognizing this, China proposed a joint withdrawal, but Japan was determined to take advantage of the situation to pursue its own expansionist ambitions. Accordingly, Japan suggested instead that the two powers jointly undertake to reform Korea's internal administration, arguing that only in this way could peace in East Asia be preserved. As Japan expected, China rejected the proposal as "preposterous" interference in the internal affairs of another nation, whereupon the talks became deadlocked and a clash between China and Japan became inevitable.

The Sino-Japanese War began with Japan's sudden seizure of the royal residence, Kyŏngbok Palace, on July 23, 1894. Japanese troops then engaged Chinese forces in a series of land and naval battles in and around Korea from late July, scoring impressive victories at P'yŏngyang and in a naval battle on the Yellow Sea in mid-September. By early October, Chinese forces had been completely driven out of Korean territory. The war ended in total Japanese victory on April 17, 1895, with the conclusion of a peace treaty at Shimonoseki.

In the first article of the Treaty of Shimonoseki, China acknowledged Korea's full independence from China, repudiating age-old Sino-Korean tributary ties. This meant that Korea had left the orbit of the Sino-centric world order for good. It did not mean, however, that Korea's independence was now secure, for Japan was not at all inclined to respect it. The treaty also called for China to cede the Liaotung Peninsula and Taiwan to Japan, revealing that Japan's territorial ambitions extended even to Manchuria and beyond. The Japanese desire to incorporate Korea and the Liaotung Peninsula into the Japanese empire, however, was for the moment foiled by the Russian-led Triple Intervention.

While preparing for war with China, Japan had demanded that the Korean government carry out internal reforms under Japanese auspices, as a first step toward gaining control over Korean governmental processes. The pro-Chinese Korean government, under the thumb of Resident Yüan Shih-k'ai, refused to yield to this pressure, demanding in turn that Japan withdraw its forces as a precondition to any reform. After seizing the Kyŏngbok Palace, however, the Japanese secured the ouster of the pro-Chinese Min government and the appointment of pro-Japanese, reform-minded officials, including Kim Hong-jip, Kim Yun-sik, Ŏ Yun-jung, Park Chŏng-yang, Yu Kil-chun, Cho Hŭi-yŏn, Kim Ka-jin, An Kyŏng-su, and Kim Hag-u, all of whom had been active in the enlightenment movement during the 1880s. In the meantime, the Japanese and the reformist officials worked together to coopt the Taewŏn'gun, the archenemy of the Min oligarchy and a hero among the Tonghak insurgents, as the nominal leader of the new government—with an eye to using his prestige in pacifying the Tonghak and in carrying out a series of sweeping reforms. The reluctant Taewŏn'gun agreed to collaborate only after securing a written affirmation from the Japanese legation in Seoul that Japan had no territorial ambitions in Korea. Then, on July 25, a special organ called the Deliberative Council (*Kun'guk Kimuch'ŏ*), composed originally of seventeen but later of twenty-three councilors, was created to inaugurate the historic Kabo ("1894") Reform (*Kabo Kyŏngjang*). By mid-August, the reformers were well entrenched as ministers or vice-ministers in the reorganized State Council (later named the Cabinet), which was headed by Kim Hong-jip, replacing members of the pro-Chinese Min oligarchy.

The Kabo Reform movement lasted for more than sixteen months, from July 1894 to February 1896—a period during which Japan dominated Korean politics as the victor in the Sino-Japanese War. The reform effort proceeded by fits and starts, reflecting the kaleidoscopic changes that occurred during this period in the political scene, when Korea experienced such wrenching events as the second uprising of the Tonghak peasant army in late 1894, the rise of a pro-Russian faction after the Triple Intervention in April 1895, and the assassination of Queen Min in October 1895.

The reform movement passed through three distinct stages of development. During the first stage, from July to October 1894, the Deliberative Council passed some 210 reform bills under the leadership of Kim Hong-jip and Yu Kil-chun with little interference from the Japanese. The second stage commenced in December 1894 when a "Coalition Cabinet," composed of the Kim Hong-jip and Pak Yŏng-hyo factions, was organized under the aegis of the new Japanese minister to Seoul, Inoue Kaoru. This cabinet stepped up the pace of the reform movement, seizing the initiative from the Deliberative Council. Pak and Sŏ Kwang-bŏm, leaders of the coup of 1884 who had now returned from long exile abroad, participated most actively during this period. The second stage came to an abrupt end on July 6, however, when Pak Yŏng-hyo lost power as a result of the resurgence of Queen Min and other anti-Japanese figures in Korean politics. The third stage of the reform began under the leadership of Prime Minister Kim Hong-jip and Home Minister Yu Kil-chun after the assassination of Queen Min on October 9, 1895, and lasted until February 11, 1896, when King Kojong fled to the Russian legation. Members of the Chŏngdong Club or the "American Party," including Pak Chŏng-yang, Yi Wan-yong and Yun Ch'i-ho, played important roles in this phase of the reform, along with like-minded associates such as Yi Sang-jae and Namgung Ŏk.

The officials who undertook the Kabo Reforms were the leading figures of the pre-1894 enlightenment movement in Korea. They had studied or lived in Japan or America and shared a common vision of modernizing Korea in emulation of Meiji Japan and the United States. Since about half of the members of the Deliberative Council were either *yangban* sons by secondary wives (*sŏja*) or belonged to the *chungin* class, they tended to be critical of traditional Chosŏn's *yangban*-dominated sociopolitical order. And there were also two Protestant Christians, Sŏ Chae-p'il and Yun Ch'i-ho, among the nominees to cabinet portfolios in mid-1895. Thus, the Korean reform officials shared a strong commitment to nationalism, egalitarianism, and modern capitalism, values fully reflected in the reform measures they adopted.

Some 660 reform documents were promulgated in the course of the reform movement. These included the 210 reform bills adopted by the Deliberative Council, a dozen royal edicts setting forth the goals of the reforms, including the fourteen-point "Great Plan" (*Hongbŏm*) promulgated by King Kojong in January 1895, and the eighty-eight point "Instruction" of the Home Ministry issued by Pak Yŏng-hyo in April 1895.

The first objective of the reform officials was to fully establish Korea's independence as a nation. Accordingly, they abolished the various privileges the Chinese enjoyed in Korea by abrogating the unequal agreements Korea had signed with Ch'ing China during 1882-1894. They forbade the use of the Chinese calendar in official documents, substituting a Korean dating method based on the year of Chosŏn's founding. They organized a modern Ministry of Foreign Affairs and made plans for establishing permanent legations in the capitals of Korea's treaty partners. Subsequently a Korean Independence Day (June 6) was celebrated for the first time and a temple was constructed for the ceremony that would elevate the Korean king to the status of "emperor." Meanwhile, efforts were made to imbue the Korean people with a sense of national identity and patriotism by using the Korean alphabet (*han'gŭl*) in major government publications and by teaching Korean history at all levels in the newly organized modern schools.

Secondly, the reform officials sought to transform the traditional political structure of Chosŏn into a cabinet-centered constitutional monarchy. After abolishing the State Council and Six Ministries, they established in December 1894 a Japanese-style Cabinet with seven ministries. In addition, they created a Royal Household Department to separate palace from state affairs, and a Privy Council whose main function, a nominal one, was "examining and certifying" enacted legislation. The real purpose of the Privy Council, however, was to provide a dignified haven for the many high officials the reformers were easing out of power. The traditional system of local administration also was thoroughly revamped, although not in the direction of granting greater local autonomy. To the contrary, the reformers were moved by two pragmatic considerations: the need to increase the power of the home minister in the central government and the desirability of replacing the local governors and magistrates of the *ancien régime* with their own men. Both these developments would serve to further their modernization effort.

A third major concern of the reformers was to develop a sound system of fiscal management and then to use the government's fiscal resources to create wealth for the country. One series of measures, then, concentrated fiscal authority in the Ministry of Finance (in part by depriving the palace of fiscal prerogatives it had hitherto enjoyed) and introduced a modern taxation system. The reformers, in addition, saw an important role for state capitalism in the development of modern industries and transportation networks under government auspices, while private capitalist ventures were facilitated by removing existing legal restrictions on the activities of merchants and artisans and by a variety of positive measures. Among the latter were the creation of a modern monetary system based on the silver standard, as well as of a modern banking system, and the standardization of weights and measures.

A fourth aim of the reformers was to improve Korea's internal security and external defense capabilities by organizing a modern police force and military establishment. Thus a Metropolitan Police Board was established in Seoul in late 1894 and, subsequently, plans were drawn up for modern police units in the twenty-three prefectural capitals and other major cities. At the same time a modern military training command was established and the old-style military units abolished. By late 1895, a new military system was created, comprising two Capital Guards Battalions in Seoul and four Local Garrison Battalions in P'yŏngyang, Chŏnju, Ch'ŏngju and Wŏnsan. And it was planned to open a Military Academy, an officers training school, in early 1896.

Fifth, a fundamental reform of the Korean educational system was carried out by abolishing the traditional government service examinations and establishing (or working out plans for) a number of modern elementary schools, high schools and colleges. In addition, the government sent some two hundred students to Japan for study, and entered into a contract with the American Presbyterian mission school in Seoul, the Paejae [Boys] School, to educate two hundred students annually in modern curricula, at government expense.

Sixth, the reformers introduced a modern judiciary system characterized by separation of the judicial and executive powers. Torture of criminal suspects and the extension of punishment to family members were banned. A system of modern courts was created and all judicial matters were placed under their jurisdiction. District courts were created at the lower level, with appellate jurisdiction assigned to high and circuit courts.

Seventh, social reform was a vital component of the sweeping changes enacted in 1894. The social status system was, in point of law, totally abolished. Class distinctions between *yangban* and commoners were eliminated, thus opening the ranks of officialdom to men of talent, irrespective of social background. The still existing institution of slavery was abolished, and the buying and selling of human beings was prohibited. Moreover, post-station attendants, actor-entertainers, the outcast *paekchŏng* and others similarly stigmatized were freed from their traditional lowborn status. These were momentous social reforms, signifying the demise, under law, of the *yangban*-dominated status structure.

In addition, legislation was enacted to do away with social evils and discriminatory practices. Early marriage was prohibited, the minimum age being set at twenty for men and sixteen for women. Widows of all social classes were allowed to remarry. Regulations governing adoption to continue family lines were revised to give sons of secondary wives the right to succeed their fathers. Sumptuary laws were changed to simplify regulations on modes of dress that had distinguished higher from lower ranks and differentiated *yangban* from commoners, and also to encourage the wearing of more practical clothing. Two final reforms of great symbolic significance were the adoption of the Western calendar and an order, enforced from late 1895, that the Korean male's traditional topknot be cut off.

The sweeping Kabo Reform enactments affected many vital aspects of the administration, economy, and social fabric of Korea, constituting a milestone in Korea's modernization process. Inevitably, however, the reforms were unpopular among various conservative elements of Korean society, especially because they were carried out under the sponsorship of the Japanese aggressors. Little wonder, then, that the reform movement encountered the bitter opposition of the conservative Taewŏn'gun, who went so far as to plot a military coup to destroy the pro-Japanese cabinet and replace the "weak-kneed" Kojong with his favorite grandson. In the initial stages of the Sino-Japanese War, the Taewŏn'gun had tried to turn the military situation against Japan by having the Chinese army, which had taken up positions in defense of P'yŏngyang, effect a pincers movement in concert with the Tonghak forces to the south of Seoul, which would again be called to arms for the purpose. Although the scheme was uncovered and came to naught, it nevertheless caused the Japanese considerable anxiety. Japan replaced its minister in Seoul with a prestigious senior statesman, Inoue Kaoru, who made use of the secret communication from the Taewŏn'gun to the Chinese—a document that had come into Japanese possession when their forces captured P'yŏngyang—to force the Taewŏn'gun to retire from the political scene. Inoue then directed the Japanese campaign to destroy the Tonghak "righteous army" in late 1894.

But after the Triple Intervention forced Japan to retrocede the Liaotung Peninsula, a prize Japan had won in the Sino-Japanese War, the situation underwent a dramatic change. Japan had been unable to withstand the Russian pressure, and a consensus arose among anti-Japanese Korean leaders that their country might be freed from Japanese domination if only Russian assistance were forthcoming. Queen Min and her kinsmen, whose power had been weakened by Japanese influence, eagerly supported the new policy of reliance on Russia to check Japan. When reports reached Queen Min that Pak Yŏng-hyo was plotting to force her removal as consort, she was able instead to drive him and his pro-Japanese cohorts from the government, in July 1895. Pak once again fled to Japan, and men of the pro-Russian faction now obtained ministerial appointments, creating a predominantly pro-Russian—and pro-American—government.

Japan naturally was loath to see the rise of Russian influence in Korea. Its policy, therefore, was aimed at eliminating the pro-Russian faction and the influence in the court wielded by Queen Min. In its desperation to restore its position of primacy, Japan was prepared to resort to any means. In the end, Inoue's successor as Japanese minister, Miura Gorō, masterminded a plot to eliminate Queen Min. The assassination was carried out in the very palace precincts on October 8, 1895. Fearing an outcry of condemnation from abroad, Japan recalled Miura and others involved in the heinous crime to stand trial in Japan, but eventually they were acquitted on grounds of "insufficient evidence."

The Kabo Reforms, carried out while the nation was in a state of shock following the murder of the queen as well as the destruction of the Tonghak "righteous army," aroused extreme popular outrage and opposition. The order for the cutting off of topknots was particular anathema, and cries were heard to "Cut off my head, but my hair—never!" The hatred of Japan was so intense that guerrilla bands, new "righteous armies," rose up throughout the country to wage an armed struggle against the Japanese troops still on Korean soil, as well as against the pro-Japanese reform officials. These bands usually were led by local literati, but sometimes by Neo-Confucian scholars of national reputation, such as Yu In-sŏk. In early 1896, the government made the agonizing decision to send most of the newly formed Capital Guards to suppress the guerrillas in rural areas. While these crack troops were fighting the local guerrillas, Yi Pŏm-jin, along with other pro-Russian and pro-American officials, succeeded in smuggling Kojong and his crown prince out of the palace, which had remained under the control of the pro-Japanese reformers, to the Russian legation. This dramatic turn of events, which took place on February 11, 1896, signaled a temporary end to Japanese dominance in the Korean Peninsula as well as the demise of the Kabo Reform Movement.

Chapter 14

Incipient Nationalism and Imperialist Aggression

The Independence Club

The king's flight to the Russian legation turned the political situation completely around. Pro-Japanese cabinet members, such as Kim Hong-jip and Ŏ Yun-jung, were murdered, while Yu Kil-chun and others fled to Japan. A cabinet was formed of pro-Russian and pro-American officials, which included such figures as Yi Pŏm-jin and Yi Wan-yong. The king remained in the Russian legation for about a year, bringing the government under strong Russian influence. Japanese employed by the reform government were dismissed, and a Russian financial adviser and military instructors were appointed in their place. A Russian language school and a Russian bank also were established. The behavior of the Russian adviser to the Ministry of Finance gave the impression that it was he who headed the ministry, and a variety of economic concessions were made to Russians and other Westerners.

As Russia gained special rights, other powers also demanded equal favors. The U.S. diplomat in Seoul, Dr. Horace N. Allen, was particularly active in seeking concessions for American businessmen. In July 1895, Allen succeeded in securing a franchise to operate a rich gold mine in Unsan in North P'yŏngan province for an American businessman, James R. Morse. Allen also helped other American businessmen obtain franchises to build the trolley lines, a city lighting plant, waterworks, and a telephone network in Seoul, in addition to the franchise to build the Seoul-Inch'ŏn railroad for Morse. (Morse later sold the franchise to a Japanese company in 1898.) Japan, England,

France, and Germany joined in the race for similar favors from the Korean government during this period, turning Korea into a "happy hunting ground for concessionaires."

The Korean people unanimously condemned the king's flight to a foreign legation and denounced the granting of economic concessions to foreigners. Their outrage crystallized in a campaign launched by the recently inaugurated Independence Club. In response, in February 1897, Kojong moved from the Russian legation to the Kyŏngun Palace (today's Tŏksu Palace) and in October he proclaimed to the world the establishment of the independent "Great Han [Korean] Empire." Korea thus formally became an empire and its monarch henceforth was referred to as emperor.

Seeing that Kojong and his top officials were prepared to rely on the support of foreign powers in the hope of preserving Korea's territorial integrity, many public-spirited Koreans attacked the government's misguided policy and fought dauntlessly to maintain the nation's true independence and freedom. The new intellectual class, men who had been exposed to Western liberalism, formed a variety of political organizations and struggled to secure the nation's independence and the "rights of the people." The Independence Club, the first of these organizations, was also the most active and effective.

The Independence Club (Tongnip Hyŏphoe) was founded on July 2, 1896 by Sŏ Chae-p'il (Philip Jaisohn), who had lived in exile in America since the abortive 1884 coup and now returned to Korea as an American citizen with a medical degree. Initially, the Club was headed by opportunistic reform politicians of pro-Western and pro-Japanese background, such as Yi Wan-yong and An Kyŏng-su, who had emerged as cabinet members during the Kabo Reform Movement. Since the Club's membership was completely open, so that anyone might join without need of recommendation or sponsor, the character of Club leadership gradually changed as increasing numbers of Seoul citizens became members. Since Club members criticized the government's policies, often harshly, politically sensitive higher-level officials, such as Yi Wan-yong, left the Club in early 1898. Constantly at odds with those in power, who hated him and the ends toward which he worked, Sŏ Chae-p'il was compelled to return to the United States in May 1898. The leadership of the Club thereupon fell to representatives of the new intelligentsia like Yun Ch'iho and Yi Sang-jae, who had been influenced by Western democratic thought through study or diplomatic service in Japan or the United States and had actively participated in the Kabo Reform Movement. The next rank of leaders was a group of incumbent government officials, including Namgung Ŏk and Chŏng Kyo, who might be characterized as Confucianist reformers. Other active Club participants included townsmen who directed trade associations, mine laborers and dock workers at the open ports, and students of modern schools. The youthful activist, Yi Sŭng-man (Syngman Rhee, 1875-1965), who had graduated from a missionary institution, the Paejae [Boys] School, figured prominently as a leader among younger members of the Club. Even some *paekchŏng* outcasts, who recently had been freed from their base social status, joined the Club and played conspicuous roles. Women formed their own organization, called the Ch'anyang Association, and supported the activities of the Independence Club.

The Independence Club originally was established to carry out two modest but symbolically important projects: first, to erect an Independence Gate on the recently razed site of the Yŏngŭn ("Welcoming Imperial Grace") Gate, through which envoys from China had been escorted; and second, to renovate the "Hall of Reverence for China," where Chinese embassies had been entertained, and to build there an Independence Hall and Independence Park. The announcement of these objectives evoked a warm response from the populace. Support and sizeable contributions came from the public as a whole and from the royal family and high government officials as well. Success seemed assured. The cornerstone laying ceremony for the Independence Gate was held in November 1896, and in May of the following year, the Independence Hall was completed.

As the Independence Club transformed itself into a citizens assembly, however, it went beyond such symbolic activities and began to initiate direct social and political programs. The Club gave first priority to the promotion of popular education through such means as a debating forum and the publication of a

modern newspaper. Several hundred Club members and spectators attended the debates, held each Sunday at Independence Hall.
The official organ of the Independence Club was the *Bulletin of
the Independence Club of Great Chosŏn*, published fortnightly.
An unoffical though more influential organ was a bilingual
newspaper printed in the native Korean script (*han'gŭl*) and
English, the *Tongnip Sinmun* or *The Independent*. Sŏ Chae-p'il
started this new paper, the first modern vernacular newspaper
in Korea, on April 7, 1896—that is, even before the Independence Club was formed. *The Independent* served as a vehicle for
the Western liberal ideas championed by the new intelligentsia.
At the same time, the daily *Hwangsŏng Sinmun* (*Capital Gazette*),
of which Namgung Ŏk was the first editor, served as a forum
for Confucianist reform elements within the Club.

The activities of the Independence Club were directed toward
three principal goals. The Club first of all wished to safeguard
the nation's independence in the face of external aggression. Needless to say, it condemned foreign interference in Korea's governmental processes; it also opposed the granting of economic
concessions and demanded that those already awarded be revoked. The Club urged Korean leaders to adopt an independent
and neutral foreign policy, favoring none of the rival powers seeking to advance their interests in the peninsula. Thus, partly as
a result of the activities of the Club, Russian advisers and military instructors were recalled, the Russo-Korean Bank was forced
to close, and the king left the Russian legation and took up residence in Tŏksu Palace.

Secondly, the Club sought to promote a self-strengthening
movement as a way of consolidating the achievements of the
Kabo Reform. Club members sought principally to establish
modern schools in every village, to build textile and paper mills,
and ironworks as well, and to develop a modern national defense
capability—all under the slogan of "Korea for the Koreans!"

Thirdly and most importantly, the Club initiated a democratic people's rights movement in order to increase popular participation in the political process. Asserting the right of the individual
to the security of his person and property, the rights of free speech
and assembly, the full equality of all people, and the doctrine

of popular sovereignty, the Club advocated the rights of the governed to participate in their governance. It sought to limit the autocratic power of the monarch and enhance instead the roles of the members of the Cabinet and the Privy Council. In October 1898, the Club organized an "assembly of officials and the people" at the Chongno intersection and adopted a six-point proposal directed toward these ends for submission to the throne. For the first time in Korea, the Club thus openly launched a movement for achieving political democracy within the framework of a constitutional monarchy.

The highlight of the Club's campaign for democracy was its November 1898 effort to convert the Privy Council, an appointive office at the highest level whose responsibilities had been left deliberately vague by the Kabo reformers, into a legislative body. Beginning in early 1898, the Club had openly advocated the need for a national legislature as a means of strengthening the bond between the government and the people. In November, it proposed that the Privy Council be reorganized into a quasi-legislature, with one-half of its fifty members appointed from among candidates elected by "public associations"—which meant the Independence Club alone "for the time being." Kojong and his conservative coterie reluctantly yielded to the Club's pressure and, on November 4, 1898, issued a new set of Privy Council regulations which were largely in accord with the Club's proposal. But this action proved to be no more than a delaying tactic to soothe public feelings while suppressive countermeasures were being readied. Presently, charging that the real aim of the Independence Club was to replace the monarchy with a republic headed by an elected president, the government ordered the Club's dissolution and arrested Yi Sang-jae and sixteen other Club leaders.

Club members immediately mounted a campaign demanding the release of those imprisoned, holding continuous mass protest meetings in the streets of Seoul day after day. As the crisis worsened, the government ordered the Imperial Association, a body of peddlers newly created as a tool of the government, to attack the demonstrators. After a bloody fight between Club supporters and the peddlers, Kojong relented once more and permitted the reestablishment of the Club. He also promised to act on the Club's proposal on the Privy Council. But when Kojong announced the formation of the new Privy Council at the end of November, it turned out to have twenty-nine representatives from the Imperial Association and just seventeen from the Independence Club—in addition to four incumbent government officials.

The reconstituted Privy Council, Korea's first attempted modern legislative assembly, survived only for about ten days. After it convened on December 16, Club members seemed to dominate the proceedings, thanks perhaps to their experience in parliamentary debate acquired through the Club's debating forums. They quickly succeeded in pushing through a resolution calling upon the government to recall Pak Yŏng-hyo and Sŏ Chaep'il from abroad and appoint them, along with nine others, to positions of responsibility in the government, to provide new leadership for the nation. This proved to be a fatal tactical blunder, made worse by the rumor that the Club intended to organize a new government under the supreme leadership of Pak Yŏnghyo. The irate Kojong reacted by ordering the "strict suppression" of the Club on December 26, for the second—and last—time. The government called in troops to clear the streets, banned further protest meetings, and imprisoned or otherwise punished the Club leaders. The patriotic efforts of the Independence Club to fundamentally reform the ailing dynasty thus came to an abrupt end by the close of 1898. Now lacking any external mechanism of restraint, Kojong's conservative government thenceforth deteriorated into a wanton autocracy of sycophantic opportunists surrounding a fickle ruler.

Japanese Aggression and the Annexation of Korea

After forcing Japan to retrocede the Liaotung Peninsula to China in 1895, Russia concluded a secret agreement with China and acquired the right to build the eastern end of the Trans-Siberian Railway through Manchuria. Next, Russia obtained twenty-five-year leases on Port Arthur and Talien (Dairen) and permission to link these two Manchurian ports by rail to the Trans-Siberian. Having thus solidified its position in Manchuria, Russia launched a powerful drive to penetrate into Korea.

Japan, more than any other nation, watched Russia's advance into East Asia with apprehension. Unprepared to oppose the Russians militarily, Japanese leaders for the time being concentrated on expanding Japan's economic interests in Korea, while looking ahead to opportunities for further aggressive military action.

The Japanese-Russian rivalry over Korea intensified following the outbreak in 1900 of the Boxer Uprising in China. Russia took advantage of the situation to send a large force into Manchuria. These troops were not withdrawn even after the uprising had been subdued, giving the distinct impression that Russia intended to remain in permanent occupation. This would constitute a grave threat not only to Japan but also to England, which remained in confrontation with Russia at points all across the Eurasian land mass. In consequence, in January 1902, Japan and England entered into the Anglo-Japanese Alliance, by the terms of which England's rights and interests in China were recognized by Japan in exchange for England's acknowledgment of Japan's special interests in Korea. The two countries further pledged to assist each other in the event either became involved in war against a third power.

Its position thus strengthened, Japan demanded that the Russian forces withdraw from Manchuria. Russia, however, reneged on a promise to do so and, moreover, in July 1903 a Russian force crossed the mouth of the Yalu and occupied the Korean river town of Yongamp'o, where they bought land and constructed housing. When Russia then formally requested the lease of a port area there, Japanese opposition compelled the Russians to back down, but they at least had achieved the opening of Yongamp'o as a trading port.

At this point, Russia and Japan entered into protracted negotiations in which each side insisted on major concessions from the other, but refused to offer much in return. Japan, for its part, was not prepared to abandon its designs on Manchuria even in exchange for Russian recognition of Japan's "preponderant" interests in Korea. In the end, unable to win all that it wanted through diplomatic means, Japan decided to seek a military solution, and, in February 1904, Japan carried out a surprise attack on the Russian installations at Port Arthur. The rivalry between the two powers now was to be resolved by war.

As war between Russia and Japan became imminent, Korea formally proclaimed its neutrality. Japan nevertheless sent troops into Seoul and by threat of force compelled Korea to sign an agreement Japan already had drawn up. This document contained the ritualistic provision that Japan undertook to respect the independence of Korea and the integrity of Korean territory, but it also required Korea to accept Japanese counsel with regard to improvements in governmental administration and authorized Japan to occupy strategic points throughout the country. A further agreement signed in August 1904 provided for Japanese or Japanese-named advisers to be installed in the strategic Korean ministries of foreign affairs and finance. (An American, Durham W. Stevens, was named as foreign affairs adviser. When Stevens returned to the U.S. in 1908 to praise the record of the Japanese Residency-General in Korea, he was assassinated in San Francisco by two Korean expatriates, Chang In-hwan and Chŏn Myŏng-un.) Subsequently, Japan also appointed advisers to the Korean ministry of defense and others to deal with police, imperial household, and educational matters—even though these were not stipulated in the agreement.

Contrary to expectations around the world, the Russo-Japanese War saw a succession of Japanese victories from beginning to end. With Russia ready to sue for peace, the U.S. president, Theodore Roosevelt, stepped in to mediate the terms. Dr. Allen, the U.S. minister in Seoul, urged his government to intervene in the Korean situation in order to block Japanese aggression. Roosevelt rejected this recommendation, taking the view that Japanese control of Korea was an appropriate means to prevent the further expansion of Russian power. Moreover, Roosevelt felt it was necessary to acquiesce in Japanese domination of Korea as a *quid pro quo* for Japan's recognition of U.S. hegemony in the Philippines. This understanding between the U.S. and Japan was contained in the secret Taft-Katsura Agreement of July 1905. England, too, in renegotiating the terms of the Anglo-Japanese Alliance in August 1905, acknowledged Japan's right to take appropriate measures for the "guidance, control, and protection" of Korea.

The Treaty of Portsmouth ending the Russo-Japanese War was concluded in September 1905, in this setting of international recognition of Japan's supremacy in Korea. Its most important provisions were Russia's acknowledgment that Japan possessed paramount political, military and economic interests in Korea, and Russia's pledge not to hinder Japan from, essentially, taking whatever action it deemed necessary in the peninsula. The treaty thus removed the last obstacle to Japan's domination of Korea. Japan could now proceed to make Korea its colony without any challenge or hindrance.

Having won recognition from Russia, England, and America of its special interests in the peninsula, Japan moved immediately to establish a protectorate over Korea. First, Japan attempted to rally public support for a protectorate treaty through a front organization that it created and financed, the Ilchinhoe ("Advancement Society"). The purpose of this charade was to create the false impression that a protectorate treaty was not a Japanese demand but rather a response to the wishes of the Korean people. But it no longer mattered what Koreans wanted. Japan sent its elder statesman, Itō Hirobumi, to conclude the protectorate treaty. Itō entered the palace with an escort of Japanese troops, threatened Kojong and his ministers, and demanded that they accept the draft treaty Japan had prepared. When the Korean officials refused, Prime Minister Han Kyu-sŏl, who had expressed the most violent opposition, was dragged from the chamber by Japanese gendarmes. Japanese soldiers then went to the foreign ministry to bring its official seal, which then was affixed to the document by Japanese hands, on November 17, 1905. Itō, who thus played the principal role in this Japanese act of naked aggression, was assassinated in 1909 by a Korean patriot, An Chung-gŭn.

The Protectorate Treaty of 1905 gave full authority over all aspects of Korea's relations with foreign countries to the Japanese foreign office. For this purpose, it provided for the appointment of a Japanese "resident-general" to a position directly under the Korean emperor. Although the wording of the treaty limited the authority of the resident-general "primarily" to matters relating

to diplomatic affairs, eventually Korea's entire internal administration would come under his control as well.

Kojong's opposition to the Protectorate Treaty was made public in an imperial letter published on February 1, 1906, in the
Korea Daily News (*Taehan Maeil Sinbo*), in which he stated that
he had not consented to the treaty and appealed for the joint
protection of the powers. The next year, when the Second Hague
Peace Conference was about to begin, Kojong secretly dispatched
a delegation to the Netherlands to expose the injustice done Korea
and to seek redress. Although the conference refused to seat the
Korean delegates or accept their petition, the world-wide publi-
city the Korean question consequently received created considerable international furor. In spite of this, Japan used the incident
as a pretext to further tighten its grip on Korea, demanding that
Kojong accept responsibility for the contretemps by yielding his
throne to the crown prince. When Kojong balked, the Japanese
indicated a willingness to allow his son to rule as prince regent,
and Kojong was thus tricked into relinquishing the throne. Sunjong, who was an imbecile, then became emperor in July 1907.

Not content with Kojong's abdication, Japan moved to put
Korea under a still harsher yoke. On August 1, 1907, a new agreement was signed giving the Japanese resident-general formal
authority to intercede in all matters of internal administration.
Japan now initiated a system of government by vice-ministers,
Japanese bureaucrats being installed in every ministry as the
second in command and in other strategic posts.

At that time in Seoul, there were about 3,600 Korean troops
in two infantry guards regiments and less than 400 men in mounted guards, artillery and transport units, while outside the capital
there were approximately 4,800 infantry soldiers in eight local
garrison regiments—a combined strength of barely 8,800. Even
so, immediately following the signing of the new agreement in
August 1907, Japan dissolved the entire remaining Korean army,
pleading fiscal stringency and claiming that it was a temporary
measure until a conscription system could be introduced. At this
point, lacking any capacity at all for self-defense, Korea became
a mere puppet, an empty shell of a nation.

The leaders of imperial Japan, who long had schemed to

annex Korea, could at last realize their ambition. In May 1910, Japan appointed General Terauchi Masatake, the war minister in the Japanese cabinet, as the new resident-general and explicitly entrusted to him the mission of effecting the planned annexation. While still in Tokyo, Terauchi secured an agreement yielding police power in Korea to Japan. Japanese gendarmerie forces then were increased by 2,000 men and given police functions. Immediately upon arriving in Seoul, Terauchi suspended the publication of Korean newspapers in order to prevent the public from learning what was taking place. Then, together with the Korean Prime Minister Yi Wan-yong, he worked out the terms of the annexation treaty, and finally, on August 22, 1910, he secured the prime minister's signature to it. For the moment, however, fearing the intensity of popular reaction against it, the Japanese did not make the treaty public. In order to prepare the ground for its announcement, Korean patriotic organizations first were dissolved and summary arrests of leading independence figures carried out. A week later, on August 29, 1910, Emperor Sunjong was forced to issue a proclamation relinquishing both his throne and his country. Thus the Korean nation, against the will of its people, was handed over to the harsh colonial rule of Japan.

Korean Resistance Against Japanese Aggression

Resistance to the Japanese aggression in Korea took many forms. First, there was the struggle of the Yi imperial house to restore its disintegrating sovereign power. The 1907 mission to The Hague was such an effort. Almost from the beginning, the emperor and his ministers had chosen to rely primarily on outside forces, seeking the support of one foreign power or another to check Japanese aggression. In the end, this policy only added to the aggressive forces with which Korea had to contend; it was not successful in securing the support Korea needed to preserve its independence.

Among the Confucian literati were those who resisted Japan in a way hallowed by tradition—offering memorials to the throne urging the adoption of a national policy of resistance. At times several hundred literati assembled at the palace gates to petition the throne for such a policy. But neither the monarch nor the government, already under the watchful eyes of the Japanese, was able to act on these pleas. In despair, a number of Korean officials chose suicide as the ultimate act of protest. Min Yŏng-hwan, for example, Kojong's military aide-de-camp, left an impassioned testament to the nation and took his life after hearing that the Protectorate Treaty had in fact been signed. Many other outraged officials—Cho Pyŏng-se, Hong Man-sik, Song Pyŏng-sŏn, and Yi Sang-ch'ŏl among others—followed Min Yŏng-hwan's example, while earlier martyred patriots included the Korean chargé d'affaires in London, Yi Han-ŭng.

There also were many Confucian literati who organized "righteous armies" and engaged in an active armed struggle against Japan. In 1905, soon after the signing of the Protectorate Treaty, Min Chong-sik organized a righteous army in Hongsŏng in Ch'ungch'ŏng province and fought against Japanese contingents. Ch'oe Ik-hyŏn and Im Pyŏng-ch'an likewise assembled forces in Sunch'ang, Chŏlla province, to fight against the Japanese. None of these acts of defiance in 1905 changed Japan's policy toward Korea, but they contributed to the formation of better-organized resistance forces in the years immediately ahead.

After 1907, soldiers from the disbanded Korean army joined those already in the field, and the righteous armies became both larger and more effective. On the day the army was dissolved in August 1907, the commander of the First Infantry Guards regiment, Pak Sŏng-hwan, committed suicide in mortification, while his officers and men took up their weapons and, supported by troops of the Second Infantry Guards regiment, engaged the Japanese occupation army in battle on the streets of Seoul. After their ammunition was depleted, the Korean troops retreated from the city to join forces with the guerrilla bands in the countryside. Garrison troops in the provinces also joined in the armed resistance against the Japanese. Most notably, the provincial garrison in Wŏnju took up arms under the leadership of Min Kŭng-ho and proceeded to inflict a series of defeats on the Japanese at Wŏnju, Ch'ungju, Yŏju, Ch'unch'ŏn and elsewhere in central Korea.

Hŏ Wi provides an example of still another dimension of the armed resistance struggle. He had formed a righteous army originally in 1896 but disbanded his force at the command of the king. He had then enjoyed a meteoric career in the central government before submitting a bitter anti-Japanese memorial and returning to his home in the Kyŏngsang province countryside. Now in 1907 he took up arms again, having received a secret message from Kojong enjoining him to do so. His activities were mainly centered in areas north and east of Seoul. Yi In-yŏng in Kangwŏn province; Yi Kang-nyŏn in the Kangwŏn-North Kyŏngsang area, his guerrilla band augmented by troops from the Andong garrison; and Sin Tol-sŏk in Kyŏngsang province were among other legendary leaders of guerrilla forces. Sin, along with Hong Pŏm-do of Hamgyŏng province, is particularly noteworthy as a non-*yangban*, a man of commoner origin, who nevertheless rose to command a righteous army.

The early righteous army forces had been moved by a fierce spirit of resistance against Japan, but they possessed neither military discipline nor weapons of any account. However, when the righteous armies were joined by soldiers disbanded in 1907, their ranks not only swelled in numbers but they acquired both the military organization and the weapons with which they could mount effective resistance. Min Kŭng-ho reputedly had several thousand men under his command and both Hŏ Wi and Yi Kang-nyŏn led over a thousand each. To be sure, none of the other guerrilla forces had the strength of more than a few hundreds, but these bands normally operated from mountainous areas, attacking Japanese garrisons and destroying railways and telegraph facilities. Supported by the populace and familiar with the local terrain, they were able to compensate for their deficiencies in manpower and weapons. The righteous armies were particularly active in Kyŏngsang, Kangwŏn, Kyŏnggi, and Hwanghae provinces, but they operated virtually nationwide. Korean guerrilla units in Kando in southeast Manchuria even crossed the Tumen River to harass Japanese garrisons in north Korea.

In 1907, Yi In-yŏng and Hŏ Wi brought together about 10,000 guerrilla troops from all over the country to attack the Residency-General headquarters in Seoul. Advance units were able to penetrate to within eight miles of Seoul's East Gate before being driven back with heavy losses. This one instance typifies the ardor and vigor, as well as the ultimate frustration, that characterized the struggle of the righteous armies against the Japanese.

Guerrilla activity reached a peak in 1908 but rapidly declined thereafter as the Japanese were able to mount large-scale and effective counterstrokes. Following the annexation, the scene of operations shifted to Manchuria and the Russian Maritime Province, and there the guerrilla soldiers became independence fighters and dauntlessly continued their war against Japan. According to official Japanese statistics, a total of 2,819 clashes occurred between Korean guerrillas and the Japanese army between 1907-1910, more than half of them in the peak year of 1908 alone. By 1910, more than 17,600 guerrilla fighters, including such commanders as Min Kŭng-ho, Hŏ Wi, and Yi Kang-nyŏn, had given up their lives in the struggle.

In the declining years of the Chosŏn dynasty, many organizations were formed with the purpose of raising the political and social consciousness of the educated class, especially in the cities. Believing that solutions to Korea's political and social problems were to be sought in the strength of the Korean people themselves, these organizations promoted programs for the edification of the people while championing the cause of protecting Korea's sovereign rights. The first such organization was the Korea Preservation Society, inaugurated in 1904. It came into being with the aim of blocking the Japanese effort to seize control for themselves over all Korea's state-owned land not under cultivation. Public opposition was aroused through a campaign of public lectures and pronouncements and succeeded in forcing Japan to withdraw its demand. Under the leadership of Yi Sang-sŏl, the Korea Preservation Society continued to grow and developed broader objectives. Before long, however, it was dissolved under Japanese pressure.

Many political and social movements of this period were concerned with issues related to internal institutional change, which was seen as a prerequisite to preserving national independence. The Society for the Study of Constitutional Government, organized in 1905 by former members of the Independence Club, was one such group, although it was best known, perhaps, for its struggle against the pro-Japanese Ilchinhoe.

In the pre-1905 milieu, the activities of political organizations such as these were anathema not only to Japan but to the Korean government as well, and before long a ban was placed on public political assembly in Seoul. When it became impossible to carry on political activities lawfully, social and cultural movements then arose, seeking to lay the foundation for the recovery of Korean independence by fostering the growth of a modern economy and by making educational opportunities available more widely among the Korean populace. The major organization with a program of this sort was the Korea Self-Strengthening Society, formed in 1906 as a successor to the outlawed Society for the Study of Constitutional Government. This organization led the opposition to Japan's demand for Kojong's abdication in the wake of the secret mission he had sent to The Hague, and in consequence it too was dissolved by the Japanese Residency-General. It soon reappeared as the Korea Association, however, and continued its social and cultural programs.

In 1907, the Association for Redemption of the National Debt was organized to conduct a campaign to repay the immense debts artfully forced upon the Korean government by Japan. The existence of these debts, it was widely believed, threatened the nation's independence, and so the notion that the national debt might be repaid through the united efforts of the Korean people gained immediate support throughout the country. The various Korean newspapers were particularly active in collecting what came to be called "pledges for the nation." Toward this common end, men donated the money they saved by giving up smoking, while women and girls responded by selling their ornamental hairpins and rings. Not surprisingly, the Residency-General looked upon this as an anti-Japanese movement and used every means to suppress it. False charges of embezzlement of contributions entrusted to the *Korea Daily News* were brought against its editor, Yang Ki-t'ak, and he was placed under arrest. Later, the charges were dropped and he was released, but the movement to redeem the national debt had been thwarted.

As both political and social movements came under further pressure from the vigilant Residency-General, Koreans finally resorted to clandestine activities. In 1907, the New People's

Association (Sinminhoe) was formed secretly by members of the press, military men, and businessmen, most of them Protestant Christians from northwest Korea, including An Ch'ang-ho, Yi Tong-hwi, Yang Ki-t'ak, Yi Sŭng-hun, and Yi Kap. The New People's Association promoted the development of modern industry and education by establishing a ceramics factory and by founding schools, while also making preparations for armed operations outside the country to promote the cause of Korean independence. The activities of the Association were brought to a halt in 1911 when a majority of the organization's directors was arrested in connection with the so-called "Korean Conspiracy Case."

The Korean press played a prominent role in fighting Japanese aggression in the last years of Chosŏn. On the day the Protectorate Treaty was signed in 1905, Chang Chi-yŏn, editor of the *Capital Gazette,* gave a detailed report of how the treaty came into being and inflamed public opinon with a scathing editorial, entitled "Today We Cry Out in Lamentation." To avoid Japanese censorship, still exercised on the basis of military security regulations put into effect during the Russo-Japanese War, Chang had the paper delivered free from house to house. When Japanese censorship tightened and newspapers lost the freedom to openly attack Japanese aggression, the English journalist Ernest T. Bethell joined Yang Ki-t'ak in founding the bilingual *Korea Daily News (Taehan Maeil Sinbo),* in 1905. Since it was controlled by an Englishman, and Japan and England were allies, the *Korea Daily News* was able to remain free of Japanese censorship. Over the entrance to the newspaper office a sign was hung proclaiming "No Entry to Japanese," and the paper proceeded to attack Japanese acts of aggression with impunity. The newspaper used the mixed Chinese-Korean script, but later it published a purely *han'gŭl* edition designed to reach a broader audience. The English language edition for foreign readers, the *Korea Daily News,* stunned the Japanese with the publication of Emperor Kojong's personal letter denying that he had approved the Protectorate Treaty and appealing for the protection of Western powers. The Japanese subjected Bethell to all sorts of harassment and even pressed charges against him in the British consular court.

Although the Englishman eventually felt compelled to sever his connection with the paper, the *Korea Daily News* continued to publish as before.

The next year, in 1906, Son Pyŏng-hŭi, O Se-ch'ang, and other leaders of Ch'ŏndogyo (the "Religion of the Heavenly Way," the new name for the Tonghak) founded the *Mansebo* (*Long Live [Korea] News*). The primary target of its attacks was the pro-Japanese Ilchinhoe. In 1909, the Korea Association began publication of the *Taehan Minbo* (*Korea People's Press*) which also set itself squarely against the Ilchinhoe.

Thus, the Korean press played a large part in raising the level of political consciousness of the Korean people prior to Japan's annexation of Korea. The first Japanese resident-general, Itō Hirobumi, once said that a single word in a Korean newspaper had greater power to move the Korean people than a hundred words from him. This is why, in 1907, the Residency-General enacted a law governing newspaper publication, by which the native Korean press was brought under strict control. After Korea's annexation in 1910, the only remaining organ that spoke for the Koreans, the *Korea Daily News,* was converted into a mouthpiece for the Government-General under the abridged name of *Maeil Sinbo* (*Daily News*). A Korean press, in any meaningful sense, for some years to come had ceased to exist.

Development of a Modern Nationalistic Culture

In 1886, the Korean government established a Royal Academy to provide education in the new knowledge from the West, and during the Kabo Reform Movement of 1894-1896 a new system of government schools was created, including primary and midddle schools, normal schools, and foreign language schools. But an even more meaningful contribution to the development of modern education in Korea was made by the numerous private schools, many of them founded by Protestant missionaries, that came into being from the later years of the nineteenth century. Private schools were founded in still greater numbers after Korea became a Japanese protectorate in 1905, a fact suggesting the close nexus in Korean minds between education and patriotic nationalist resistance to Japanese aggression.

The first modern private school was the Wŏnsan Academy founded in Wŏnsan in 1883. It was established by the county magistrate, a man of progressive views, in response to the request of the Wŏnsan Traders Association and other local residents. Three years later, in 1886, the Paejae [Boys] School and several other private institutions were founded by American Protestant missionaries. Then, after 1905, private schools were established by Koreans in almost unending succession. In the few years before Korea fell completely under Japanese colonial domination, some 2,250 private schools were founded, a great many in the northern half of the country. Meanwhile, with the founding of the Ihwa (Ewha) [Girls] School by American missionaries in 1886, Korea's first educational institution for women came into being. Subsequently, several other girls schools were established under Korean auspices, and these schools performed a vital role in freeing Korean women from their subservient position in traditional *yangban* society.

The curriculum in these private schools emphasized the new Western learning and thought. There were courses in history, geography, politics, and law, as well as arithmetic and algebra. The schools not only disseminated the new learning but also served as hotbeds of the nationalist movement. Debates, oratorical contests, and campaigns of various sorts were held under school sponsorship, fanning the patriotic ardor of the students. Conservative elements in Korean society remained convinced of the unworthiness of the new-style education, but the private schools nevertheless continued to flourish, wrapped in a mantle of growing nationalist fervor.

Japan was not at all pleased with this educational phenomenon. Accordingly, a law was enacted during the Residency-General period stipulating that private schools be operated only with government sanction and that only authorized textbooks be used. As a result, many private schools were forced to close. After the annexation, Japan's educational policy became even less favorable for Korean schools. Nevertheless, some private schools managed to survive even under Japanese colonial rule, continuing to serve as key instruments of Korean national education and as a locus of Korean nationalist activity.

Christianity, Protestantism in particular, exerted a tremendous influence on political and educational activities in Korea from the early 1880s. In 1884, Dr. Horace N. Allen, an American Presbyterian missionary, arrived in Korea, followed by Horace G. Underwood of the same denomination and Henry G. Appenzeller of the Methodist Episcopal Church the next year. Thereafter, representatives of many other Protestant sects joined them in conducting a variety of missionary activities in Korea.

As one means of propagating their faith, the missionaries engaged in medical work, contributing much in this way to Korean society. By spreading Western liberal ideas, missionaries also played an important role in arousing a national consciousness among the Korean people. The political activities of Korean converts like Sŏ Chae-p'il and Yun Ch'i-ho, two central figures in the Independence Club, were both inspired and informed by their Christian beliefs. Moreover, Protestant private schools gave every appearance of being organs for the propagation of Korean nationalist thought. Other Christian organizations, such as the Seoul Young Men's Christian Association, founded in 1903, carried on active political and social programs and provided the stimulus for the formation of similar Korean youth organizations. These groups did not confine their ativities to politics and education but contributed significantly to arousing new social awareness with their campaigns against drinking, smoking, and superstitious practices.

Protestantism was most warmly embraced by the non-*yangban* intellectual class and the business community, particularly in regions where the development of a capitalist economy was well underway, such as P'yŏngan province. *Yangban* intellectuals were relatively slow to abandon their attachment to Confucian values and accept Protestantism. From the early 1880s, however, some *yangban* literati officials converted to the Christian faith while studying or in political exile in Japan, China, and the United States. Later, on the eve of the the Russo-Japanese War, a group of political prisoners of *yangban* background underwent conversion while being held in a Seoul prison. Protestantism thus became a religion of all classes. The growing vitality of the Protestant church in Korea was demonstrated in 1905 with the inauguration of large-scale Bible study conferences, at which participants recited Bible passages to stir their audience to self-reflection. In 1909, the "Million Souls for Christ Campaign" was successful in bringing about mass conversions to the Protestant faith. The remarkable appeal of Protestantism in Korea was partly due to a psychological factor: the feeling of many Koreans that conversion to Christianity was an act of penance for the failings of their traditional society that had led to the loss of Korea's nationhood.

On a lesser scale, there were other religious movements that also served to instill in Koreans a keener sense of nationalism. After the Tonghak lost a number of its more alienated members to the pro-Japanese Ilchinhoe, its third patriarch, Son Pyŏng-hŭi, led the Tonghak mainstream into active participation in the nationalist movement under the newly created name of Ch'ŏndogyo, or Religion of the Heavenly Way.

Confucianists on the whole adhered to their tradition by taking a conservative stance, often opposing the trends toward modernization. But they too believed strongly that the Japanese must be expelled from Korea. To this end, they continuously memorialized the throne and raised "righteous armies" to fight against Japan. Meanwhile, efforts were made to reform Confucianism, that is, to adapt it to the changing conditions of the times. This Confucian reform movement, as has been observed, joined forces with the Christian members of the new intellectual class and participated in the activities of the Independence Club and the New People's Association. Within Buddhism, too, a reform movement arose, one fruit of which was the appearance in 1913 of Han Yong-un's work, entitled *On the Revitalization of Korean Buddhism.*

Finally, seeking to inculcate the ancient belief in Tan'gun as the divine progenitor of the Korean race, Taejonggyo (Religion of Tan'gun Worshippers) was founded in 1909, a conservative religious movement with strong chauvinist-nationalist overtones.

In the years preceding 1910, a number of scholarly organizations came into existence to further nationalistic ends. Some were formed around scholars in particular provincial areas, such as Yi Kap's North and West Educational Association, Yi Kwang-

jong's Kyŏnggi-Ch'ungch'ŏng Educational Association, Chang
Chi-yŏn's Kyŏngsang Educational Association, Yi Ch'ae's Chŏlla
Educational Association, and Namgung Ŏk's Kangwŏn Educational Association. More broadly based bodies of this kind
included Yu Kil-chun's Society for Fostering Leaders (Hŭngsadan), Kim Yun-sik's Korean Confucian Association, and Chin
Hak-sin's Association for Women's Education.

Most of these scholarly or educational organizations published
journals that helped to slake the public's thirst for knowledge.
Many other educational magazines also were published, such as
the monthly organ of the Independence Club, the *Korea Self-
Strengthening Society Monthly,* and Ch'oe Nam-sŏn's *Youth
(Sonyŏn).* A number of commercial publishing companies were
founded and put out numerous books whose contents reflected
the new learning.

New ground in the study of the Korean language was broken
toward the end of the nineteenth century with Yu Kil-chun's
Grammar of Korean, the first such modern work. Subsequently,
Chu Si-gyŏng founded the Society for the Standardization of
Korean Writing, and Chi Sŏg-yŏng formed the Society for Study
of the Korean Script. Both organizations devoted themselves to
studying the problems of spelling and writing in *han'gŭl.* In 1907
the Ministry of Education, acting upon the proposal of Chi Sŏg-
yŏng, established a Korean Language Institute and work was
begun in earnest on the fundamental task of standardizing Korean
spelling and usage. Among the scholars who joined in this
effort, the one with the most outstanding record of accomplishment was Chu Si-gyŏng, who authored such works as *A Korean
Grammar* and *A Phonology of Korean.* His many disciples later
organized the Korean Language Society (Chosŏnŏ Hakhoe),
which remains today, under the name Han'gŭl Hakhoe, the leading scholarly body in its field.

Scholars of Korean history active during this period were Chang
Chi-yŏn, Pak Ŭn-sik, and Sin Ch'ae-ho. Through their research
and writing, these men strove above all to foster a sense of
national pride and self-respect. This is evident from the prominence among their publications of such works as the *Biography
of Ŭlchi Mundŏk, Biography of Kang Kam-ch'an, Biography*

of Ch'oe Yŏng, and *Biography of Yi Sun-sin*—all accounts of the lives of heroes who fought against foreign invaders. There also was much interest in historical geography; work in this field too laid stress on the love a people must have for the land of their forebears. Efforts were made to rediscover old texts and to gain a new understanding of their value. The outstanding example of work of this kind was that done by Ch'oe Nam-sŏn, who founded the Society for Refurbishing Korea's Literary Legacy and published a series of reprints of old Korean texts under its auspices.

Koreans of this period showed great interest in world history as well, particularly in the histories of nation-building that might serve as a model in their own situation, and in accounts of the fall of nations that could offer salutary lessons upon which to reflect. Thus, there appeared such works as *The Creation of the Swiss Nation, History of American Independence, History of Italian Independence, Poland's Final Struggle,* and *The Fall of Vietnam.* Biographies of heroic world figures—*Three Heroes of Italian Nationhood, Biography of George Washington, Peter the Great, Biography of Joan of Arc*—also were read avidly by the Korean public.

It was during this period too that the "new novel" (*sin sosŏl*), a transitional literary mode that served as a bridge between the old novel and modern Korean literature, was born. The new novel was written entirely in *han'gŭl,* largely in vernacular style, and so could be read for pleasure by everyone. Clearly, therefore, the new novel was evolving toward the modern form that presently would emerge. The characters in the new novels cried out for Korean independence by both word and deed. In addition, the novels called for a new family morality based on equality between the sexes, and argued for the new education, the eradication of superstition, and the construction of a rational, enlightened society.

In short, the new novels reflected the values of the contemporary enlightenment movement. They therefore represent an important stage of development in Korean literature. Yi In-jik was the pioneer figure among the new novelists, with such representative works as *Tears of Blood, Pheasant Mountain,* and

Voice of a Demon. Yi Hae-jo's *Liberty Bell* and *The Peony Screen*, Ch'oe Ch'an-sik's *Color of the Autumn Moon*, and An Kuk-sŏn's *Proceedings of the Council of Birds and Beasts* appeared at about the same time. The new novel constituted the mainstream of fiction writing in Korea until around the time of the March First Movement in 1919.

So-called *ch'angga,* songs of a new type sung to Western melodies, were immensely popular from around 1900. *Ch'angga* owed their beginning to the introduction of Protestant hymns, but they became songs of the whole people and were sung everywhere throughout Korea. Many *ch'angga* inspired love of country, glorifying independence and the new education and culture. Such *ch'angga* were sung joyously by students and by independence fighters, to uplift their spirits. In this respect the *ch'angga* songs, one among many cultural innovations that characterize this otherwise doleful period in the history of the Korean people, clearly mirror the age in which they were created.

Chapter 15

The First Phase of Japanese Rule, 1910-1919

The Theory and Structure of the Colonial State

A generation of Japanese economic, political, and military interference on the Korean Peninsula culminated in Korea's formal annexation to Japan on August 22, 1910. Korea became a Japanese colony with Prime Minister Yi Wan-yong's signing of the Treaty of Annexation, and the treaty was announced to the Korean people by Emperor Sunjong in a proclamation on August 29 marking the end of the 518 year rule of the dynasty of Chosŏn. Annexation inaugurated a thirty-five year period of social and economic change directed to the ends of the Japanese state that has left a bitter legacy to this day. The experience under Japanese rule in the twentieth century heightened Korean enmity towards the Japanese that dated from the Hideyoshi Invasion of the late sixteenth century. But no previous experience could have prepared the Korean people for the dramatic changes in the next thirty-five years.

The Japanese assumed control of Korea with purpose and decisiveness. They created a powerful, intrusive state unprecedented in Korean experience. By the end of Japanese rule in 1945, there was not one aspect of Korean life that lay unaffected by the pervasiveness and will of Japanese rule. Thus, the events of this period are crucial to an understanding of post-World War II Korea. The political dilemma created by the loss of sovereignty affected the direction of Korean nationalism. The cultural and educational policies of the Japanese skewed cultural development and compounded ideological division amongst elites. And economic programs and development under Japanese rule intensified class contradictions that continue to influence Korean society. Although Japanese rule stimulated Korean national identity and political consciousness, the very success of its cooptive political control policies exacerbated internal cleavages among Korean independence fighters. Such contradictory effects have left a mixed legacy among Koreans to this day.

Terauchi Masatake, first Governor-General (1910-1916), legitimated Japanese rule by asserting that there was a natural affinity between the Korean and Japanese peoples. Terauchi noted the historical and cultural ties between the two countries and posited that assimilation of the Korean people into Japanese society was the long-term goal for the colony. This paternalistic rhetoric justified the Japanese seizure of Korea in the name of progress, protection, and brotherly ties. But irrespective of the formal ideology, Japanese rule was rooted in political and economic reality. Since 1876 Japan had inexorably strengthened its strategic and economic ties to the peninsula and through wars with China (1894-5) and Russia (1904-5) had gained international acquiescence in the pursuit of its aims in Korea. Moreover, Japan had solidified its international position by forming the Anglo-Japanese Alliance (1902) and signing a memorandum of understanding with the United States (Taft-Katsura Memorandum, 1905) by which means Japan secured recognition of its ascendancy in Korea. The annexation simply formalized the preexisting Japanese position and created the political machinery for carrying out future colonial policies. From 1910, then, Korea ceased to exist as an entity in the world of nation-states.

The annexation provoked an intense reaction by the Korean people and their leaders. Patriotic officials and nationalist leaders vilified Yi Wan-yong as an arch traitor, but demonstrations against the annexation were stifled with preemptive arrests and a heavy show of police force. In the countryside, the annexation provoked a revival of "righteous army" (*ŭibyŏng*) activity. Guerrilla bands led by local literati had fought the Japanese intermittently since 1905, and the demobilization of the Korean army in 1907 strengthened these resistance forces. Japan was compelled to substantially increase its commitment in Korea in order to pacify the countryside. By the end of 1910, however, a reinforced and better trained and equipped Japanese military police force had subdued the guerrilla fighters. According to Japanese records, 17,600 guerrillas were killed in the fighting between 1907 and 1910.

In their first year of rule, the Japanese moved swiftly to pacify the colony. The Protectorate Treaty which created the Residency-General (1906-10) had already established the legal basis for a full-scale repression. Terauchi suspended publication of all Korean newspapers, disbanded political organizations and prohibited public gatherings of all types. With the countryside pacified and political opposition in the cities stifled, Terauchi was in position to finish constructing the political institutions of the colonial state, a process begun during the Residency-General period.

As latecomers among imperialist powers, the Japanese were able to draw upon several centuries of world colonial experience. Their knowledge of other colonial systems and the unique geographical proximity of their Korean colony provided them with certain advantages. By colonizing their immediate neighbors, the Japanese occupied a unique niche in colonial history. Close proximity to the metropole encouraged Japanese emigration and intensified economic ties to the colony (by 1940, there were 708,418 Japanese residents, 3.2 percent of the population). In the political sphere, proximity led Japanese planners to envisage a tight, highly centralized governance for Korea. This was not a remote colony, far removed from the daily concerns of Japan proper. The Japanese conceived their presence in Korea as vital to the general strategic and economic fortunes of the homeland.

Additionally, unlike the Western colonial powers, the Japanese did not have the luxury of carving out an artificial state entity in a political vacuum. They had to establish their control over an ancient state and society with a long historical experience and high degree of racial, ethnic, cultural, and linguistic homogeneity. Moreover, responding to external pressures, Korea had already begun the process of transforming its traditional institutions, and in consequence the annexation disrupted the indigenous political movement to create a modern Korean nation-state. The traditional political system thus was largely discredited, and in any case it had been marked by incomplete centralization and local autonomy, characteristics unsuited to the plans of the Japanese colonizers. Their ultimate creation, the Government-General of Korea (Chōsen Sōtokufu: Chōsen is Japanese for Chosŏn the name of the last Korean dynasty) was a powerful state that penetrated to the lowest levels of Korean society. Power was centralized in a large bureaucratic order backed by impressive coercive force. Able to establish only weak connections to traditional elite elements, Japan chose to rule Korea directly.

The authority vested in the Governor-General, the chief colonial administrator, was absolute. As a direct appointee of the emperor, the Governor-General could operate with considerable autonomy. Moreover, the office was filled by a succession of officials, all, except one, high ranking military officers on active duty, who were well-connected to the highest levels of Japanese politics.

The administrative machinery of the colony was created by imperial ordinance, but the administrative authority that in Japan proper would have belonged to separate ministries was concentrated in the person of the Governor-General. The Governor-General controlled the military police as well as colonial civil police, issued legislative directives, oversaw the judicial system, had fiscal independence, and exercised total control of appointments within his bureaucracy. Nominally required to report to the Japanese Home Ministry, the Governor-General possessed special powers that gave him virtual independence and tremendous flexibility with regard to policy. Although the home government reorganized the Government-General of Korea in 1919 and again in 1942, these actions did not effectively alter the authority and autonomy of its chief.

The colonial bureaucracy expanded rapidly. Starting in 1910 with roughly 10,000 officials, by 1937 the bureaucracy employed 87,552 (52,270 Japanese and 35,282 Koreans). If a broader calculation of all public and private positions important to the colony is made, the totals for 1937 would be 246,000 Japanese and 63,000 Koreans. These numbers are even more significant when a comparison is made with Western colonies. In 1937 the French in Vietnam ruled a colony of roughly 17 million with 2,920 administrative personnel, 10,776 regular troops and about 38,000 indigenous personnel, a small number compared to the Korean situation where 42 percent of Japanese residents were involved directly or indirectly in government.

The Japanese expanded the system of local administration after 1910. From the center, Japanese control penetrated downward in an elaborate system of administrative levels. There were thirteen provinces (increased from the eight provinces of the former Chosŏn dynasty), 218 counties, eighteen cities, 2,262 townships, and two islands. By directly appointing chief officials of these units, the Governor-General extended his control over local affairs. This situation was in great contrast to the presence and power of central government officials in Chosŏn. While inefficient and often corrupt, traditional governance had allowed considerable local autonomy, and it had rested for the most part lightly on the populace. Under Japanese rule, however, the most trivial of matters became issues of official concern. The expansion of the local administration also provided the central administration with an efficient intelligence apparatus. And in the next thirty-five years, the colonial bureaucracy produced a prodigious number of reports on local conditions in Korea.

Full power to legislate in accordance with the special conditions found to exist in Korea also had been given to the Governor-General. This meant that Koreans were bound not only by Japanese law but by colonial decrees and promulgations as well. Japanese citizens in Korea, on the other hand, were governed by the laws of their homeland and enjoyed the rights guaranteed to them by Japan's Meiji constitution, rights that were not extended to the Korean population. Eventual assimilation, with its implication of equal treatment under a common law, had been proclaimed to be Japan's ultimate goal in Korea, but the realities of colonial rule made a farce of such lofty pretensions. What Japan in fact instituted was a dual system of laws that created an atmosphere of pervasive legal discrimination against its Korean subjects.

Virtual exclusion from meaningful participation in colonial governance mirrored the weak legal position of the native population. While the Japanese did hire large numbers of Koreans in the colonial bureaucracy, Japanese officials outnumbered them almost two to one. Moreover, at middle and upper levels in the bureaucracy, Japanese dominance was even more pronounced.

Discriminatory hiring practices made it difficult for the increasing numbers of educated Koreans to find jobs in the expanding government or in the many quasi-official sectors of the colonial structure. Ultimately, this contradiction alienated educated Koreans and drove them into the anti-Japanese, nationalist movement.

Behind all the rhetoric of assimilation and pronouncements of benevolent intent lurked the powerful force of the Japanese colonial police. Whenever persuasion and negotiations failed to secure Japanese interests, the last resort was compulsion. The build-up of the colonial police force began with the pacification campaigns against the "righteous armies" during the Protectorate period and continued until the end of Japanese rule. In 1910, the Governor-General had 6,222 military and civilian police at his disposal, half of them Korean. By 1922, the force had more than tripled to 20,771, and it tripled again by 1941. The 1941 figure of over 60,000 police represented one policeman for every four hundred Koreans.

The broad latitude given police in the conduct of their mission augmented the power of numbers. The police presented themselves in military uniform replete with swords; indeed, all government officials, including teachers, were required to wear swords as symbols of authority. The powers granted the police allowed them to intrude into every aspect of colonial life. They were the controlling agency of politics, education, religion, morals, health and public welfare, and tax collection; even the slaughtering of animals came under their scrutiny. The police also had summary powers with regard to misdemeanors, and this allowed them to adjudicate, pass sentence, and execute punishment for minor offenses. And in a burst of self-serving cultural sensitivity, ancient Yi dynasty whipping laws were kept on the books to deal with petty offenders (Koreans only).

In the end, the colonial police became a major focus of Korean resentment. This resentment was compounded by the fact that the police recruited large numbers of Koreans, often from the lower classes. Roughly half of the police force was Korean, and the colonial thought police also employed a vast network of native informers. The use of Koreans in the police force turned

Korean against Korean and poisoned the atmosphere of colonial society. Perhaps more than any other colonial institution, the memory of the intrusive, arbitrary, and often brutal conduct of the colonial police remains one of the most bitter legacies of the colonial period.

The First Decade of Colonial Rule, the "Dark Period," 1910-19

The first decade of Japanese rule has been called the "dark period" (*amhŭkki*) because of the comprehensive repression of political and cultural life in the colony. The Japanese banned political organizations and the right of assembly, using the existing 1907 Peace Preservation Law. After 1910, it was illegal to assemble without police permission for almost any purpose. During the Protectorate period a series of restrictive press laws had been passed to gain control of Korean newspapers. The 1907 Newspaper Law and 1909 Publication Law gave the government the power to grant permits for publication of newspapers, magazines, and books. This meant publishing was a privilege, not a right, and practically speaking the Korean press disappeared during this decade. A small number of scholarly journals, youth magazines, and religious bulletins received permits, but the major Korean newspapers such as the *Korea Daily News* (*Taehan Maeil Sinbo,* 1905-1910) ceased publication. In addition, publications that received permits had to endure prepublication censorship.

The blackout of the Korean press constricted public dialogue among literate and politically conscious elements in Korean society and hampered political leaders' efforts to mobilize opposition to Japanese rule. The press blackout was only part of the Japanese strategy to cripple the political opposition to colonial rule. In the first months of their rule, the Japanese attempted to gain allies among conservative ex-officials and aristocrats. They offered noble titles and direct stipends to eighty-four high Yi dynasty officials and important *yangban* elite and seventy three accepted. In addition, the Imperial Household pensioned off 3,645 Chosŏn officials of all ranks. The Japanese based their selections on pre-annexation police analysis of key factions in the former political elite. Such treatment of conservative elements offers early evidence of what was to become a persistent Japanese strategy of dividing the political and social leadership of Korea. Many of these prominent individuals were later called upon to organize and lead pro-Japanese organizations.

The Government-General dealt harshly with the active political opposition. As we have seen, military force was used to pacify the righteous army resistance. In the cities, the police carefully watched intellectuals, religious leaders, and nationalist politicians, and arrests for political activities mounted. In 1912 alone, there were over 50,000 arrests for all crimes including arrests for illegal political activity and assembly. The discovery of a plot to assassinate Governor-General Terauchi involving An Myŏng-gŭn, brother of An Chung-gŭn (assassin of Itō Hirobumi), precipitated an intensive round-up of nationalists in December of 1910. Charging that the assassination attempt was only the tip of a wider conspiracy, the police arrested over six hundred people. Of the original group arrested, one hundred and five were ultimately indicted for conspiracy. The "Case of the One Hundred Five," as this incident subsequently became known, struck a decisive early blow to the nationalist movement.

The list of indicted included important members of the Korean nationalist leadership. Prominent leaders of the New People's Association (Sinminhoe) such as Yun Ch'i-ho, Yang Ki-t'ak, and Yi Sŭng-hun were among the indicted conspirators. The New People's Association had been formed in 1907 by An Ch'ang-ho to serve the ends of the Korean nationalist movement. Rather than direct resistance to Japanese rule, it advocated a program of cultural activities, education, and native economic development that would lay the foundation for later nationhood. After 1910, the organization had had to go underground in order to continue its operations, now explicitly directed toward regaining independence. Although they were not involved in the attempt on Terauchi's life, the incident served as a convenient pretext to arrest active Sinminhoe members. The arrests also decimated the progressive Christian leadership and involved prominent educators and intellectuals.

The Japanese convened a show trial to try the alleged conspirators, an event that gained considerable attention in the world press due to the efforts of foreign missionaries in Korea. The trial served notice to all opponents of Japanese rule, whether moderate or radical, that the Japanese would tolerate no opposition. In the course of the arrests and trial many of the indicted Koreans were brutally interrogated and, although little proof of conspiracy surfaced, many of the accused were sentenced and imprisoned.

Between 1910 and 1919, the Government-General also moved to solidify the foundation on which its rule rested by developing an educational system that would socialize Koreans to be good citizens of the Japanese Empire. While less spectacular than military pacification or prosecution of political criminals, the creation of the education system had an even more profound long-run effect on Korean society. The colonial education system served several purposes. It was designed to train a literate labor force for future economic development and to educate Koreans to Japanese customs, culture and language. More importantly, perhaps, it provided a mechanism for the broad transmission of Japanese cultural and political values in order to legitimate Japanese rule. The Educational Ordinance for Chōsen summarized the intent of the system as follows: "Common education shall pay special attention to the engendering of national [Japanese] characteristics and the spread of the national language; the essential principles of education in Chōsen shall be the making of loyal and good subjects by giving instruction on the basis of the Imperial Rescript concerning education."

Japanese efforts to control the educational system in Korea had begun during the Protectorate period. In a series of ordinances promulgated after 1906, the Japanese established government control of textbooks and curriculum in public schools. In 1908, the Private School Ordinance required licensing and annual reports for all private schools. After 1910, codes regulating all public and private schools were unified. The tight regulation of private schools was significant because after 1906 the private schools, operated by Korean nationalists and foreign missionaries, had encouraged intellectual freedom and had provided cover for political activity. With regulation it became more difficult to operate private schools, and the numbers of such schools decreased as the public system expanded. For example, in 1907 missionaries alone operated 508 primary schools, 22 high schools and two theological schools; by 1917 this number had been halved, and by 1937 only 34 missionary schools of all types remained. Korean-operated private schools suffered a similar fate.

The Government-General built hundreds of schools in the first decade of its rule, and the numbers of students attending all schools increased dramatically. In 1910, 110,800 students attended some sort of school (excluding the traditional village schools, *sŏdang*). By 1941, this number had increased to 1,776,078. The vast increase in numbers of students, however, obscured an important pattern of discrimination. There were two sets of schools in Korea, one set for Koreans, another for Japanese. These separate and unequal systems were differentiated by quality of instruction, facilities, and curriculum. One emphasis of the common schools for Koreans was basic literacy in the "national language" (Japanese), and Korean was taught as a "second language." The common schools were also thought of as terminal programs for most students. The system limited higher educational opportunities for Koreans, and even then higher education for Koreans focused on vocational training. Only five percent of Korean students passed beyond the primary level, and although there was a tremendous expansion of student numbers over time, in 1945 only about twenty percent of the population had received some schooling, while the general rate of literacy was still below fifty percent.

For Koreans, the experience in the Japanese schools engendered ambivalent feelings toward their own language, history, and culture. Knowledge of the Japanese language expanded rapidly. The percentage of Koreans able to speak and read Japanese increased from one half of one percent of the fifteen million total population in 1913 to about fifteen percent of 25 million in 1945. Morals education, the Japanization of Korean history and culture, and the spread of the Japanese language and values subtly eroded Korean cultural identity and confidence. Indeed, in the 1920s, many intellectuals felt compelled to devote themselves full-time to organizing movements for the maintenance of Korean cultural identity and Korean language use.

Concurrently, the Japanese education system also stimulated

political consciousness by spreading literacy in both Korean and Japanese. Increased literacy created a base for a larger group of politically mobilized individuals whose experience of discrimination within the Japanese system drove them to active opposition to Japanese rule. Indeed, by limiting access to college and university education in the colony, the Japanese encouraged an exodus of bright Koreans to Japan. Once in Japan, these students were exposed to radical political literature unavailable in Korea and rubbed shoulders with activist students from other countries. Ultimately, the expansion of the education system and the peculiar limits on opportunities within it engendered a new generation of political activists who formed the core leadership of the nationalist opposition during this period.

Although the Japanese had silenced the daily press and forced political organizations to disband, intellectual life in the colony could not so easily be stifled. Chu Si-gyŏng and his disciples carried forward the work of standardizing Korean vernacular grammar and orthography, thus laying the groundwork for the emergence of a Korean language movement in full force in the 1920s. Experimentation with modern literary forms, begun after 1900 by writers such as Yi In-jik, Yi Hae-jo, and Ch'oe Ch'an-sik, continued. The publication of the widely read new novel, *Mujŏng* (*The Heartless*, 1917), by Yi Kwang-su established the respectability of the modern novel. In journalism, Ch'oe Nam-sŏn's youth magazines *Youth* (*Sonyŏn*, 1907-1911) and *Young Years* (*Ch'ŏng-ch'un*, 1914-1918) provided popular forums for social commentary, Western literature and history, and literary experimentation. While intellectual life had been constricted in the 1910-1919 period, it did not die.

The Japanese Land Survey

Land was the most important form of wealth in traditional Korea. The division between landed and landless was the major marker of class relations, landholding being the principal support of the traditional *yangban* class. While distinctions can be made between *yangban* with official position and those without close or recent connection to office-holding, the control of land led to the wealth necessary for the maintenance of status or upward mobility. The pattern of the land tenure system had been well-established long before the advent of Japanese rule. Agriculture was organized, especially in the wet paddy regions of the south, into large private or state-owned landholdings cultivated by tenants. To be sure, there was a variety of land tenure relationships: resident and absentee landlord, owner-cultivator, part-owner-tenant, pure tenant, and agricultural laborer. That tenancy already had reached major dimensions was proved by the last land survey undertaken by the Yi dynasty between 1898-1904 (the Kwangmu Land Survey). Indeed, the power of the landed aristocracy was a major reason for the dynasty's inability to assert tax rights and maintain accurate land registers. Evasion of taxes and removal of land from government control had been widespread abuses for centuries.

In the late nineteenth century there was no strong indication that land tenure relations had been substantially altered by the rise of a market economy and commercialization. Moreover, the landlord class represented the traditional aristocracy, not a group of peasant-entrepreneurs such as emerged in eighteenth century Japan. While it is pleasant to assume that traditional interpersonal relations and village communalism might have mediated economic relations between landlord and tenant, the tenant's lot, by and large, remained one of helplessness and uncertainty. At the beginning of Japanese rule, the land system remained what it had been for centuries, many large holdings concentrated in the hands of a small wealthy class with the remainder of rural society divided among small holders, tenants, and agricultural laborers.

The rationalization and codification of the land system was an important policy of the Government-General. Understanding the land system, its productivity and ownership, were vital to establishing a rational land-tax. With this end in mind, the Government-General conducted a comprehensive land survey between 1910-1918. The newly established Land Survey Bureau mapped all plots of land, classified it according to type (upland, dry land agriculture, paddy, etc.), graded its productivity and established ownership. The survey created a reporting system that required all owners to claim and prove title to their land. Partial owners, tenants, and squatters with traditional "cultivation rights" were in a poor position to claim title to land. Consequently, many small owners unfamiliar with reporting regulations lost their land by failing to register it. Generally speaking, however, major landowners were able to report and maintain legal claim to their valuable land.

Contemporary nationalists and post-liberation historians have characterized the land survey as a Japanese "land grab." Indeed, by seizing the late dynasty's office land, forest and river bed land, and a large portion of the holdings of the Yi Royal Household, the Government-General became by far the largest landowner in Korea. In 1930, the state held a total of 8,880,000 *chŏngbo* (21,756,000 acres; one *chŏngbo* equals 2.45 acres), almost 40 percent of the land area of Korea itself. The amount of land held by Japanese private and corporate investors also grew, as the Government-General sold off land at bargain prices. But Korean landowners also increased the size of their holdings; over time, most who owned land in 1910 maintained or increased their holdings during the period up to 1945.

At the turn of the century, the Chosŏn dynasty was trying to reassert its control over the land system and register "hidden" lands on the tax rolls. The Kwangmu Land Survey (1898-1904) effected a partial survey of agricultural land for this purpose. In addition, the dynasty strictly controlled foreign ownership of land up to the Protectorate period. After 1904, however, Japanese gained the right to own land and several large projects were proposed that sought to buy farmland in order to bring Japanese settlers to Korea. One such project in 1904 was defeated by widespread Korean opposition, but after 1907 Japanese land companies began to purchase large tracts of land.

The most infamous of these corporations was the semigovernmental Oriental Development Company. Chartered in 1907, by 1930 the company had acquired 110,000 *chŏngbo* (269,500 acres) of agricultural land. Its ambitious plan to settle 30,000 Japanese emigrants a year in Korea failed, but it remained throughout the colonial period a major foreign landlord in Korea. The activities of these companies and the intrusion of Japanese private investors added to the already tense atmosphere produced by increasing tenancy, widespread absentee ownership, and growing rural poverty. But the presence in significant numbers of Japanese owners did not change the reality of class relations in the countryside.

It must be remembered that most landlords continued to be Korean. A 1930 study of land conditions divided landlords by the amount of land owned. Small landlords, holding 5-50 *chŏngbo,* were mostly Korean, and in the large category, 50-100 *chŏngbo,* there were two times as many Koreans as Japanese. Only in the largest category, 100-plus *chŏngbo* did Japanese outnumber Koreans, and this was due to the presence of the large Japanese financed land companies. The main consideration is that Government-General rationalization and codification of the land system strengthened all owner's rights, Japanese and Korean. The worsening conditions that led to strained class relations between owners and tenants after 1920 cannot be blamed solely on the Government-General land survey.

The land survey and subsequent deterioration of rural life in Korea is a highly sensitive issue in modern Koren historiography. With considerable justification, nationalist historians have criticized the exploitative nature of the colonial land system in Korea and the vast dispossession of small-holders and partial tenants. As we shall see below, the colonial system, in combination with market forces, drove small-holders off the land, and tenancy rates approached eighty percent in the fertile paddy regions of the southwest in the 1930s. The widening gap between the landed and landless created tremendous tensions in Korean society. Yet these tensions were not simply a distillation of the resentments and misery of landless Koreans directed against a landed, Japanese ruling elite. The land situation was a problem of class; the fact of foreign imperialism also made it a problem of nation. Nevertheless, even if nationalist forces had overthrown Japanese imperialism in 1920, the class problem in the Korean countryside would have continued to fester until resolved by a land reform.

Ultimately, the Japanese land survey rationalized and codified a preexisting situation. It strengthened the rights of all owners and provided a legal and administrative stability that encouraged

Japanese investment in land. Strengthened owner rights interacted with market forces and population expansion to increase tenancy rates. Population increase created more demand for access to land and created upward pressure on rents. The average length of tenancy agreements decreased as owners maneuvered to renegotiate contracts at higher rents. Already by the beginning of the twentieth century, owners had begun to shift production costs onto their tenants. By the 1930s, the burden this represented for tenants was staggering. This meant that in addition to rent, tenants had to pay for tools, seeds, water rights (including the costs of public irrigation projects), and fertilizer. Few tenants could finance an entire year's investment without borrowing, and this led to increased indebtedness compounded by widespread usury.

H.K. Lee's important study of the land situation in the early 1930s determined that rents averaged fifty percent of the harvest. The rent-in-kind system of tenancy insured that the bulk of the harvest would be marketed, making it available for export. This fit the economic policies of the Japanese because they had looked to Korea as a source of rice for the Japanese homeland. Japanese efforts to increase rice production were ultimately successful and, particularly after the 1918 rice riots in Japan, Korean rice production expanded dramatically, even to the point of depressing the price of rice in Japan proper. The tragedy of this system was that, while increased production enriched landlords through rents, it did not benefit the common tenant who was forced to market his rice as soon as it was harvested for cash to service his debt. Studies of rice consumption in the 1930s confirmed that poor peasants were consuming cheaper grains such as millet and barley in order to sell their more valuable share of the rice crop.

The Government-General's land policy consolidated its power in the first decade of colonial rule. It both confirmed the existing land system and strengthened it, by resting it on solid legal underpinnings. One result was the creation of a stable tax base after 1918, as land tax revenues steadily grew to account for 45% of total revenues by 1930. At the same time, the interests of the important, conservative landowning class had been assured. Having accomplished these primary objectives, the Japanese now turned their attention to other aspects of the economic infrastructure in Korea.

Communications and Economic Development

In the first decade of their rule, the Japanese also consolidated their grip on communications, public services, and economic activity in general in the colony. The first telegraph had been laid in 1885 between Seoul, Inch'ŏn, and Ŭiju on the Chinese border at the mouth of the Yalu. The establishment of this line was a product of aggressive Chinese policies in Korea in this decade. At Japanese insistence, the Korean government expanded telegraph links between Seoul and Pusan in 1888. This link was connected to Japan by an undersea cable. By 1905, the Japanese had assumed control of Korea's telecommunications and had expanded the system.

Railroads were even more important to the long term interests of the Japanese. Particularly after the Sino-Japanese War, the Japanese rushed to build railroads that would link the homeland with the continent. Convenient and rapid communications, through Korea, between Manchuria and Japan were considered vital for strategic and economic reasons. The late dynasty had tried to forestall Japanese involvement in railroad construction by entering into a joint venture with American interests to build the first railway between Seoul and Inch'ŏn in 1896. In 1900, however, this project was completed by Japanese interests. The extensive capital and modern technology requirements for railway construction hampered Korean governmental and private rail building projects. Pak Ki-jong's Pusan and Southwest Perimeter Railway Company failed in 1898 because of lack of capital. The Korean government attempted to coordinate rail projects by establishing a railroad agency in 1902, but the effort was poorly planned and failed in the wake of the Russo-Japanese War.

In the end, political ascendancy led to Japanese domination of railway building. For strategic reasons during the Russo-Japanese War, Japan raced to complete the Pusan-Seoul-Ŭiju railway. After 1910, now using its power of eminent domain, the Government-General proceeded to construct railroads, build harbors, and improve telegraph and telephonic communication in Korea. All this activity was closely coordinated with similar development in Manchuria, to undertake which Japan had created the South Manchurian Railway Company (SMRC) in 1906. The SMRC was a semi-governmental company charged with railroad management, harbor construction, and the provision of other public services in the Kwantung leased area. Increased Japanese economic dominance of Manchuria in the next decades was a direct result of the SMRC's aggressive investment and infrastructure development. By the time of the Japanese takeover of Manchuria in 1931, the SMRC had evolved into a powerful communications and industrial conglomerate.

In 1933, the SMRC took control of the Korean rail network, and by 1945 the combined system had 6,200 kilometers of track, over fifty percent of which was in Korea (the Korean portion alone equalled the length of about one third of all railways in China). While not comparable to railroad development in Western nations, it was very impressive when compared to China or another colony such as Vietnam. Korea was no larger than a medium-sized Chinese province, but its annual ridership was about half that of the entire Chinese system. In further contrast, Vietnam had only a few coastal railroads and one major branch inland in 1945. The Government-General also built a motor road network, and in 1945 there were 53,000 kilometers of improved roads. In short, the Japanese poured vast amounts of capital into the expansion of transport and communications facilities on the continent. Thus, by the end of the colonial period, Korea boasted extensive modern networks of both kinds. These systems were integrated with those in Manchuria, a design calculated to best serve Japan's economic needs and strategic interests in northeast Asia.

The Government-General also assumed control of mining and forest management. Korea had significant deposits of important minerals, but the extraction of these resources required modern technology and large amounts of capital. The Chosŏn kingdom had attempted to utilize these resources in the late nineteenth century by leasing concessions to a variety of foreign companies. The plan was to gain access to technology and to train native engineers in order to exploit these resources. After the fall of the dynasty the way was open for Japanese exploitation of Korea's gold, silver, iron, tungsten, and coal. The extractive industries in Korea expanded dramatically during World War I as Japanese companies began supplying war-heated Japanese industrial production as well as the allied powers with strategic raw materials. Only in the 1930s did Korean raw materials begin to supply heavy industry on the peninsula, and then large Japanese companies consumed most of the output.

Forest resources and fisheries were also controlled tightly by the Government-General. Most forest lands were owned outright by the Government-General, and logging leases were given predominantly to Japanese companies. Although there was an elaborate reforestation program, a combination of over-logging and population pressure, which led to increased illegal firewood cutting, depleted the forests during the period of Japanese rule. By the 1940s, forest cover remained only in the more remote regions of the peninsula. At the end of Japanese rule the bare hills, denuded of even brush cover and pocketed with gullies spawned by erosion, were another legacy of dramatic economic and demographic change after 1910. Korean fisheries also suffered as the larger and better equipped Japanese fleet gained the lion's share of the catch.

The advent of Japanese rule created a very favorable climate for Japanese commercial interests. After the Kanghwa Treaty of 1876 the Korean economy had been opened to international trade and increasing foreign participation in its markets. The traditional Korean commercial class was very weak, and handcrafted production dominated industry. The rice market was the first area of the economy to be affected by the intrusion of capitalism in the late nineteenth century. Chinese and Japanese rice merchants gained an increasing share of the rice milling industry and its distribution networks. Foreign imports, and particularly those from Japan following its victory in the Sino-Japanese War, also began to dominate Korea's consumer markets. Native handmade goods, particularly textiles and home essentials, could not compete with cheaper, high quality foreign imports.

While Koreans at first were slow to participate in the rapidly changing economy of the late nineteenth century, there soon was a notable shift in attitudes toward commercial investment. Land-lords first began to invest in small banks and the profitable rice milling industry, but by 1900 some were shifting their surplus wealth into other commercial ventures. In the fateful decade 1900-1910, entrepreneurial activity often was looked upon as one facet of the struggle to maintain Korea's independence. Progressives were quick to see the link between economic power and political autonomy, and investment in railroads, shipping, textiles, and other manufactures was viewed as a patriotic act. By 1900, Korean shipping lines—Korea Joint Mail and Shipping, Inch'ŏn Mail and Shipping, and the Inhan Steamship Company—competed with Japanese, American, and Chinese companies. Around the turn of the century textile manufacturing was a growth industry. Among prominent Korean companies were the Chongno Textile Company (1900), and the Kim Tŏk-ch'ang Textile Company (1902). The numbers of Korean entrepreneurs active in other industries such as ceramics, tobacco products, and milling increased as well.

In spite of such increased participation in the modern economy, Korean enterprises based on native capital were insignificant compared to those of the Japanese. While the Korean companies outnumbered Japanese, in terms of amount of paid-in capital, modern production facilities, and scale of operation, Japanese companies clearly dominated. After 1910, Government-General regulations insured the continuation of this pattern. The no-torious Company Law (1911) required Government-General approval for the formation of private and public corporations. In fact, few Korean entrepreneurs obtained such approval. Although the pre-1910 tariffs were maintained until 1920 (a con-cession to foreign pressure at the time of annexation), Japanese companies still had a distinct advantage over Korean and other foreign competition. Strong ties to the colonial administration and easier access to financing provided the edge.

By 1900, most of the major Japanese banks had offices in Korea, and after 1905 Japanese finance on the peninsula domi-nated the economy. In 1904, a Japanese bank, the Daiichi Ginkō, was chosen to carry out currency reform and later empowered to issue currency. After 1910, the Daiichi Ginkō became the Bank of Chōsen and assumed the role of central bank for the colony. The Bank of Chōsen and another large Japanese bank, the Shokusan Ginkō (Industrial Bank) dominated the world of finance in Korea. The central bank issued government bonds, regulated currency, and financed large government projects. The Shokusan Ginkō supported Japanese business and agricultural investments. Smaller Korean banks continued to exist during the colonial period, but these banks never developed the major capital resources required to compete at the level of the major Japanese banks. As the colonial period wore on, larger Korean entrepreneurs became dependent on the Japanese banks as well, and by the 1930s big industrialists, whether Korean or Japanese, were linked inextricably to Japanese finance.

The Korean Nationalist Movement in Exile

The harsh repression that accompanied the advent of Japanese rule drove many political activists into exile. Although overt political resistance had been stymied inside Korea, a growing number of organizations emerged abroad, many of them supported by large Korean communities in Manchuria and Russia, and by a smaller number of émigrés in the United States. The movement in exile continued throughout the period of Japanese rule, and although it was fragmented, it played an important role in maintaining a minimum level of political opposition against the Japanese.

Worsening economic conditions and continued political instability had led to increased Korean emigration since the late nineteenth century. A series of droughts and bad harvests in the 1860s had driven Koreans in the far northern provinces over the Yalu and Tumen rivers in search of land and better living conditions. The Korean community in the Kando (Chien-tao) region in southeast Manchuria, already numbering 65,000 in 1894, had increased to 109,000 by 1910. In the first two years of Japanese rule the Korean population there increased by another 60,000 residents. Tens of thousands of Koreans also emigrated to the Russian Maritime Province. In 1902, the first group of Korean contract laborers were recruited to work in Hawaiian sugar and pineapple plantations. Between 1902-1910 roughly 7,000 Koreans went to Hawaii; subsequently many of the original contract laborers moved to the west coast of the United States, settling in the environs of Los Angeles and San Francisco.

These communities outside the homeland provided sustenance for a burgeoning number of exiled political groups. In the Kando area of Manchuria, Yi Si-yŏng, Yi Tong-nyŏng and Yi Sang-nyong established the Military School of the New Rising (Sin-hŭng Mugwan Hakkyo, 1911) in order to train a fighting force against the Japanese. In 1914, Yi Sang-sŏl and Yi Tong-hwi organized another military unit called the Government of the Korean Restoration Army (Taehan Kwangbokkun Chŏngbu). Although these early groups soon faltered, the Manchurian base area provided shelter to political groups and guerrilla forces throughout the colonial period.

Other exiled activists attempted to gain assistance for the Korean independence movement through diplomatic channels by lobbying foreign governments. Sin Kyu-sik's Mutual Assistance Society (Kongjesa) established contacts with the Chinese Nationalists. In the United States, Syngman Rhee (Yi Sŭng-man) had already formed the Korean National Association (Taehan Kungminhoe) in 1909 in Hawaii. From his original base in Hawaii, Syngman Rhee continued a dogged lobbying effort in the United States for the next thirty-five years. Another exile in America, Pak Yong-man, organized military training for Korean youth beginning in 1910. An Ch'ang-ho, founder of the New People's Association (Sinminhoe) which had been destroyed by the arrests associated with the alleged conspiracy "Case of the One Hundred Five" in 1911, also found his way to the U.S. An was opposed to reliance on military means to achieve independence, and he continued his gradualist educational program aimed at the cultivation of future national leaders by organizing chapters of the Young Korean Academy (Hŭngsadan) in overseas Korean communities.

Although this organizational activity and international lobbying had little impact on the internal situation in Korea, it did have propaganda value and created a loose network of Korean political activists in exile. Even if the exile movement could only embarrass the Japanese in the world press, it achieved a small victory for the otherwise demoralized and disorganized nationalist movement. After 1914, World War I preoccupied the major powers, and Japanese participation in the alliance against Germany did not help the cause of Korean independence. Korean representatives continued to lobby their cause at international meetings such as the International Socialist Congress in Stockholm and the World Conference of Small Nations in New York, both in 1917, but few would listen seriously to their appeals for aid.

As World War I drew to a close, nearly a decade of Japanese rule had smashed political opposition in Korea and had set in motion policies that would transform Korea economically and socially. The harsh Japanese policies, however, created conditions for a broad nationalist reaction in Korea. The political and economic repression engendered strong anti-Japanese sentiment at all levels of the population. Expansion of the education system also provided a larger pool of potential recruits for political activity. Ironically, many of the new activists came from the large numbers of students attending school in Japan. The limits on higher education in the colony had stimulated a student exodus to Japan. In 1909, there already were 790 Korean students in Japan, and by 1912 the number had swelled to 3,171. Living together and studying subversive political literature available in Japan, Korean students became increasingly radicalized. In addition, the bonds between Korean and other foreign students were intensified by first-hand experience of ethnic discrimination in Japanese society. They also forged ties with leftist Japanese students who were alienated by the politics of the older generation. Ultimately, it was in this hot-house atmosphere that Korean students in Japan contributed to the dramatic political renaissance of Korean nationalism in 1919.

Chapter 16

Nationalism and Social Revolution, 1919-1931

The March First Movement

An expectant world breathed a sigh of relief as World War I drew to a close. Suffering the least casualties and with its economy intact, the United States went to the Versailles Peace Conference as a true international power. Woodrow Wilson had set the stage for American involvement in the post-war peace on January 8, 1918, in a stirring declaration that sketched his agenda for the post-war settlement. In his famous fourteen points Wilson declared that the principle of humanism, respect for the self-determination of peoples, and international cooperation must become the basis of a new era of peace. By championing the concept of national autonomy and self-determination, Wilson lifted the spirits of colonized peoples around the world. Although Wilson's points were made in the context of the post-war disposition of the Austro-Hungarian Empire and the remaking of the political boundaries of Europe, Asians struggling under colonial rule felt they had found a world power willing to guarantee political self-determination for all people.

Korean nationalists in exile had watched the war's course closely and were quick to seize upon Wilson's principles as proof of major power interest in the plight of oppressed nations the world over. In Hawaii, the Korean National Association (Taehan Kungminhoe) resolved to send Syngman Rhee to the Versailles Peace Conference to plead the case for Korean independence, but as colonial subjects of Japan the delegation was refused passports. Yŏ Un-hyŏng and Chang Tŏk-su's New Korean Young Men's Association (Sinhan Ch'ŏngnyŏndang), organized in Shanghai in the summer of 1919, succeeded in dispatching Kim Kyu-sik to Paris to lobby for Korean independence. Korean students in Japan formed the Korean Youth Independence Corps (Chosŏn Ch'ŏngnyŏn Tongniptan) and on February 8, 1919 passed a declaration written by Yi Kwang-su demanding immediate independence for Korea. Over 600 Korean students attended the Tokyo meeting and representatives were sent to Korea to speak with nationalist leaders in the colony. Thus, the entire exile community experienced a heightened sense of hope that foreign assistance, might help loosen Japan's hold on Korea.

The moderate tone of Wilson's fourteen points and his appeal for a new era of humanism and peace also found a receptive audience in Korea among religious leaders and moderate nationalists. With most radical leaders either in exile or in jail, what remained of the nationalist leadership in the colony was centered in the religious community. Church related assembly and organization had been guaranteed in the name of religious freedom and thus became a shelter for covert political activity. Aware that exile groups were represented at the Versailles Conference and inspired by the Korean students' Tokyo declaration, leaders of the Christian, Ch'ŏndogyo (Religion of the Heavenly Way), and Buddhist churches began to plan a national movement to appeal for independence. Son Pyŏng-hŭi of the Ch'ŏndogyo, the Christian leader Yi Sŭng-hun, and Han Yong-un of the Buddhist church had been contacted by younger nationalists and were convinced that the Tokyo students' lead must be followed in Korea. Ch'oe Nam-sŏn, Song Chin-u, Ch'oe Rin, and Hyŏn Sang-yun all played important roles in galvanizing religious organizations to provide aid to a domestic movement.

The Ch'ŏndogyo, the modern offshoot of the nineteenth century Tonghak religion, provided funds and leadership to the movement. The death of the former emperor, Kojong, on January 22, 1919, and the subsequent plans for his funeral on March 3 provided a convenient focus for the planned demonstrations. Many Koreans who were uninvolved in the nationalist movement and unaware of the international drama unfolding at Versailles were mobilized by the death of Kojong. Rumors of Japanese involvement in his death had inflamed anti-Japanese sentiments, as thousands of mourners poured into Seoul for the funeral. Accordingly, the demonstration planners resolved to use the Emperor's funeral to widen participation.

Throughout February, leaders debated the proper course for the movement. After some controversy over whether to petition the Japanese for independence or simply declare independence unilaterally, leaders decided on the latter approach as an appeal to the conscience of the world powers. Plans called for a declaration of independence (drafted by Ch'oe Nam-sŏn), petitions to foreign representatives in Tokyo, a message to President Wilson, and for all documents to be submitted over the signatures of representatives of the people and former Chosŏn dynasty officials. The movement was to be non-violent, reflecting the conservative bent of its organizers. The declaration itself was a very mild document. It asserted Korea's liberty and equality within the world of nations and claimed the right to pass such status on to posterity, with the words: "This is the clear leading of God, the moving principle of the present age, the whole human race's just claim."

With preparations nearly complete, the date of the demonstrations was advanced to March 1 in order to avoid police discovery. Student intermediaries had been enlisted to organize demonstrations in provincial cities. On March 1 twenty-nine of thirty-three "national representatives," signers of the Declaration of Independence, gathered at a Seoul restaurant, dispatched a student with a copy of the declaration to the Governor-General, and notified the police of their intentions. Simultaneously, the declaration was being read at Pagoda Park in downtown Seoul. The widespread demonstrations that ensued on this day drew people from all walks of life into a celebration of Korean national will, as demonstrators paraded through the streets shouting "Taehan tongnip manse" ("long live an independent Korea"). The peaceful demonstrations on March 1 sparked a nation-wide movement in the following months. Over a million people participated in demonstrations, with the Japanese police reporting "disturbances" in all but seven of Korea's 218 counties.

The demonstrations caught the Japanese by complete surprise, a tribute to the meticulous organization of its leadership as well the careless hubris of the police. Demonstrations on such a scale were without precedent, and it was clear that the Japanese had not thought the Koreans capable of such concerted action. The police response to the demonstrations bordered on hysteria, and by May, military reinforcements had been summoned to help quell the rioting. No doubt frightened by the electric spontaneity which brought masses into the streets, the Japanese reacted to subsequent gatherings with an orgy of arrests, beatings, and even village burnings. Japanese brutality invited Korean reprisals, and in the following months there were frequent, bloody clashes between crowds and police. Estimates of casualties range from the official Japanese count of 553 killed, 1,409 injured, and 12,522 arrested between March and December to a Korean nationalist estimate of over 7,500 deaths, roughly 15,000 injured, and some 45,000 arrests.

The demonstrations failed entirely to rid Korea of the hated Japanese rule, and the appeal to the world powers was greeted with indifference. Possessing their own colonies, the powers of the great alliance of which Japan was a member were unwilling to consider implementing Wilson's idealistic formula for world peace in Asia. After all, to do such would be to endanger their own international and domestic political interests. This was a crushing blow to the moderate leadership of the March First Movement, some of whom had believed naively that Wilson's self-proclaimed new era would include provisions for Korean independence. Therefore, in terms of liberation from colonial oppression, the movement failed absolutely.

Short of independence, however, the movement provided a catalyst for the expansion of the nationalist movement as a whole. Before 1919, Korean nationalism had been divided into separate and poorly coordinated movements. From the late nineteenth century, progressive elites had accepted the vision of Korea as a nation in the world of nation-states, and they had attempted in a variety of ways to join the force of Korean national identity to a system of politics that would derive its sanction from this very awareness of the Korean people of their common Korean-ness. Failing in reform, progressive elites had devised programs for raising national consciousness, for education, and for economic development, in order to bring into being, as they saw it, the fundamental conditions under which mass support might be mobilized for the creation of a modern nation.

This elite strain of Korean nationalism had been complemented by the emergence of mass reaction to outside interference in Korean society. The Tonghak movement of the 1890s, the "righteous army" guerrillas until 1910, and after 1910 the entrenchment of anti-Japanese sentiment in Korean society represented the power, still largely in potential only, of national patriotism. The problem for Korean nationalism up to 1919 was that the separate stream of mass nationalism had remained largely untapped by the progressive political elite. One accomplishment of the March First Movement was the temporary joining of these two streams and the advent of a purposeful, mass nationalist movement in Korea.

The success of the demonstrations also produced a round of organizational activity among the widely separated exile groups. For the first time since annexation, nationalists abroad attempted to create a government in exile to unify the many disparate elements and to link up with the growing movement in Korea. The result was the Provisional Government of the Republic of Korea (Taehan Min'guk Imsi Chŏngbu) formed on April 9, 1919, in Shanghai. Formed as a republic, the Provisional Government established links to organizations in Korea and, in order to establish its legitimacy, elected as its ministers the absent leaders of all established independence groups abroad. With Syngman Rhee as president and An Ch'ang-ho, Yi Tong-hwi, Kim Kyusik, Mun Ch'ang-bŏm, and Ch'oe Chae-hyŏng all given cabinet posts, the major figures of exile organizations in China, Manchuria, Siberia, and the United States were brought together in a single government. With its principals enroute to Shanghai or busy abroad, the Provisional Government had yet to demonstrate its viability, but with post-March First euphoria many assumed a workable coalition had been formed. And the leadership of the domestic and exile movements moved with optimism and purpose to exploit the forces liberated by the March First Movement.

In Korea, the Japanese colonial administration was in disarray. The recently elected premier of the home government, Hara

Kei, watched the crisis in Korea with concern. Hara's government had inaugurated party rule in Japan in the fall of 1918, and it was clear that the heretofore heavy-handed policy in Korea was not in keeping with Hara's style. By June, Tokyo realized that police suppression was inadequate and that fundamental policy changes would be necessary. The Hara government, therefore, passed the Revised Organic Regulations of the Government-General of Korea in August 1919. Sensitive to charges of Japanese brutality and unenlightened colonial rule, Hara took measures to reorganize colonial rule under the slogan "harmony between Japan and Korea" (*Nissen yūwa*). As we shall see, this did not represent a weakening of Japan's will to rule Korea. Hara cleaned house in the colonial administration, chose Admiral Saitō Makoto as his new Governor-General, and charged him with revamping the administration of Korea. Saitō's appointment and his reforms altered the style of Japan's governance in Korea.

The March First Movement occupies an important place in the collective memory of the Korean people that transcends its central role in the dramatic events of 1919. The nationalist reform and later independence movement had always been plagued by divisive factionalism, and the March First Movement stood out as a decisive point of unity during the colonial period. It also has come to symbolize the awakening of the entire nation to the accumulated political, cultural and economic inequities inherent in Japanese imperial rule. In terms of the maturation of Korean nationalism, however, March First only suggested the potential of a nationalism fully supported by the mass of the Korean people. It remained for Korean leadership elements to unite behind a general program that could enlist mass participation. Meanwhile, Saitō's administration strove to remove the more obnoxious outer trappings of colonialism while at the same time further entrenching Japanese rule. The new policies significantly altered the political climate in Korea, and it is to these important changes we must now turn.

The Cultural Policy Reforms

From the outset the new team of colonial administrators knew their task would be difficult. After all, a bomb had been exploded at Seoul Station the day of Saitō's arrival. Saitō was an urbane, well-traveled diplomat of high repute within government and military circles. Mizuno Rentarō, former home minister (1916-1918), assumed the duties of Director-General of Political Affairs, second in command. Maruyama Tsurukichi, a young and talented civil servant who had become an expert on colonial police affairs, completed the brain trust as police superintendent. The abilities and experience of the new colonial leadership were in stark contrast to the army background and narrow vision of the previous Governor-Generals. Saitō and his team began their task with an exhaustive round of consultations with colonial officials, prominent Koreans, and missionary elements in order to shape their policies.

Saitō had a dual charge. For one, he needed to change the image of the colonial administration in the eyes of Koreans and world opinion. Second and more important, administration and police control had to be made more efficient. Saitō meant to replace terror and coercion with a more subtle policy of cooptation; this meant finding ways to manipulate "cooperative" elements within Korea and to rely on selective repression of more dangerous groups such as militant nationalists and social revolutionaries. The stance of conciliation was for public consumption; behind the scenes, Saitō strove to upgrade the efficiency and sophistication of the control apparatus.

In the political sphere a number of concessions were made in highly visible areas. Saitō redressed major Korean grievances with regard to discriminatory laws. Whipping for minor offenses was abolished. Saitō also modified unpopular laws regulating traditional burial practices as well as police interference with peasant markets and slaughtering. The dual pay scale for Korean and Japanese civil servants was readjusted nominally; Japanese officials, however, were placed on a bonus system insuring superior pay levels. Saitō also promised to recruit more Koreans in the civil service, appoint Koreans to judgeships, and provide more local autonomy.

The question of Korean participation in governance was of fundamental importance. Saitō finessed this issue by creating an advisory council with representatives from the provinces. Excluded from matters of political consequence, the advisory council ended its first year by drafting a report on Korean burial customs. Saitō expanded the city, county and provincial councils to include some carefully chosen Koreans. More importantly, he decentralized decision making in administration to increase its efficiency. This gave governors and county administrators more autonomy. To pay for the expansion of local government, however, the Government-General shifted fiscal responsibility downward, resulting in increased indirect taxes.

The Saitō reforms came to be known as the Cultural Policy (*Bunka Seiji*). This label denoted a general relaxation of controls in the cultural and political life of the colony. Saitō responded to critics of the educational system by promising equality of opportunity in the schools and an expansion of common schools, one school for every district within four years. Publication controls were relaxed as well, and the Government-General began to issue permits for Korean language newspapers and magazines. In 1920, two Korean newspapers received publication permits, the *Chosŏn Ilbo* (*Korea Daily News*) and the *Tonga Ilbo* (*East Asia Daily News*). Although all publications were subject to strict censorship, hundreds of popular magazines and more specialized political publications appeared in addition to the two new dailies. Saitō also removed restrictions on organizations that had been in effect during the Terauchi and Hasegawa administrations. Saitō's Cultural Policy was designed to allow more freedom of association, but only if this did not result in new challenges to the legitimacy of Japanese rule or, worse yet, threaten the peace and security of the colony. Consequently, there was a mushrooming of youth, religious, educational, academic, social, and labor/peasant organizations after 1920.

The conciliation policy had strived to mollify public opinion through selected legal reforms. In addition, the policy had attempted to curry favor with elites by removing restrictions on publishing and organizational life. Behind the policy of conciliation, however, Saitō assiduously worked to strengthen the colonial police. Under Maruyama's direction the military police system was reorganized along civilian lines, military uniforms being discarded by police and all public officials. Concurrently, the size of the police force was increased and its reach in Korean society broadened. While Saitō only promised a school in every district (*myŏn*) within four years, Maruyama was given the resources to expand the police network into every district within a year. In 1919, there were 151 stations and 686 sub-stations in the entire country; by the end of 1920, there were 251 stations and 2,495 sub-stations. In order to control the new press and organizations, Maruyama reorganized police intelligence. The High Police (*Kōtō Keisatsu*) became the instrument of censorship and internal political security. Using an army of informers and intelligence officers, the Japanese police worked to subvert and crush political opposition before it took shape, thus to prevent a repeat of incidents such as March First.

The Cultural Policy also featured several fundamental changes in economic policy. There had been massive protests in Japan over the sharp increase in rice prices at the close of World War I. The Rice Riots of August 1918 in Japan stimulated increased interest in raising rice production in Korea. In response, the Government-General invested tens of millions of yen in irrigation works and agricultural extension activities in order to increase Korean rice yields and make more rice available for export. The plan was ambitious and called for a 9.2 million *sŏk* (one *sŏk* equals 5.119 bushels) increase in production, of which somewhat less than half was to be retained for Korean consumption. While falling short of the plan's target, production did increase by forty percent between 1920-35, but most of the increase found its way to the export market. Moreover, inadequate government financing forced irrigation associations to raise the price of water, thus further burdening the small farmer. The increased availability of Korean rice in Japan helped the food situation at home, but Korean per capita rice consumption continued to drop during the colonial period.

A second major economic change was the rescinding of the Company Law. Hereafter, whether Korean or Japanese owned, companies had only to register their existence, not receive permission to be formed. While this encouraged native entrepreneurs, the main intent was to open Korea to private investment from Japan. Flush from the economic boom of World War I, Japanese companies greedily eyed the cheap, abundant labor in Korea. At the same time, the tariff barriers between Japan and Korea were largely eliminated. Japanese firms already in Korea protested that fledgling colonial companies needed subsidies to protect them from larger, well-financed competitors investing in Korea after 1920. This issue of subsidies was an explosive one, because Korean capitalists were demanding equal treatment.

In 1920, Saitō had established a policy to try to forge a "bridge between Japanese and Korean capitalists." The following year he invited important Korean businessmen to participate in the Chōsen Industrial Commission. Ultimately, selected Korean companies did receive subsidies, most notably Kim Sŏng-su's Kyŏng-sŏng Spinning and Weaving Company. The subsidies came at a time when Korean capitalists were participating in the nationalist Korean Production Movement that will be discussed below, and they were clearly intended to dilute Korean capitalist enthusiasm for nationalist political programs, even those devoted to the development of national (Korean) capital.

The Saitō-Mizuno policies established a more effective administration in Korea by assuaging those Korean grievances whose redress would not disturb the basic patterns of Japanese rule. Henceforth, the Japanese would use a policy of divide and rule, conciliation for non-threatening activities and a more skillful repression of dangerous nationalist and social revolutionary elements. The Government-General's stance during the next decade or so was characterized by flexibility, not the dogmatic harshness of the 1910-1919 period. Saitō courted all elements in Korean society that he felt could be mollified. He impressed American missionaries with his fluent English and protestations of good will. He encouraged, even subsidized, pro-Jpanese organizations formed by conservative Korean leaders. And he worked hard to gain the trust of moderate, middle-of-the-road nationalists, those who most directly benefited from the new climate of tolerance in the crucial areas of freedom of speech and assembly. The Cultural Policy reforms created a very different atmosphere in the colony, and the Japanese waited for the Korean response in the broadened cultural and political area.

The Cultural and Political Renaissance

If 1910-19 had been a dark period in the cultural and political life of the Korean people, the first part of the 1920s was, in contrast, a true renaissance. The Cultural Policy provided new opportunities for Koreans, and in the heady atmosphere of the post-March First period there was a tremendous upsurge of political and cultural activity. Politically, there was every reason to be optimistic. The exile movement had formed a government in Shanghai, and links were being forged with emerging nationalist groups in the colony. The new nationalist press provided a voice for the heretofore silenced stratum of articulate opinion in Korea. Ten years of increases in school attendance and expanding literacy, while still affecting only a small percentage of the population, had widened the pool of potential recruits for political mobilization. Moreover, the development of communications provided increased physical mobility and broke down barriers between town and countryside.

The domestic nationalist revival was most obvious in organizational life. In 1920, there were 985 organizations of all types registered with the colonial police. These were youth groups, religious sects, study groups, academic societies, and social clubs. By September 1922, the number of organizations had swelled to 5,728; the Japanese police provided the following breakdown:

Registered Korean Organizations, 1922

Political and intellectual	48
Labor	204
Youth	1,185
Church youth	639
Religious	1,742
Tenant	26
Children's	40
Academic	203
Industrial	470
Health	6
Anti-drinking/smoking	193
Self-improvement	235
Recreation/social	348
Women's	56
Savings and purchasing cooperatives	53
Other	280

Most of these groups restricted their activities to "safe" social or enlightenment projects; Japanese officials, however, worried about the activist potential of the new youth, tenant, political, and labor groups. As early as August 1920, Saitō had publicly warned Korean organizations to guard against radical tendencies. In addition to the proliferation of organizations, there was a significant structural change in their interrelations. Increased operational freedom led similar groups to form national federations and leagues. In June of 1920, 600 groups joined together to form the Korean Youth League (Chosŏn Ch'ŏngnyŏn Yŏnhaphoe). Other federations came later, particularly among youth, labor, and tenant groups. Political leaders within the nationalist movement competed with each other to gain control of these new federations. As we shall see below, this was particularly significant as ideological struggles began to divide the nationalist movement.

The expansion of vernacular publications at this time gave voice to the goals and ideological orientation of these new organizations and publicized their activities. The legal framework required prepublication inspection of daily newspaper galleys, and all magazines and books had to be approved prior to distribution. The High Police was responsible for maintaining censorship standards that were similar to, but more inclusive, than those in Japan proper. The police gave certain categories special attention: defamation of the emperor or imperial institutions, military matters, radical ideology, Korean-Japanese relations, and Korean nationalism. The main weapons of the censor were warnings, erasure, and in the most serious cases, publication ban. Furthermore, authors and publishers could be prosecuted for thought crimes, the first such case occurring in early 1923. Actual censorship was quite frequent, but in the 1920-25 period it was relatively casual. There was an atmosphere of trial and error as Koreans tested the limits and censors tried to cajole publishers into following the guidelines. Therefore, for the first few years after 1920 the Korean press was relatively open, and Koreans responded accordingly.

Between 1910-1919 under forty magazine permits had been issued, while in 1920 alone, the Japanese issued 409 permits for magazines and books. The two new vernacular dailies, *Choson Ilbo* and *Tonga Ilbo* were granted permission to print articles on current affairs. Such a permit allowed publication of articles on politics, social problems, and international events, a privilege granted also to six magazines in the early 1920s. By 1929, combined circulation of the two newspapers reached 103,027, a tenfold increase over circulation for the entire nationalist press in 1909.

The two nationalist newspapers helped resuscitate Korean nationalism. For the next twenty years they served as the major foci of political and social life in the colony. The papers attracted many of the brightest Korean intellectuals as editors and reporters. Here indeed was an honorable career for politically conscious and patriotic Korean youth. Moreover, youth was the watchword on the new papers. For example, the founder and president of the *Tonga Ilbo,* Kim Sŏng-su, was barely thirty years old in 1920, and the majority of the writers were in their twenties. The new papers were more sophisticated than the pre-colonial press. They featured serialized novels, short stories, essays on social problems, international news, political catoons; in short, daily reading of either newspaper was *de rigueur* for any informed citizen.

After 1920, a new type of magazine appeared. In contrast to pre-1910 issue-specific, privately financed, and narrowly distributed intellectual magazines, mass-circulation magazines of wider appeal emerged in the 1920s. In particular, magazines granted the coveted current affairs permit provided a forum for discussion of burning social and political topics. *Creation (Kaebyŏk), New Life (Sinsaenghwal), Eastern Light (Tongmyŏng), New World (Sinch'ŏnji),* and *Light of Korea (Chosŏn chi kwang)* are examples of such magazines.

If the new newspapers were the heartbeat of the nationalist renaissance after 1920, the intellectual journals were its soul. Just as the March First Movement marked the advent of mass nationalism in Korea, the emergence of the nationalist press marked the maturation of a new generation of nationalist intellectuals. While the appearance of a new generation of such leaders was a hopeful development, it was not without problems, for the increased sophistication of Korea's leadership elite inevitably generated conflicts over ideology and tactics.

Cultural Natonalism: Gradualism and National Independence

Within Korea, the major nationalist movements of the early 1920s were based on the assumption that direct confrontation with the Japanese was a self-defeating proposition. For this group, the lesson of the first decade of Japanese rule was that the nationalist movement needed to raise the general level of national consciousness, literacy, and economic development in Korean society in order to develop a mass base. Tactically, cultural nationalism chose a gradualist approach to solving the problem of independence. This approach sought to take advantage of the relatively relaxed political atmosphere of the Cultural Policy period by mounting major educational and economic campaigns to strengthen the base of Korean nationalism. Moderates theorized that even if the movement could not directly confront the Japanese, it could still lay the foundations for future independence.

The cultural nationalist approach as it evolved in the 1920s was a logical outgrowth of earlier nationalist ideology. The Independence Club (Tongnip Hyŏphoe, 1896-98) had supported education, national consciousness raising, and the cultivation of future national leaders as a means to bring more people into direct participation in politics. In the period after 1900, the progressive reform movement that had earlier failed to substantially alter dynastic politics had turned ultimately to indirect enlightenment activities. In many ways, the fall of Chosŏn confirmed the beliefs of the leaders of these early movements. Sŏ Chae-p'il, Syngman Rhee, and Yun Ch'i-ho of the Independence Club, and An Ch'ang-ho and Yi Sŭng-hun of the New People's Association (Sinminhoe) a decade later, all had looked on the West as their model of the nation-state. What they and their later disciples observed in Korea did not compare favorably to the democratic institutions, strong middle-class, developed capitalist economies, and widespred education of the West, and it was their conclusion that a strong nation-state must be based on such attributes. Indeed, had not Japan been able to avoid colonization by the West because it had harnessed economic wealth, education, military power, and national patriotism to the service of the state?

Moderate nationalists of this temperament pursued a variety of projects that the press lumped under the sobriquet of the "cultural movement" (*munhwa undong*), from which derives the name cultural nationalists for this group. Although not confined to a single organization or under a common leadership, the cultural nationalists were unified by an ideology of nonconfrontation, grdualism, and social development. Perhaps more than any other statement, Yi Kwang-su's well-known and later controversial essay in *Creation* of May 1922, "A Treatise on National Reconstruction" (*Minjok Kaejoron*) embodied the ideology of cultural nationalism. Yi, novelist and author of the Tokyo Student Declaration, had returned to Korea from Shanghai in 1922 determined to work within the broadened political and cultural framework created by the Cultural Policy. He had been appalled by the factional disputes in the Korean Provisional Government and was searching for a common program that would unify all nationalists into a single force. While many disagreed with his gradualist, indirect program for independence that stressed action within the legal bounds of Japanese rule, his statement crystallized the thinking of many moderate nationalists.

The two largest projects mounted in the wake of the Cultural Policy reforms fit the cultural nationalist thesis closely. The first, the National University Movement led by the Society for the Establishment of a National University (Minnip Taehak Kisŏng Chunbihoe), was the natural outcome of the intelligentsia's interest in educational issues. The heavy stress in the colonial schools on Japanese language acquisition, cultural values, and Japanized Korean history had outraged nationalist intellectuals from the beginning. Even more galling was the fact that with few opportunities beyond middle school available in the colony, college-bound Koreans increasingly ended up in Japan to complete their education. To counter the undesirable socializing effect inherent in such a system, nationalists mounted a drive to establish a truly Korean university. This was planned as an institution that would feature the scholarship of the best Korean academicians and at the same time serve as a center for the training of future national leaders.

A venerable ex-Chosŏn official, Yi Sang-jae, was chose as leader of the Society for the Establishment of a National University in November 1922. Song Chin-u, then editor-in-chief of the *Tonga Ilbo,* helped to prepare the organizational framework for a national fund-raising campaign. The goal was to raise ten million yen for the university, and the low, one yen subscription meant that if every Korean donated the goal would be met. The movement generated a national network of offices that worked closely with youth groups, social clubs, temperance groups, and churches. Representatives were sent to Manchuria and the United States to solicit funds. Within six months, however, what had become the largest movement since March First began to falter. Mismanagement of donations, infighting between chapters, and vitriolic criticism from more radical nationalists, including the withdrawal of support from the important All Korean Youth League, slowed the early momentum of the movement. Japanese authorities also announced plans for the building of an imperial university in Seoul (Keijō Imperial University) by 1926, which further diminished public interest. Before long, then, the movement had become moribund.

A second important movement coalesced around the issue of national economic development. The combination of worsening economic conditions, Government-General economic reforms, and renewed discussion of Korea's economic dependence spawned what would become the largest movement of the early 1920s, the Korean Production Movement (Chosŏn Mulsan Changnyŏ Undong) of 1923-24. Korean businessmen were already fighting for subsidies and freedom to participate on an equal footing with Japanese businesses, but moderate nationalists approached the economic crisis on a different tack. Their plan was to mobilize national sentiment in support of Korean industry and handicrafts, thus to encourage self-sufficiency and the development of national capital in competition with Japanese capitalism. They were joined immediately by Korean businessmen who saw the advantage of such political support.

Patriotic appeal for economic development was not a new idea. Nationalists had been quick to see the link between economic power and political autonomy; the Repay the National Debt Movement (Kukch'ae Posang Undong) during the Protectorate period had raised money using patriotic appeals. The first Korean joint stock company, the Masan Porcelain Company in P'yŏng-yang (1908), was a project of An Ch'ang-ho's New People's Association. In fact, the company's founder, Yi Sŭng-hun, became one of the leaders of the Korean Production Movement. The situation in the early 1920s was peculiarly suited to the launching of a large, sustained economic movement. Korean enterprises were reeling under competition from large Japanese companies. Consumer goods from abroad, cheaper and of higher quality than Korean goods, dominated the Korean market. The discriminatory regulations of the 1910-1919 period had seriously inhibited the growth of Korean corporations. With the upsurge of nationalistic fervor after 1919, the time was ripe for a movement that would combine patriotism with the promise of Korean-generated economic growth.

The idea of self-sufficient national economic development had already fostered a number of consumer cooperatives. In P'yŏng-yang, Cho Man-sik, often called the Gandhi of Korea, had created the Society for the Promotion of Korean Production in July 1920. Cho had come in contact with the Gandhian ideas of non-violence and self-sufficiency while attending college in Japan. Cho later joined with Yi Kwang-su and Yŏm T'ae-jin, and the leaders of other consumer cooperatives, to form a national league that in turn gave birth to the Korean Production Movement in December 1922. The addition of businessmen to the usual coalition of intellectuals, students, and journalists was an important development. Kim Sŏng-su, president of the *Tonga Ilbo* and the Kyŏngsŏng Spinning and Weaving Company, and Kim Tong-wŏn, President of the Kyŏnggi Spinning Company, both played important roles in the genesis of the movement. An auxiliary association (T'osan Aeyong Puinhoe) mobilized Korean women to work toward the common end. The plan was simple. The time had come for all Koreans, rich and poor, to support exclusively native producers by patronizing Korean stores whenever possible and using Korean-produced clothing, foodstuffs, and other daily necessities. The movement stressed the positive value of preferring Korean production out of a desire to avoid the confrontation that a boycott of Japanese goods would surely engender. More significantly, the movement's leaders wanted to stress native Korean production for its spiritual effect on national unity.

The Korean Production Movement generated tremendous initial enthusiasm. Rallies and parades in provincial cities opened the campaign, but the police banned all demonstrations in Seoul. In its first year, the movement rode the crest of an upsurging patriotism and was so successful that prices for increasingly scarce Korean goods soared. The movement published a monthly magazine, *Industrial World* (*Sanŏpkye*), to further publicize its activities, and branch offices appeared in every province. At its height in the summer of 1923, the Korean Production Movement had become the most successful mass mobilization of Koreans since the March First Movement. It heightened mass awareness of economic issues, and it altered, at least temporarily, Korean consumption habits.

The movement threatened the Japanese in a curious way. It was not illegal, but it was clearly directed against their interests. Accordingly, the police blocked rallies in Seoul and suppressed advertisements in the national press. Perhaps more effectively, the Japanese continued with the planned tariff restructuring and negotiations on subsidies for selected Korean companies. They also discussed economic concessions with key business leaders in a behind-the-scenes campaign to undermine the resolve of the movement's leadership. Ultimately, it foundered on the same structural problems that had inhibited the growth of Korean industry already in place. Over time, the combination of financial sacrifice entailed in buying more expensive Korean goods, scandals over price gouging, the staying power of Japanese merchants, and the ambivalence of important Korean business leaders undermined the movement. Although the Korean Production Movement continued into the 1930s, it was unable again to muster the enthusiastic support given it in its first year. The movement was also a target for Korean leftists, who charged that to aid Korean businessmen, even in the name of developing national capital, eventually tightened the grip of imperialism and Japanese monopoly capitalism on Korea. These charges impugned the patriotic motives of the movement's leadership, and the resulting controversy marked the beginning of serious ideological cleavages within the nationalist movement.

Although the National University and Korean Production movements had run afoul of organizational problems and political differences, intellectual and cultural activities must be credited with sustaining the spirit of Korean nationalism throughout the 1920s. Under the Cultural Policy new vistas were opened to cultural and intellectual life, and a welter of academic, literary, and artistic societies emerged in the post-March First period. These societies were at the nucleus of an emerging modern, national culture in Korea, and they nurtured the development of Korean national consciousness in historiography, literature, drama, music, and film. While this represented only an indirect form of resistance to the cultural assimilation policy of the Japanese, it was also the most difficult to repress.

Linguists and educators concerned with the standardization and spread of the Korean vernacular banded together in 1921 under the banner of the Korean Language Research Society (Chosŏnŏ Yŏn'guhoe). In the following twenty years the society published standardized grammar and spelling rules, began the compilation of a comprehensive Korean dictionary, and, in alliance with the nationalist press, led mass literacy campaigns in the late 1920s. The society also lobbied Japanese officials to improve Korean language texts and to increase the hours devoted to Korean instruction in the colonial schools. Thus nationalist linguists combined academic interests with a populist concern for raising national consciousness and mass education. Indeed, the success of the Korean Language Society might be measured by the fact that its leading members were arrested and put on trial during World War II essentially for the heinous political crime of compiling a dictionary!

The first modern novels began to appear in the first decade of Japanese rule, and after 1920 there was a flurry of literary production. Early modern novels had often been didactic and critical of traditional Korean social norms. After 1920, the new literature flowered in journals such as *Creation (Ch'angjo,* 1919), *Ruins (P'yehŏ,* 1920), and *White Tide (Paekcho,* 1922). Kim Tong-in and Yŏm Sang-sŏp were two leading novelists whose work appeared at this time. Han Yong-un, best known for his poem "Silence of Love" (*Nim ŭi ch'immuk*), was also becoming active during this period. As time went on, new trends emerged. Concurrent with the rise of leftist thought in the colony after 1920, a flourishing proletarian literature movement appeared. Of whatever ideological complexion, the new literature gave voice to the frustrations of Korean intellectuals aroused by political repression and the many serious social problems arising out of Korea's rapidly changing society. Censorship and/or jail was the fate of many a novelist and poet, but such repression only served to heighten the political flavor of much of the literary production of this period. In addition to literary activity, other cultural organizations such as Ch'oe Nam-sŏn's Kwangmunhoe continued to champion the study and appreciation of Korea's unique cultural heritage.

The cultural renaissance of the 1920s also witnessed the development of Korean drama and cinema. Modern drama in Korea dated back to the first productions of the Wŏn'gaksa Theater established in Seoul in 1908. Since then, new Korean plays and productions of Western plays had been popular among the growing urban intelligentsia. The Japanese police repeatedly closed productions because of their nationalist content, but as soon as one company was disbanded others sprang up to meet the demand for theater entertainment. Cinema in Korea also dates from the 1920s. Perhaps the best known Korean actor of stage or cinema of this period was Na Un-gyu, whose productions were dogged by controversy. *Arirang* (1926), his best known film, was a blatant attack against Japanese rule; for this reason *Arirang* and many other Korean films were banned at this time.

Although artists and intellectuals of the new urban society created a distinctive, modern Korean culture, setting it against the Japanese policy of cultural assimilation as a self-conscious means of asserting Korean national identity, their work could not come to grips with the deeper political issues of the times. The political movements of the moderate nationalists and the cultural achievements of the artists and intellectuals were activities very largely limited to an elite stratum of society. The National University and Korean Production movements in the end were unable to create a mass base for their programs, and so failed to sustain them. The developments in scholarship and the arts, while a valuable intellectual underpinning for Korean nationalism, did not represent a means of enlisting the mass of the Korean people in the service of liberation. Unless political leaders found a way to first awaken, and then to channel into political action the energies of the vast majority of Koreans, the peasantry and growing laboring class which formed eighty percent of the population, independence would remain a dream for nationalist visionaries.

In the aftermath of the March First Movement, social revolutionary ideology had begun to gain popularity among young Korean intellectuals. The spread of leftist ideology brought new ideas to the discussion of the problem of Korean independence. By focusing on the class structure of colonial society and its economic underpinings, social revolutionary thought encouraged criticism of the more moderate nationalist politics that had heretofore dominated the Korean independence movement. The rise of socialist thought, and the connection between its adherents within Korea and the growing communist movement in exile, ultimately led to a serious ideological split within the nationalist leadership that weakened the drive for national liberation.

Leftist Thought and Political Controversy

Just as World War I had begun a process of disillusionment with Western liberalism in East Asia, the Russian Revolution and emergence of the Soviet Union as a champion of oppressed peoples generated increasing interest in social revolutionary thought. Korean intellectuals were not immune to the excitement, and the rise in popularity of socialism at home and in exile was rapid. Socialism offered an alternative world view and a different mode of analysis for those concerned with the problems of socioeconomic reform and national liberation.

After 1910 it was not surprising to see the spread of socialism, first among Korean exiles in the Russian Far East, Siberia, and

China, and then among Korean students in Japan. Nationalists abroad were freer to read and discuss radical ideas and join groups professing principles of Marxism-Leninism, and some of them were attracted to the insights these ideas lent to the problem of national liberation. After 1920, it became increasing difficult to separate social revolutionaries from nationalists, because most Korean intellectuals studied radical ideas as patriots, intensely concerned with overthrowing Japanese rule. The first formal socialist Korean organizations emerged in Russia and Manchuria, while the Bolsheviks attracted Korean nationalists in Eastern Siberia to the common cause of fighting the remnants of Czarist forces and their Western and Japanese allies. In 1918 Yi Tong-hwi formed the first Korean Socialist Party (Hanin Sahoedang), at the same time that Nam Man-ch'un formed a Korean section of the Communist party in Irkutsk.

These two groups ultimately clashed over the issue of Soviet support. Yi Tong-hwi had temporarily joined the Shanghai Provisional Government in 1920, only to become disenchanted with its moderate political line. Yi and his group were among those nationalists in Shanghai who advocated armed struggle and social revolution, and at the height of the factional struggles within the Provisional Government he formed the first Korean Communist Party (Koryŏ Kongsandang). However, a split had developed between the Shanghai and Irkutsk groups, and the competition between the two factions eventually escalated into a bloody armed struggle at Alexeyevsk, Siberia, June 1921. The Alexeyevsk incident disillusioned many Korean communists who had seen the Soviets as allies in the struggle against Japan. Nevertheless, these early groups spread the idea of social revolution and out of them came a number of smaller organizations interested in anarchism and other radical ideologies.

Japan was the second major spawning ground for radical ideology among Korean intellectuals. Always the primary destination for Koreans studying abroad, by 1922 there were several thousand Korean students in Japan. In Japan, Korean students encountered a society that was reeling from the effects of a generation of rapid economic and social change. Moreover, at this particular point in time, the post-World War I recession had brought considerable hardship and increased labor and tenant organization to Japanese laborers and peasants. Social revolution was a hot topic in the tea rooms and bars of Tokyo, and Korean students were drawn into the whirl of new ideas. Korean students in Japan had always been tightly organized, and now many radical organizations emerged that introduced these students to revolutionary ideology. Among them, the Korean Self-Supporting Students' Fraternal Association (Chosŏn Kohaksaeng Tonguhoe) established itself as the first avowedly socialist organization. Its magazine, *Comrade* (*Tongu*), emphasized student and worker relief and the importance of direct involvement with the cause of class struggle.

Students returning from their Japan sojourns brought home with them their radical schooling, and after 1920 they established a number of study groups, youth organizations, and labor and tenant unions. The members of one such group, the Seoul Youth Association (Seoul Ch'ŏngnyŏnhoe, 1921) broke away from the more moderate All Korean Youth League because of their interest in socialism; this group later spawned the Socialist Alliance (Sahoejuŭi Tongmaeng) in 1924. Another radical group with links to Japan was the Proletarian Alliance (Musanja Tongmaenghoe), which later split to form several leftist study societies including the Saturday Society (T'oyohoe, 1923) and the Tuesday Society (Hwayohoe, 1924). Such groups popularized radical ideas and many of their members subsequently were active in Korean communist circles. Other returned students joined existing organizations such as the All Korea Youth League, published journals, or established contact with representatives of exile socialist groups. Already by 1922 the Japanese censors were working overtime to excise the increasing number of radical articles appearing in the nationalist newspapers and new intellectual journals. While individual articles could be suppressed and writers jailed—the first "thought-crime" prosecutions came in 1923 in the wake of the suppression of the *New Life* (*Sinsaenghwal*) magazine, the Japanese were unable to halt the general spread of these ideas within political circles.

The increasing popularity of social revolutionary ideas in Korea led to bitter debates within the nationalist movement. Leftists criticized the moderate nationalists for playing into the hands of the Japanese by avoiding confrontation. Even more vehemently, leftists such as Kim Myŏng-sik and Sin Il-yong lambasted moderates like Yi Kwang-su for daring to suggest that Koreans must work within the colonial system to prepare the groundwork for future independence. They attacked the National University Movement as a useless project that would only benefit the sons of landlords and middle class elements while ignoring the crying ignorance and poverty of the masses. The Korean Production Movement came under attack as a transparent device that used patriotism to enrich Korean capitalists. The distinction made by the ideologues of the Korean Production Movement that national capital was in competition with foreign capital was ridiculed by leftists. They questioned the patriotism of Korean businessmen by asserting that the movement simply served the class interests of rich Koreans at the expense of the poor.

Such charges had split the nationalist movement by the middle 1920s. The leftist attack placed moderate nationalists increasingly on the defensive; radicals, however, were unable to establish their own political movement because of heavy Japanese repression. Radical publications such as *Proletariat* (*Musanja,* 1922) and *New Life* (*Sinsaenghwal,* 1922) were closed down; even the mainstream Ch'ŏndogyo journal, *Creation* (*Kaebyŏk,* 1920-26) was suppressed in 1926 for its radical content. Although radicals were unable to organize themselves successfully and remained, for the most part, aloof from the masses for whom they purported to speak, they decisively affected the nature of political discourse in Korea. By 1925, the Korean communist movement was only beginning to become organized within Korea, but the ideological controversies spawned by social revolutionary thought had already seriously divided the nationalist movement.

United Front Tactics and Korean Communism

The growing split within the nationalist movement coincided with a renewed crack-down by the Japanese police. The new Peace Preservation Law of May 1925 provided the police with broadened powers to control political life in the colony. In November of the same year, the Japanese police arrested a number of Korean communists and leftist leaders. In June 1926 the funeral of the last Yi Emperor, Sunjong, was the focal point of widespread anti-Japanese riots (the June 10 Incident), which precipitated additional police reprisals against nationalist organizations. Concurrently, the High Police began to eliminate radical publications as well as increase censorship actions against the nationalist newspapers. The number of editions suppressed jumped from 27 in 1923 to 151 in 1925. 1926 brought a close to the period of relative freedom of publication as incidences of censorship, seizure, and total suppression of journals mounted.

Internal political struggle and the rising number of arrests heightened tension within the nationalist movement and encouraged a renewed discussion of a united front. Although the split in the movement was serious in 1925-6, there was evidence of willingness to reunite. The moderates had attempted previously to create a broad coalition, but their lack of credibility among the more radical wing of the movement hampered this effort. The discussion then shifted to how ideological differences between groups might be reconciled. By joining the discussion, radicals indicated a new willingness to abandon dogmatic insistence on socialist principles and search for pragmatic solutions to the problem of unity.

At this time, both the Right and Left were anxious that the movement enter a phase of concrete organizational activity. Each worried about the aimless drift of the cause, the Right stung by the failure of the Korean Production and National University movements, and the Left concerned about factional infighting and increasing Japanese repression, which had also targeted the Left's efforts to organize laborers and tenant farmers. The debate over the role of the Korean agrarian masses in the anti-Japanese struggle had precipitated the united front dialogue. Moderates had argued for gradual enlightenment and future participation of the masses. Leftists wanted to harness the potential power of the masses for the struggle against imperialism and, later, for social revolutionary upheaval. This debate had marked a turning point for Korean nationalism in general. Each side realized that the nature of the liberation movement had to change from one driven by elites to one powered by the masses. Finally, early in 1927, the decisive move for a united front came from the forces of the Left.

Practically from its inception, the Korean Communist Party had been directed to establish a presence in the colony, eliminate its factional divisions, and participate in united front tactics. Between 1920 and 1925, however, various factions competed for Comintern (the Communist International, directed from Moscow) recognition and patronage and the party, such as it was, failed to gain a toehold in Korea. Thus, the work of proselytizing Marxism-Leninism had fallen on the shoulders of leftist intellectuals and radical nationalists. Their attack on the moderate wing of the nationalist movement as "accommodationist" had made united front tactics difficult. But by 1925, and in spite of extreme pressure from the Japanese police, the Korean communists had finally established a party in the colony and labored to follow the Comintern line of united front tactics.

The Sin'ganhoe (New Korea Society), active between 1927-31, was the culmination of the search for a united front organization. Founded in 1927 with top posts going to prominent moderate nationalists, the Sin'ganhoe provided a common base for moderates, radicals, and Korean communists. The Japanese tolerated the organization because of its moderate leadership, and they undoubtedly took advantage of its formation as a means to further penetrate the nationalist movement. Once formed, however, the leadership, especially at the branch level, fell to radicals and communists. By 1930, according to nationalist sources, the Sin'ganhoe claimed 386 branches and 76,939 members. It had established a national network that coordinated youth groups, labor and peasant groups, and intellectual societies, and it had become a vehicle for coordinated nationalist activity that served the ends of both the Right and Left.

The struggling and faction-ridden Korean Communist Party found its salvation in the Sin'ganhoe. It provided a mechanism for expanding communist activities, and its participation brought the party in line with Comintern directives. The success of Korean communists and their radical nationalist allies within the Sin'ganhoe local branches demonstrated that conditions were ripe for grassroots organization. Nevertheless, their domination of local

Sin'ganhoe chapters provoked the resistance of the moderate central leadership as well as repression by the Japanese.

The Japanese police carefully watched the Sin'ganhoe from the beginning. Its national conventions were prohibited, and periodic roundups of leftists within the leadership excerbated factionalism within its ranks. Factional struggles had arisen in its first year when leftists had proposed a number of radical amendments to the original Sin'ganhoe charter, calling for exemption of student fees for the poor, the withdrawal from Korea of Japanese companies such as the Oriental Development Company, and the abolition of all laws inhibiting free speech and assembly. The Sin'ganhoe's support of student demonstrations in Kwangju in 1929 (the Kwangju Student Movement) and its role in expanding the incident into a nation-wide disturbance was the beginning of the end of the united front. In the wake of the Kwangju Student Movement a number of communists were arrested, bringing a shift to the right in the Sin'ganhoe leadership. The communist-dominated local branch leadership, already under the influence of changing Comintern directives to avoid domination by reformist elements, began to consider dissolving the organization. In May 1931, the first national conference to be allowed by the police was convened. The moderate leadership fought to save the organization, but they were ultimately defeated by radicals voting for dissolution. The Japanese police watched the process of disbanding with relief as, ironically, their interets coincided with those of the communists bent on pulling out of the organization.

The Sin'ganhoe represented the joining of two streams, each in search of a mass base. For the communists' part, the Sin'ganhoe represented a legal facade under which they might work to create and, ultimately, seize control of a mass national liberation movement. Unlike their Chinese communist contemporaries they were not joining an existing, strong nationalist organization, and this explains, perhaps, their initial success in gaining control of a portion of the movement. Indeed, the success of the communists and radicals might well indicate that they were being perceived as the true leaders of the national liberation movement. Futhermore, it was the Japanese, not bourgeois nationalists, that posed the greatest threat to the existence of a viable Korean Communist Party. Therefore, even after the 1927 debacle for the Chinese communists (Chiang Kai-shek's bloody purge that year of communists in the KMT), the Korean Communist Party continued to pursue united front tactics because, for them, it represented the most promising approach under the circumstances in Korea at the time.

After 1930 the Comintern shifted its line toward an emphasis on a "united front from below" and eschewed collaboration with national reformers of all stripes. The Comintern, however, had only a tenuous hold on the very weak and constantly shifting leadership of the Korean Communist Party. Moreover, its directives to the Korean Communist Party at this time showed how little the Comintern knew about conditions in Korea. The well-known "December Thesis" (1928) had admonished the party—even though the arrests in the Fourth Party Incident of that year left virtually no party to admonish—for failing to distinguish between a revolutionary and national reformist movement and for being isolated from the proletarian elements in society.

In the end, the downfall of the Sin'ganhoe stemmed from the original inability of the nationalist leadership to create a mass-based movement. Both the Left and the Right had failed in this regard. The moderate nationalist movement of the early 1920s had never been able to forge strong links to the vast Korean underclass, and efficient Japanese repression made it impossible for the communists to maintain a viable party apparatus, let alone effectively organize a mass base. It is no wonder, then, that united front tactics failed in Korea. The serious split in the nationalist movement had already weakened the impulse for national liberation, and the common commitment to the Sin'ganhoe could not be expected to reconcile, or even gloss over, the deep ideological divisions and tactical differences that had plagued the movement for so long.

After 1931, nationalist resistance continued, but its thrust had been blunted by the failure of the united front and the disunity of its leadership. Spontaneous demonstrations, isolated terrorism, underground agitation, and widespread sullen resistance still remained, but overt political opposition now was mounted primarily by the exile movement. Outside the peninsula as well, however, the nationalist movement was fragmented, and separate groups each professing its own goals carried on the struggle in relative isolation from one another. Not until World War II did the movement make another concerted attempt to unify forces.

In 1931, the Japanese occupied Manchuria and the next year established the puppet state of Manchukuo. Expansion of the Japanese Empire into Manchuria led to important policy changes in its Korean colony. As we shall see, the 1930s was a momentous period in Korean society, as the accumulated changes of the 1920s were compounded by new economic policies and a forced assimilation campaign that struck at the very existence of a separate Korean cultural identity.

Chapter 17

Forced Assimilation, Mobilization, and War

The Japanese Advance in Asia

In September of 1931, the Japanese Kwantung Army, having manufactured a minor pretext, attacked Chinese troops in Manchuria and expanded their control over the entire province. The Manchurian Incident and the home government's inability to restrain their military leaders in China signaled a decisive change in Japan's foreign policy. Conservatives in Japan had rankled throughout the 1920s at the limitations imposed on Japanese naval power by the Washington Treaty system. The combined effect of the world depression of 1929, which caused a fifty percent drop in Japanese exports, and the advance of Chinese nationalist forces threatening Japanese continental interests, created the political and economic backdrop to the seizure of Manchuria. After 1931 Japan became increasingly isolated in the world community and, at home, the military assumed greater influence within government.

These changes had a profound effect on Korea because, with Japan's renewed advance on the continent, its Korean colony would be required to assume the role of strategic and economic keystone within the framework of Japan's overall Asia policy. In 1931 the Japanese formed the puppet state of Manchukuo and began to develop the rich natural resources of Manchuria. The economic motivation for the seizure of Manchuria was obvious. A vast area rich in natural resources, Manchuria represented an easily exploited storehouse of raw materials for Japanese industry. With protectionism prevailing in world trade the addition of Manchuria to its empire contributed greatly to Japan achieving its goal of economic and political self-sufficiency.

In the years before the outbreak of the war with China in 1937 the Japanese began developing Manchuria as an industrial base, and this led to a reconsideration of overall economic policies in Korea. Korea would be integrated into Japan's northeast Asian development plans by extending its communications across the Yalu, linking its hydroelectric capacity in the north to Manchurian industry, and utilizing its supply of excess labor in new extractive and manufacturing industries. There were already more than a million Koreans in Manchuria. Political domination in Manchuria gave the Japanese authority over these emigre imperial subjects as well as a free hand to deal decisively with the lingering problem of Korean guerrilla resistance centered in North China and Manchuria.

The events in 1931 foreshadowed the end of the period of the Cultural Policy in Korea. As we have seen, since 1926 the Government-General had already begun tightening its control of political and cultural life in the colony. By 1930, the Government-General was beginning to lay the groundwork for a more persistent policy of rapid assimilation. The renewed advance in Asia after 1931 created conditions that demanded more active participation of Koreans in the development of the expanding Japanese Empire, Such imperatives called into question the wisdom of the velvet gloved Cultural Policy and its relative toleration of Korean cultural and intellectual autonomy. What the Japanese required after 1931 was active support and participation in their economic and military plans, not the indirect support of a portion of the elite and the grudging, sullen passivity of the Korean common man. To guarantee such support, Japan set in motion policies in the 1930s to mobilize the Korean population to support its economic, political, and military campaigns. By 1945, the ensuing massive mobilization led to the uprooting of millions of Koreans from their homes and to a disastrous program of cultural oppression that attempted to obliterate the very identity of the Korean people.

Agriculture, Industry, and Labor Mobilization

In July 1931, the new Governor-General, Ugaki Kazushige,

assumed his post, and early in his stewardship he began to readjust economic policies in the colony. The program to increase rice production in Korea had been moderately effective. As has been seen, however, the increased production had generally found its way into the export market, thus, enriching landlords and rice merchants but not the peasant producers. Quite the contrary: the nature of the land tenure system and market forces already operating at the beginning of Japanese rule, by now greatly exacerbated, had resulted in greater concentration of land ownership and a vast increase in tenancy.

Increases in Tenancy During the Colonial Period in Percentages of Farming Households

Year	Landlords	Self-Cultivators	Self-Cultivators/ Tenants	Tenants
1913	3.1	22.8	32.4	41.7
1918	3.1	19.7	39.4	37.8
1924	3.8	19.4	34.6	42.2
1930	3.6	17.6	31.0	46.5
1932		16.3	25.3	52.8
1936		17.9	24.1	51.8
1939		19.0	25.3	55.7
1943		17.6	15.0	65.0
1945		14.2	16.8	69.1

After the world depression, the situation in rural Korea worsened. Increased tenancy was compounded by the rapid increase in the Korean population after 1920. Between 1910-1940 there was an increase of roughly 60-65 percent, from about 15 to over 24 million, a high but not unusual rate of expansion. Because of the more itense pressure on available land resources, landowners could raise rents almost at will, further exacerbating peasant distress. In this situation, large numbers of peasants were forced off the land in search of jobs as casual laborers or as workers in service industries and factories.

Another indicator of rural distress was evident in the increase in landless peasants resorting to upland slash and burn agriculture, the so-called fire-field people (*hwajŏn*). In 1936 over 300,000 families were engaged in such marginal farming, triple the number in 1916. The deterioration of life in rural Korea was also indicated by the increase in landowner-tenant disputes. Disputes recorded by the Government-General increased from 667 in 1931 to 7,544 in 1934; a year later they had more than tripled to 25,834. Although the Government-General revised its tenancy laws and arbitration procedures in the early 1930s to address this problem, the new laws continued to support landowners' interests over those of tenants.

An increased number of absentee landlords was the hallmark of ownership concentration. With owners in absentia, more tenants came under the supervision of landlord agents, who often worked under an incentive system which tied their income to the amount of rents collected. This system further depersonalized owner-tenant relations already strained by the impersonal market. An increase in Japanese investment in Korean land in the 1930s had the same deleterious effect; although relatively few in number, many Japanese absentee landlords possessed very large holdings. But a more tragic consequence of the colonial agricultural economy was that it served the economic interests of Korean landowners so well, and in so doing removed them as a possible source of support for nationalist politics. Furthermore, although a few large landowners invested in banks, bought stocks, and participated in small commercial ventures, and fewer still made a successful shift to industry, in the main the land owning strata continued to profit from secure investments in land without transforming itself into a successful commercial class.

In 1934, Governor-General Ugaki formally ended the rice production program under pressure from Japanese agricultural interests who were demanding relief from the downward pressure on prices caused by the influx of cheap Korean rice. Ostensibly to meet the food problems in the colony, he now instituted a self-regeneration campaign to encourage rural self-sufficiency and frugality. In 1933, however, Ugaki had inaugurated an agricultural diversification plan under the banner of "cotton in the south, sheep in the north." The expansion of acreage devoted to cotton displaced dry field acreage that had formerly been devoted to cereals. The campaign thus served Japanese demand for cotton fiber and wool, but it reduced the amount of food available for feeding the population.

Although the program to increase rice production had been the key economic policy of the Government-General in the 1920s, manufacturing and industry also expanded. Low labor costs in Korea had attracted investors in light manufacturing areas such as textiles. Indeed, although dwarfed by the domination of Japanese capital, Korean entrepreneurs Kim Sŏng-su and his brother Kim Yŏn-su had created the largest Korean industrial group from a beginning in textiles. Other important Korean entrepreneurs in light manufacturing were Chŏng Yong-ch'ŏl (Mokp'o Rubber Co.) and Yi Chin-sun (Kongsin Hosiery), while in trading and retailing An Hŭi-je (Paeksan Trading Company) and Pak Hŭng-sik (Hwasin Department Store) were preeminent. In addition to the expansion of light manufactures, the government investment in irrigation works, roads, and railways stimulated growth in the construction and cement industries. Although modestly, by 1930 the share of the industrial and manufacturing sectors in the heretofore agrarian economy of Korea had increased.

With the new Company Law and removal of most tariffs in 1920, there was increased Japanese investment in the Korean economy. In 1926, the industrialist Noguchi Jun began operations in north Korea by spearheading hydroelectric development on the Pujŏn River. Noguchi's harnessing of the rich power resources in northern Korea paved the way for later industrialization. The coupling of this inexpensive energy source to abundant, cheap Korean labor was the potent selling point that attracted additional investment in the 1930s. The establishment in Hŭngnam of the Chōsen Nitrogenous Fertilizer Company, and later an entire related chemical industry, was a logical corollary development, given the extensive energy required by chemical manufacturing technology. The Japanese search for secure sources of raw materials led to an expansion in mining and related extractive industries. Particularly after 1937, the Japanese undertook intensive development of Korean ore and timber resources. The discovery of high-grade iron ore deposits in the north attracted the Japan Steel Corporation, and the production of pig-iron and steel expanded dramatically after 1934. From a base of 59,700 tons of pig-iron in 1934, by 1943 over 450,000 tons of pig-iron and 100,000 tons of steel were being produced in Korean foundries. With the war in China, the Government-General, working closely with private industry, intensified exploitation of strategic ores such as gold and tungsten.

By 1940 the structure of the Koran economy had been decisively altered. The share of the manufacturing sector (including mining and timber) increased from 17.7 percent in 1931 to almost 40 percent by 1939. Within manufacturing, the chemical, tool, and metal industries increased most dramatically, and there was a corresponding drop in the percent share of the food processing industry.

Manufacturing Output by Industry (in percentages)

Industry	1930	1936	1939
Textile	12.8	12.7	13.0
Metal	5.8	4.0	9.0
Machine and Tool	1.3	1.0	4.0
Ceramic	3.2	2.7	3.0
Chemical	9.4	22.9	34.0
Lumber and Wood	2.7	2.7	1.0
Printing	3.1	1.8	1.0
Food	57.8	45.2	22.0
Gas and Electric	2.4	5.6	2.0
Others	1.5	1.4	11.0

The increased level of economic activity also further bound the economies of the metropole and colony. In 1934, 95 percent of all Korean exports went to Japan, and 80 percent of imports to Korea came from Japan. Indeed, the Korean market assumed major importance for the Japanese home economy as, by 1939, it had come to absorb 34 percent of all Japanese exports. A further dimension of the economic picture was the participation of Korea-based Japanese companies, Korean entrepreneurs, and Korean labor in Manchuria. With Japanese political control and previous communications development, capital and labor flowed freely over the Korean-Manchurian border, and by the outbreak of war in China, the close-knit economic linkage between Japan-Korea-Manchuria envisioned a decade previously by Japanese businessmen and economic planners was becoming an accomplished fact.

The economic development of Korea during the 1930s had a profound effect on the Korean population. As industry expanded hundreds of thousands of peasants found themselves in factory jobs. In the decade of the 1930s, the factory work force in Korea doubled, and after the outbreak of the Pacific War in 1941, the war economy hastened this trend.

Koreans Employed in Industry within Korea, 1932 to 1943

Year	Number of Persons	Index of Increase
1932	384,951	100
1934	483,396	126
1936	594,739	154
1938	585,589	152
1940	702,868	183
1942	1,171,094	304
1943	1,321,713	343

If laborers in mining and transportation were added, the increase would be even more dramatic. These figures also ignore the enormous numbers of Koreans working in Manchuria and Japan. The labor requirements of the new industrialization in north Korea and Manchuria were largely met by the movement of Korean labor from the populous Kyŏngsang and Chŏlla provinces in the south.

The increasing numbers of landless peasants driven off the land by the worsening situation in the agricultural sector provided the pool of labor needed for the industrial expansion. As we have seen, the concentration of landownership and spiraling indebtedness of the rural peasantry combined to drive people into the new cities and toward low-paying jobs in the burgeoning industry of the colony. Before 1937, private industry campaigned to recruit peasants, and their task was simplified by the increasingly desperate situation in the Korean countryside. Recruitment by the market, however, was insufficient after the outbreak of war in China.

After 1937, therefore, Korean labor became a pawn to be moved at will by central planners in Tokyo and Seoul.

Just as Korean entrepreneurs were handicapped in their efforts to compete with their Japanese counterparts, especially in the area of large-scale industry, in the labor force as well Koreans found themselves largely relegated to secondary jobs in an ethnically demarcated work place. Koreans formed the bottom of the labor hierarchy, and before the war only a small percentage were able to rise into leadership or technical positions. The foremen of most factories were Japanese, and the skilled trades were dominated by Japanese labor. Wages were also differentiated by ethnicity with Koreans generally being paid less than Japanese laborers for similar duties. Similarly, Koreans were found less in management, mostly restricted to middle levels of authority or to clerical positions. With the coming of war and the draining away of Japanese personnel through army conscription, Koreans were able to advance to higher positions on the factory floor and in offices. But the dimensions of this phenomenon have yet to be fully determined.

The tenure of Governor-General Ugaki (July 1931-August 1936) was a time of growth and relative optimism for landlords, industrialists (both Korean and Japanese), and colonial officials. For nationalists, radicals, and even apolitical intellectuals, it was a period of deep disillusionment and depression. Arrests for political crimes mounted and the High Police continued to harry publications and organizations of all kinds. And for Korean laborers and peasants the situation was becoming increasingly desperate, as tenant and labor unions formed in response to the worsening conditions were smashed by the Japanese police.

In spite of the long odds, a resistance of sorts continued. In the northern provinces continguous to the Manchurian border, Korean communists organized underground Red Peasant Unions that violently attacked landlords, their agents, and Japanese police units. Although generally unsuccessful and not on the scale of the famous Wŏnsan General Strike in 1929, labor strikes and stoppages were frequent. The Kwangju Student Movement of 1929 had provoked nation-wide riots, but after 1930 student led demonstrations were sporadic and localized. After 1931, the

Japanese police used brutal tactics to wipe out the guerrilla threat in Manchuria and North China, yet some groups survived. Among them, small guerrilla units led by Yi Hong-gwang, Kim Il-sŏng (Kim Il Sung) and Ch'oe Hyŏn managed to survive into the late 1930s. The domestic political efforts, however, never again achieved the breadth of the movements of the early and mid-1920s.

Political histories of this period often ignore the fact that in the cultural realm life continued—that, in fact, while political activity decreased, the period between 1931-37 was one of cultural growth in Korea. After 1931, the nationalist newspapers began to publish mass-circulation monthly entertainment magazines. Magazines like *New Asia* (*Sindonga*), *Korean Light* (*Chogwang*), and *Three Thousand Leagues* (*Samch'ŏlli*), appealed to a general urban, middle class audience. While enduring heavy censorship, these magazines managed to present social commentary, current events, serialized novels, new poetry, movie reviews, and gossip columns to an avid readership. The growing sophistication of publishing led to segmented marketing strategies, as the monthlies spawned women's editions and youth and farmer's publications. A glance at the articles and advertisements within the entertainment press provides a vivid picture of the growing urban culture of Korea. However depressed the political life of the colony had become, a picture emerges of a vital and creative culture that flourished in conjunction with Japanese rule. Indeed, modern Korean urban culture developed in resonance with Korea's increasing importance within the Japanese Empire. It is no surprise, then, to observe the profound influence of Japan on its style and content.

Advertisements for nostrums, radios, vocational and correspondence courses, books, and an increasing array of retail items revealed a growing consumer culture, at least among the urban middle class. Much of the new consumer culture was of Japanese origin, yet its presentation and design was a synthesis guided by Korean tastes. There was a decidedly schizophrenic flavor to these developments as Koreans were alternately attracted to and repelled by the cultural influences of their Japanese overlords. The tensions inherent in such a situation were revealed in social commentary that was characterized by biting sarcasm, wit, and parody. In fact, the problem of integrating cultural and material influences from the outside with indigenous tastes and sensibilities remains in contemporary Korea. In the present day, it is crystallized in student debates over the evils of Western materialism and the search for a truly Koreanized, modern cultural identity.

During this period, academic societies were also active. One notable example was a unique organization devoted to the study of Korean history. In 1934, a group of nationalist scholars that included Yi Pyŏng-do and Yi Sang-baek formed a society for the study of Korean history and literature called the Chindan Society (Chindan Hakhoe). The society strove for nearly a decade to promote Korean historical and literary scholarship. This was a self-conscious effort to counter Government-General sponsored studies that deliberately deemphasized unique aspects of Korean history and culture in order to foster cultural assimilation. The Chindan Society was ultimately suppressed by the Japanese thought police for engaging in "activities deleterious to the promotion of harmony between Japan and Korea."

The Ugaki administration provided only a preview of what was to come. The appointment of Minami Jirō (August 1936-May 1942), former Minister of War and one of the leading generals of the Manchurian Incident, foreshadowed a period of unremitting bleakness that would continue until liberation in 1945. Minami's authoritarianism set the tone for a period of forced assimilation and mobilization as Japan rallied its empire to the support of the adventure in China after 1937. From this point forward, the material and human resources of Korea were directed to the war effort. And because of the importance of its Korean colony to the prosecution of the war in China, the Japanese began a systematic program of cultural assimilation to insure the participation of the Korean populace as loyal and self-sacrificing members of the imperial family.

Forced Assimilation and War Mobilization

The move to accelerate the assimilation of Koreans into the cultural and political life of the Japanese Empire had begun under Governor-General Ugaki. In 1934, he revamped educational policies under a new Rescript on Education and introduced a revised curriculum for the colonial schools. The new curriculum featured extended hours of instruction in Japanese language, ethics, and history. Minami continued the educational reforms by integrating regulations for all schools, introducing the Pledge for Imperial Subjects, and combining Korean and Japanese normal schools. The intent of these policies was to forcibly inculcate Japanese values and consciousness of empire among Korean students. To this end, the number of common schools (grades 1-6) was increased to maximize the reach of Japanese propaganda. Perhaps most objectionable to Koreans, the new educational regulations eliminated the study of Korean and use of Korean in general instruction. Later, the policy of forced Japanese language use was expanded by regulations requiring exclusive use of Japanese in all public offices. By the 1940s, the Government-General forced all businesses and banks to keep records exclusively in Japanese.

Forced language use struck at the heart of the Korean cultural identity, but it was only the beginning. In 1935, Ugaki began a policy that required student and government employee attendance at Shintō ceremonies. Led by the Christian community, a storm of protest greeted the Shintō shrine order. The forced attendance policy split the Korean Christian church. Many Christians closed their schools and churches rather than accede to the order. Some foreign missionaries were expelled and several thousand ministers arrested between 1935-38 as a large portion of the Korean Christian community continued to resist. The Japanese policy assumed that as imperial subjects Koreans should also celebrate the imperial mythology that had been spun around the Japanese emperor. Yet in the view of Koreans of all faiths, forced attendance at Shintō ceremonies was deeply objectionable, an invasion of that most sacrosanct area—personal religious beliefs.

The impossible aim of the policies Governor-General Minami was charged with carrying out was the ultimate eradication of all differences between the citizens of the Japanese homeland and the population of colonial Korea. In fact, of course, this end would be achieved only when Koreans had been completely stripped of their Korean cultural identity (and indeed of their very racial memory) and had become Japanese both in name and in reality, in body and in soul. Under the slogans of "Japan and Korea as one body" (*Nai-Sen ittai*) and "harmony between Japan and Korea" (*Nissen yūwa*), Minami embarked on a breathtaking program to mobilize Koreans of all walks of life. The mobilization was designed to insure total obedience and enthusiastic participation—the fiction was that, as full-fledged imperial subjects, Koreans would feel the same fervor as their brethren in the sacred homeland. The forceful assimilation of Korea was only a part of the grand plan to bring all of East Asia under the benevolent blanket of Japanese rule. According to the logic of Japanese assimilation, the "fortunate" Koreans were to be a special part of the inner empire within the vast area propagandized as the Greater East Asian Co-Prosperity Sphere.

After 1937, the Government-General began to shut down Korean organizations of all types. As the freedom to associate was removed, the Japanese created mass organizations to bring all Koreans into the war effort. In fact, they now began to apply to Korea the same policies that had begun to mobilize the entire population on the home islands. In 1938, the Government-General formed the Korean Federation of Youth Organizations, Local Youth Leadership Seminars, and Training Institutes for Children's Organizations, thereby binding all students and youth into interlocking organizations directed by the central government. Intellectuals were brought together into an All Korea Writers Federation, while similar nationwide associations organized laborers, tenant farmers, and fishermen. Different mass organizations focused directly on the war effort in China, such as the Korean Defense Association, the Association for Study of Policy Dealing with the Critical Situation, and the Korean Association for Imperial Rule Assistance. The Japanese used these organizations to facilitate labor and military recruitment (the Japanese army began to accept Korean volunteers in 1938), to collect cash and in-kind contributions to the war effort, and for the staging of patriotic rallies. By the 1940s, every Korean was associated with at least one mass organization.

Pro-Japanese organizations had been active since 1910, but

their members had incurred the suspicion and reprobation of most Koreans. There had long been a home rule movement as well, begun in the 1920s by Ch'oe Rin, that had sought to gain political rights under the Japanese constitution for Koreans. Now, with the forced assimilation campaign, pro-Japanese organizations operated boldly, assured of official blessing, and already in 1937 Minami created the National Association of Koreans to unite such groups under a single banner. The campaign to enfranchise Koreans in the Japanese Diet continued, and the Diet passed resolutions permitting Korean representation in 1938-39 and again in 1941. The cabinet, however, refused to act. Only at the end of the Pacific War did select Korean representatives sit in the Diet, but the plan for general representation beginning in 1946 was negated by the Japanese defeat in 1945.

The assimilation policy required the Japanese to change their recruitment practices within government. However, although the total numbers of Koreans working within the Government-General increased after 1931, the percentage of higher Korean officials actually dropped due to an expansion of the number of positions. About fifty percent of the 87,552 central government, provincial, municipal, and educational officials in the Government-General were Korean in 1943. Yet, eighty percent of high officials and over sixty percent of middle rank officials were Japanese. Banks, businesses, semi-governmental organizations, the police force, and the Japanese army represented other avenues for real participation in the colonial system. As in the government bureaucracy, however, Koreans continued to be relegated to inferior positions, and to the jobs most offensive in their impact on the Korean populace. The notorious example of the colonial police highlighted the warped effects of such discriminatory inclusion: while the recruitment of lower class elements to the force provided a limited mobility for some luckless Koreans, at the same time it engendered tremendous resentment among the general population, turning Korean against Korean.

The forced assimilation policy of the 1930s reached its apex on the eve of the outbreak of the wider war in the Pacific. In

1940, all Korean language newspapers save the Government-General organ, the *Daily News* (*Maeil Sinbo*) were shut down, thereby closing one of the few remaining channels of Korean expression. A year earlier, however, the Japanese had struck at the most personal, and perhaps the most cherished, source of Korean identity, family and personal names. The Name Order promulgated in late 1939 "graciously allowed" all Koreans to change their names to Japanese style surnames and given names. One could carefully choose Chinese characters to retain or suggest similarity with the original name, or an entirely new name could be devised, but all proposed changes had to have Japanese approval. Pressure was applied to all Korean government employees and the employees of semi-governmental corporations such as the Manchurian Railway Corporation. Soon the heartrending spectacle of Koreans abandoning ancient family names became a daily event at local registry offices as, in the end, over eighty-four percent of the population complied with this cruelly insensitive edict.

Even changed names, however, did not mean true inclusion, whatever the implications of the ideology of assimilation. In spite of registration of a new Japanese name, nationality distinctions were maintained on the public records. Public documents, domicile registration, school and job applications all required two sets of names, lest a Korean "pass" as a genuine Japanese. It is hard to imagine what Japanese leaders were thinking when they devised the Name Order. In a society where deep reverence for lineage had been a way of life for millennia, such a policy could only engender the most profound resentment. Nearly a half century after liberation, the memory of this policy remains burned in the consciousness of Koreans, and the psychological trauma it engendered is embedded in literature and song.

The Japanese had in mind the extinction of the separate cultural identity of the Korean people when it devised its forced assimilation policies in the 1930s and 1940s. For the survival of the Japanese Empire, its imperial subjects had to be encouraged to act and think like Japanese citizens. By combining forced assimilation with continued discrimination and exploitation, however, Japanese authorities insured the ultimate failure of their policies. While some few Koreans were happy to participate, the vast majority of the population only suffered the contradictions inherent in the wartime policies.

The forced assimilation policy was based on the dubious proposition that Koreans and Japanese could become as one in a system that continued to discriminate on the basis of ethnicity. Racism is a significant feature of all colonial systems, and, in the words of Albert Memmi, "all efforts of the colonist are directed toward maintaining social (racial) immobility." The Japanese justifed their rule with the sophistry that their mission in Korea was to bring modern values and economic development to Korea. The maintenance of their privileged position, therfore, was only just and legitimate. That they chose to obfuscate their policies with the rhetoric of benign assimilation was subtly confusing and psychologically damaging. To have to cast off one's primary identity for that of the colonizer demeaned Korean culture in a profound way. To intensify this process as was done in the 1930s in Korea added another level of trauma to what was, at bottom, a harsh and brutal system of colonial rule.

For most Koreans, assimilation remained an abstraction, but for those Koreans who attempted to succeed in the colonial system, it posed a real dilemma. Even partial inclusion in the bureaucracy or a Japanese company required language skills and acceptance of Japanese ways. For the Korean elite and middle class, it was often necessary to adopt a dual personality. Yet no matter how hard one tried to emulate the habits, values, language, and culture of the colonizer, exclusion from the system was always only a hair's breadth away. Thus, those who tried to participate could succeed at best only in part and at the price of alienation from their native culture and identity, and from their countrymen.

Nevertheless, many Koreans chose to collaborate in the colonial system. Life under Japanese rule begged difficult decisions. To remain completely faithful to one's Korean identity and to refuse to accept Japanese ways in all things limited one's life chances. But to actively assimilate meant to implicitly accept the colonizer's debased view of the value of one's own culture and heritage. An ambitious Korean had few choices, as most avenues of upward mobility lay in Japanese dominated institutions. The emerging Korean bourgeoisie had to work with Japanese banks and government offices or have their prospects significantly diminished. Office personnel perforce were clothed in the institutional identity of the government bureaucracy or corporation in which they worked. The fact was that there were few appropriate avenues of opportunity for educated, ambitious Koreans that did not involve some compromise. Rejection and open defiance of the system meant limited access to a decent job, ostracism, jail, or exile, each with its terrible consequences for one's self and family.

In the 1930s, the line between political purity and collaboration became blurred, as everyone was forced to participate in some measure. The great tragedy of the colonial period was that at its end so many had been compromised. Not only had the Japanese imposed a vast program of cultural and social mutilation on Korea, but they had also turned Koreans against one another. Class conflict would have been severe enough at the end of Japanese rule, but resentments rooted in class antagonisms were heightened by this issue of collaboration and the cultural betrayal it implied. Entrepreneurs who profited in the Japanese system, landlords, and Korean policemen were obvious targets of resentment. But the mobilization in the 1930s spawned another whole group of targets as the Japanese cajoled or dragooned a number of Koreans prominent in social and intellectual circles to front mass organizations devoted to the war mobilization. The political and cultural apostasy of such opinion leaders was psychically damaging, particularly at a time when there seemed so little hope for a resurgence of Korean nationalism. Ultimately, this issue of collaboration caused deep wounds in Korean society that would continue to fester long after liberation.

The Last Phase of Colonial Rule, 1941-1945

For Koreans already sore beset by the mobilization campaigns of the 1930s, the widening of the war after the attack on Pearl Harbor in December of 1941 meant increased hardship. Having declared war on the Allied powers, Japan found itself fighting on fronts stretching from the South Pacific across New Guinea to Southeast Asia, in addition to the commitment of its forces in China. By the war's end in 1945, Japan's manpower needs for the war effort had also scattered Koreans far and wide. Koreans worked in the mines and factories of Japan and Manchuria. They guarded prison camps, built military facilities, and served Japanese troops in a variety of ways on all fronts. Within Korea, people were moved about in an extraordinary mobilization of labor to insure production for the war effort. The consequence was still more misery for most of the Korean population, as lives were interrupted and often endangered at the caprice of military planners.

In 1940, the Japanese organized the entire colony into 350,000 Neighborhood Patriotic Associations. Each association consisted of ten households, and this became the basic unit for a variety of government programs for collection of contributions, imposition of labor service, maintenance of local security, and for rationing. The contribution campaigns appealed for monetary or in-kind donations, and avoiding contributing was difficult. With war shortages in metals, gold and silver jewelry and brass table services were collected through these organizations. The resort to neighborhood organizations crowned the Japanese effort to mobilize the labor and personal wealth of the entire colony for the war effort.

The schools also became prime targets of the war mobilization. The Government-General reduced the number of classroom hours in 1941 so that students would be free for various war-related activities such as ceremonies for departing troops and labor service in construction or in the fields. All youth under military age were expected to participate in such programs. In 1944 the Japanese passed a special Student Labor Mobilization Ordinance that turned students into half-time workers. While onerous, the labor requirement for younger students did not take them away from their homes; this was not the case for Korean college students who, after 1943, were required to serve in the Japanese military.

The Japanese Imperial Army began accepting Korean volunteers in 1938. This was not, however, the beginning of Korean involvement in the Japanese military, from 1910 on, select Koreans had been included and trained in the Japanese armed forces. After 1930, small numbers of Koreans were admitted to the regular course of the Japanese Military Academy in Tokyo and a larger number found their way into the new Manchurian Military Academy. Pak Chŏng-hŭi (Park Chung Hee), Republic of Korea President 1963-1979, no doubt is the best known graduate of the Manchurian Military Academy. The mass recruitment of Koreans after 1938, however, was not on the elite track; the volunteers found themselves doing labor duty on airstrips and guard duty at prisoner of war camps in China. The war's continuous drain on Japanese manpower ultimately required the general conscription of Koreans after 1943. In a shameful development related to military conscription, the Japanese even organized the so-called Comfort Corps, made up of Korean young women sent to the front to service the sexual needs of the troops.

While thousands of Korean men found themselves in military service, by far the greater Korean contribution to Japan's war effort was made by ordinary Koreans mobilized to work in factories and mines in Manchuria, northern Korea, and Japan. The numbers of such laborers uprooted in the war mobilization were staggering. In what has been called a "population hemorrhage," perhaps as many as 4,000,000 people, an astonishing 16 percent of the Korean population, were living outside the borders of their country in 1944. This does not count those moved from the southern provinces to work in the industrializing north. The drainage of manpower into the Japanese army had created desperate labor shortages in Japan. To fill the gap, Koreans, particularly from the southeast Kyŏngsang provinces, were recruited to go to Japan to work in menial positions. Some of the most arduous labor duty was in the mines, where tens of thousands of Koreans labored throughout the war. With the onset of aerial bombing of Japanese industry, planners began to move war production off the home islands. The resultant expansion of industry in Manchuria and northern Korea required the further migration of hundreds of thousands of laborers.

The internal and external migration of Korean labor during the war years left a bitter legacy. The urban population of Korea increased from three to ten prcent of the population between 1930-1945. The mass movement of so many raised the political and social consciousness of the population. The heretofore rural-based population of Korea was shaken up, dispersed, and brought back together in the space of a decade. This movement had a politicizing effect, particularly for rural Koreans who returned to missing families, lost land, unemployment, and crowded conditions in the new cities. Expectations for life chances and the perception of class differences were irrevocably altered. And beneath the accumulated psychological trauma lurked a deepening resentment of the Japanese and their collaborators.

The war effort developed the industry of Korea in a curious way. The chemical industry in the north became a prime source of munitions and ordnance for the Japanese army. Textile companies found an inexhaustible demand in the needs of the Japanese armed forces. And from a meager beginning, a sophisticated tool and machinery industry emerged to manufacture a host of war-related parts. Korea and Manchuria were largely spared Allied bombing during the war, and so the Japanese shifted the production of many industrial and manufacturing needs to these safe havens. Understandably, the war also brought opportunities to some Korean industrialists. Indeed, Korean entrepreneurs had ready networks for labor recruitment, and the wartime economy provided additional access to the capital resources needed to expand production facilities. Those in a position to take advantage of the needs of the war effort thus profited enormously, to the disgust of many of their countrymen after the war.

While the domestic political resistance had been driven underground after 1931, the outbreak of war stimulated increased activity in the movement in exile. At this time there was an increase in contacts between Korean exile leaders, including those still with the moribund Shanghai Provisional Government, and the nationalist government of Chiang Kai-shek. Although the Provisional Government had been dormant after 1925, nationalists had continued to be active in China. Kim Ku's Korean National Party and the more leftist Korean Revolutionary Party of Kim Wŏnbong now emerged, each representing distinct factions of the nationalist movement. In 1931 they briefly came together in an unsuccessful effort to form another united front, this time in league with the Chinese Nationalists. The Chinese were particularly interested in a Korean role in the struggle against the Japanese, and after 1937 Kim Ku and Kim Wŏn-bong joined forces and allied themselves with the Chinese war effort.

The Korean exile movement in China had remained factionalized through the 1930s. Kim Ku trained military forces and organized assassinations and bombings in China and Korea proper, but he had little sympathy with the Korean left and their revolutionary programs. Kim Wŏn-bong had emerged in the 1920s as the leader of the anarchist Righteous Brotherhood (Ŭiyŏltan) and by the 1930s had won the respect of the Korean communist left. At Kim Wŏn-bong's urging in 1938, leftist units were consolidated into the Korean Volunteer Corps. Although this solved temporarily the issue of working together with the KMT, the Corps continued to be torn over the issue of whether to concentrate its efforts in North China (the stronghold of the Chinese communists) or to work in the KMT controlled area in the south.

The majority of Korean communists were working then with the Chinese Communist Party. In 1939-40 a Korean communist, Mu Chŏng, emerged as a leader of Korean units within the Chinese communist movement. But Korean communism had to maneuver within the complicated politics of the KMT-CCP united front in the 1940s. This further exacerbated the factionalism within the overall Korean liberation movement. While Kim Ku and other nationalists worked with the KMT and struggled to unite their forces, Korean communists found allies within the Chinese communist movement in the north, and the distrust between the major forces of the Chinese united front fueled the antagonism between Korean resistance groups.

In 1940, the major Korean non-communist resistance forces came together again to form the Korean Restoration Army (Han'guk Kwangbokkun). The Restoration Army was one of the largest Korean military groups ever formed in China, with a force that ultimately reached about 3,000 regulars under its command. The Restoration Army worked with the KMT and, later United States military advisors. Koreans were in high demand for intelligence and espionage work, and they also participated in guerrilla operations, propaganda activity, and helped to organize underground resistance in North China and Manchuria.

Nevertheless, The Korean independence movement, whether of the Left or Right, remained fragmented during the War. By the eve of liberation there were a number of leaders, each commanding the loyalty of small groups, waiting for the ultimate Japanese defeat. Korean communists working with the Chinese gained valuable military and organizational experience in North China. The nationalist elements of the Korean Restoration Army solidified their Chinese Nationalist contacts. Abroad, Syngman Rhee continued his feverish diplomatic activity in his efforts to establish himself as the leader of a Korean government in exile. The Manchurian guerrillas, Kim Il Sung among them, who had survived the Japanese extermination campaigns of the late 1930s, were in hiding in the Soviet Far East. All these numerous factions of the Korean resistance began planning to return to their homeland as the inevitability of Allied victory over Japan became more obvious. But clearly no one group would be able to claim responsibility for removing the Japanese from Korea. Thus, in the aftermath of Japanese rule, dozens of leaders from the domestic and exile movements emerged in competition for leadership of a liberated Korea.

In the last years of Japanese rule, Korean society reeled under the weight of the war mobilization and political repression. With almost any act defined as a crime against the state, from linguistic scholarship to sabotage, the prisons of the colony overflowed with tens of thousands of political prisoners. By even a modest estimate several million Koreans had been uprooted from their homes and sent to work abroad or in the northern provinces. War-related shortages made life unbearable. The state rationed dwindling food supplies, melted down personal effects in the smelters of war production, and apparently even destroyed film prints, the creative product of the entire early Korean film industry, for their silver content. Korean language publications all but disappeared. The Korean people thus waited impatiently for the end of the war, the increasingly bizarre demands of the Japanese overlords a signal to many, no doubt, of the growing desperation of the imperial cause. By the last months of the war,

Korean society thrashed about as if in a gruesome nightmare, longing for the relief and clarity of a new dawn.

Chapter 18

Liberation, Division,
and War, 1945-1953

August 15, 1945 was a day of jubilation throughout the Korean peninsula. Japan's surrender, unimaginable only a few years earlier, seemed to open the way for Koreans themselves to shape their own destiny for the first time since 1905. Koreans differed, however, in their visions of a postcolonial state and society. While most Koreans welcomed the prospect of independence, forty years of Japanese rule had engendered socioeconomic, political, and ideological cleavages within the country that made national unity problematic. And in 1945, as in the late nineteenth century, it was not only Koreans who were interested in Korea. If the Japanese defeat in World War II had brought liberation to the peninsula, it had also created a geopolitical vacuum in northeast Asia that neither of the two great powers of the postwar era, the United States and the Soviet Union, was willing to relinquish to the other, or to the Koreans themselves. In less than five years, the interaction of these forces, internal and external, led to national division and devastating civil war.

The Colonial Legacy, and the Transfer of Power

It is impossible to comprehend the events and significance of the period of liberation without reference to the previous four decades of Japanese rule. Colonial policies had shattered the foundations of a remarkably stable nineteenth-century bureaucratic agrarian society and unleashed, new forces in conflict with the old and with each other. Korean society in 1945 was a maelstrom of old and new classes, political groups, and ideologies. About eighty percent of the population still lived on the land, but in

addition to landlords and tenants, the Korean social scene was
now dotted with an assortment of capitalists, white-collar professionals, factory wage workers, and hundreds of thousands of
landless peasants who had been uprooted from their villages by
wartime mobilization policies and were now returning home from
other provinces or parts of the crumbling Japanese empire.
Colonialism had spawned both an active and passive Korean
resistance, including numerous nationalist groups, both in Korea
and abroad, each with its own history, personal connections, and
political agenda. It had also created a variety of collaborators:
Koreans who had openly and enthusiastically supported Japanese
rule, those who had unwillingly acquiesced, and a whole range
of people in between. Communism in Korea had also developed
as a radical response to colonialism, and like other nationalist
groups, the Korean communists were also divided by their
experiences and goals.

In this jumble of sometimes overlapping, more often antagonis-
tic, forces and ideas, one can draw a heuristic line between two
basic political orientations at the time of liberation—keeping in
mind, of course, that there was a whole range of opinions and
interests on either side with a grey, possibly even apolitical, area
in the center. To the right of the line were the majority of propertied and educated Koreans, many of whom had cooperated in
one way or another with the colonial regime and were therefore
inclined to be lenient on the issue of collaboration. Most were
resistant to fundamental social change such as land reform.
Others, including some of the more progressive landlords who
had transferred a portion of their assets into industry, regarded
change as inevitable, but were anxious to control and contain
it so as to preserve their privileged positions in the society. Also
on the right were those Koreans with less education and little or
no property who had faithfully served the Japanese state, such
as the Koreans who comprised about forty percent of the colonial
police force.

On the left side of the spectrum were Koreans of varying backgrounds, including students, intellectuals, peasants, and workers
who had been politicized by the colonial experience. Some were
actual members of the Communist Party or felt an affinity

toward communism as a force that had opposed Japanese rule and advocated justice for the poor and oppressed. All were committed first to a thorough purge of collaborators from positions of power and influence. They sought, in addition, some form of redistribution of wealth, such as land reform, that would redress the inequities of the past and transform Korea into a more egalitarian society.

As early as the 1920s the basic antipathy between right and left had already burst forth in the form of an intellectual debate in Korean magazines and newspapers. It had grown in the 1930s as more and more Koreans found themselves participating in the Government-General's economic development programs as junior partners or victims. The wartime mobilization between 1938 and 1945 had sharpened the differences between the two sides and brought the animosity to a new height. By the end of the war, and long before any artificial geographic lines had been drawn at the thirty-eighth parallel, Korea was already an ideologically bifurcated society, held together by the power of the colonial state. The great question of liberation was what would happen once that state was gone.

In August 1945, with the outcome of the Pacific War no longer in doubt, the main concern of the Japanese authorities in Korea was with maintaining order and protecting the lives and property of Japanese citizens until one or more of the Allied victors arrived. For this they needed Korean help.

They turned first to Song Chin-u, a political moderate closely associated with Kim Sŏng-su, his boyhood friend and patron, and with other Korean landlords, businessmen, and "cultural nationalists," many of whom had gradually accommodated themselves to the colonial regime. Like many of his associates, Song had acquired a certain reputation in Korea as a nationalist for his role in the March First Movement of 1919 and its aftermath in the 1920s. Unlike most of them, however, Song had managed to keep a low profile during the war, and by 1945 he was something of a rare commodity in Korea: a politician with elite Korean and Japanese colonial connections who had some relatively untarnished, if modest, nationalist credentials. Between August 9 and 13 the Government-General entreated Song to head up an interim administrative committee to preserve law and order. For reasons that are not entirely clear, but may well have had to do with Song's fear of compromising his already delicate political position, he refused the offer, and the Japanese were forced to consider an alternative candidate.

On the morning of August 15 the Japanese made the same offer to Yŏ Un-hyŏng. Yŏ was a highly respected and popular political figure with impeccable nationalist credentials. A populist at heart, he was politically far to the left of Song and much less attractive in that sense to the Japanese. On the other hand, although he was willing to work with the communists, he had never joined the Communist Party and claimed he could never embrace a materialist view of history. At this point, moreover, the Japanese still expected that the Soviets, who had already attacked the northern port cities of Unggi and Najin on August 10, would be occupying all of the peninsula, and they reasoned that Yŏ's more radical political stance would give them some leverage with that most dreaded enemy.

The Government-General's hopes that Yŏ would be a pliable figurehead were immediately shattered. Yŏ accepted the offer, but only on condition that the Japanese immediately release all political prisoners, guarantee the food supply for the next three months, and absolutely refrain from interference in any Korean peace-keeping, independence, and mobilization activities. The Japanese reluctantly agreed, and Yŏ quickly set up the Chosŏn Kŏn'guk Chunbi Wiwŏnhoe or Committee for the Preparation of Korean Independence (CPKI). From its headquarters in Seoul, the CPKI established contact with a wide range of prominent Koreans throughout the country, and Yŏ called upon Koreans to act together in unity and to refrain from violence.

The CPKI developed rapidly from a temporary peace-keeping organ as envisioned by the Government-General into a new national government. Branches of the CPKI, called "people's committees" (inmin wiwŏnhoe), sprang up all over the country almost overnight and assumed control of the local administrative apparatus. All thirteen provinces had provincial committees within a few days after liberation. By the end of August there were committees in most of the major cities and a total of 145

throughout the peninsula. Within three months, there were committees at all administrative levels down to the smallest villages.
At each level the people's committees were supplemented by indigenous workers' and peasant unions, and by peace-keeping,
student, youth, and women's groups which affiliated themselves
with the local committees. Drawing on this nationwide base, the
CPKI convened a representative assembly in Seoul on September 6, and several hundred delegates announced the formation
of the Chosŏn Inmin Konghwaguk or Korean People's Republic (KPR) and scheduled future national elections.

Scholars disagree about the political character and legitimacy
of the KPR. Standard South Korean and American scholarship
has tended to view the KPR as a communist front whose popularity was directly proportional to the degree it was able to
camouflage its real intentions, i.e., the establishment of a revolutionary communist state. According to this view, Korea in 1945
lacked the necessary requirements for socialism and Koreans were
generally unwilling to espouse the program of the Korean Communist Party. Revisionist studies of the period, on the other hand,
have suggested that the KPR represented a genuine attempt at
a leftist coalition government and that it had strong popular backing. Scholars of this view do not dispute the fact that Korean
communists, many of whom had considerable experience as
political organizers in the decade before liberation, played an important role in the formation of the people's committees and the
KPR, but they contend that the prevailing mood of the country
at the time was revolutionary and that the communists consequently felt confident enough to allow a moderate segment of
the right a place in the new government for the sake of national
unity.

The KPR's roster of cabinet officers and its platform tend to
lend support to the revisionist view. Both suggest an effort toward
the establishment of a workable national coalition in which the
left, to be sure, would predominate. Cabinet posts went not only
to leftists like Yŏ and Hŏ Hŏn, but also to Kim Sŏng-su and
to right-leaning nationalist exiles associated with the early independence movement and the Korean Provisional Government in
Chungking. Syngman Rhee (Yi Sŭng-man), a former member

of the old Independence Club and onetime president of the
Korean Provisional Government when it was in Shanghai, was
chosen as the KPR chairman.

A twenty-seven-point platform, announced on September 14,
also left a certain niche for the right. The land reform plank called
for confiscation without compensation (and redistribution to the
peasants who worked it) only of land belonging to the Japanese
and to the so-called national traitors who had collaborated with
them. Unconfiscated land was to be subject to a tenancy rate
reform on a 3-7 basis, by which rent would be capped at 30%
of the crop. Nationalization was to be applied only to major industries such as mining, large-scale factories, railways, shipping,
communications, and banking, most of which were already
owned or controlled by the state; small and medium commerce
and industry would be allowed to continue and develop, although
under state supervision. Labor provisions for an eight-hour day,
prohibition of child labor, and a minimum wage were basically
reformist and echoed the demands that Korean workers had been
making throughout the colonial period. The platform also gave
the franchise to all Koreans, both male and female, with the sole
exception again of the collaborators, and promised freedom of
speech, assembly, and religion.

While the KPR thus strove for coalition, it can hardly be denied that the new government's platform, if carried out, would
have constituted a social revolution in the Korean context. The
proposed confiscation of land alone would have been a virtual
deathblow for the core of Korea's propertied class, because so
many in this group were major landowners and collaborators.
It is not difficult to imagine, however, that the majority of
Koreans, for whom colonialism had been a bitter and degrading
experience, would have been supportive of such a measure, and
there is, indeed, much evidence of such support. Throughout the
country between August and November 1945, Koreans proceeded to dismantle the colonial administration at every level and to
expel those judged as collaborators from positions of political
power and influence. Although communists played an often significant part in these dramas, they were not invariably the leaders, and observers noted that there was always rapid participation

by the local population. The KPR program thus seems to have been a reasonable reflection of popular sentiment.

Soviet-U.S. Rivalry and the Division of the Peninsula

During World War II Americans had gradually become accustomed to hearing their president speak of the "gallant Red Army" and to thinking of the Soviets as allies, but such warm regard for the Soviets was a new phenomenon. Between 1918 and 1920, the United States had sent 9,000 troops to Siberia as part of an allied expeditionary force to crush the Russian Revolution, and it was not until 1933 that the United States had officially recognized the new Soviet state. Hostile foreign policies toward the Soviet Union, moreover, had always tended to find support in longstanding American fears of socialism and communism. The wartime alliance, in spite of all the rhetoric and seeming goodwill, was for both nations essentially a military marriage of convenience. As the war wound down, the old suspicions, never far below the surface, started to break through again, and one of the first areas to be affected was Korea.

For the Soviet Union, Korea had long been an area of strategic interest. It had all begun in the late nineteenth century as the Tsarist empire had expanded east with the Trans-Siberian Railway into its new Maritime Province (betwen the Ussuri River and the Pacific), acquired from the Chinese in 1860. The concern with Korea was natural, dictated by geography: the two countries shared a common ten-mile border near the mouth of the Tumen River and not far from the new Russian naval port of Vladivostok. Russian concern with Korea, however, had been more than matched by similar Japanese imperialist ambitions and anxieties. After a decade of failed mutual attempts to reach a satisfactory accord on both Korea and Manchuria, including a secret proposal in 1896 to partition the peninsula along the 39th parallel, the two countries found themselves edging ever closer toward war, finally launched by the Japanese with a surprise attack on Port Arthur in 1904. In the end, the result had been the eclipse of Russian influence in Korea for forty years. At the end of World War II, the imminent collapse of Japan once again made Korea an object of attention in Moscow.

American interest in Korea before the 1940s had been confined for the most part to a few Protestant missions and even fewer businessmen. For that reason, although the United States had been the first Western nation to sign a formal diplomatic treaty with Korea in 1882, it had also been the first foreign embassy to leave in November 1905 after the Japanese had forced the Koreans to sign a protectorate treaty. This policy of acquiescence in the Japanese seizure of Korea had been formalized in the Taft-Katsura Memorandum of 1905, by which Japan had agreed, in turn, to respect America's control of the Philippines. It had remained the basic American policy toward Korea until Pearl Harbor. Thereafter, however, long-range American policy on Korea had undergone a gradual shift. By late 1943 it was clear that Japan's anticipated defeat in the war would make the United States a great new power in East Asia, and former American indifference to Korea was replaced by the same fear of Russian control of the peninsula that had tormented the Japanese at the turn of the century.

While the issue of Korean security was never forgotten, American policy makers in the State Department were temporarily forced by military imperatives to bow to the views of the War Department. Anticipating a long and difficult battle for the Japanese home islands, the United States desperately sought Soviet participation in the war against Japan on the Asian mainland, and U.S. military leaders, including General MacArthur, were willing, if necessary, to pay the price of Soviet control over Manchuria and Korea. An agreement for Soviet participation in the war that left the invasion of these two areas entirely in Soviet military hands was reached at Yalta and Potsdam in 1945.

Subsequent events, however, allowed State policy planners to regain the upper hand. By August 10, after the atomic bombings of Hiroshima and Nagasaki, it was clear that the war was over and that a land invasion of Japan would be unlikely. Concern now centered on the continent, where Soviet armies had already begun to sweep into Manchuria and Korea. At this point there was nothing to stop a complete Soviet occupation of the peninsula; American troops could not be moved quickly enough to prevent it. Nevertheless, at a meeting of the State-War-Navy

Coordinating Committee on the evening of August 10-11, a decision was made to divide the peninsula into two occupation zones and hope the Soviets would agree. Dean Rusk, a major at the time, and Colonel Charles H. Bonesteel, later a commander of American forces in South Korea, were given thirty minutes to select an appropriate dividing line. They chose the thirty-eighth parallel, a boundary that gave control of Seoul to the Americans and minimally disturbed the existing administrative divisions. Suggestions were made to rush American troops to Pusan if the Soviets refused to accept the partition, but to everyone's surprise the Soviets agreed, and the Americans did not arrive in Korea until September 8.

Even today a Cold War perspective from the 1950s continues to inform much of the popular perception of the Soviet and American occupations of Korea. A critical reassessment of this perspective is now underway, especially in the United States and South Korea, and the debate will undoubtedly continue as more and more evidence comes to light. In the midst of what can sometimes seem like a quagmire of conflicting interpretations, it is perhaps useful to keep several points in mind. First, both the American and Soviet forces were anxious to insure that whatever political form Korea ultimately took would be friendly, or at least not inimical, to their respective security interests. Second, Americans have often tended to regard communism as a monolithic force centered in the Kremlin rather than as a congeries of localized nationalist and socialist movements with their own historical and cultural roots. Third, Koreans in 1945 were not merely pawns in a great power game: just as Korean actions were affected by the presence of the two foreign armies, so too were the Americans and Soviets influenced and constrained by the Korean milieu.

On arrival in Korea both the Americans and the Soviets were confronted with the existence of the KPR and its people's committees. Their reactions to the fledgling government, however, were very different.

Any discussion of the Soviet occupation must include a caveat about sources. American government and military archives are extraordinarily open and provide an abundance of information about the aims and actions of the U.S. in Korea in 1945. Such access to Soviet files, however, is impossible, at least for now. Nevertheless, a combination of available American and Korean sources suggests the following broad story. The Soviets accepted the Japanese surrender and moved temporarily into the background, allowing the ongoing process of de-Japanization and social revolution to continue at the local levels through the channel of the people's committees. At the same time, they kept a guiding hand on affairs at the top in P'yŏngyang, although they never set up a formal occupation government. This relatively lighthanded approach to Korea by the Soviets undoubtedly reflected both empathy with the Korean revolution and a pragmatic calculation that the revolution was not contrary in any way to their own strong interest in having a friendly state on the other side of the Tumen River.

The result of Soviet policy was the complete overturn within a few months of the colonial bureaucratic and social structure. Collaborators were thrown out of office, and in March 1946 a sweeping land reform was implemented that destroyed the basis of landed wealth that had existed in Korea for centuries. In addition to the confiscation of Japanese landholdings, about 5,000 Korean landlords lost most of their land in the redistribution process, although those who were not deemed pro-Japanese traitors were given the option of either retaining enough of their land to work themselves (*5 chŏngbo* or 12.25 acres) or of moving to another district where they would be given a similarly small plot. Atrocities did occur, but in general the reform appears to have been carried out with surprisingly little violence, perhaps because most of the larger landowners were in the south and because many of the northern landlords had already fled by the time the reform was announced.

Other social changes followed in the wake of land reform. Major industries were nationalized, although small and medium businesses were encouraged to remain active. Labor reforms included an eight-hour workday, social security insurance, higher pay, and equal pay for equal work regardless of sex. The equality of women was also protected in a law prohibiting such practices as concubinage and prostitution, female infanticide, and other forms of female exploitation. Such reforms were executed under Soviet auspices, and there is no doubt that Soviet intervention and patronage gave the Korean communists a political edge not only over the right—which they really did not need— but also over the moderate left. Nevertheless, the reforms were led and carried out by Koreans and reflected to a considerable degree the original leftist spirit of the KPR.

The American Occupation

The American thrust in Korea contrasted sharply with the Soviet political push. Playing Iago to an already suspicious Othello, the Japanese authorities in Seoul had passed the word along to the American command in Okinawa in early September that Korean communist and independence agitators were plotting to subvert Korean peace and order and had warned of possible sabotage and mob violence. Thus even before leaving Japan, the Americans were already distrustful of Korean intentions and inclined to regard the anti-colonial revolution taking place there as a Soviet-inspired communist conspiracy antithetical to American interest. Once in Korea, the American occupation force, the XXIV Corps commanded by General John R. Hodge, refused to recognize the KPR (Hodge was, in fact, under orders from Washington not to recognize any Korean government) and eventually outlawed it. Instead, the U.S. set up a formal United States Army Military Government in Korea (USAMGIK) and proceeded to resurrect much of the discredited colonial administrative structure throughout the country. Briefly, at the beginning of the occupation, USAMGIK even attempted to make use of existing Japanese personnel, but this policy was abandoned when it stirred up an inevitable uproar from Koreans. The Americans then began to appoint more Koreans to USAMGIK posts, but many of the most important joint or subordinate positions went to Koreans who only a few weeks earlier had been serving the Government-General before being removed by the people's committees. Such Koreans were often promoted to fill positions formerly held by the departing Japanese and included thousands of Korean colonial policemen who had been in flight or in hiding when the Americans had landed. While the Americans were not unaware of the problem of collaboration, they chose largely to ignore it for the sake of administrative efficiency and because they distrusted the leftist character of the KPR.

Many of the Koreans who came to fill the higher echelons of the military government, including the two top Korean police officials, Cho Pyŏng-ok and Chang T'aek-sang, were affiliated with the Korean Democratic Party (KDP). The KDP had been founded on September 16 by a group of wealthy landlords and businessmen with close ties to Kim Sŏng-su and Song Chin-u. Some of its more moderate elements, like Kim and Song, had originally gone along with the KPR in the interest of self-preservation when it had still appeared that the Soviets would be occupying most or all of the peninsula. As soon as it had become clear, however, that the Americans would be occupying the southern half, including Seoul, Kim and Song and their associates had set up their own political organization, which eventually became the KDP, and had issued a denunciation of the KPR for its communist activities. With little or no appreciation of the historical context in which they were operating, General Hodge and his officers tended to equate the Koreans in the KDP, who were property-owning and anticommunist—in addition to being well-dressed, educated, and often even English-speaking—with the middle class that formed the political basis for American democracy. Unfortunately, what seemed middle-class and democratic by American standards was more often than not upper class, reactionary, and collaborationist by Korean standards in 1945.

It was one thing to deny recognition to the KPR as a legitimate government; it was another to extirpate the KPR's nationwide structure of people's committees and their supporting organizations, including labor and peasant unions. The process was long and violent, exacerbated by ill-conceived USAMGIK economic policies, and reached a climax in September 1946 with a general strike by railroad workers in Pusan. The strike quickly spread to mass demonstrations in Taegu and eventually turned much of the southern occupation zone into a hotbed of insurrection. Korean rightist forces, including the National Police and a Korean constabulary established by USAMGIK the previous year, put down the rebellions with the support of American troops and materiel, and by the end of 1946 most of the people's committees in the south were gone. At least one, however, managed to survive into 1949. On Cheju Island that year the people's committee was finally rooted out only after a sustained assault that destroyed three fourths of the island's villages and left tens of thousands dead.

Economic and social reform under American military rule reflected USAMGIK's basic political orientation toward the right. Although the Americans moved quickly to reduce tenancy rates from one-half to one-third of the crop, land reform of any kind was continually postponed at the urging of USAMGIK's conservative Korean advisors in the KDP, many of whom were large landowners. It was thus not until March 1948, in the last months of military rule, that the Americans finally carried out a land reform, but it was limited to those rental lands formerly owned by the Japanese, less than twenty percent of the total. USAMGIK also instituted labor laws banning child labor (children under the age of fourteen) and limiting employment to sixty hours per week (with overtime rates for work in excess of forty hours). From the beginning, however, USAMGIK took a dim view of labor unions and strikes, often incorrectly assuming them to be the work of communists; such an attitude, in turn, encouraged rightist-controlled police and private goon squads to deprive Korean workers of many of the basic rights enjoyed by their counterparts in the United States.

The Emergence of Separate States

Neither the Soviet Union nor the United States had envisioned the formation of two separate Korean states in the summer of 1945. At the Cairo Conference in December 1943, the United States, Great Britain, and China had agreed that Korea should become free and independent "in due course," and Stalin had concurred in this sentiment when Roosevelt told him about the Cairo discussions soon afterwards in Teheran. Koreans who learned of the Cairo declaration took the phrase "in due course" to mean immediately after liberation, but the great powers, at Roosevelt's initiative, were actually thinking in terms of a four-power trusteeship that might last as long as forty or fifty years. The trusteeship question was discussed again at Yalta and Potsdam in 1945 and was finally resolved in December of that year at the Moscow Conference. The Moscow accords stipulated a four-power trustee-ship of Korea for up to five years and provided for a Soviet-U.S Joint Commission to work toward the establishment of a uni-fied provisional Korean government.

The Joint Commission met in 1946 and again in 1947, but it was already clear by the end of the first set of meetings that the commission was in trouble. The stumbling block was the ques-tion of whether or not Korean political parties and organizations who opposed trusteeship should be consulted in connection with the formation of a provisional government. The underlying cause of the trouble, however, was the right-left polarization of Korean politics as a result of Soviet and American occupation policies. At first the opposition to trusteeship had cut across Korean political lines, as one might have expected in a country that had just suffered four decades of foreign rule. But the communists suddenly reversed their original anti-trusteeship stance as a result of calculated self-interest and probable urging from the Soviets, and anti-trusteeship subsequently became a rallying point for the right, one of the few genuinely popular rightist issues during the entire liberation period. Although the communists made a point of saying that they supported trusteeship in the context of the entire Moscow agreement, which specifically enjoined the U.S. and the Soviet Union to work toward the establishment of a provisional Korean government, the rightists seized upon the op-portunity to denounce the communists as "country-selling Soviet stooges," and USAMGIK added to the confusion and ferment by deliberately implying that trusteeship was solely a Soviet policy.

The fact was that while both the United States and the Soviet Union were committed at the highest levels to an internationalist solution to the Korean problem through trusteeship, their occu-pation forces on the ground were being allowed to pursue na-tionalist policies that envisioned a unified Korean government only on terms that excluded, respectively, either the right or the left, a view that was encouraged by Koreans themselves on both extremes of the political spectrum. Such a position naturally in-clined each occupation force and its Korean allies to prefer two separate Korean states to a unified state in which power had to be shared. Indeed, even before the first meeting of the Joint Commission in March 1946, both the Soviet and the American occupation forces had already moved in that direction by sponsoring separate Korean advisory and administrative bodies in Seoul and P'yŏngyang.

The process had begun as early as the fall of 1945, when each occupation command had publicly welcomed back its own favorite Korean patriot-in-exile. In the north the Soviets gave their support to Kim Il Sung, famous to many Koreans—and notorious to the Japanese police—for his guerrilla activities with the Chinese communists in Manchuria in the 1930s. Kim's history between 1941 and 1945 is obscure, but he appears to have retreated to Soviet military training camps in Khabarovsk and Barabash to wait out the war. There is evidence to suggest that Kim landed at Wŏnsan on September 25, and on October 14 he was accorded a public welcome by the Soviets as "General Kim Il Sung." Although only 33 years old, Kim's unblemished reputation as an anti-Japanese fighter, the backing of a loyal band of armed partisans, personal charisma, and—not least of all—unequivocal backing of the Soviet occupation force allowed him to gain control of the north's politics over older and more established communist leaders who had stayed in Korea throughout the colonial period. (The southern communists remained largely under the control of Pak Hŏn-yŏng, an important communist activist in the country since the 1920s.) In February 1946 a *de facto* provisional central government, the Interim People's Committee, was inaugurated in P'yŏngyang with Kim at its helm, and non-communist northern political leaders like Cho Man-sik, who had originally supported Kim, were gradually squeezed out of the political process. In the fall of 1946 a northern army also began to take form.

Almost simultaneously with such centralization in the north, USAMGIK was laying the foundations for a separate rightist provisional government in the south. On October 20, 1945, the American command presented Syngman Rhee to the Korean public with great fanfare. Rhee, who was 70 years old in 1945, had acquired a reputation as a patriot for his work in the Indepen-

dence Club and the Shanghai Provisional Government and had
spent most of his adult life in the United States, where he had
received advanced degrees from both Harvard and Princeton. He
was a fervent anticommunist and proceeded immediately upon
his return to Korea to denounce not only the Soviets and the
Korean communists but any Korean group, such as the KPR,
that was willing to work with them.

Such rhetoric was too extreme at the time even for General
Hodge, who was still under pressure from the State Department
to cooperate with the Soviets, but it endeared Rhee to the political right, centered in the KDP, and gave him an advantage over
Kim Ku, his main rival for rightist affection: although both Kim
and Rhee possessed the requisite nationalist credentials that the
KDP so desperately needed to make a bid for political power,
Kim was less tolerant of the KDP for its collaborationist past
and willing, if necessary, to strike a deal with the left to insure
a unified Korean government. Rhee thus soon became the rightist favorite, and General Hodge, in spite of a growing personal
dislike for Rhee, eventually came to acknowledge his importance
to those Koreans most favored by the military government. In
February 1946, just as Kim Il Sung was forming the Interim People's Committee with Soviet approval and help in the north,
Syngman Rhee was in the process of founding the Representative Democratic Council, which USAMGIK seemed to regard as
a possible forerunner of a Korean provisional government.

After the breakdown of the first Joint Commission in the summer of 1946, General Hodge, still hoping for an acceptable
political alternative to Rhee, and under pressure from the State
Department, launched an eleventh hour attempt to put together
a centrist political body that would be acceptable to the Soviet
Union and thus save the Moscow accords. The idea was to ex-
clude extremes of both the right (Syngman Rhee) and left (Kim
Il Sung in the north and Pak Hŏn-yŏng in the south) in favor
of a coalition of the moderate left (Yŏ Un-hyŏng) and moderate
right (Kim Kyu-sik). In the polarized Korean political atmosphere
that had developed during the first year of foreign occupation,
however, there was little support for such a coalition, and it came
to nought. Relations between the United States and the Soviet

Union, moreover, were beginning to undergo a major change, as Roosevelt's internationalism was gradually replaced by Truman's policy of containment. By the summer of 1947, USAMGIK had moved even closer to a separate southern government with the inauguration of a South Korean Interim Legislative Assembly (December 1946), the Truman Doctrine had been officially proclaimed (March 1947), and the Soviet-U.S. Joint Commission had become moribund.

Given both the Korean and international political climate at this time, it was all but inevitable that two separate Korean regimes would now eventually emerge. The final step in this tragic process was taken in September 1947, when the United States announced its intention to move the Korean question to the newly created United Nations. There, despite Soviet protests, the United States succeeded in obtaining approval in the General Assembly for the establishment of a United Nations Temporary Commission on Korea (UNTCOK) to supervise general elections leading to the formation of an independent Korean government. P'yŏngyang disputed the UN's authority to undertake such a mission and refused UNTCOK entry to the northern zone. At American insistence, the United Nations then voted to proceed with elections only in the south. In spite of objections from both P'yŏngyang and from southern nationalists like Kim Ku and Kim Kyu-sik, who feared a permanent division of the country and still hoped for an accommodation with the north, the elections were held in May 1948. Two months later a constitution was adopted by the new National Assembly, and on August 15 the Republic of Korea (ROK) was established with Syngman Rhee as its first president. On the basis of the UN-supervised elections, the ROK claimed legitimacy as the only lawful government in Korea and was promptly recognized by the United States and its allies. P'yŏngyang responded to these events by holding its own elections on August 25, and the Democratic People's Republic of Korea (DPRK), also claiming to be the only legitimate government on the peninsula, was proclaimed in September with Kim Il Sung as premier. In late 1948 the Soviets withdrew their troops from Korea, and the Americans followed suit in June 1949. The stage had now been set for civil war.

The Korean War, 1950-1953

Each of the two Koreas has consistently blamed the other as the sole aggressor in the Korean War of 1950-1953, but expert opinion today suggests a far broader and more complex view of the war's origins rooted in the 1945-1950 period described above. While there is little room for doubt that the north actually launched the attack across the 38th parallel on June 25, 1950, it is also important to place that attack in the context of the increasingly violent political polarization of the peninsula in the previous five years, especially in the two years following the establishment of separate Korean regimes in 1948. Between the end of 1948 and June 1950 South Korea was the scene of a bloody, and ultimately unsuccessful, indigenous leftist guerrilla war that erupted on Cheju Island and in Yŏsu-Sunch'ŏn in South Chŏlla and spread throughout much of the country. During this same period military conflicts along the 38th parallel between northern and southern forces, many of which appear to have been initiated by the south, became increasingly frequent and intense and continued right into the spring of 1950. Both Rhee and his generals, moreover, spoke openly during this period of retaking the north by force. In the end, the crucial factors affecting the DPRK decision to attack in June 1950 were probably the failure of the southern guerrilla movement, the return to North Korea in 1949 of tens of thousands of battle-hardened Korean veterans of the Chinese civil war, and North Korean fears of a major preemptive attack from the south.

Following the blitzkrieg attack on June 25, the well-trained and more experienced DPRK troops, equipped with World War II tanks and fighter planes obtained from the Soviets, soon overwhelmed the ROK army. They took Seoul in three days and continued to sweep south. By early August they had captured all but a small, fifty-by-fifty mile slice of the peninsula extending east from the Naktong River to the port city of Pusan (the so-called Pusan Perimeter). The United States moved quickly to intervene militarily under UN auspices, and the course of the war changed dramatically in September when General MacArthur, commanding the UN and ROK forces, carried out a successful amphibious assault on the port of Inch'ŏn near Seoul, thus cutting the northern army in two. Seoul was retaken on September 28, and within weeks the UN and ROK troops had pushed north to the Yalu River.

In late November, however, the course of the war was abruptly reversed again, when hundreds of thousands of Chinese soldiers who had been gradually crossing into Korea since mid-October, launched a major counter-offensive, pushing the UN and ROK forces back down the peninsula. On January 4, 1951, Seoul fell for the second time. Although UN forces succeeded in recapturing the capital city in March, a stalemate between the two sides subsequently developed around the 38th parallel. After two years of negotiations a truce was finally signed at P'anmunjŏm on July 27, 1953. Since then the Chinese have withdrawn their forces (1958), but the United States has continued to maintain about forty thousand or more troops on the peninsula, even down to the present day.

Three years of fighting had solved nothing and brought ruin to both halves of the country. The toll in human lives was staggering. In the south alone, the combined total of military and civilian casualities—Koreans who had been killed, executed, wounded, kidnapped, or gone missing—was about 1.3 million people. Nearly half of the industrial capacity and a third of the housing in the south were destroyed along with much of the public infrastructure. Although precise figures are not available, the human and physical destruction of the war appears to have been even greater in the north. With a population base of about only one-half that of the south, the north suffered military and civilian casualties estimated at 1.5 million people. Intense aerial bombardment of the north throughout the three-year period ravaged the countryside and reduced cities like P'yŏngyang to ashes and rubble.

Those who experienced the war know that such numbers do not even begin to convey a sense of what it was like. Those who did not can only try to imagine: the terror of alien armies and incendiary bombing; the separation of families, often to be permanent; the frantic flight to refugee camps up and down the peninsula; the subsequent struggle for survival in a swirling mass of similarly displaced and desperate people; the fear of reprisal from one side or the other, or from a neighbor taking advantage of the chaos or politics to settle an old score. The war killed and maimed millions of Koreans, but it also left its scars on an entire generation of survivors, a legacy of fear and insecurity that continues even now to affect the two Koreas both in their internal development and in their relations with each other.

Chapter 19

Authoritarianism
and Protest, 1948-1990

Since 1948 and until only very recently the politics of South Korea have been characterized by two expanding and opposing forces. Controlling the society at the top has been an increasingly oppressive and systematic authoritarian coalition of political, bureaucratic, economic, and security groups, dominated by a single dictatorial leader. Confronting this massif of power has been a growing and ever more diverse and sophisticated collection of opposition groups, both within and outside the formal political structure.

Three times during this forty-year period the opposition has shaken or broken through the authoritarian framework to create an opening for more liberal forces to transform the system: first in 1960-61, again (indirectly) in 1979-80, and most recently in 1987-88. On the first two occasions, the opposition victory proved to be ephemeral. A new strongman soon appeared who seized control of the political system and ended the brief period of freedom, simultaneously raising the stakes for both sides. The final denouement of 1987-88 remains to be seen. Political paralysis and serious disorder so far have been forestalled, initially by a popular desire for a successful summer Olympics in Seoul and by what most South Koreans hoped would prove to be a genuine commitment to reform by the new government. Ultimately, of course, political stability in Korea will depend on the extent to which the government is willing and able to follow through on its public promises.

Syngman Rhee and the First Republic

South Korean politics of the 1950s tended to revolve around or against one man: Syngman Rhee. While a definitive biography of Rhee remains to be written, the broad lines of his personality and politics have already been sketched by various authors. In 1948 Rhee was 73 years old, and although he had spent much of his adult life in the United States, his political behavior was more reminiscent of a late Chosŏn monarch than of Woodrow Wilson, his teacher at Princeton. Supremely self-confident and a genius of political manipulation, he was clearly more of a Yŏngjo or a Chŏngjo than an ineffectual Kojong, but he seems to have shared with all Korean kings a conception of sovereignty as something more properly invested in a head of state than in a popular electorate or its representatives. By late nineteenth-century standards, Rhee had been something of a progressive. In 1898 he had even suffered imprisonment for supporting the Independence Club's call for a popularly elected national assembly. The kind of assembly that Rhee and his fellow Club members had advocated, however, was essentially an expanded advisory group to the king that would not have ultimately threatened royal supremacy. Rhee's early liberalism, moreover, does not seem to have evolved much in the succeeding fifty years and was clearly anachronistic by 1948. His ambition for personal power was also in sharp conflict with the political system he had been forced to adopt as the price for continued American support after 1948: an elective democracy with various constitutional safeguards against arbitrary executive power. Rhee's subsequent emasculation of this system, and the opposition thus provoked, were the hallmarks of the political history of the First Republic.

One of Rhee's key weapons in subverting the political system was the National Security Law (NSL), passed by the National Assembly in November 1948 in the wake of an allegedly communist-led sedition in Yŏsu and Sunch'ŏn the previous month. Like similar laws enacted during the colonial period, the NSL defined sedition in so vague and broad a way that the law could easily be used as a political tool by the authorities to suppress virtually any kind of opposition. Clearly against the spirit of the 1948 constitution, the NSL was nevertheless legal under a clause which prohibited any restrictions on freedom of speech, press, assembly, and association, "except as specified by law."

The first casualty of the new law was what remained of the South Korean left. Armed with the NSL, Rhee embarked on a campaign of anticommunist witch hunts that eventually affected tens of thousands of people, most of whom had no connection with the Communist Party. All major organizations, including the military, the press, and educational institutions, were subjected to scrutiny and purge. Out of rightist zeal, intimidation, or concern about eventual reappointment, Korea's judges bowed to the regime's wishes, and by the spring of 1950, the country's prisons held nearly 60,000 people, 50-80% of whom had been charged with violation of the NSL. Soon thereafter the Korean War provided Rhee with untold opportunities to eliminate suspected leftists and their supporters on an even more massive and brutal scale. One of the most notorious incidents of this kind occurred in February 1951 in the Kŏch'ang area of South Kyŏng-sang province, where a contingent of ROK troops led by Colonel "Tiger" Kim, a Rhee favorite who later became head of the national police, rounded up and massacred about 500 villagers for allegedly harboring communist guerrillas.

The NSL was also invoked to dragoon National Assembly members themselves into compliance with Rhee's will. In early 1949, the assembly began a series of wide-ranging special investigations, arrests, and trials of Japanese collaborators, action that struck at the heart of Rhee's rightist support. Rhee naturally objected to the trials but, given the public's enthusiasm, could not at first oppose them openly. Several months later the assembly also overrode a presidential veto on land reform and demanded the resignation of the entire cabinet. Rhee finally struck back. By October 1949, sixteen assemblymen were in jail for violation of the NSL, the assembly trials had fizzled out, land reform was still unimplemented, and the cabinet stood basically intact.

In 1952, when Rhee was up for reelection, he employed similar tactics in Pusan, the temporary wartime capital. His goal was to coerce the assembly into diluting its own powers by passing constitutional amendments for a popular election of the president—the 1948 constitution had given the right to elect the president to the National Assembly—and for the creation of a bicameral legislature. After declaring martial law and arresting several dozen assemblymen who had subsequently voted to lift it, Rhee had both the assemblymen under arrest and also their colleagues, who were boycotting the legislature in protest, herded into the assembly building and locked up until the amendments were passed.

In 1954 Rhee again acted to amend the constitution. This time his main object was to obtain a special exemption from the two-term limitation on presidential tenure. By then, however, he had developed a new and more subtle tool for controlling the National Assembly: his own political party. The Liberal Party, as it was called, had been established by Rhee in late 1951 and was composed of a motley assortment of opportunists held together by a desire for power and loyalty to Rhee. At its core was a group of Koreans who had earlier served the colonial bureaucracy. Electoral victories at the polls were guaranteed by the general public's unfamiliarity with democratic processes and by a combination of nationwide police surveillance, strong-armed thugs and gangs, fraud, and, when necessary, use of the NSL. By 1954 the Liberals had achieved a clear majority in the assembly and were able to bribe, blandish, or threaten enough independents to achieve the two-thirds vote required to pass the amendment. Four years later, when Rhee sought to expand the criminal reach of the NSL in order to preclude virtually any public criticism of his regime, the Liberal majority in the assembly again proved effective. Although the police eventually had to be called in to break up a sit-down strike by the opposition, the new criminal laws were passed.

In addition to the Liberal Party, Rhee's power structure included the government bureaucracy and the national police, both of which suffered from the taint of colonial collaboration in their higher ranks and were dependent on Rhee for their continued existence. With their respective national networks of central and local offices, both were crucial not only for social control but also for electoral success, because the Liberal Party lacked a strong popular base. Since the late 1940s Rhee had also made use of various rightist associations with extensive national networks. These included such groups as the Korean Youth Corps led by Yi Pŏm-sŏk, which was later absorbed into a larger youth association when Rhee came to regard Yi as a potential rival; the Federation of Korean Trade Unions; the Federation of Korean Farmers' Cooperatives; the Korean Women's Association, and various other compliant religious and professional groups. Although he relied mainly on a group of younger officers of north Korean birth, Rhee also kept the army in line by deliberately pitting various individuals and factions against each other through a skillful manipulation of assignments and promotions. Control over lucrative import licenses, American aid funds, credit allocation, and over the disposition of former Japanese properties that had been vested in the ROK by USAMGIK in 1948, also allowed Rhee and the Liberal Party to dominate the private economic sector and to cultivate a group of wealthy businessmen captive to Liberal interests.

By the late 1950s Rhee had made the political system largely his own. The legislature had been turned into a classic rubber stamp, and there were no serious rivals to Rhee himself on the right or left. Assassination had eliminated a number of potential competitors: Song Chin-u, apparently at Kim Ku's order, in 1945; Yŏ Un-hyŏng in 1947; and Kim Ku himelf in 1949, probably with Rhee's complicity or approval. The north-south division and war had removed others: Pak Hŏn-yŏng had fled to the north in October 1946, and Kim Kyu-sik had reportedly died after being taken to the north during the war. Illness had struck down Kim Sŏng-. su in 1955, and Sin Ik-hŭi, Rhee's main presidential opponent in 1956, had suffered a fatal heart attack only a week before the election that year. Another possible threat had been Cho Pong-am, a popular socialist candidate who had run for the presidency in 1952 and 1956 and had surprised the Liberals in 1956 by garnering more than 30% of the total vote and winning a majority in several major cities, including Taegu, Ch'ŏngju, Mokp'o, Chinju, and Chŏngŭp. In 1959, however, eight months before the 1960 presidential election, Cho had been executed for alleged violation of the NSL.

Rhee's victory in the March 1960 presidential election thus

seemed assured, especially when the main opposition candidate, Cho Pyŏng-ok, like his predecessor in 1956, died shortly before the election. Given these circumstances and Rhee's advanced age (85), public attention became focused on the vice-presidential race, a separate contest by South Korean law. The Liberal candidate and heir-apparent was Yi Ki-bung, whose first son had been adopted by the childless Rhee to cement and symbolize the special personal and political bond between the two men. Rhee's enthusiasm for Yi, however, was far from shared by the Korean public, and when the Liberals resorted to blatant, wholesale fraud to win the election, the country's students erupted in protest and were quickly joined by a substantial segment of the populace.

The April Revolution (1960) and the Second Republic

Resistance to Rhee inside the assembly had proven largely ineffectual during the First Republic. The main reason was Rhee's willingness to use intimidation and force to achieve his ends, but a second reason lay with the nature of the opposition itself, especially after Rhee's anticommunist campaigns and civil war had decimated the left in the 1948-53 period. The main opposition group in the latter half of the decade was the Democratic Party, which had emerged in 1955 from efforts by the old KDP to confront the Liberals with a broader political base in the assembly. In fact, however, the new party was an unstable alliance of two contending groups known as the Old Faction and the New Faction, who tended to fight each other as much as they fought the Liberals.

The Democrats also suffered from an extremely weak social base in the population and made little attempt to expand it. In that sense they differed little from their Liberal opponents. Both parties drew their key membership from essentially the same pool of landowners, businessmen, bureaucrats, and professionals who had formed the core of the late colonial social elite and who had never had shown much inclination or ability to develop genuine grass-roots political support and organization. The Democrats' basic similarity to the Liberals in this respect was reflected in the kind of program they continued to advocate in the National Assembly. Instead of focusing on fundamental social and economic problems, they chose to devote most of their energy to promoting a constitutional amendment that would have changed the government to a parliamentary system and thereby given them some leverage over the executive.

While the formal opposition to Rhee and the Liberals was being frustrated inside the assembly, an informal opposition was mounting in the society outside. Land reform had finally been carried out, largely as a result of the Korean War, and the countryside, though still poor, remained relatively quiet. But the cities were another matter. Between 1945 and 1960 the proportion of South Koreans living in cities of 50,000 or more had nearly doubled (to almost 30%), and urbanization had been both stimulated and accompanied by post-colonial and postwar booms in education. Educational facilities of every kind mushroomed, some with American assistance, and school enrollments at all levels posted phenomenal increases. The literacy rate more than tripled in the fifteen years after liberation, and by 1960 over 70% of the population could read and write. With urbanization and education came a corresponding growth in communications, especially newspapers and magazines. Circulation figures for *Tonga Ilbo,* South Korea's foremost newspaper, went from less than 20,000 after the war to about 400,000 in little more than a decade, with the bulk of new subscriptions coming in before 1960. In spite of Rhee's attempts to curtail it, moreover, the press adopted an increasingly hostile attitude toward the government. After twelve years of election rigging and political repression, South Korea's educated urban elite, especially in Seoul, was finally beginning to lose its patience with the existing political system. The strong showing of Cho Pong-am at the polls in 1956 and the election to the vice-presidency that same year of Chang Myŏn, a New Faction Democrat, were an indication of the shifting political mood of South Korea's cities.

At the center of this new urban discontent were South Korea's college and university students. By 1960 student protest in Korea already had a long and heroic tradition behind it that reached back through the colonial era deep into Korean history. Students saw themselves in good Confucian fashion as guardians of state virtue, and they identified that virtue in 1960 with many of the ideals of constitutional democracy that they had been taught since 1945 but had never seen practiced by their own government. Korea's first post-colonial generation come of age, they looked at the entrenched network of fraud, corruption, and coercion that linked Rhee and his party to the bureaucrats, police, and big businessmen and saw the decadence and failure of an older and less enlightened generation that needed to be swept away.

Student disaffection was also exacerbated by a socioeconomic system that seemed unable to absorb or accommodate its own university graduates. Between 1948 and 1960 the number of institutions of higher education had doubled and their enrollments had increased by a factor of twelve. As many as sixty percent of those graduating, however, were finding it difficult or impossible to obtain employment, and even those who did often wound up taking jobs they regarded as unsuitable or unsatisfactory. Unlike other more settled and necessarily pragmatic elements of the educated urban opposition, moreover, the students could afford to give their idealism and frustration full rein. Under such circumstances, it is hardly surprising that it was they who acted as the vanguard of the protests and demonstrations that eventually brought down the Rhee government.

Rhee's downfall in the spring of 1960 came swiftly, in little more than a month after the March 15 elections. Anger had gradually been building throughout the country after the flagrant rigging of Yi Ki-bung's victory when on April 11 a seventeen-year-old boy's body was discovered in the bay around Masan, a South Kyŏngsang port city. The boy had apparently been struck and killed by a tear gas canister in March during one of the demonstrations against the elections, and his body had been dumped into the bay by the police to protect themselves from charges of brutality. This ghastly discovery, which immediately brought the citizens of Masan into the streets and into confrontation with the police, provided the spark that ignited the rest of the country.

Rhee attempted to play down the boy's murder as a crime committed by "thoughtless people" and placed the main onus on communist infiltrators, who he claimed were responsible for inciting and engineering the Masan demonstrations. On April 18, however, students of Korea University in Seoul held a demonstration and were attacked by a gang of thugs from the Anticommunist Youth Corps. On the following day, April 19, which was to become a national holiday in South Korea, some 30,000 university and high school students marched toward the presidential mansion in Seoul and were fired upon point blank by the police. The students in Seoul then began to riot and were joined by other students in major cities. By the end of the day, about 130 students had been killed and another 1,000 wounded in Seoul alone, and the country had been placed under martial law.

The public shooting of peaceful, unarmed students had taken away whatever vestige of legitimacy the regime had still possessed, and a demand for Rhee's resignation began to grow. Three main factors finally combined to bring it about: a shift in U.S. policy after April 19 from a reluctant tolerance of Rhee's excesses to a public condemnation of the regime's repression (and a simultaneous American call for democratic reform); a demonstration for Rhee's resignation in front of the National Assembly building on April 25 by 300 university professors—a signal of support for the students from the broader educated urban elite; and the refusal of the Martial Law Command under General Song Yoch'an to fire on demonstrators. On April 26 Rhee resigned, leaving the government in the hands of his foreign minister, Hŏ Chŏng (Chang Myŏn, the vice-president, had already resigned to protest the March 15 elections). On April 28 the elder son of Yi Ki-bung shot his father, mother, younger brother, and himself in a family suicide pact, and a month later Rhee left for Hawaii. The First Republic was over.

In the early months following Rhee's resignation Koreans enjoyed a euphoria of release, freedom, and hope that had not been seen since liberation. Restraints on the press and political activity were removed, followed by an immediate profusion of new newspapers, magazines, and interest groups. Hŏ Chŏng's interim government moved quickly to draft a new constitution creating a bicameral parliamentary government centered on a premier and cabinet who were responsible to the National Assembly. The presidency was retained, but it was subject to indirect election by the National Assembly; except for the president's right to nominate the premier, the post was largely ceremonial. The new constitution was announced on June 15, and elections were held on July 29. The Democratic Party won a clear majority in both houses in what was deemed by both Korean and foreign observers to have been a relatively free and fair election. The assembly then went on to elect Yun Po-sŏn as president and to approve Yun's nomination of Chang Myŏn as premier. In December, an historic step toward political decentralization was taken with the holding of local elections for provincial governors and for the mayor of Seoul. In spite of this bright beginning, however, in less than a year after its inauguration the Second Republic had fallen to a military coup with surprisingly little protest from the urban educated elite who had originally helped bring it into being. What had happened?

A number of elements had worked together to bring down the new government. One of the most important was the weakness of the Democratic Party itself. Factionalism continued to plague the party throughout the Second Republic, culminating in a major schism between the Old and New Factions and the former's establishment of the New Democratic party (NDP) in September 1960. Under such circumstances cabinet members tended to have an average tenure of only about two months, and the formulation of coherent, long-range policies was difficult.

Even more important, perhaps, than the party's disunity was its lack of commitment to revolutionary change. The party had suddenly and unexpectedly come to power on the back of a revolutionary movement that demanded a rapid, thorough, and unequivocal purge of all people and groups closely associated with the Rhee government. In its first months of power, however, the party moved too slowly and cautiously against the remnants of the *ancien regime* to satisfy this demand, and the National Assembly was eventually forced by public opinion to take stronger action by enacting a series of constitutionally questionable special laws. Even then, Chang and his party continued to temporize in certain areas, especially with respect to any significant reprisals against high-ranking military officers and big businessmen. The Democrats' tentativeness in moving against the Rhee forces was perhaps not surprising in view of the common social background of both groups and their close personal and professional interaction over the years; the businessmen were also important to Chang and the party as a source of election funds. Nevertheless, the result for the Second Republic by early 1961 was a severe loss of credibility. Widespread official corruption at high levels also seemed to demonstrate the new government's basic affinity with the old.

One of the Rhee groups that the Chang regime did take relatively strong action against was the police force. But the dismissal of about 17,000 policemen, however necessary and just, also created new problems that ironically helped to hasten the government's end. Reduced, demoralized and fearful of further retribution, the post-Rhee police force often showed itself either unwilling or unable to preserve normal public order. The result was a disenchantment on the part of the property-owning and security-conscious urban elite on which the regime's stability rested. Initial urban enthusiasm for the regime was gradually replaced by alarm that the government might be losing its grip on the society.

Such fear was fueled by economic insecurity in the wake of the government's devaluation of the *hwan,* which sent prices spiraling and frightened the business community. It was also heightened by the psychological impact of continual public demonstrations of one kind or another throughout the entire period. Especially alarming to the urban elite was the fact that many of the demonstrations, especially those by students, elementary and secondary school teachers, and workers, all seemed to be moving rapidly to the left. Student calls in 1961 for immediate negotiations with North Korea on reunification and for a north-south student conference at P'anmunjŏm were also startling to a populace that still vividly remembered the civil war.

A third factor in the government's eventual demise may well have had to do with a general ambivalence about democracy among South Koreans in 1961, both inside and outside the government. Few people desired a return to the oppression of Syngman Rhee, and those advocating change, including the students, tended to speak in the language of American liberal democracy. But too few also made a genuine attempt to practice what they preached. Members of the Chang regime and the Democratic Party, most of whom had seen Rhee's abuse of the law at close hand, nevertheless sought, as Rhee had done, to brand their opponents in the National Assembly as communists and to place legal restrictions on the free speech and association of individuals and groups they considered too radical. The Chang regime even authored a new National Security Law, which retained the vague language of the old NSL and provided draconian penalties for any expression of support or praise for the North Korean communists. On the other hand, students who had earlier decried Rhee's abuse of constitutional government did not hesitate to invade the new National Assembly and demand the passage of retroactive legislation that also violated other's civil liberties. The political tolerance so necessary to a viable democracy seemed missing in the charged atmosphere of 1960-1961. As a result, to many South Koreans at the time democracy itself appeared to be the problem. For some, like the radical students, it did not go far enough; for others, like many of the urban educated elite and even the government itself, it ultimately seemed to pose a threat to the social order.

In the end, however, it must be noted that the Second Republic did not actually collapse from its own weaknesses or from a lack of popular support; it was overthrown by the military, a new and powerful force in South Korean society that had been growing throughout the 1950s. The South Korean constabulary organized by the American military government in late 1945 (officially established in January 1946) had expanded from a small core of about 5,000 men to an army of 50,000 by 1950. By the end of the war, South Korea had one of the most impressive standing armies in the world: over 600,000 troops, trained, equipped, and maintained by American military aid and expertise as a northeast Asian bulwark against communism.

Like the Democratic Party, the officer corps was riven with factionalism, reflecting the different ages, backgrounds, and regional affinities of its various members. In the late 1950s a gap also developed between the senior officers, who traced their roots for the most part to the Japanese Army, and their juniors, generally of major and colonel rank, who had graduated from the ROK Officers Candidate School, later the Korean Military Academy. Disaffection in the lower ranks was fed by financial and political corruption in the upper ranks, which controlled the flow of American military aid, and by discrimination in the promotion system. Much of the discontent came from the military academy's large eighth class of 1949, which had borne the brunt of combat in the Korean War. Its main advocate was a lieutenant colonel named Kim Jong Pil (Kim Chong-p'il), whose attempt to persuade the Chang regime to reform the military cost him his commission in February 1961. Three months later, on May 16, Kim and his uncle-by-marriage, Park Chung Hee (Pak Chŏnghŭi), a major general who had the trust of the junior officers, seized control of the government in a relatively quiet coup that placed the Korean military at the center of the country's politics for the first time since the late fourteenth century. Although Kim had planned and engineered the coup, it quickly became clear that Park was the key figure in a new configuration of power that would last nearly two decades and which continues, in modified form, even today.

The Park Chung Hee Era

In the course of his long rule, Park ran the political gamut from military totalitarianism to party politics before finally establishing what he called a "Korean-style democracy," a harsh authoritarian system with, in fact, barely a suggestion of democracy about it. These political shifts, culminating in the Yusin Reforms of 1972, were a function both of Park's character and also of the changing domestic and international circumstances in which he found himself.

Like Rhee, Park was torn between a desire to maintain personal power and a need for crucial American economic and military support that depended minimally on his formal adherence to civilian democratic government. Democracy had also been the theme of the April Student Revolution, and although many South Koreans had been disappointed with the form it had taken in the Second Republic, it was still a popular ideal that Park was obliged to acknowledge. Park also shared Rhee's anticommunism and hostility toward the north, although he seems, in his foreign policy at least (including his policy toward the DPRK), to have been more flexible than Rhee in this regard; in the realm of domestic affairs, he showed as little compunction as the former president in using stringent security legislation, when necessary, to castigate and arrest political opponents.

In clear contrast to Rhee, however, Park was committed to a vision of national wealth and power through economic development that reflected both his need for legitimacy in the absence of other credentials, and also his early training and experience as an officer of the Japanese Army during the militarism of the late 1930s and 1940s. Like his Japanese mentors, he had little patience with the institutional inefficiencies of democracy, and while he recognized the necessity of popular mobilization for national goals, he did not welcome widespread popular participation in the political decision-making process. His very commitment to continual rapid economic growth, moreover, pushed him toward greater authoritarianism in the 1970s, as the new socioeconomic system he had created became increasingly complex, difficult to control, and vulnerable to external forces in the international capitalist system.

The Park era divides naturally into three periods. In the first, between 1961 and 1963, Park ruled through a military junta called the Supreme Council for National Reconstruction (SCNR) that had been superimposed upon the existing structure of civilian government after the coup. Park moved quickly to consolidate his control over the SCNR and went on to carry authoritarianism in South Korea to a level that had not been seen since the late colonial period. The country was placed under martial law, and a special military tribunal was appointed to purge the military, government, and society of people the junta regarded as corrupt or undesirable. Thousands of arrests, trials, resignations, and forced retirements soon placed a new generation of officers, many from the eighth class of the military academy, in positions of power and in Park's debt. Many more thousands of politicians and bureaucrats were similarly removed from power. Anyone even suspected of being a communist was arrested, and thousands of petty thugs and gangsters who had flourished under the Second Republic were sought out, arrested and paraded through the streets in public humiliation. The National Assembly was dissolved, political activity of any kind was forbidden, and the press was severely trimmed and censored. Initially exhibiting a puritanical zeal that would gradually cool and then disappear, the junta also issued sumptuary regulations, broke up prostitution rings, and closed down bars, dance halls, and even coffee shops.

In June 1961, the SCNR also created the Korean Central Intelligence Agency (KCIA) with Kim Jong Pil at its head. Kim, whose military training and experience in the 1950s had been in the ROK Army Counterintelligence Corps (KCIC), was, in fact, the architect of the new organization, and he made use of the existing KCIC as a base on which to build the KCIA. The powers granted to the KCIA went far beyond those of its American counterpart and included domestic as well as international surveillance, in addition to the right to investigate other official intelligence agencies such as the KCIC itself. Within three years, the KCIA had established a vast network of agents in South Korea and abroad. It was this organization above all others, including the military itself, that eventually came to symbolize the more sophisticated and systematic repression of the Park era.

The period between 1963 and 1972 represented an attempt by Park and his military cohorts to operate within the more confined structure of democratic party politics. From the beginning, the junta had pledged to restore civilian government and return to the barracks as soon as it had accomplished its avowed revolutionary tasks of strengthening anticommunism, rooting out corruption, and laying the foundation for a self-reliant national economy. Although this promise may well have been sincere, there is no doubt that the coup leaders were also aware of the need to assuage domestic and international concern about their unlawful seizure of power. They were particularly sensitive to pressure from the United States, whose aid programs at the time accounted for over 50% of the national budget and more than 70% of defense expenditures, and the United States had clearly let it be known that it favored a swift return to civilian rule.

On August 12, 1961 Park publicly announced that the SCNR

would turn over power to a civilian government in 1963, following a referendum on a new constitution, and he ordered the release from prison of thousands of former political leaders; a month later President Kennedy responded with an invitation for Park to visit Washington in November. In December 1962, after the lifting of martial law, a constitutional referendum was approved for a third republic with a strong, popularly-elected president and a party-centered unicameral legislature (all assembly candidates had to receive the endorsement of a political party, and parties were awarded additional seats in proportion to the popular vote they received in the elections). Two months later, in January 1963, limited political activity was again permitted in anticipation of presidential and national assembly elections later in the year. In March Park attempted to renege on his promise by announcing the extension of military rule for another four years, subject to a national referendum, but American pressure, including a threat to withhold $25 million in economic aid, forced him to proceed as originally planned.

Park and his fellow officers in the SCNR were now determined, however, to effect a shift from military to elected constitutional government with as little change in the actual power structure as possible. The transition was already well underway by the end of 1962. A political "purification" law passed by the junta in March of that year had banned over 4,000 former politicians from political activity for a period of six years. Even though a number of these people had their political rights restored the following year, many of the military's most serious civilian rivals continued to be excluded from political competition. In December 1962 Park had also declared that he intended to retire from the military and run for office in the 1963 elections and that all other SCNR members were free to do the same.

In the meantime, even while the ban on political activities was still in effect, Kim Jong Pil had been using the organizational structure and network of the KCIA, together with a large reservoir of funds whose precise sources have never been conclusively identified, to create an extensive and highly centralized new political organization, the Democratic Republican Party (DRP), through which the junta intended to control the new party-centered assembly. Only after the party had already been set up was the prohibition on political activities lifted. Even then, the actual date of the presidential election, October 15, was not announced until mid-August, and political parties were given only a month thereafter in which to produce a slate of candidates.

In the subsequent election, Park, the DRP's candidate, won over his main rival, Yun Po-sŏn, with about 47% of the vote. A month later the DRP itself acquired a majority of the seats in the new national assembly, despite winning only 32% of the popular vote, thanks to its strong organization, a divided opposition, and the new system of proportional representation that automatically awarded up to two-thirds of the at-large seats to the party winning the most seats in the general election. In spite of the DRP's natural leverage, the election was generally regarded as fair, and Yun Po-sŏn publicly congratulated Park on his victory. At the end of 1963 it looked as though Park had succeeded in devising a system of elective civilian government that he could accept.

By 1972, however, a number of factors had converged to make Park change his mind. Even with the DRP's majority in the National Assembly, party politics proved to be more time-consuming and disruptive to the regime's policies than Park was willing to tolerate. In 1965, for example, when the opposition in the assembly used every delaying tactic at its disposal to keep the government's proposed normalization treaty with Japan from reaching the floor, the DRP used force to end the debate, and the treaty was finally ratified in the assembly only after the opposition had walked out in protest. In 1969, with the opposition itself now forcibly holding the rostrum, the DRP called a secret early-morning session of its own in the assembly's annex in order to pass a constitutional amendment that would permit President Park to run for a third term in 1971.

By the early 1970s, moreover, the two factions of the old Democratic party had joined hands again in new and stronger version of the New Democratic Party (NDP), and the party itself was being regenerated by a gradual shift in leadership to a younger generation in its forties: in addition to older figures like Yu Chin-san, the party now boasted two new leaders, Kim Young

Sam (Kim Yŏng-sam) and Kim Dae Jung (Kim Tae-jung), both of whom were outspoken in their criticism of the Park regime.

Election trends also showed that the new NDP challenge was being translated into popular support, especially in urban areas. In the 1971 presidential election, Kim Dae Jung, the NDP candidate, took about 45% of the vote, about 4% more than Yun Po-sŏn had received four years earlier. In the assembly elections that year the NDP gained 44 seats, while the DRP lost 16—and with them the two-thirds majority that had allowed it to pass constitutional amendments. Kim also carried the cities by about 52%, including nearly 60% of the Seoul vote. Although both Park and the DRP remained in power after the 1971 elections and the NDP suffered a post-election relapse of chronic factionalism, the potential for future obstruction and problems from the opposition remained strong.

Watershed changes in the international sphere during this period were also giving Park cause for concern: the enunciation of the Nixon Doctrine in 1969 and the retreat of the United States from Southeast Asia, the breakdown in 1971 of the dollar-gold international financial system established at Bretton Woods in 1944, and the American rapprochement with China and detente with the Soviet Union. All seemed to portend the beginning of the end of the global system of American economic and military hegemony on which the ROK had been founded and continued to depend. Especially disturbing to the authorities in Seoul was Nixon's decision in 1970 to withdraw one of the two American combat divisions (about 20,000 troops) that had been in the country since the end of the Korean War.

Finally, economic factors may well have played an important role in Park's decision to return to a more authoritarian system. Park's export-led industrial growth experienced a slowdown in the early 1970s related in part to increasing American protectionist pressures on textiles, South Korea's key export industry at the time. In the fall of 1971, for example, the Park government finally bowed to U.S. threats to impose unilateral import quotas and agreed to double the number of its textile products subject to restrictions. Park was also laying the groundwork at this time for a Third Five-Year Plan (1972-1977) that targeted heavy and chemical industries such as steel, shipbuilding, petrochemicals, automobiles, and even nuclear industries. Recession combined with a decision to deepen the industrial structure could have persuaded Park and his advisors of a need for firmer controls over potential dissent from labor and small-medium businesses.

Citing domestic and international insecurity, Park abruptly declared a state of emergency in December 1971. Ten months later, on October 17, 1972, he proclaimed martial law and carried out what has been aptly described as a "coup in office." The constitution was suspended, and the National Assembly and all political parties were dissolved. Further political activity was forbidden, and restrictions were placed on other civil liberties, including free speech.

Park then announced a series of "revitalizing" reforms—*yusin* in Korean (the same word used in Japan for the Meiji "Restoration")—that sounded a death knell for the Third Republic and for whatever progress toward a more liberal polity had been made in South Korea since 1961. The new Yusin Constitution, formally approved through public referendum by an intimidated populace in November 1972, transformed the presidency into a legal dictatorship. Under its terms the president was to be chosen indirectly by an easily manipulated elective body of several thousand nonparty members called the National Council for Unification (NCU), which was headed by the president himself. The president was also empowered to appoint one-third of the National Assembly, thus enabling him to control the legislature in a more direct and personal way than before. Ultimate safeguards against any serious challenge to presidential authority were supplied by further constitutional provisions for national plebiscites, and for special emergency measures covering the whole range of state affairs to be enacted at the president's sole discretion. By the end of 1972, with Park more firmly entrenched than ever as the president of a new Fourth Republic, it looked as though the former head of the SCNR had succeeded in a bold bid to retrieve in civilian guise the power he had wielded in the 1961-63 period. For seven years thereafter the system held. But the price was an increasing disaffection in the society and finally, for Park himself, personal tragedy, betrayal, and death.

Park did not remain in power for eighteen years through coercion alone; his authoritarianism was grounded in the support of a number of institutional, social, and international forces. Like Rhee, Park could count on the backing of the national police and bureaucracy, both of which had been purged and filled with loyalists after the 1961 coup, especially at the higher levels. The KCIA also provided a new institutional bulwark for Park, although in time it became so.pervasive and powerful as to rival the executive itself, and one of its heads finally pulled the trigger that ended Park's life. Under Park's rule, moreover, a new and studiously apolitical group of technocrats assumed a pivotal role in the country's economic development; well-educated, articulate, and urbane, they tended to exert an influence in Korea's status-oriented society that far outweighed their actual numbers and by their very presence abetted the regime's quest for legitimacy. After an initial purge, the military also came under Park's firm control, and a process of rewarding the retired military faithful with lucrative civilian posts in the bureaucracy, National Assembly, and the private sector became an institutional feature of South Korean society. Though not immune to factional strife, especially between the supporters of Park and Kim Jong Pil, the DRP also generally functioned as Park's creature in and out of the National Assembly, and nearly 40% of its members were ex-military officers in the late 1970s.

Economic development also gave certain elements in the society a vested interest in Park's continued rule. In spite of a public outcry against the "accumulators of illicit wealth" that had arisen in the aftermath of the April Revolution and been echoed by the military junta itself in 1961, Park had ultimately taken no criminal action against the country's businessmen and had worked out a compromise that allowed many of them to grow even richer. These businessmen, together with a number of new entrepreneurs, became the leaders of Park's export drive in the next two decades and were accordingly favored with a cornucopia of tax and investment incentives, inexpensive government credit, and government-guaranteed foreign loans. By the end of the 1970s, they comprised about fifty major conglomerates with legions of management personnel and were the mainstay of the regime's support in the private sector.

The increasing prosperity of the Park years also engendered a middle class of small-medium businessmen, lower-level white-collar workers in government and industry, and intellectuals whose growing affluence gave them some reason to tolerate the regime, if not actively support it. The post-land-reform peasantry also continued to be a conservative force in South Korean politics and the main base of Park's electoral victories, despite the fact that his economic policies were clearly geared toward the export manufacturing industries rather than agriculture. Whatever discontent existed in the countryside seems to have been largely dissipated by strong anticommunist feeling, by migration to the cities (leaving the rural population older and more conservative), and by greater government attention to rural development with the launching of the Saemaŭl (New Village) Movement in the winter of 1971-72.

Certain external factors also tended to buttress Park's position. The unsettling presence of a hostile Korean state immediately to the north continued to lead many South Koreans to accept political conditions they would otherwise have found intolerable—a fear the government constantly and skillfully manipulated. Such manipulation was facilitated, moreover, by periodic international incidents such as the North Korean seizure of an American intelligence ship in 1968 (the so-called *Pueblo* Incident) and the DPRK's shooting down of a U.S. reconnaissance plane in 1969. Two events in particular, a North Korean commando attack on the presidential mansion in January 1968 and a second, allegedly DPRK-inspired assassination attempt in August 1974 that took the life of Park's highly respected and popular wife, also generated public sympathy for Park and lent some credibility to his authoritarian policies. The unwillingness of the United States government to put public pressure on Park, particularly after the ROK entered the Vietnam War in 1965, also strengthened his hand against any moderates that might have existed inside the Yusin power structure, including within the military itself, and enhanced his status among those South Koreans who still tended to think of the United States as a benevolent older brother.

Opposition, Mutiny, Insurrection, and Coup

In spite of such support for the Park regime, the new Yusin system established in 1972 eventually came to alienate many segments of the population. Kim Dae Jung, Park's popular rival for the presidency in 1971, continued his criticisms of the government and became a potent symbol and rallying point for a variety of formal and informal opposition groups in South Korea, the United States, and Japan.

The most important players in the anti-government movement, however, were once again the students. By the Yusin period, the anti-Park student opposition had already accumulated a decade of experience, punctuated by dramatic and prolonged episodes of violent struggle, as in 1965, against the ROK's normalization treaty with Japan, and again in 1969, against the constitutional amendment for a third-term presidency. Yusin gradually galvanized the student movement and kept it at an intense pitch. By 1979, the movement had begun to assume the character of an underground institution in South Korean society, with its own extensive organization, heroes and martyrs, patois, and culture. Works by dissident musicians, writers and other artists, together with the artists themselves, became icons of the new subculture and gave it both emotional strength and intellectual substance. Two artists in particular seemed to capture the students' imagination and respect during this period: Kim Chi-ha, a poet, and Kim Min-gi, a student at Seoul National University's College of Fine Arts turned singer and composer. Kim Chi-ha's poems, including his "Five Bandits" (1970), "Groundless Rumors" (1972), and "Cry of the People" (1974), provided a stinging indictment of the Park regime's political abuses and obsession with statistical economic growth at the expense of broader social concerns. Kim Min-gi's "Morning Dew" (1971), a plaintive pre-Yusin hymn of universal struggle and hope popularized by the folk singer Yang Hŭi-ŭn, became the unofficial anthem of the student movement.

During the Yusin period the opposition also expanded to include new groups of people. Although the urban intelligentsia and middle class had prospered economically under Park, a number of such people were also beginning to question the government's policy of providing economic growth without, and, indeed, in lieu of, political participation.

Even more important was a new force of regional and class dissent arising from the skewed character of Park's economic development. Economic growth had tended to follow a Seoul-Pusan axis, favoring the capital area and the southeast, the home base of many of the ruling elite, including Park himself, and grossly neglecting the two Chŏlla provinces of the southwest. The economic development had also been based to a large extent on low wages, and on the suppression of organized labor through the use of both physical force and an elaborate and oppressive legal structure that gave special attention to the needs of foreign enterprises investing or otherwise doing business in South Korea. Since a large proportion of South Korea's urban workers were inevitably migrants from the Chŏllas, regional and class disaffection also tended to overlap. In the 1960s, the structural foundations of the new export economy were only just being laid, and the workers remained relatively quiet. On November 13, 1970, however, a garment worker named Chŏn T'ae-il immolated himself in a public protest against labor exploitation, an act that became part of South Korea's labor history and signified the beginning of a new working class activism. By the mid-1970s, union membership was beginning to boom (topping one million in 1978), and workers were becoming increasingly more assertive, often encouraged and supported by students, intellectuals, and Christian groups like the Young Catholic Organization and Protestant-sponsored Urban Industrial Mission.

The anti-government movement was also strengthened, ironically, by Park's ruthless and inflexible response to political dissent. The existing National Security Law had been supplemented by an Anticommunist Law in 1961, and by a subsequent barrage of security legislation enacted as presidential emergency decrees under the Yusin Constitution. Most infamous of all was Emergency Measure No. 9, announced in May 1975, which made criticism of the president, or of the measure itself, a criminal act. Arbitrary arrests, prolonged detentions, forced confessions under torture, and sham trials followed by imprisonment or execution became the order of the day for anyone who dared to take a stand against the Yusin system: politicians, religious leaders, intellectuals, university professors, students, labor leaders, and workers. In spite of press controls, however, the truth about Yusin spread both within South Korea and abroad and expanded the number of people actively or passively opposed to the regime. Those who were victimized thus often triumphed in the end by becoming symbols both of the regime's brutality and also of inspiration to those who continued to resist. Two of the most famous of these symbols during the period were Kim Dae Jung and Kim Chi-ha, whose outspoken criticism and defiance of the Yusin system not only cost them their freedom (and nearly their lives), but also attracted international attention and sympathy. Kim Dae Jung in particular became a *cause celebre* in 1973 after surviving a sensational abduction (from Japan) and murder attempt by the KCIA, then headed by Lee Hu Rak (Yi Hu-rak).

By the late 1970s Park had become somewhat isolated, even from his own supporters. The Yusin system had made the president into a figure responsible only to himself, and even the DRP had been reduced in stature by the new constitution. Park had cultivated no clear successor; he had, in fact, removed Kim Jong Pil, his most likely successor, but also a serious potential rival, from the premiership in 1975 and replaced him with an unthreatening professional bureaucrat named Choi Kyu Hah (Ch'oe Kyu-ha). Access to Park, moreover, was being strictly controlled and manipulated by two successive heads of the Presidential Security Force, Pak Chong-gyu (1964-74), and later Ch'a Chi-ch'ŏl.

Although American presidents, including Jimmy Carter, continued to embrace Park as an Asian ally, even relations with the United States began to deteriorate in the late 1970s in the wake of a complex influence peddling scandal dubbed "Koreagate" that began to break in the spring of 1975. The scandal led to a wide-ranging congressional investigation of the ROK-U.S. relationship and to revelations about illegal KCIA activities in the United States, including the KCIA's harassment and intimidation of Korean-Americans and South Korean nationals, and attempts by the ROK government and KCIA directly and indirectly to influence the U.S. executive and legislative branches and the American academic community.

Despite such signs of weakness and paranoia at the heart of

the Yusin system, so clear in retrospect, the sudden and violent end of the Park regime in 1979 took most South Koreans and the world by surprise. The end came swiftly on the heels of a combined economic and political crisis. Economic problems that had been accumulating since the early 1970s were exacerbated in 1979 by the second oil shock and caused a number of middle class South Koreans who were already harboring doubts about the government's politics to question its handling of the economy for the first time. South Korean workers, the main victims of the economic downturn, also expressed their anger in the form of increasingly militant labor disputes and strikes, and in August 1979 about 200 female textile workers from the Y.H. Trading Company gained considerable public attention and support after the police brutally broke up a demonstration they were staging inside the opposition party's headquarters. In the melee that followed, one woman leapt or was pushed to her death.

Two months later, in the midst of a deepening recession, an outspoken anti-government faction of the NDP headed by Kim Young Sam succeeded in gaining control of the opposition party, and the DRP reacted by voting to expel Kim from the National Assembly on October 4. A week later the main opposition parties walked out of the assembly in protest, and demonstrations by thousands of students, workers, and other urban residents demanding not only Kim's reinstatement, but also Park's resignation and an end to the Yusin system, soon erupted in Pusan, Kim's hometown.

The demonstrations quickly spread to Masan and other cities and threatened to get out of control. Martial law was declared in the Pusan-Masan area, and a basic disagreement on how to handle the situation apparently arose between Park and his KCIA director, Kim Jae Kyu (Kim Chae-gyu). Kim reportedly argued for compromise and reform, but Park, encouraged by his chief bodyguard, Ch'a Chi-ch'ŏl, insisted on dispatching paratroopers, if necessary, to quell the demonstrations. Finally, on the evening of October 26, Kim shot and killed both Park and Ch'a at a private dinner in a KCIA compound near the presidential Blue House. Choi Kyu Hah became acting president and immediately declared martial law.

Park's assassination initially stunned the country and evoked mixed feelings among the people. More than any other single political figure, Park had shaped the modern South Korean political economy, and his legacy was both admirable and appalling. Shock and confusion, however, soon gave way to hope and expectation that the Yusin system would finally be dismantled and that the country would be able to match its remarkable economic achievements with a corresponding development in the political sphere.

There were reasons for optimism. Although Choi immediately incurred public criticism for retaining the Yusin Constitution and allowing himself to be elected president in his own right by the NCU on December 6, he also promised that a referendum on a new constitution would be held within a year, to be followed by a general election. On the day after his election, he also rescinded the hated Emergency Measure No. 9 and released some fifty people who had been imprisoned under the decree. Hundreds more in prison, on parole, or under arrest were freed on December 8, including Kim Dae Jung, who had been under house arrest since his release from a prison hospital at the end of 1978. On February 29, 1980 Choi also restored Kim's civil rights, together with those of about 700 other former political prisoners.

As the months wore on, the optimism began to fade. Choi seemed unable or unwilling to move fast enough to satisfy the popular demand for constitutional revision. A complex power struggle also ensued, pitting the National Assembly against the administration and the DRP against the NDP. Interparty strife, moreover, was more than matched by fierce intraparty struggles. In the DRP, Kim Jong Pil faced a challenge for control of the party from Lee Hu Rak, and a bitter personal feud developed in the NDP between Kim Young Sam and Kim Dae Jung. Supporters of the so-called three Kims carried these various disputes loudly, and sometimes violently, into the city streets and countryside, thus further heightening the personal antagonisms and political tension. Not a few South Koreans were disturbed by such discord, and some drew uncomfortable parallels with the period of relative freedom that had followed the collapse of the Rhee regime.

Nevertheless, it was not such jockeying for power that caused the most concern. There was, in fact, a strong feeling, especially among the anti-Yusin forces, that such political conflict, however unfortunate or unseemly, was natural under the circumstances and represented an inevitable period of tumult in the transition to a more democratic government. The question of real concern for most people at the time was not so much whether the civilian politicians had the ability to put together a viable new government, but whether the military would let them.

The answer, as it turned out, was negative, and it came with a violence that had not been seen since the Korean War. When it was all over, a new junta of army officers led by Major General Chun Doo Hwan (Chŏn Tu-hwan) was in control of the state. Other key figures included Major General Roh Tae Woo (No T'ae-u), and Major General Chŏng Ho-yong. All three men were from the Kyŏngsang region and graduates of the eleventh class of the Korean Military Academy in 1955. They seized power in three steps in the course of a ten-month period following Park's assassination, and two of the steps were drenched in blood.

The first, which took place on the evening and early morning of December 12-13 and thus became known as the 12-12 Incident, was a mutiny against the army itself. Chun, who was in charge of the Army Security Command and the investigation into Park's assassination, ordered the arrest of General Chŏng Sŭnghwa, Army Chief of Staff and head of the Martial Law Command, for alleged complicity in the assassination. Other key military officials, including the Capital Garrison Commander and the Commander of the Special Forces, were also arrested, and a regiment of crack troops from Roh's Ninth Division that guarded the approaches to Seoul, moved in with tanks, armored cars, field artillery, and anti-tank missiles to occupy crucial strategic areas in the capital. They were joined by other forces supporting Chun, bringing the total number of soldiers to about 6,000, and after seven hours and a bloody shoot-out at ROK Army Headquarters and the nearby Ministry of Defense, the army was subdued. Yi Hŭi-sŏng, a lieutenant general, was appointed Army Chief of Staff and Martial Law Commnder, Roh became head of the Capital Garrison Command, and Chŏng was made

Special Forces Commander. The army now belonged to Chun.

The next step was an assault on the state and society. In April 1980 Chun illegally assumed control of the KCIA, the most powerful civilian organization in the country, without giving up his military status and posts. Chun's appointment touched off a wave of student demonstrations calling for his resignation and that of Prime Minister Sin Hyŏn-hwak, the lifting of martial law, and a more rapid abolition of the Yusin system. The demonstrations increased in size and intensity, culminating in a protest in Seoul on May 15 involving 30 universities and an estimated 70,000-100,000 students. Fearing possible military intervention, the students then decided on May 16, with the encouragement of Kim Dae Jung and Kim Young Sam, to call off further demonstrations for the time being, but it was too late. On May 17 Chun made his move. Acting through the Choi government, Chun proclaimed Martial Law Decree No. 10, which extended the already existing martial law even to Cheju Island, dissolved the National Assembly, closed down all colleges and universities, banned labor strikes, and prohibited all political discussion and activity. On the following day twenty-six people, including key politicians in both the ruling and opposition parties, were arrested on charges of influence peddling and social disruption.

The political drama now shifted to the city of Kwangju, the capital of the province of South Chŏlla that was home to Kim Dae Jung. On the morning of May 18, a small group of Chŏnnam National University students demanding Kim's release and an end to martial law suddenly found themselves facing a contingent of black-bereted paratroopers, sent into the city by Special Forces Commander Chŏng Ho-yong. Apparently informed by their superiors that Kwangju was being overrun by communists, the paratroopers began indiscriminately clubbing and bayoneting both demonstrators and spectators with a brutality that shocked and outraged Kwangju's citizens. After two days of atrocities, the students and citizens began to commandeer weapons wherever they could find them and to take over the city. By May 21, a full-scale insurrection had broken out, forcing the paratroopers to retreat, and anti-government demonstrations were spreading to other cities in the area. Kwangju remained tense, surrounded by a cordon of thousands of troops, while a council of citizens attempted to negotiate a truce with the army and appealed, without success, to the United States for mediation. Finally, on May 27 regular troops from the ROK Twentieth Division invaded the city and reimposed martial law. When it was all over, hundreds, perhaps thousands, of Kwangju citizens were dead. The official number given was about 200. Witnesses to the tragedy, however, claimed a much higher number, usually around 2,000 and a 1986 Asia Watch report noted that the city's death statistics for May 1980 were 2,300 over the monthly average. Whatever the correct figure, which awaits determination by a thorough investigation, Chun had clearly demonstrated to the country the terrifying force at his disposal and his even more frightening willingness to use it.

After May 18 and Kwangju, the third and final step in Chun's rise to power was anticlimactic, a mere matter of rearranging the civilian government in accord with what was already political reality. On May 31 Chun set up a combined military-civilian Special Committee for National Security Measures. The committee was chaired by Choi and included a number of cabinet members, but it was in fact merely a front for Chun and his key supporters, including Roh and Chŏng Ho-yong, who constituted the committee's military component. Less than two months later, Chun dispensed with this facade. On August 16 Choi resigned as president, and two weeks later Chun, who had resigned from the army on August 22 after promoting himself to four-star general, was elected to succeed him by the NCU. A revised constitution drafted by the government was approved by a plebiscite conducted under martial law in October, and in February 1981 Chun ran again for president under the new constitution and was elected. A new national assembly was also elected the following month.

The Fifth Republic of Chun Doo Hwan, 1981-88

Chun's coup and transition to civilian rule in 1979-81 followed a pattern established earlier by Park Chung Hee in 1961-63. In the army, the loyalty of younger officers, both from Chun's class and later classes of the Korean Military Academy, was secured through promotions, and any potential threats to Chun's position like Paek Un-t'aek's alleged conspiracy in 1982, were promptly crushed. Like Park, Chun made a bid for legitimacy by denouncing past corruption and promising a new age of economic growth, probity, and justice. Like Park, he also used this pledge as a justification for banning political activity by former politicians who could challenge his regime in the civilian sphere, including the three Kims. Kim Dae Jung, in fact, was tried and sentenced to death for alleged sedition in connection with the Kwangju Incident, and although the sentence was later commuted to life imprisonment in 1981, then to a twenty-year term in 1982, Kim remained barred from active politics in South Korea throughout most of the Fifth Republic. Chun also followed Park's pre-Yusin strategy of cultivating a strong centralist political party in the National Assembly, both as a means of controlling the legislative process and also as a vehicle for the military's continued hegemony in civilian politics. Like Park's DRP, Chun's Democratic Justice Party (DJP) relied on its inherent advantages as the ruling party and the proportional representation system to acquire and then retain a majority in the National Assembly with only about one-third of the popular vote.

The correspondence with the Park regime was hardly coincidental. Chun and Park both faced a similar problem of transforming a military coup into a legitimate civilian government, and Chun probably hoped to duplicate Park's successes while avoiding his mistakes. Thus Chun continued the basic Yusin policy of stressing economic growth over political development, but he also allowed political parties to assume more importance than had been possible under the Yusin system, and the ban on political activities by former politicians (except Kim Dae Jung and a handful of others, who remained under suspended criminal sentences) was gradually, if grudgingly, lifted over a five-year period. To blunt criticism that he intended, like Park, to keep extending his rule for life, Chun included in the new constitution a stipulation that the president could serve only a single seven-year term, and, he repeatedly emphasized his intention to turn the office over to an elected successor in February 1988. Chun also carried out a number of minor but highly visible social changes that conveyed the impression of greater liberalization, including the abolition of a curfew that had been in effect since the Korean War and the relaxation of an originally colonial dress code for middle and high school students that required severe haircuts and black uniforms complete with caps. The apparent assumption of Chun and his group was that continued economic growth, coupled with a few, largely cosmetic, political changes to distinguish the Fifth Republic from the Yusin system, would in time allow the new regime to gain public acceptance, just as Park's pre-Yusin regime had come to be more widely accepted in the late 1960's.

There were several basic problems with such a strategy, however. The first was that Chun was not Park. Throughout his eighteen-year rule Park had been regarded by South Koreans with great ambivalence. Even those people who had disliked, or even despised, him for his politics, had been willing to acknowledge his intelligence and his receptivity to expert advice, at least in the economic sphere, as well as his ability to accomplish economic goals. He had also been reputedly austere in his lifestyle and personally honest, and his family had remained relatively free from any taint of scandal or corruption. Indeed, his wife, Yuk Yŏng-su, had been widely revered in South Korea, and after her murder in 1974 (in an assassination attempt on Park), Park's elder daughter Kŭn-hye had assumed many of her mother's official duties with a filiality that touched a deep chord in South Korea's still Confucian public. Chun, on thè other hand, suffered from a widespread reputation for dullness, obstinacy, and arrogance, and his family, including his wife and his younger brother, continued to be implicated in financial scandals that are only now, since Chun's retirement, being more openly discussed and investigated. By 1987, if not long before, it required considerable effort to find anyone—regardless of socioeconomic background or political affiliation—who genuinely liked and respected Chun and his family.

A far more serious problem for Chun than his personality and family, however, lay in the means by which he had come to power in 1979-81. Like Park, he had led a revolt in the army and eventually deposed the existing civilian government. But there was

one crucial difference: Park had carried out his coup with relatively little bloodshed. Chun's coup had involved not only the
deaths of numerous soldiers on December 12, 1979, but also a
murderous attack on a major South Korean city. The government's refusal, moreover, to acknowledge any responsibility for
the Kwangju Incident, officially tagged a communist-inspired rebellion, or to evince any compassion for the victims of the tragedy, only served to raise anti-Chun passions even higher, both in
and beyond the city of Kwangju itself. The anger was especially
strong among people of the two Chŏlla provinces, who tended
to see Chun's assault on Kwangju as final, brutal proof of a continuing official policy of contempt for the southwestern part of
the country, but the anger also came to embrace many other people throughout the country who learned what had happened in
spite of the government's attempts to suppress the facts. The
Kwangju Incident continued to haunt Chun throughout the Fifth
Republic and, more than any other single factor, denied him the
legitimacy he sought.

A third and related problem that Chun had to confront in
attempting a successful transition to civilian rule was the enormous socioeconomic change that had occurred in South Korea
since 1961 (discussed in Chapter 20). The social effects of nearly
twenty years of rapid economic growth had helped topple the
Yusin system in 1979, and Chun erred in assuming he could continue Park's repressive policies into the next decade with only
superficial changes. In spite of problems, most notably in 1979-80,
most South Koreans now took economic growth for granted;
what they wanted, in varying degrees and proportions, was more
political freedom and greater equity. Despite his rhetoric, Chun
offered neither to any substantial degree. Indeed, under Chun
the security forces were strengthened as tens of thousands of
young conscripts were trained as riot troops and attached to the
national police force; their conspicuous presence in residential
and public areas served to intimidate average citizens as well as
students and workers and suggested a country under siege by its
own government. Even Chun's pledge to step down in 1988 began to ring hollow to many South Koreans as it became increasingly clear that he was paving the way for his former classmate

and fellow conspirator Roh Tae Woo to succeed him.

Chun also had to face a more radical and determined student movement than his predecessors. Before the 1980s the student movement had been geared largely toward liberal democratic goals, which were seen not only as good in themselves but also as preconditions for resolving the great problem of national division. The gradual absorption of Western neo-Marxist and dependency literature, both directly and through Japanese translations and commentaries, and the failure to achieve reform in the 1979-80 period pushed student leaders much further to the left than ever before. The ideological shift was historical and profound, reflecting the rise of a new generation of South Korean youth whose politics had been shaped not by the Korean War or even by the April Revolution of 1960, but by Yusin and Kwangju. For the new student leaders, liberal democracy was no longer a sufficient goal, either in itself or as a necessary step toward unification of the peninsula. They regarded South Korea's major political and social ills, including the national division, as structural problems embedded in the country's sociopolitical system, or in its "neocolonialist" relationship with the United States—impervious, in either case, to reform at the top. The logical task, from the students' perspective, was revolution against these two evils, usually seen as interconnected.

This new, philosophically grounded anti-American sentiment was intensified by a widespread feeling among the students that the U.S. played a major role in Chun's seizure of power in 1979-80. Of particular importance here was the students' belief that the U.S. shared responsibility for the Kwangju Incident by having approved Chun's dispatch of troops to the city. (A 1978 agreement creating the U.S.-ROK Combined Forces Command gave operational control of selected units of the ROK regular army to the commander of the American forces in South Korea.) There is no evidence that the U.S. conspired with or directly supported Chun during this period, and the dispatch of the savage paratroopers who provoked the Kwangju Incident was outside the operational control of the US forces, a fact generally unknown or ignored by the students. Nevertheless, neither the State Department nor the American military seems to have made any serious attempt to impede the coup process at any stage, and General John A. Wickham, the commander of the American forces in South Korea during this period, did in fact respond positively to a query from the South Korean authorities about deploying elements of the ROK Twentieth Division in Kwangju after the citizens had taken over the city in self-defense (with the hope, according to Wickham, that the use of regular troops, rather than paratroopers, would allow a retaking of the city with a minimum of violence if negotiations between Kwangju's citizens and the ROK military broke down). In August 1980, moreover, Gen. Wickham further inflamed anti-Americanism in South Korea by suggesting in an interview with the *Los Angeles Times* that the U.S. had, in effect, decided to support Chun as the country's next president and that all the South Korean people were lining up behind Chun like "lemmings." Several months later, on February 2, 1981, President Reagan himself also seemed to confirm the students' worst suspicions about the United States by according Chun the honor of being the first head of state to visit the Reagan White House.

The students were also strengthened in their new world view by support from South Korean academic and intellectual circles, themselves undergoing a similar process of radicalization in the 1980s, and the efficacy of their movement during this period was greatly enhanced by major changes in organization and tactics. A cellular organizational structure was adopted that helped protect the anonymity of key leaders and preserve the organization as a whole in spite of individual arrests and imprisonments, and the students turned to flexible hit-and-run tactics against the police that allowed them to avoid becoming trapped inside or around the universities and to take their protests into the heavily populated downtown areas.

Public antipathy toward the Chun regime deepened in 1986. That year the country witnessed a rash of unprecedented student suicide protests, and massive, violent confrontations broke out between the police and demonstrating students and workers, especially in the industrial port city of Inch'ŏn in May and at Seoul's Kŏn'guk University in late October. Led by the main opposition party (renamed the New Korea Democratic Party/NKDP in 1985 and reformed as the Reunification Democratic Party/RDP in 1987), a broad-based popular movement emerged with the goal of amending the constitution to permit direct election of the president in 1987. A direct presidential election, it was believed, would insure an opposition victory and prevent Chun from transferring power to one of his cronies.

The catalyst that finally touched off a popular explosion was Chun's abrupt suspension on April 13, 1987 of any further public debate on the constitutional revision issue, followed on June 10 by the DRP's selection of Roh Tae Woo, Chun's favorite, as its candidate in the forthcoming presidential race. Two other events, however, also played a role in pushing public anger to the boiling point. One was the centrifugal effect of a popular revolution in the Philippines in February 1986. Although the socioeconomic conditions of the two countries were vastly different, the sudden overthrow of the entrenched Marcos dictatorship by a largely spontaneous popular uprising created a sensation in South Korea that bolstered hopes for political change through direct popular action. Even Chun felt the force of this sentiment. Before the Philippines revolution, he had insisted that any discussion of constitutional revision would have to wait until 1989 and threatened to arrest anyone who signed an NKDP petition for direct presidential elections. In April 1986, however, he changed his mind and agreed to permit formal discussions leading to a constitutional revision before the end of his tenure in 1988. When he then reversed himself again a year later, he raised the political tension in the country even higher than it had been in early 1986.

Another critical event occurred in early 1987. For decades international human rights groups had been citing South Korea for routine and systematic torture of political prisoners, but the government had always denied such charges. The charges were also difficult to prove because victims who lived showed few visible signs of torture and those who died were always declared dead of natural causes or suicide by the authorities. In January 1987, however, the police picked up a Seoul National University student named Pak Chong-ch'ŏl for questioning about the whereabouts of a radical student leader. During the interrogation Pak was suffocated to death by policement who repeatedly shoved his head into a tub of water and finally crushed his throat against the rim.The police initially claimed that Pak had died of "shock." His death, however, attracted considerable attention in the press, and the police finally admitted that he had been tortured after an attending physician publicly questioned the official cause of death. Chun had the two policemen involved charged with murder, and as public protests increased, he dismissed the Home Minister and the head of the National Police. Nevertheless, the damage had been done. For the first time in its history, the South Korean government had publicly acknowledged the fact of police torture and thereby called into question all its previous denials.

On June 10, the day Roh assumed the DRP mantle, Seoul erupted in the worst street fighting since 1979-80, with riot police showering demonstrators with a stinging tear gas and students responding with rocks and homemade gasoline bombs. The fighting quickly spread to other major cities throughout the country, including Taejŏn and Ch'ŏnan in South Ch'ungch'ŏng province, Taegu, Pusan, Masan, and Chinju in the southeast, Kwangju and Chŏnju in the Chŏllas, and even Wŏnju in normally quiescent Kangwŏn province. After more than two weeks, there was still no end in sight. The RDP, led by Kim Young Sam, rejected as too little and too late an offer by Chun to allow resumption of debate in the National Assembly on the question of direct presidential elections, and speculation mounted in South Korea and abroad about the possibility of a military crackdown or coup.

Finally, on June 29, Roh Tae Woo stunned the country by announcing an eight-point program of reform that began with an endorsement of direct presidential elections and included restoration of civil rights for Kim Dae Jung and other political prisoners, protection of human rights, the lifting of press restrictions, the encouragement of local and campus autonomy, the promotion of political parties, and a call for "bold social reforms." Roh pledged to take his program to Chun and resign from all public duties if the president refused to accept it. Two days later, Chun publicly accepted Roh's proposals, and the atmosphere of crisis that had prevailed for so long immediately began to abate.

The declaration of June 29 was completely unexpected, and

its underlying dynamics are not precisely known. There were a number of factors, however, that surely figured prominently in Roh's decision to opt for reform, and in Chun's willingness to go along with it. One was the fact that the Chun regime had made the holding of the 1988 Summer Olympic Games in Seoul the centerpiece of both its domestic and international policies. For seven years the government and, indeed, the entire country, had been mobilized toward this overriding goal, whose attainment, the government hoped, would bring South Korea—and the government itself—a new international recognition and respect commensurate with the country's growing economic power. Continuing political instability raised the specter of Olympic disruption or even cancellation and made the idea of reform more palatable.

Another factor the government could not ignore was the depth of support for the students from ordinary citizens. Much of the fighting took place in downtown areas, such as around Seoul's Myŏngdong Cathedral in the center of the city, and whitecollar workers, housewives, college professors, Christian ministers, .priests and nuns, and Buddhist monks actively joined in the demonstrations or cheered the students on from the sidelines. Even taxi drivers stopped and honked their support for the students in the midst of their struggles with the riot police. As the fighting continued, ordinary citizens were also increasingly affected and angered by the virulence of the tear gas employed by the police, which often lingered in the air for days.

Finally, the Chun government was under strong pressure from the United States to eschew a military solution to the problem of popular dissent. Gaston J. Sigur Jr., the U.S. Assistant Secretary of State for East Asian and Pacific Affairs visited South Korea only days before Roh's announcement and met with all the key political figures, including Chun, Roh, Kim Young Sam, and even Kim Dae Jung, who was still under house arrest. Although it is difficult to know exactly what effect, if any, Sigur's visit had upon the government, his unequivocal public statements against military intervention and in favor of political reform, together with his willingness to meet with opposition leaders, were clearly intended as a message to Chun and Roh that the U.S.

was going to be less tolerant of strong-arm political interference by the South Korean army than in 1979-80. That Chun was sensitive and responsive to changes in official American foreign policy was also suggested by his initial turnabout on the question of constitutional revision the previous year, after the Reagan administration's abandonment of support for the Marcos dictatorship.

Roh's June 29 announcement was followed by a six-month period of frenetic political activity. A new constitution providing for direct presidential elections was drafted in the National Assembly by the ruling and opposition parties and approved in a national referendum on October 27. Elections for president were scheduled for December 16. Ironically, however, the great hope of the liberal forces to displace the political establishment through direct presidential elections was thwarted by a personal and party split between the two main opposition leaders, Kim Young Sam and Kim Dae Jung (Kim Dae Jung's civil rights had been fully restored on July 9). In spite of repeated public pledges to work together and numerous negotiations toward that end, the two Kims finally went their separate ways, and Kim Dae Jung formed his own new Party for Peace and Democracy (PPD) in November. The following month Roh won the election with only about 37% of the vote, with Kim Young Sam and Kim Dae Jung taking about 28% and 27% respectively. At first both Kims claimed the election had been stolen, and there were, in fact, numerous instances of vote-buying, intimidation (including death threats), and fraud reported by both domestic and foreign observers. No one was able to produce conclusive evidence of systematic rigging, however, and the election results were generally accepted by a South Korean public weary of demonstrations and disgusted with the two Kims. Roh Tae Woo, whose nomination as the ruling party candidate seven months earlier had ignited a popular revolt against the government, was peacefully inaugurated as South Korea's president on February 25, 1988.

The Sixth Republic and Prospects for Democracy

It is still too early to assess the impact of the Sixth Republic on South Korea's turbulent political history. So far the record has been mixed. Roh is far more relaxed, personable, and accommodating than his predecessor and many South Koreans have responded to his new "common man" style with enthusiasm.

The new constitution is also arguably the most liberal in the country's history. It specifically enjoins the military from political activity and provides new safeguards against official abuse of civil and human rights. Presidential tenure is limited to a single five-year term, and the president's powers have been substantially reduced. No longer does the president have the right to dissolve the National Assembly; the assembly, however, may inspect or investigate affairs of state and has the right to approve the president's choice of Supreme Court justices.

More important than the new constitution itself, however, has been Roh's apparent willingness to allow the system it envisions to function. In the National Assembly elections of April 1988, the ruling party failed for the first time in its history to secure a majority in the legislature, and the opposition has used its new power to begin probing into the financial scandals of the Chun administration and to reject Roh's nominee for Chief Justice, the first parliamentary repudiation of a Supreme Court nominee in South Korean history. So far the administration has accepted these defeats gracefully. It has also adopted a more laissez-faire attitude toward labor disputes since the June 29 declaration, precipitating over 3,000 strikes in the last months of 1987 alone and forcing businessmen to work out compromises with workers that have involved wage increases of over 20% in 1987 and 1988. Numerous political prisoners have also been freed since the summer of 1987, including Kim Kŭn-t'ae, a Seoul National University student in political economy who had been arrested in 1985 for alleged violation of the National Security Law and subsequently tortured, and whose release was regarded by many human rights groups as an important test of Roh's sincerity. The press has also been noticeably freer under Roh, as indicated by recent appearance of an outspoken new newspaper called *Han Kyŏre,* independent of government or *chaebŏl* connections and published by a group of journalists who had been dismissed and/or imprisoned under the Park and Chun regimes. In late June 1988, Roh also proposed a restructuring of relations with P'yŏngyang that would seek to integrate rather than isolate the north from the international capitalist economy in which the south has been so successful. While such a policy clearly reflected the government's desire to foster both a domestic and an international atmosphere conducive to a successful Olympics, it may also augur a new confidence and fundamental shift on the part of the South Korean government in its attitude toward the north. If implemented, it could greatly reduce tensions between the two Koreas and pave the way for further political liberalization in the south.

Despite such important changes, problems and questions persist. While Roh has acquired a certain popularity and public acceptance that had always eluded Chun, his selection of cabinet officers was an early disappointment for many South Koreans who had hoped for a cleaner break with the past. It also raised questions about where Roh actually stands in the political spectrum; even those South Koreans who wanted to believe in his liberalism found themselves wondering to what extent the new president would be his own man, able to sever his former ties with Chun and the military right wing. In that respect it is important to note that a considerable number of political prisoners remain incarcerated at the time of this writing. All the old security laws and forces are, in fact, still intact, and even since Roh's June 29 declaration, the government has continued to use them as harshly as in the past, though perhaps with less frequency and more discretion. Only two days after the 1987 presidential election, for example, thousands of riot police stormed the Kuro Ward Office in Seoul, which was being occupied by students demanding an investigation into a suspicious movement of absentee ballot boxes there on the day of the election. By the time the so-called Kuro Incident was over, the ward office building, a huge five-story edifice, had been virtually gutted, and the surrounding working-class residential area had been terrorized.

Even if Roh is serious about reform, he will still have to face certain basic problems, one of which is likely to be the activist right wing of the military. Can Roh control the more conservative officers who tend to see any form of political liberalization—particularly in conjunction with a more relaxed policy toward the north—as a threat to national security, and, not incidentally, to their own personal interests? Another problem will be the National Assembly, with its new opposition that can now exercise a veto over Roh's programs and investigate his administration. Will he continue to tolerate such disruption and loss of face? Finally, perhaps the greatest challenges for Roh will come from within the society itself. In his inaugural address, the new president said his main goal was "national reconciliation." It is a noble cause, resonant with Confucian overtones. But the regional and socioeconomic conflicts of South Korean society run deep and will not disappear without serious disturbance to vested interests. How far is Roh willing to take his reforms? And does the pursuit of "national reconciliation" include tolerance for the opinions of radical dissenters who demand revolutionary changes that Roh himself undoubtedly regards with alarm? The answers that the Roh regime provides to such questions will ultimately determine its mark on South Korea's political history.

Chapter 20

Economic Development in Historical Perspective, 1945-1990

The development of the South Korean economy is one of the great stories of the post-World War II era. It is a tale whose drama is heightened by breathtaking contrasts: a per capita GNP of about $100 in 1963 versus a figure of nearly $5,000 as the year 1990 began; a war-ravaged Seoul of gutted buildings, rubble, beggars, and orphans in 1953 versus the proud, bustling city of the 1988 Summer Olympics with its skyscrapers, subways, plush restaurants, boutiques, first-class hotels, and prosperous middle class; a country abjectly dependent on foreign aid in the 1950s versus a 1980s economic powerhouse—a factory to the world for everything from clothes, shoes, and electronic goods to steel, ships, and now even automobiles and semiconductors. Given these remarkable facts, it is not surprising that many popular writers and even a few scholars have taken to calling South Korea's economic transformation "the miracle on the Han."

The term "miracle," however, actually fails to do justice to the complexity of the story by implying that South Korea's growth was somehow contrary to reason or extraneous to history. Nothing, of course, could be further from the truth. Growth was stimulated and conditioned by a number of international, social, political, and cultural factors—all deeply grounded in Korean history. Indeed, even though the most visible and striking aspects of South Korean development occurred after 1961, the post-1961 period of rapid growth can be fully understood only in the context of a long historical process that began in the late nineteenth century. The process and impact of economic growth, moreover, have also posed some fundamental problems and challenges for

South Korean society, culture, politics, and international relations that the "miracle" sobriquet tends to obscure.

International Factors

While the credit and responsibility for South Korean development ultimately rests with the Koreans themselves, the influence of foreign powers in shaping the country's economy has been extraordinary. Korea's crucial geopolitical position at the crossroads of northeast Asia has brought the peninsula into intimate and sustained contact with the two most dynamic and expansive economies of the twentieth century, Japan and the United States. From the Korean viewpoint especially, the contact has not always been a happy one, and many scholars in South Korea, let alone in the north, have argued that foreign interference before and after 1945 has worked to distort a natural development of the economy that was already underway in the late nineteenth century. Such a view is deeply tinted with nationalist feeling and laden with presuppositions about the nature of economic development, but it correctly emphasizes the extent to which economic growth on the peninsula has been conditioned by external forces. What can hardly be denied, however, is that Korea's special historical relationships with the major core countries of the international capitalist system have played a key role in fostering economic growth, even if a number of Koreans have found certain aspects of that growth objectionable. What, then, were these special relationships? And how have they affected the development of the South Korean economy?

Before the late nineteenth century, Korea's international orientation was toward China, and the interaction between the two countries was less economic than diplomatic and cultural. After the Hideyoshi Invasions of the late sixteenth century, Koreans regarded Japan with a wary eye, and even though diplomatic relations were restored with the Tokugawa shogunate in 1609, Japanese were never permitted to go beyond Pusan, and the shogun was obliged to communicate with the Korean court either through sporadic Korean embassies to Edo or through the medium of Tsushima, a Tokugawa island domain that also maintained a semi-tributary relationship with Korea. From the Korean per-

spective, moreover, Japan was a peripheral, even culturally inferior, member of the Sinitic world order, and although the shogun was formally accorded a status equal to the Korean king by
Korean diplomats, Koreans in general never demonstrated the
kind of interest in and respect for Japan that they historically
showed for China.

All this changed with the Western invasion of East Asia in the
1800s. The dynamo of Western power and imperialism was its
great capitalist industrial base, and East Asian history since the
1840s has to a large extent been an attempt to come to terms
with this new global economic force. Japan's early success in this
regard gave it military and economic superiority in the region and
compelled the surrounding countries, including Korea, to emulate Japan's achievement or face the threat of Japanese hegemony. By the turn of the century, there were signs that both Korea's
government and private sectors were finally beginning to reform
the economy and society along Western (and Meiji Japanese)
lines, but it is impossible to say where such reform would have
led had it been allowed to continue. In the end, it proved to be
too little and too late to stem the Japanese advance, and Korea
became a Japanese colony in 1910.

It was thus Japanese colonialism that ultimately laid the foundations for a modern transformation of the economy. To be sure,
colonial development was geared to Japanese, rather than Korean,
goals and needs. But the changes effected were nevertheless historic. To appreciate how far reaching they were, one need only compare photographs of Seoul in the late Chosŏn period with similar
photographs taken in the mid-1930s. The former show a city
that seems distant and alien to the modern eye—less a city, in
fact, than an overgrown village of thatched-roof cottages that
the famous nineteenth-century explorer Isabella Bird Bishop
likened to an "expanse of overripe mushrooms." By contrast,
pictures of Seoul in the 1930s show a city that is distinctly modern
and familiar.

The altered face of Seoul was part and parcel of a general physical transformation of the country that occurred as colonial industry expanded with Japan's penetration of the Asian continent,
especially in the 1930s and 1940s. Railways, roads, rice mills,

textile factories, hydroelectric plants, smelters, oil refineries, shipyards, and even new cities were built to service the empire. The growth of manufacturing, in fact, averaged about 10% per year, and by 1940 about half of all factory production was in heavy industry, located mainly in the north. By any standards such industrial growth was impressive; in the context of colonial rule, it was exceptional, a clear reflection of Korea's vital strategic role as Japan's military-economic link to the Asian mainland. Much of this industrial base was later lost to South Korea through the peninsula's partition and civil war, but some important elements, including the railway system and the textile industry (centered in the south), remained as a framework for reconstruction in the 1950s and for rapid export-led growth in the 1960s.

The physical changes wrought by colonialism, however, were probably less important for later South Korean development than the accompanying social changes. A small population of Japanese dominated the modern, urban sector of the colonial economy, but by 1945 millions of Koreans had been induced or forced into new modes of life and thought by the industrialization process. Between 1910 and 1941, the number of Koreans living in cities of 20,000 people or more increased over threefold, from about 6% to 20% of the total population. Perhaps four million Koreans (about 16% of the population) were in Japan and Manchuria by 1945, and many of these people, especially the two million or more in Japan, were also living in cities.

Most of the new Korean urban populace consisted of factory wage workers who only a short time before had been tilling the land literally in the footsteps of their fathers and forefathers. As a political safety valve, however, the Japanese had also opened the door for a small number of Koreans to develop into a urban elite of businessmen, bureaucrats, white-collar workers, technicians, lawyers, doctors, and other modern professionals. Together the workers and the urban elite provided the social core and framework for a new capitalist society that continued to develop with American support and aid in the south after 1945.

Liberation ended Korea's colonial tie with Japan, and regular diplomatic relations between Seoul and Tokyo were not resumed until 1965, in part because of an implacable anti-Japanese stance by President Syngman Rhee. Private personal and professional relationships formed by Koreans and Japanese during the colonial period were by no means entirely severed, however, and for South Korea's elite, largely educated in the Japanese language, Japanese newspapers, magazines, and books continued to be a source of the latest information on everything from fashion to economic trends and industrial technology. Japan itself, moreover, remained a model of national and economic development for such people, especially as it began to reemerge as an important international economic force in the late 1950s and early 1960s. In that sense at least, the ROK-Japan Normalization Treaty, when it finally came in 1965, was less a break with the past than a resumption of an historic relationship under new conditions and on different terms. Indeed, although such a treaty had long been urged by the United States, South Koreans themselves took the initiative when the opportunity presented itself. Soon after Rhee was overthrown in 1960, South Korean official and private contacts with Japanese counterparts mushroomed, with Japanese-speaking Korean bureaucrats and businessmen of colonial vintage leading the way and working through a network of ex-colonial officials in Japan. And President Park Chung Hee, who was himself an elite product of the colonial military system, fluent in Japanese and deeply influenced both intellectually and emotionally by his training during Japan's period of Asian military-industrial supremacy, seems to have needed little or no persuasion to continue this process after seizing power in 1961.

The normalization treaty of 1965 signaled the beginning of the second period of major Japanese influence on the Korean peninsula since the late nineteenth century, and opponents of the treaty in fact compared it to the forced Korea-Japan Kanghwa Treaty of 1876 that had first opened Korea's ports to international trade. In one sense the comparison was misleading, since it was the South Koreans who were initiating normalization in the early 1960s, though the Japanese themselves certainly welcomed such a treaty for both political and economic reasons. On the other hand, normalization once again opened the door to widespread Japanese activity in Korea, and the results in terms of economic ties between the two countries were immediate and dramatic.

ROK-Japan trade had been growing since the 1950s despite the lack of formal diplomatic relations, but until 1965 the preponderance of South Korea's trade had been with the United States. Within little more than a year after the signing of the normalization agreement, however, Japan surpassed the United States as South Korea's most important trading partner and continued to hold this position throughout the period of rapid growth in the 1960s and 1970s. Since 1971, moreover, Japan's investment in South Korea has been considerably greater than that of any other country, accounting for about 54% of all foreign investment since 1962 (compared to about 26% for the U.S.).

The benefits of normalization for South Korean economic growth were enormous. At a time when American aid was being reduced and the Park government was desperately seeking alternative sources of capital to finance its new development plans, the treaty provided South Korea with $300 million in grants, $200 million in public loans, and $300 million in commercial credits (raised to $500 million in 1967) over a ten-year priod. In 1982 the Chun Doo Hwan regime negotiated a second loan agreement for $4 billion with the Nakasone government that reaffirmed the Japanese economic commitment to South Korea and eventually helped pay for the 1988 Summer Olympics in Seoul. Since 1965 Japanese private capital and technology have also flowed into South Korea in large quantities, propelling economic development. The recent triumph of the Hyundai subcompact car in the United States is a case in point: Mitsubishi owns about 10% of the Korean company and provides the car's engine and other key components.

The close economic interaction between South Korea and Japan has clearly been facilitated by geography. Seoul and Tokyo are only two hours apart by air and in the same time zone, and the economic advantages for both countries in terms of shipping costs and delivery times are obvious. Geographic proximity has also made the peninsula a continuing object of Japanese political and strategic concern and given Japan an incentive for contributing to the growth of a cooperative capitalist economy in South Korea.

Cultural similarity stemming from both countries' historical involvement with Chinese civilization and from the more recent heritage of colonialism has also played an important role in creating a special economic relationship. Language, for example, has been more of a bond than a problem. Since Korean and Japanese grammar and syntax are very similar in many respects and both written languages make use of borrowed Chinese characters, Koreans and Japanese can master each other's languages with relative ease; with its comparatively simple sound system, Japanese is in fact particularly easy for Koreans to learn, and more and more younger South Koreans have been studying Japanese in schools, universities, and private institutes as economic relations between the two countries have progressed. The generation that has dominated South Korea over the last twenty-five years, moreover, was educated for the most part in the Japanese language, and key government and business figures in both countries have consequently been able to deal with one another comfortably and confidently in the Japanese language.

In addition to a relative absence of language problems, the Japanese have found in South Korea a government-business structure and culture that is strikingly like their own—even down to the informal parties of wine, women, and song that invariably follow serious business discussions in both countries. They have also found a people who, though generally more direct and outspoken, possess a similarly keen sense of hierarchy and status. Indeed, there is surely no other foreign country in the world—perhaps not even Taiwan—where the Japanese have felt more at home doing business than in South Korea.

Today as Seoul is sprouting flashy new suburbs like Apkujŏng-dong that increasingly resemble Shinjuku and other districts of Tokyo, plans are being laid by American and South Korean authorities to move the American military command out of the central part of Seoul which it has occupied since 1945 and to return the command's 700-acre compound of offices, barracks, schools, landscaped homes, and myriad recreational facilities (including clubs, movie theatres, swimming pools, a full-scale library, a baseball diamond, and an 18-hole golf course) to South Korea. Somehow this conjunction of events seems appropriate and symbolic: in the long-term judgment of history, America's total economic impact on Korea will probably shrink in comparison with

Japan's. Nevertheless, for a period of about thirty years between 1945 and the mid-1970s, the U.S. played a critical role in the South Korean economy. Most of this complex story has yet to be written, but the following points seem clear.

The first and perhaps most important point—so obvious as to be forgotten—is that the United States since 1945 has been the decisive factor in the creation and maintenance of a political environment on the Korean Peninsula in which South Korea's particular capitalist development has taken place. Such a political framework was first established in 1945-1948 by the United States Army Military Government in Korea (USAMGIK), and the story of how this came about is recounted in Chapter 18. What needs to be emphasized here is that without American backing in 1945, Korea's nascent capitalist class, tainted by colonial collaboration, would in all likelihood have been severely purged or swept away in the politics of liberation, and the capitalist system itself would, at the very least, have been greatly modified.

In 1950, the United States again intervened in Korea to push back a North Korean invasion and saved the existing capitalist system a second time. Since then the U.S. has signed a mutual defense treaty with South Korea (1953) and maintained tens of thousands of American troops and even tactical nuclear weapons on the peninsula, while pouring vast sums of money into the development of South Korea's own military forces. The construction of this massively fortified political citadel has been an important prerequisite for continued capitalist development on the peninsula, especially in the first two decades after liberation.

In addition to insuring a political environment conductive to capitalist development, the U.S. has directly or indirectly sought to foster economic growth in South Korea. To be sure, interest in Korea has from the beginning been political and strategic rather than economic: support for South Korea since 1945 has been part of a global containment (and occasional rollback) of international communism centered on the Soviet Union. Nevertheless, American policymakers have also tended to see the development of a strong capitalist economy in Korea (and elsewhere) as an integral part of their anticommunist strategy and have consequently provided South Korea with large amounts of the two things it has needed most: capital and technology.

Between 1946 and 1976 the U.S. supplied a total of $12.6 billion in economic and military assistance to South Korea—more dollars per capita of aid than to any other foreign country except South Vietnam and Israel. Although the growth rate achieved in the 1950s as a result of such assistance was only about 4%, American aid was clearly the crucial factor in South Korea's post-colonial economic survival between 1945-50 and in the country's postwar reconstruction after 1953. Indeed, between 1953 and 1962 American aid financed about 70% of South Korea's imports and accounted for nearly 80% of total fixed capital formation, mainly in the areas of transportation, manufacturing, and electric power. One of the most notable aid accomplishments was the resuscitation of the South Korean textile industry. Building on its colonial base, the textile industry experienced its most rapid expansion in history between 1953 and 1957, with growth rates averaging about 24% per year; by 1957 the industry had achieved complete import substitution in cotton, woolen, rayon, and knitted textiles and was beginning to explore possible export markets. Also worth noting is that nearly all of the American aid to South Korea before 1964 was provided on a grant basis, thus making it possible for the country to begin its export-led growth in the 1960s without a backlog of debt. Since then South Korea has gradually freed itself from a reliance on American economic grants, but it has continued to depend on U.S. support for concessional and commercial loans from the World Bank, the International Development Bank, the International Finance Corporation, and other international public and private lending institutions. American military aid, moreover, which totaled about $6.8 billion in the thirty years after liberation (not including the military equipment supplied during the Korean War), has also been an important factor in economic growth by freeing domestic resources for development.

The influx of American capital into South Korea has been accompanied by a corresponding flow of American technology and technical expertise. Aid has helped finance technology transfers from American firms and the creation of official research and development organizations like the Korea Development Institute

(KDI) and the Korea Institute of Science and Technology (KIST), while the U.S. itself has since 1945 been the primary training ground for South Korean economic and industrial technocrats, many of whom have been supported by aid funds.

American economic experts and technicians associated with the U.S. AID Mission in South Korea have also played a key role in shaping the South Korean economy through their allocation of aid funds for specific projects and their participation in the formation and implementation of South Korean government development plans. While the full dimensions of this particular American contribution are only now being investigated by scholars, it is clear that the direct and personal involvement of Americans in the South Korean economy has been extraordinary. Indeed, in the early 1960s the U.S. AID Mission in South Korea was one of the largest in the world, and AID officials had full access to South Korean government information and personnel. American experts spoke of "tutoring" President Park in economics and did not hesitate to use aid funds as leverage to force the South Korean government into compliance with their economic suggestions.

The special U.S.-ROK relationship also gave South Korea privileged access to U.S. markets. Until recently the U.S. more or less accepted South Korean protectionist policies as a necessary part of the growth process and accorded many South Korean exports duty-free status under the General System of Preferences (GSP), a program instituted in 1976 to promote trade with developing countries. Although the U.S. has gradually been withdrawing such favors as ROK development has proceeded, the economic gains to South Korea over the years have been considerable. In 1987, when the U.S. drastically reduced the scope of the GSP, South Korea accounted for about 14% of all GSP preferences. Today South Korea sends about 40% of its exports to the U.S., and in 1987 it enjoyed a $10 billion trade surplus with its former aid donor.

South Korea also reaped important economic benefits from its role as America's chief ally in the Vietnam War. In 1964-65 the Lyndon Johnson administration launched a major diplomatic effort to secure troop commitments for the war from European and Asian countries, both to create the impression of international solidarity with the United States on the war issue and also, secondarily, to reduce the burden on U.S. combat forces. Only Australia, New Zealand, the Philippines, Thailand, and South Korea responded positively, and South Korea eventually emerged as the most important contributor by far, dispatching a total of about 300,000 troops to Vietnam between 1965 and 1973.

In return, the South Koreans demanded and received a remarkable package of military and economic payments and perquisites formalized in the so-called Brown Memorandum of 1966 (Winthrop Brown was the U.S. ambassador to the ROK at the time). In addition to agreeing to equip, train, supply, and pay all the ROK forces used in Vietnam, the U.S. further agreed to modernize the ROK forces in South Korea itself and to suspend the program, instituted by the U.S. in the early 1960s, to shift the burden of American military aid to the ROK defense budget. The U.S. also promised additional AID loans to the ROK and pledged itself to procure from South Korea insofar as possible and practicable supplies, services, and equipment for the various military forces in Vietnam, as well as a "substantial amount of goods" required by the AID Mission in South Vietnam for its work in rural construction, pacification, relief, logistics, and other areas. South Korean contractors, moreover, were to be given "expanded opportunities" to participate in American construction projects in South Vietnam and to provide other services, including the employment of skilled Korean civilians.

Vietnam quickly developed into an economic bonanza for South Korea. Although rapid export-led economic development was already underway in the country by 1965, the Vietnam War boom, like the ROK-Japan Normalization Treaty, gave the economy an important lift during the critical take-off period—similar, in that sense, to what the Korean War did for Japan in the 1950s. In 1966 the war accounted for 40% of South Korea's crucial foreign-exchange receipts, and by 1970, the last year for which we have published data, the total U.S. payments to South Korea under the Brown Memorandum were estimated by the U.S. Department of Defense to be nearly $1 billion.

The economic effects of South Korea's Vietnam's venture,

moreover, went far beyond the simple acquisition of foreign exchange. Many South Korean business firms, including two of the largest business conglomerates or *chaebŏl*, Hanjin and Hyundai (Hyŏndae), got their first big economic boost from the war. Cho Chung-hun, Hanjin's founder, set up a land and marine transport company in South Vietnam and eventually assumed responsibility, with the blessing of the U.S. Army, for the whole operation of the port of Qui Nhon. In 1967 Cho also established an air and sea transport firm in South Korea, mainly to carry South Korean products and workers to South Vietnam; two years later he took over an ailing Korean Air Lines from the government and used the Vietnam trade to help turn the company around and elevate Hanjin into the ranks of the major *chaebŏl* by the mid-1970s.

The Hyundai story was no less spectacular. Hyundai and other South Korean construction companies became major contractors for the U.S. army in South Vietnam and later made use of their Vietnam contacts and experience to expand into the international construction business, most notably in the Middle East. Between 1974 and 1979 South Korea's top ten *chaebŏl* took home nearly $22 billion in Middle East construction sales, of which Hyundai's share alone was over $6 billion.

Internal Social and Political Factors

External influence, however important, is not sufficient to explain South Korea's economic growth; internal factors have also been crucial. In many countries the existence of a powerful landed elite opposed to agrarian taxation and reform has been a serious historical impediment to industrialization, and we can appreciate the significance of this point by looking at the Philippines and numerous Central and South American countries even today. On the other hand, the fact that Japan's traditional elite was a stipended urban bureaucracy without binding economic ties to the land has often been cited as one of the main underlying reasons behind Meiji Japan's rapid transformation into an industrial society. Another problem for many countries has been the lack, for a variety of reasons, of a dynamic class of entrepreneurs and/or of a class of dependable, efficient industrial workers; without such critical social elements to support and sustain the growth process in a developing country, the injection of foreign capital and technology into the economy is likely to be a wasted effort.

In the late nineteenth century Korea had one of the most entrenched landed aristocracies in the world, and the refusal of this class as a whole to countenance any serious change in the economic and political status quo was a major factor in the country's ultimate inability to meet the challenges of imperialism and ward off colonial domination. Colonialism removed this class from political power but strengthened and sustained it economically, so that in 1945, in spite of the existence of a new urban industrial sector built up largely by imported Japanese capital, the countryside was still dominated by the old landed elite. Nevertheless, by 1945 a progressive segment of this class had already begun to transfer some of its landed wealth into commerce and industry, and subsequent land reforms in South Korea under the American military government, North Korean occupation during the war, and the Syngman Rhee regime finally eliminated the landlords as a class and opened the door to full-scale industrialization of the South Korean economy.

Many post-reform landlords were, in fact, highly successful in making the transition to industrial society: a Harvard study conducted in 1976, for example, concluded that the vast majority of the country's business leaders have come from the land-based traditional elite. The process of transition, however, was not simply one of shifting assets from the land to urban enterprise. South Korean landlords were given government bonds denominated in rice as compensation for reform, but the bonds eventually lost about 90% of their value in the marketplace, largely because of the government's failure to redeem on schedule; they thus never provided a financial basis for landlord reinvestment in industry. Nevertheless, many landlords, anticipating reform, had already concluded satisfactory private sales with relatives and tenants by the time the reform was actually implemented, and even those landlords who were wiped out by the reform continued to retain the high level of education and the personal connections that have always been important factors for success in Korean society. In any case, by the mid-1950s not only was landlordism no longer an obstacle to economic growth, but former landlords themselves and their children were already well on their way to becoming businessmen or white-collar professionals of one kind or another.

Korean entrepreneurs have, in fact, been an important and constant part of the country's modern history, skillfully availing themselves of every major economic opportunity since the late nineteenth century. With the opening of Korea's ports in 1876, Korean landlords and commercial agents called *kaekchu* or *yŏgak* made fortunes in the new international trade in export rice and imported manufactures, thus initiating a process of capitalist accumulation and growth on the peninsula that continues in South Korea today. By the turn of the century, a number of these newly enriched Koreans were beginning to establish modern banks and commercial enterprises, but it was really the colonial period (especially after 1919) that saw the emergence of a nascent industrial capitalist class, which developed in cooperation with Japanese colonial economic interests. This story is perhaps best epitomized by the rise of the Kim family of Koch'ang County in North Chŏlla province from small enterprising landlords in the late nineteenth century to commercial and industrial magnates by 1945, but there were other similar, if less dramatic, cases of colonial entrepreneurship whose importance we can now more fully appreciate. No less than three of South Korea's top four *chaebŏl*, for example, were founded by men who began their business careers during the colonial period: Yi Pyŏng-ch'ŏl (Samsung), Ku In-hoe (Lucky), and Chŏng Chu-yŏng (Hyundai).

Since 1945, and especially since 1961, the process of capitalist growth has greatly accelerated in South Korea. Although there has been considerable entrepreneurial continuity throughout the post-1945 period and even extending back into the colonial period, each new economic opportunity since 1945 has also tended to spawn additional entrepreneurs, and some in each case have generally been able to carve out a lasting place in the economy. Broadly speaking, the main opportunities have come in connection with the following circumstances or events: the gradual sale of former Japanese properties by the South Korean government at exceptionally favorable prices during the 1950s; the demand for goods and services (at inflated wartime prices) during the Korean War; the political economy of aid dependency and import substitution during the Rhee years, when fortunes could be made through the acquisition of foreign exchange, exclusive import licenses, public contracts, aid funds and materials, and cheap bank loans—all government-controlled; the new policies of export promotion after 1961, which gave exporters in targeted industries special licensing, tax, and financial privileges; the aforementioned economic environment created by South Korea's participation in the Vietnam War, and the subsequent construction boom in the Middle East, where South Korea captured almost 7% of the market and became the sixth largest international contractor in the region. By the mid-1980s, the combined sales of South Korea's top five *chaebŏl* (excluding intrafirm transactions) accounted for nearly 66% of GNP, and two of them, Samsung and Hyundai, were, according to *Fortune* magazine, among the fifty largest business firms in the world.

Equally if not more important than such entrepreneurship in the development process has been the contribution of South Korea's workers. The growth of elementary and secondary schools during the colonial period and the participation of millions of Koreans in the pre-1945 industrialization of Korea, Japan, and Manchuria left the peninsula with an impressive pool of literate and experienced workers by 1945. Since then this pool has been continually enlarged in conjunction with the proliferation of new schools and the reconstruction and expansion of the manufacturing industry. Very few countries have been as blessed as South Korea with such a well-educated and adept working class in their early stages of development. Indeed, for so-called late- or late-late-developing countries like South Korea, where success in the international market depends to no small degree on the ability of the country's workers to adapt quickly to changing foreign technologies, the existence of such a work force is a special desideratum.

South Korea's workers have not only been quick and skillful; until recently they have also been cheap. A number of factors have made this possible: the country's low standard of living in the early stages of the growth process; the workers' low pay relative to business profits; poor working conditions (especially at the smaller factories); the longest average work week in the world (about fifty-four hours); workers' forbearance in the face of such hardships, especially in the 1960s and early 1970s; and until recently the refusal of the South Korean government to permit workers freely to organize and take collective action in their own interests. For the past twenty-five years low labor costs have consistently been South Korea's chief, if not only, comparative advantage in the international export market; one of the main reasons, for example, that South Korean companies were able to compete so successfully in the Middle East construction market in the 1970s was their ability to offer package deals that included the utilization of thousands of experienced and inexpensive South Korean workers.

By the early 1960s South Korea already had many of the essential ingredients for rapid economic growth: international political support, access to foreign capital and technology, a small core class of entrepreneurs, and a reserve of actual and potential workers, quick to learn and cost-competitive in the international market. As the economist Alexander Gerschenkron has pointed out, however, late development assumes an active economic role for the state, and until 1961 South Korea did not have a state structure committed to and capable of galvanizing all its valuable international and social resources toward economic growth.

The problem of creating such a state had plagued Korea since the late nineteenth century. The late Chosŏn state had lacked both the necessary vision and the autonomy from civil society to take the lead in the industrialization process, and it was the Japanese who finally provided Korea with the kind of strong, autonomous, and developmental state that could initiate and carry out industrialization. The American military passed this state structure on virtually intact to the newly inaugurated ROK in 1948, but Syngman Rhee converted it into a political tool to perpetuate his own power, thus fostering a pattern of nonproductive interaction among the ruler, bureaucracy, and social elite that was reminiscent of the late Chosŏn dynasty. The ill-starred Second Republic that followed Rhee made economic growth a priority and began to revive a development plan that the Rhee government had originally drafted and then neglected, but the new government was overthrown before the plan could be implemented. Even if the Second Republic had continued, however, there is considerable doubt whether the new ruling Democratic Party of Chang Myŏn, with its intimate ties to existing socioeconomic interests, would have been able to carry out the kind of economic transformation effected by the military under Park Chung Hee.

The Park government represented a return to the relatively autonomous and economically-oriented state of the colonial period. The relative autonomy was a function of the Park group's position outside the South Korean socioeconomic, and even military, elite. Like the political leaders of Meiji Japan and the Kuomintang on Taiwan after 1949, Park and his followers were comparatively free of entangling personal and economic connections with the civil society and thus under far fewer constraints than their immediate predecessors with regard to making economic changes. This point, of course, should not be exaggerated—hence the term "relative autonomy." Park never carried out what can be described as a genuine social revolution, and from the beginning he was to some extent dependent on the goodwill and cooperation of various key sectors of the society— especially the business elite whom he disliked and distrusted (at least at first), but who were important in his plans for economic development. The South Korean state, moreover, has never enjoyed the same degree of autonomy vis-à-vis the international political and economic order that it has with respect to domestic forces. Nevertheless, the point to be noted here is that compared to the Chang Myŏn, or even the Rhee, government, the Park regime was notably unhampered by ties to the existing South Korean establishment.

Such freedom allowed Park and his officials to devise a series of five-year economic development plans beginning in 1962 that were based largely on perceived economic efficiency, with initially little input and no serious interference from the civil society. Economic planning and monitoring were centered in a new Economic Planning Board (EPB), established in 1961, which was composed primarily of professional economists and other so-called technocrats, and headed by a Deputy Prime Minister who was himself a prominent technocrat. Probably the most important economic policy change of the Park government was its shift in the early 1960s from an import-substituting to an export-led economy, a move that both the Rhee and the Chang Myŏn government, with all their vested social, economic, and bureaucratic interests in import-substitution would have found difficult if not impossible to carry out. Since then, the state has continued to act as the general manager of the economy, supervising a major transition in the 1970s from an emphasis on labor-intensive light industries like textiles to capital/technology-intensive heavy industries like shipbuilding, petrochemicals, heavy machinery, electronics, and automobiles.

Official development plans were implemented in all the relevant sectors of society through a combination of state controls and incentives. As in the colonial period, labor and business were treated very differently. When workers, for example, began to demand better conditions and more freedom in the late 1960s and early 1970s, the labor laws were structured into an elaborate system of restraint on union activity, and the workers themselves were ruthlessly put down by the police and other security forces; only recently has the government modified its harsh treatment of workers to some extent. Businessmen too have ultimately been subject to the state's monopoly of violence, but in general Park and his successors have chosen to cultivate a cooperative relationship with business leaders, gradually bringing them into the economic decision-making process through both formal and informal channels, lavishing public praise and honors on them for achieving or exceeding development goals, and selectively allowing them to become rich.

At the same time, however, the state has been able to make businessmen adhere to its official development programs thorugh the manipulation of a number of key economic controls, three of which have been particularly effective. One has been the state's allocation of business licenses, which precisely define and limit the scope of a firm's activity; all businessmen have been required to obtain such licenses from the appropriate government ministry or department in order to establish, modify, or expand a company. A second lever of control has been the government's domination of the financial system; through its ownership or supervision or all the country's banks and its power to set interest rates, the government has been able to direct capital into industries targeted for development and to make or break even large conglomerates. Even commercial loans induced from foreign countries have generally required approval and guarantee by the government. Finally, a third government control over business has existed in the Office of National Tax Administration (ONTA), which has been used by the government to insure that business expenditures and profits flow into approved areas, and to penalize or even ruin businessmen who have seriously violated the official guidelines and regulations or somehow offended the government authorities.

The Role of Culture and Timing

The correlation of economic development with such things as access to international capital and technology, entrepreneurship, industrial labor, and a strong, developmental state seems direct and unequivocal. The role of culture and timing in this process, though probably no less significant, is far more difficult to pinpoint and delineate. Nevertheless, it is important to try, and the following general observations may be regarded as a tentative step in that direction.

Nationalism has often been cited as a cultural factor in economic growth, especially in late-developing countries, where it can function as an ideology of popular mobilization and legitimacy during the hardships and social disruption of rapid economic growth. Certainly nationalism has played such a role in the historical development of Japan, and to some extent in Taiwan after 1949; and although it does not seem to have been an important factor in the growth of Hong Kong or Singapore, perhaps this is because both are really city-states rather than nations. On the other hand, the absence of a strong national identity and pride or, conversely, the presence of deep subnational loyalties to a particular tribe, religion, or region has proven to be a serious obstacle to economic growth in many parts of the world.

In Korea there has been no such obstacle. One of Korea's most striking characteristics has been its long and continuous existence as a unified country, from the triumph of the Silla state in the seventh century A.D. to the artificial political division of the peninsula in 1945. Between 668 and 1910, moreover, there were only three Korean dynasties, and the third alone lasted over 500 years. Linguistic, ethnic, and religious divisions among the population have had little impact on the country's history, and only in the last decade or so has regionalism become an important socioeconomic and political issue as a result of South Korea's geographically skewed pattern of economic growth (discussed in Chapter 19). In spite of numerous invasions and occupations, the Koreans have remained remarkably homogeneous, so much so in fact that they use the same term, *Han minjok,* to mean both "Korean nation" and "Korean race," and, indeed, do not clearly differentiate between the two ideas. (The Japanese also fail to make this distinction, but the Chinese in the PRC, at least since 1949, use the term "Chinese nation" or *Chung-hua min-tsu* to embrace a variety of ethnic minorities.)

Korea was not only unified for well over a millenium before 1945; until the twentieth century it was an active and leading participant in East Asia's Sinitic world civilization. If Japan's cultural achievements came largely from a departure from Chinese culture, Korea's came from a process of creation within the Chinese tradition, and its accomplishments often rivaled, and sometimes even surpassed, those of China itself. In the realm of Neo-Confucian culture alone, Korea's contributions were "stellar," to borrow the adjective used by Columbia scholar Wm. Theodore de Bary, and were creatively adapted to Korean conditions and needs. Indeed, Chosŏn Korea's aristocratic elite were both self-consciously cosmopolitan and Korean at the same time, and they were capable, during China's Ch'ing dynasty, for example, of looking down on China for abandoning cultural standards they themselves continued to uphold.

Although extra-familial loyalties in traditional Korea were focused on the ruling dynasty rather than on the abstract idea of Korea as a nation state, the country's essential homogeneity and historically based sense of cultural attainment helped pave the way for modern Korean nationalism, which gradually developed in reaction to foreign imperialism and occupation in the late nineteenth and twentieth centuries. Colonialism, in particular, intensified nascent nationalist feeling by providing a clear external enemy and by leaving many Koreans with a passionate post-colonial resolve to match or outdo the economic achievements of their former colonial overlords. The very fact, moreover, that the colonizer had been Japan, a culturally similar—indeed, from the Korean perspective, inferior—country, rather than a totally alien Western nation, gave Koreans confidence in their ability to duplicate Japan's economic success. All these feelings—the continued strong sense of national unity and destiny and the catalytic bitterness and anger (*han* in Korean) of the colonial experience—have been consciously and effectively harnessed in the service of economic growth by South Korea's developmental state.

The postwar economic rise of East Asia (especially Japan, Korea, Taiwan, Hong Kong, and Singapore) has spurred a new interest in Confucianism, and there are presently a number of academic projects underway in the United States to explore the role of Confucianism and Confucian institutions in the process of rapid economic growth. Everyone involved seems to agree that Confucianism has indeed played such a role, but defining it—indeed, defining Confucianism itself—has proved to be more difficult than many people had originally anticipated. Nevertheless, such projects have already gone a long way toward raising some of the fundamental questions that need to be confronted in dealing with this complicated topic, and substantive studies are likely to be published in the next few years. Such Western interest in Confucianism is of course highly ironic, since for decades scholars had followed the lead of Max Weber in considering Confucianism the main cultural impediment to economic development in East Asia; even research on the cultural origins of development in Japan, the only East Asian country at the time that seemed to demonstrate a capacity for economic growth, was focused primarily on Japan's indigenous cultural roots, especially those that were most reminiscent of the complex of values associated with Weber's so-called Protestant ethic.

In the case of Korea, perhaps the best way to approach this issue is through a few caveats, some of which may apply to one or more of the other East Asian countries as well. First, despite the recent focus on Confucianism, it is important to keep in mind that it is only one of several great religious or philosophical traditions in Korea. Two others which predate Confucianism and continue to exist in South Korea today are Buddhism and shamanism, but so far no one has seriously investigated their role, if any, in the country's economic growth. Nor has anyone sufficiently considered the impact of Christianity in this regard (Christianity has been growing in Korea since the late Chosŏn period and now embraces about 25-30% of South Korea's population). As the anthropologist Vincent Brandt has suggested, moreover, the communitarian values that are generally associated with Confucianism and regarded as an ethical resource in late development (in contrast to the spirit of individualism associated with the original industrial revolution in the West) are only half of the Korean story; Brandt has pointed to an equally deep and persistent countervailing tendency in Korean culture toward individual self-assertion, and it may well be that this combination of opposing values and the tension between them, rather than communitarianism alone, provide a better explanation of Korea's particular type of development, with its aggressive entrepreneurship and, simultaneously, its close government-business relations.

A second point to remember is that many of the so-called typical Confucian values now seen as factors in South Korea's economic growth—filial piety and family loyalty, a perception and acceptance of the state as an active, moral agent in the development of society, a respect for status and hierarchy, an emphasis on self-cultivation and education, and the concern with social harmony mentioned above—were already present in varying degrees in Korean culture long before Neo-Confucianism became the country's ruling ideology in the Chosŏn dynasty. What the Chosŏn state's adoption of Neo-Confucianism seems to have done is to have given these values a more richly constructed philosophical framework and to have diffused them throughout the society at much deeper levels than ever before.

A third point to be considered in assessing the impact of Confucianism on South Korean growth involves coming to terms with the phenomenon that finally led Weber to conclude that Confucianism was a hindrance to economic development: the failure of a country like China or Korea to achieve an economic breakthough at a time when Confucian influence in the society was at its peak. One might argue, of course, that strong negative factors, such as the existence of a powerful land-based aristocracy, overrode the positive force of Confucianism, but history does not really support such a view; Korea's aristocratic elite, for example, were well-educated Neo-Confucians and opposed economic and social reform on solid Neo-Confucian grounds.

A much more convincing explanation of this problem has been put forward by Harvard historian Tu Wei-ming. Tu avoids positing any kind of direct causal relationship between Confucianism and economic growth and even acknowledges the likely debilitating effect of a conscious, studious commitment to Neo-Confucian ethics on the development process. He suggests, however, that once the orientation of a society has shifted toward modernization, many of the values mentioned above, now internalized and no longer conscious, can provide a cultural basis for the requisite economic transformation. Following Tu, one may therefore conclude that the effect of Confucianism on East Asian economic growth has been a case of "unintended consequences," similar in that sense to the effect of Calvinism on early Western capitalists. A good example of such an "unintended consequence" in South Korea has been the country's development of an exceptionally well-educated population, capable of rapid assimilation and adaptation of foreign technology and economic expertise. Instead of reading Mencius and Chu Hsi, ambitious South Koreans now read Paul Samuelson and Martin Feldstein, but the respect for education and commitment to self-improvement through study remain much the same as in the Chosŏn dynasty.

Timing, even more than culture, is one of those elusive variables of development that tend to defeat economic model-making and give the whole process of growth a stubbornly fortuitous cast. The reason, of course, is because timing, by definition, involves a conjunction or concatenation of events or situations that are usually unpredictable and unique. One good example of such timing was South Korea's economic opportunity in Vietnam, which came precisely at a time when the country was in dire need of new sources of foreign exchange. Another was the construction boom in the Middle East, which came just as the Vietnam War was winding down, and after South Korean firms had already acquired a decade of experience in the international construction industry in Southeast Asia as a result of the Vietnam War.

There have been other such examples, but two in particular deserve mention because their impact has been even more continuous and profound than the benefits from Vietnam and the Middle East. One concerns the international market as a whole. Until recently South Korea has been able to keep its own markets relatively closed to the world while having wide, and often preferential, access to the international market, both as a source of capital and technology and as a destination for South Korean exports. The importance of such access can hardly be overestimated for a country whose rapid growth since 1961 has been fueled almost entirely by exports. For some time now, however, the international market has been growing increasingly tighter for Korea, a function of the economic decline of the United States and the rise of a number of other low-wage economic competitors (Thailand, Malaysia, and China), and there seems to be a perceptible drift toward protectionism and the development of regional economic blocs centered in East Asia, North America, and Western Europe. In retrospect, it seems that South Korea has been doubly fortunate, first in that its period of reconstruction in the 1950s came at a time when the United States was still willing and able to channel large amounts of concessional aid to developing nations, and second, in that its subsequent period of export-led growth occurred when the international market was still relatively open and outside pressures to open its own domestic market were slight to nonexistent.

South Korea's important cooperative economic relationship with Japan since 1965 has also been deeply affected by factors of timing. First, the relationship was initiated, structured, and developed by what was, in effect, Korea's last colonial generation, i.e., Koreans who had reached maturity (age 20 and above) while the country was still under colonial rule. Many of these Koreans already had personal connections dating from the colonial period with Japanese who were, or had subsequently become, influential elements in Japan's political and business elite. All spoke Japanese fluently (in some cases even better than Korean) and were well accustomed to, even genuinely comfortable in, Japanese social and cultural settings.

Second, the South Korea-Japan economic relationship has also grown because of the complementary nature of the two countries' economies, a function largely of the different historical timing of each country's industrialization. Since the colonial period Japan has been the moving force in the development of what some scholars have suggested is a transnational northeast Asian political economy. Both in the colonial period and again after 1965, Korea has in fact developed more in conjunction than in competition with the Japanese economy, often serving, like Taiwan, as a base for declining Japanese industries as Japan has moved upward through each product cycle and through progressively more advanced stages of industrialization. One sees this phenomenon perhaps most clearly in textiles, the oldest industry in both countries, but it has also been present in steel, shipbuilding, automobiles, and other industries as well.

Problems and Prospects

South Korea's transformation into an urban industrial society has raised the country's general standard of living far beyond the dreams of even the most visionary of the Chosŏn dynasty's statecraft writers and justly commanded the attention and respect of the world. The legacy of this great change, however, has been mixed. A look back over the past one hundred years or so, for example, shows a history of industrialization that has been intimately connected with invasion and foreign occupation, war and other forms of organized violence, political repression, and the immiserization of millions of people.

The problems and issues raised by the country's economic

growth have also been numerous and profound, and many are in fact a natural outgrowth of the various factors, discussed above, which have contributed most to the growth process. Reliance on foreign capital has given South Korea's business firms exceptionally high debt-equity ratios (some in the range of 8-1) and the country as a whole one of the largest foreign debts in the developing world, equal in 1986 to about 50% of South Korea's total GNP. A similar dependence on foreign technology (as late as 1980 only about six-tenths of 1% of GNP was spent for research and development) has also left the country with a weak indigenous technological base at a time when international economic competition is making the acquisition of new foreign technology increasing difficult, even at the high prices South Korea is now willing and able to pay. As noted above, South Korea's strategy of export-led growth is also beginning to run into protectionist barriers, especially in the crucial U.S. market.

South Korea's strong developmental state, which has jealously planned and guided the economy since 1961, has now become as much of a problem as a boon to continued growth. The increasing complexity of both the domestic and the international economy suggests a pressing need to transfer more of the economic decision-making power to the private sector, but even apart from the knotty problem of infringement on vested political interests that such a shift would pose, there is some question as to the ability of the private sector in certain key areas like commercial banking, so long under the control or protection of the government, to adjust quickly or easily to such a change.

The main social problem of South Korean development involves the question of economic justice in the distribution of wealth. In promoting export-led growth, the state has cultivated a junior partnership with the country's entrepreneurs and simultaneously kept workers' wages down to maintain comparative advantage in the international market. Although since 1961 both entrepreneurs and workers have benefited from the general rise in living standards and absolute poverty has been notably reduced, the entrepreneurs have reaped a disproportionate share of the new national wealth, especially in view of the workers' crucial contribution to the rapid growth of the economy. In the first decade of rapid growth, for example, annual business profits averaged about 20%, but real wages rose only about 9%. Since 1970, moreover, there has been a perceptible trend toward income inequality (as measured by the Gini coefficient), a significant increase in relative poverty (income less than one-third of the national median income), and a striking concentration of national wealth in the hands of the business elite; between 1974 and 1984, for example, the estimated combined GNP share of value-added for South Korea's top five *chaebŏl* alone grew from 3.6% to 12.1%. None of these statistics would make any difference, of course, if South Korean workers were satisfied with what most U.S. and South Korean economists have praised as a relatively equitable distribution of wealth compared with other developing countries. But recent political events (discussed in Chapter 19) suggest that the workers are in fact far from satisfied, and South Korea's residual Confucian culture has always been much less tolerant of such income disparity than Western capitalism.

The contradictory linking of nationalist ideology and external dependency in the growth process has also posed cultural and political challenges for South Korea. The cultural challenge has been to retain and develop a uniquely Korean identity while absorbing a constant amd intense barrage of foreign cultural influences. Given the enormity of this task, it is hardly surprising that South Koreans in the last twenty-five years have tended to shift uncomfortably between two extremes: indiscriminate cultural imitation on the one hand, and militant cultural chauvinism on the other. Recently the pendulum has moved toward the latter, and traditional culture (both high and low), disdained as late as the 1960s by many South Koreans as unprogressive or simply embarrassing in a Western-oriented world, has been enjoying a renaissance of interest and respect. Folk culture in particular has become a new source of pride and inspiration, especially to nationalist (*minjok*) or populist (*minjung*) artists who have consciously identified the core of the nation with the history of the common people (or masses). Nevertheless, the question of how to be both modern and Korean at the same time remains a deeply felt problem in the society and is often reflected in South Korean newspaper and magazine articles, as well as television programs, that attempt to define—if only to celebrate—those things which are indisputably Korean.

The contradiction between nationalism and foreign dependency has also made potential political instability a structural problem for the state, the capitalist class, and perhaps even for South Korean capitalism itself. To understand why, one first has to remember that the whole process of capital accumulation in South Korea has taken place largely through the establishment of transnational state and class relationships, and that although actual foreign ownership of South Korean assets has been strictly controlled and limited by the state since 1948, such external linkages have kept both the state and the private sector in a relatively vulnerable economic position with respect to the outside world, and especially vis-à-vis the United States and Japan. South Korea's market liberalization in the past decade has been a case in point: although domestic as well as international forces have moved the country toward liberalization, there is no question that South Korea's heavy dependence on the U.S. as an export market has also limited its ability to withstand U.S. pressures to liberalize certain sectors of the economy, especially agriculture and services.

The economic relationship with Japan in the past two decades has been far more dependent and uneven than with the U.S. Indeed, according to Chang Key-young (Chang Ki-yŏng), former Deputy Prime Minister and head of the EPB in the period of transition to rapid export-led growth, the Park government consciously sought to promote an "organic division of labor" betwen Japan and South Korea that would marry Japanese capital and technology to cheap and unorganized South Korean labor. Park was, of course, successful in this endeavor, and the result has been a highly unbalanced relationship: South Korea's own economic growth has now become structurally linked to Japan's, both through the product cycle, mentioned above, and through an exceptional South Korean reliance on imported Japanese intermediate goods (between 60% and 100% of the total required, depending on the product). Ironically, U.S. pressures on South Korea to liberalize the economy have actually increased Japan's economic leverage in South Korea because of American inability to compete effectively with Japanese products.

The existence of such inherently unequal economic relationships with external powers is a politically volatile issue in South Korea because of the peninsula's history of foreign invasion and domination since the late nineteenth century and because successive South Korean governments since 1961 have not only fanned nationalism in South Korean society as a mobilizing ideology, but also consistently used nationalist themes, including economic self-reliance, as a justification for official policies. Many South Koreans have been disturbed and dismayed by the country's external economic dependency and by the apparent contradiction between official words and deeds, but the sharpest criticism has come from a small but growing radical left.

In the past decade or so, the radical left has carved out an important niche in nearly all of South Korea's major intellectual circles and has gradually been redefining Korean nationalism within the discourse of Western/Japanese neo-Marxism and dependency theory. The result has been a scathing attack on the government and the capitalist class for foreign toadyism, and even treason, and a scholarly investigation into what is perceived to be the anti-nationalist historical origins of Korean capitalism itself. Curiously, most of this criticism has been focused on South Korea's economic relationship with the United States rather than with Japan, even though the latter is much deeper, more unequal, and, in the long run, probably more important. Such myopia is understandable, however, in view of America's overarching political and military role in South Korea since 1945 and its direct and critical involvement in the economy through at least the mid-1960s. With some 40,000 troops stationed throughout the country, the U.S. has also been a highly visible and, especially since the Kwangju Incident, controversial, presence in South Korea, whereas the Japanese economic influence has so far been more subtle and hidden. If, as expected, Japan's economic penetration of South Korea grows in the next decade as a result of South Korea's current liberalization and Japan's new and increasingly important role as a financial, as well as an industrial, superpower, the imbalance in the ROK-Japan economic relationship may well become more conspicuous, more widely debated, and more politically uncomfortable for the South Korean government.

Through most of the 1980s the South Korean economy seemed strangely immune to these deep and complex problems. Economic development continued to advance at a rapid pace (over 12% between 1986 and 1988), thanks in large part to a decline in international oil prices and interest rates, the revival of the U.S. economy, and the increased competitiveness of South Korean exports following an appreciation of the Japanese *yen*. A current account surplus, first registered in 1986, allowed the government to reduce its foreign debt from a peak of about $47 billion in 1986 to about $35 billion in 1988, and there was even widespread talk among government officials of South Korea's becoming a net creditor as early as 1992.

By the end of the decade, however, it was clear that some of the structural weaknesses of the economy were beginning to take their toll. Political reform in 1987 opened the door to a long-suppressed social conflict between capital and labor that interrupted production, raised wages (in some cases by as much as 30% in a single year), and unnerved a business community accustomed to unequivocal support from above and no interference from below. At the same time, economic liberalization, especially in the form of a steady appreciation of the *wŏn* after 1987 (including a 15.8% increase in 1988), exacerbated an already difficult situation by reducing the competitiveness of South Korean exports and raising the cost of imports. By the end of 1989, South Korea's current account surplus had plummeted by 64%, and the national growth rate had fallen to only 6.5%, the lowest such figure since 1981, when the economy was still reeling from the shocks of presidential assassination, social upheaval, and military coup. Not surprisingly, the country's trade deficit with Japan, which had been gradually decreasing from a 1986 high of $5 billion, also expanded by 1.5% in 1989.

Such problems do not beget quick or easy answers. The continuing bitter confrontation between labor and management, probably the most serious obstacle to growth the country presently faces, is a product of nearly thirty years of institutionalized oppression and distrust, and it will take much time and effort on both sides before a new institutional arrangement is devised that strikes a satisfactory balance between a commitment to productivity and a concern for the rights and needs of the working class. But the prospects are by no means bleak. Barring a major economic or military crisis, a return to the authoritarian past is not likely to be tolerated by the general public. And if the current economic problems are allowed to run their course in an atmosphere of free speech and association, they may well turn out to be no more than a necessary transition to a period of new growth, less dramatic, perhaps, than in earlier decades, but ultimately more equitable and stable.

Index

A

I